INDIANA UNIVERSITY ASIAN STUDIES RESEARCH INSTITUTE

Oriental Series

Editor, Denis Sinor

Volume 5

TIBET. A HANDBOOK

The research reported herein was performed pursuant to a contract with the United States Department of Health, Education, and Welfare, Office of Education (under the provisions of Section 602, Title VI, P.L. 85-864), Grant No. U.S.O.E. OEC 4130-14 Sinor.

Project Director: Denis Sinor

TIBET
A Handbook

HELMUT HOFFMAN
in collaboration with
Stanley Frye
Thubten J. Norbu
Ho-chin Yang

0737893

Published for the
Asian Studies Research Institute
by the
RESEARCH CENTER FOR THE LANGUAGE SCIENCES
Indiana University, Bloomington

Copy Editors: Karin Ford, Carol Hale Harm, Robbin McInturff

ISBN 87750-180-7
Library of Congress Catalog Card Number 73-90141

Research Center for the Language Sciences, 516 East Sixth Street, Indiana University, Bloomington, Indiana 47401.

Printed in the Unites States of America

This book is dedicated to His Holiness the Fourteenth Dalai Lama, Tenzin Gyatso, as a small contribution to the overwhelming and important task of keeping alive in the West the knowledge of and respect for Tibetan civilization and religion.

TABLE OF CONTENTS*

*The Index to this volume will be published separately.

FOREWORD

The aim of this *Handbook* is to present the most pertinent of extant factual and bibliographic information on Tibet, past and present. Essentially, the book is conceived as a tool to be used in American higher education.

Those who, without being experts themselves, have tried to incorporate Tibetan data into courses on Inner, East, or South Asia, know full well the difficulties caused by the lack of reliable and accessible information. To be sure, there is no lack of general, sometimes superficial material on Tibet and its people. Neither is there a dearth of scholarly articles; but many of them are written in foreign languages and published in learned journals accessible only to those fortunate enough to work near a major, specialized library. They are, therefore, out of the reach of all but the specialist; and this is one of the reasons why it was thought that a reference work like *Tibet: A Handbook* would be useful to a number of instructors teaching a great variety of courses.

The research reported herein was performed pursuant to a contract with the United States Department of Health, Education, and Welfare, Office of Education, under the provisions of Section 602, Title VI, P.L. 85-864. According to the original plan, the research was to have been completed some two years earlier. Extraordinary misfortune presided over the preparation of this *Handbook*. The project director suffered two heart attacks, and the principal investigator fell victim to a bad accident which all but immobilized him for many months. But there were other problems caused by the very nature of the work.

We discovered in the course of writing the *Handbook* that to be really useful, the volume would have to be much larger than originally envisaged. In fact, it incorporates twice as much material as had been initially conceived. Even so, the personnel engaged on the project are painfully aware of the many imperfections of the final product. Among the more disturbing of these, in the opinion of the project director, are the inconsistencies in the spelling of some proper names. However, this flaw has the redeeming feature of giving the nonspecialist reader a foretaste of the inconsistencies he would encounter were he to peruse more than one work. In the course of preparation we have at least learned what this *Handbook* should ideally have been. To come nearer to our ideal would have meant yet another year of work, a year which no one presently engaged in this project could afford. We sincerely think that even as it stands now, the *Handbook* will be of use to those for whom it has been written. We also hope that demand for it will justify a second edition in which account will be taken not only of our own suggestions for improvement but also of those kindly proposed by others.

Essentially, the work reflects the scholarship of the principal investigator, Professor Helmut Hoffmann, who wrote all but three of the chapters. Mr. Stephen A. Halkovic, Lecturer in the Department of Uralic and Altaic Studies of Indiana University, wrote Chapter I. Chapter IV, "The Present Political Framework," is the work of Dr. Yang Ho-chin, and Chapter VIII, "The Social and Economic Structure in Traditional Tibet," was written by Professor Thubten J. Norbu. Dr. Stanley Frye, formerly a Ph.D. candidate in the Department of Uralic and Altaic Studies at Indiana University, was the principal editor of the text. He was assisted in this task by Mrs. Karin Ford, who also checked the bibliography. With angelic patience, Mrs. Jane Thatcher typed and retyped the manuscript. As project director, I did my best to coordinate the activities of all engaged in the project, which in many ways reflects my own concept of what this *Handbook* should be.

The whole team is very much indebted to Mrs. Julia A. Petrov of the Office of Education for her sympathetic handling of our problems to the bitter end.

Indiana University   DENIS SINOR
Asian Studies Research Institute

LIST OF ABBREVIATIONS

AA	Artibus Asiae
AAs	Arts asiatiques
ADAW	Abhandlungen der Deutschen Akademie der Wissenschaften
AFS	Asian Folklore Studies
AKBAW	Abhandlungen der (Königlich-) Bayerischen Akademie der Wissenschaften, I. Klasse
AKM	Abhandlungen für die Kunde des Morgenlandes
ALAW	Abhandlungen der Leipziger Akademie der Wissenschaften
AM	Asia Major
ANL	Accademia Nazionale dei Lincei
AO	Acta Orientalia
AOH	Acta Orientalia Hungarica Budapest
AÖAW	Abhandlungen der Österreichischen Akademie der Wissenschaften
ArOr	Archiv Orientálni
APAW	Abhandlungen der Preussischen Akademie der Wissenschaften
AS	Asiatische Studien, Zeitschrift der Schweizerischen Gesellschaft für Asienkunde
ASi	Academia Sinica. The Bulletin of the Institute of History and Philology
AV	Archiv für Völkerkunde, Wien

BA   Baessler-Archiv

BEFEO   Bulletin de l'École française d'Extrême Orient

BSOAS   Bulletin of the School of Oriental and African Studies

BSOS   Bulletin of the School of Oriental Studies

BT   Bulletin of Tibetology, Namgyal Institute, Gangtok

CAJ   Central Asiatic Journal

EA   The Eastern Anthropologist

EI   Epigraphia Indica

EORL   Études d'Orientalisme publiées par le Musée Guimet à la mémoire
              de Raymonde Linossier, Paris 1932

ETML   Etudes Tibétaines dédiés à la mémoire de Marcelle Lalou, Paris
              1971

EW   East and West

FF   Forschungen und Fortschritte

HJAS   Harvard Journal of Asiatic Studies

IA   Indian Antiquary

IHQ   Indian Historical Quarterly

IIJ   Indo-Iranian Journal

JA   Journal Asiatique

JAF   Journal of American Folklore

JAH   Journal of Asian History

JAOS   Journal of the American Oriental Society

JASB	Journal of the Asiatic Society of Bengal
JBORS	Journal of the Bihar and Orissa Research Society
JBTS	Journal of the Buddhist Text Society
JIBS	Journal of Indian and Buddhist Studies
JMVL	Jahrbuch des Museums für Völkerkunde, Leipzig
JPASB	Journal and Proceedings of the Asiatic Society of Bengal
JRAS	Journal of the Royal Asiatic Society of Great Britain and Ireland
JRCAS	Journal of the Royal Central Asian Society
JWCBRS	Journal of the West China Border Research Society
JWCRS	Journal of the West China Research Society
MASP	Mémoires de l'Académie des Sciences de St. Pétersbourg
MASB	Memoirs of the Asiatic Society of Bengal
MCB	Mélanges chinois et bouddhiques
MIO	Mitteilungen des Instituts für Orientforschung Deutsche Akademie der Wissenschaften, Berlin
MN	Monumenta Nipponica
MS	Monumenta Serica
MSOS	Mitteilungen des Seminars für Orientalische Sprachen
NAE	National Archives of Ethnology
NAM	Neue Allgemeine Missionszeitschrift
NAWG	Nachrichten der Akademie der Wissenschaften in Göttingen

OE	Oriens Extremus
OS	Orientalia Suecana
OZ	Ostasiatische Zeitschrift
PEW	Philosophy East and West, Honolulu
RAA	Revue des arts asiatiques
RCAJ	Royal Central Asian Journal
RHR	Revue de l'Histoire des Religions
RSO	Rivista degli studi orientali
SBAW	Sitzungsberichte der Berliner Akademie der Wissenschaften, Phil.-Hist. Klasse
SBHAW	Sitzungsberichte der Heidelberger Akademie der Wissenschaften
SMAW	Sitzungsberichte der Münchener Akademie der Wissenschaften
SÖAW	Sitzungsberichte der Österreichischen Akademie der Wissenschaften
SWJA	South-Western Journal of Anthropology
TP	T'oung Pao
TSB	The Tibet Society Bulletin
UJ	Ungarische Jahrbücher
WZKM	Wiener Zeitschrift für die Kunde des Morgenlandes
WZKSA	Wiener Zeitschrift für die Kunde Süd-Asiens
ZDMG	Zeitschrift der Deutschen Morgenländischen Gesellschaft
ZE	Zeitschrift für Ethnologie

ZfM   Zeitschrift für Missionswissenschaft

ZII   Zeitschrift für Indologie und Iranistik

ZS   Zentralasiatische Studien (Bonn)

I. THE GEOGRAPHICAL SETTING OF TIBET

The Tibetan Highlands (historical Tibet) cover an area of about 900,000 square miles, roughly one-fourth of the total area of the United States. As the highest and most extensive plateau on earth, the Highlands extend from approximately the 79th through the 102nd degree of east longitude from Ladakh in the west to Dar -rtse mdo (Chin. Ta-chien-lu) in the east, and from approximately the 28th through 39th degree of north latitude from the Himalayas in the south to the Kunlun and Altyn-Tagh ranges in the north. The Tibetan Plateau constitutes the hub of the so-called Central Mountain Barrier, the great divide of Asia, running from east to west and cutting off the south of the continent from the north. Owing to the inverse curvature of the great mountain ranges to the north and south the shape of Tibet is somewhat oval.

Political Tibet includes a smaller territorial area of about 500,000 square miles, roughly the size of Texas, New Mexico, and Utah combined. The boundaries of political Tibet are much reduced on both the north and east extending only as far as approximately the 79th degree of east longitude and the 36th degree of north latitude.

The Tibetan Highlands are not only rimmed by mountain ranges, but are also traversed by many mountain chains. The western border region has the highest elevation, especially in the area of Mount Kailas (Tib. Ti-se) and Lake Manasarovar (Tib. mTs'o ma-p'ang), (both old pre-Tibetan names). The Tibetans call it sTod-P'yogs ("Upper Region"). The descent to the west, to Maryul or the Low Country, i.e., Ladakh, is over passes reaching 19,000 feet.

On the Tibet-Ladakh border, where the Kunlun and Karakoram ranges meet, at an altitude of 17,000 feet lies the desolate plateau of Aksai Chin through which passes the old caravan- and modern motor-route linking Sinkiang to Tibet. Possession of Aksai Chin was one of the key issues of the Sino-Indian conflict of 1962.

The Altyn-Tagh, together with the largest mountain system in Asia, the Kunlun, forms the northern boundary of Tibet. The Nan Shan range forms the northwestern boundary traversing north of Lake Koko Nor. The eastern border is composed in part of the Bayan Kara, Amne Machin, and the Ta-Hsüeh ranges; in addition, a series of rugged chains extending north to south separates the highlands from China proper. The lofty Himalayan range forms the southern frontier of Tibet. The Himalayas act as a barrier to the monsoons from the Indian Ocean. The most important range traversing Tibet are the Trans-himalayas, composed in the west of the Kailas and in the east by the Thangla (Tib. gNyan-c'en t'ang-la).

Tibet can be divided into several physical regions. Southern Tibet comprises the valleys of the Upper Indus and the Sutlej flowing west and that of the gTsang-po or Brahmaputra flowing east. The gTsang-po is the longest flowing river within the borders of Tibet, running through Tibet for about 800 miles. The valley of the gTsang-po has an altitude generally of 12,000 feet or lower, and is located between the Himalayas and Transhimalayas. Within this river valley region are located the main cities of Tibet including Lhasa, Shigatse, and Gyangtse as well as the ancient Tibetan cultural center of Yarlung; in the western region watered by the Indus the urban center of Leh should be mentioned. This southern area, composed of the provinces of dbUs and gTsang, comprises what was called central Tibet. From an historical, cultural, political, and economic perspective this region is the center of Tibet.

North of the Transhimalayas lie the thinly populated northern plains, Chang Tang, a windswept, tangled mass of valleys and plains studded with lakes. This arid, desolate region has an elevation averaging 15,000 feet. Because it has only internal drainage, most of its lakes are salty. The largest lake in the Chang Tang is the Tengri Nor (Tib. Nam Tso).

Along the northern limit of the Tibetan plateau stretch the Kunlun Mountains, which consist of two systems of ranges. Their western part separates Tibet from the Taklamakan desert of the Tarim basin, but further east the Kunlun's northern slopes descend into the swampy Tsaidam depression, today part of the Chinese province Tsinghai.

The Nanshan Mountains constitute the northern border of the Tsaidam region and, at the same time, of historical Tibet. South of them, at an elevation of over 10,000 feet, lies Lake Koko Nor, approximately 40 miles wide and 66 miles long. On its shores can be found some excellent pasturage, famous in ancient as well as in modern times. The surrounding mountain slopes, unsuitable for permanent settlement but good for pasture land, are called 'Brog and their nomad inhabitants 'Brog-pa. This entire northeastern area is called Amdo. The southern border for this region is the Bayan Kara Range. The great Yellow River (Chin. Huang-Ho, Tib. Rma-chu) has its source in the eastern portion of Amdo.

Eastern Tibet, Kham, is the most fertile region of the country. The Bayan Kara Mountains constitute its northern boundary, to the south of which flow the Salween, the Mekong, and the Yangtze. In their upper courses within Tibet they are called, respectively, Nag-chu, rDza-chu, and 'Bri-chu. The three great rivers which rise in the Tibetan Highlands run almost parallel for several hundred miles. Their deep valleys, separated by ranges reaching 15,000 feet or more, are in places as close as 20 to 30 miles.

BIBLIOGRAPHY

The most important and comprehensive work on Tibetan geography is Sven Hedin, *Southern Tibet*, 9 vols., Stockholm 1917-22. An excellent and up-to-date picture of the physical geography of Tibet is included in *The Physical Geography of China, I-II*, prepared by the Institute of Geography, U.S.S.R. Academy of Sciences, Praeger Special Studies in International Economics and Development, New York 1969. A short description of Tibetan geography has been written by B. W. Yussov, *Tibet*, Moscow 1953 (in Russian).

The following books deal with special areas of Tibet: Sven Hedin, *Transhimalaya*, 2 vols., London 1909-13; Albert Herrmann, "Der Manasarovar und die Quellen der indischen Ströme," *Zeitschrift der Gesellschaft für Erdkunde zu Berlin*, 1920, pp. 193-215; Swami Pranavanda, *Kailas-Manasarovar*, Calcutta 1949; Joseph F. Rock, *The Amnye Ma-chhen Range and Adjacent Regions*, Serie Orientale Roma 12, Rome 1956; Albert Tafel, *Meine Tibetreise*, 2 vols., Stuttgart-Berlin 1914 (deals with eastern Tibet).

A very useful study is Emmanuel de Margerie's "L'oeuvre de Sven Hedin et l'orographie du Tibet," *Bulletin de la section de géographie du Comité des Travaux Historiques et Scientifiques 1928*, Paris 1929.

For historical geography of Tibet, see Albert Herrmann, *Das Land der Seide und Tibet im Lichte der Antike*, Leipzig 1939.

Concerning the history of the exploration of Tibet: John MacGregor, *Tibet. A Chronicle of Exploration*, New York–London 1970; and Ernst Schafer, *Tibet und Zentralasien*, Stuttgart 1965.

An indigenous work on Tibetan geography: Turrell V. Wylie, *The Geography of Tibet According to the 'Dzam-Gling-Rgyas-Bshad*, Serie Orientale Roma 25, Rome 1962 (text and English translation).

A good resumé of the geographical setting of Tibet will be found in F. W. Thomas, *Nam, An Ancient Language of the Sino-Tibetan Borderland*, London 1948 ("Geographical Considerations," pp. 1-25).

II. TIBETAN AND ITS RELATION TO OTHER LANGUAGES

Tibetan, a branch of the great Sino-Tibetan family of languages, may be called a monosyllabic and isolating language. Normally a Tibetan word consists of only one syllable: each word contains as a minimum a consonant, namely the base letter, and a vowel, although it often contains one or even two prefixes and one or two suffixes. Both prefixes and suffixes may have originally been separate, independent words, which hints at ancient polysyllabism in Tibetan. Actually the language even now contains words which, aside from prefixes and suffixes, show a disyllabic form but are written as two separate syllables. It is not, of course, always easy to distinguish between compound and disyllabic words, as in many cases the single components of the compound may no longer be used by themselves. But undisputed examples of genuine disyllabic words such as *ra-gan* ("brass") and *yi-ge* ("script, letter") do exist. If such words are combined with another word in a compound, the first component is given in an abbreviated form, e.g., *rag-dung* ("brass trumpet"), *spring-yig* ("written message"). Many scholars assume that the so-called monosyllabic languages of the Sino-Tibetan family were originally polysyllabic and that the present monosyllabic structure is a result of degeneration. One important group of Sino-Tibetan, Kukish, still contains disyllabic and even trisyllabic words.

Tibetan, like Chinese and other languages of the same family, does not inflect nouns or verbs. The construction of the Tibetan sentence therefore must totally rely on particles for the marking of subordinate verbs and for what are case endings in other languages. These particles, of course, became very closely connected in different euphonic forms with the main word, so we may speak of a pseudo-inflection which prevails in the Tibeto-Burmese subgroup. There are also particles which designate a word as noun or adjective (e.g., *pa, ba, ma, po, bo, mo, ka, kha, ga*) or express plurality (e.g., *rnams, tshogs*). The latter two particles may be traced back to independent words, the first meaning "piece," the second "multitude." The above-mentioned particles *pa, ma, po,* and *mo* may also denote natural gender.

Because Tibetan is an isolating language no real difference exists between a noun, adjective, or verb. Words were orignially multifunctional: *nyams-pa* may thus mean "damage," "damaged," and "to be damaged." Consequently there is no active or passive: *rgyal pos mi de ral-gris bsad* may be translated "the king killed that man with a sword" or "that man was killed by the king by means of a sword." Many verbs in classical Tibetan as adapted for the writing of Buddhist texts developed a system of prefixes and suffixes to indicate present, preterit, future, and the imperative, the latter being characterized—if phonetically

5

possible—by aspiration; while in the oldest secular texts, the use of those is much rarer, and the verb very often appears only in *one* form. Actually, verbs are neither active nor passive but impersonal; hence, the foregoing example would really mean: "a killing by the king as to that man by means of a sword came to pass." *bTang ba'i mi* may mean "the man who sent" as well as "the man who was sent."

The real meaning of a sentence will invariably depend on the context. The predicate of the sentence is always given at the end, while at the beginning a local or temporal adverbial expression occurs followed by the subject, which may consist of the following parts in the following order: a so-called genitive preceding the noun, the noun itself, one or several adjectives, a pronoun, a numeral, and an indefinite article (originally the word for "one"). If there is a transitive verb, a postposition meaning "by" is affixed to the subject which will not occur if the verb is intransitive.

Classical Tibetan ("Old Bodic" according to Robert Shafer) was recorded at a time when the old prefixes and suffixes were still pronounced, and it is due to this archaism that Classical Tibetan if often called "the Sanskrit of Sino-Tibetan." But even the language of the first half of the ninth century shows a degeneration of that system of pronunciation. The inscription of the Sino-Tibetan treaty of A.D. 822, in which the names of the Tibetan officials who had sworn to it are given in both Tibetan script and Chinese phonetic transcription, is evidence that most of the prefixes and suffixes were no longer pronounced. The old system of writing has been maintained down to the present, but phonetical changes imply a very different pronunciation. Quite naturally, the dialect of central Tibet and of the capital Lhasa was the most subject to change, whereas the districts in the far East and West still retain the pronunciation of many of the old prefixes (Balti and Purig in the West, Amdo and Khams in the East). Verbs which in the classical language employed the four tenses now use the preterit for all forms. In modern speech the letter Tibetans call *'a-chung,* which carries the vowel sign and serves as prefix (and in the oldest texts even suffix), becomes a sign for prenasalization ("magical circle," *dkyil-'khor,* becomes *khying-khor*; "downpour," *char-'bab,* becomes *chambab*).

Concerning the tonal system found in other Sino-Tibetan languages, we have insufficient data on the early stage of the language. In the modern Lhasa dialect, words beginning with unvoiced consonants *k, c, t, p, ts, kh, ch, th, ph, tsh, sh, s,* and *'a-chung* are high-toned; whereas *g, j, d, b, dz,* the nasals *nga, nya, na, ma,* the bilabial *wa,* the semivowels *y, r, l,* the voiced sibilants *zh* and *z,* and the voiced *h* are low-toned. There is also a phoneme which is a high-toned unvoiced *l,* written in Tibetan orthography as *lh.* An *r* subscribed to a base letter implies lingualization, a subscribed *y* results in palatalization. In some cases the disappearance of a final *g* leads to tonal changes: classical *sGang-tog* becomes *Gang-to⁻*, the second syllable higher than the usual high tone level. The genitive after a final vowel produces umlaut of *a, u, o,* and a rising tone (*klui*, "of the water-spirit," becomes *lü/*). On the other hand, the disappearance of final *d* and *s* produces only umlaut but no change in tone; thus the instrumental may be distinguished from the genitive (*klus*, "by the water spirit," becomes *lü_*).

In the field of comparative linguistics Tibetan (Bodic) is classified as one of the six main divisions of the Sino-Tibetan family: Sinitic (Chinese), Daic (Thai) recently excluded from the family by P. K. Benedict, Bodic (Tibetan), Burmic (Burmese, including the linguistically important Old Kukish), Baric (a group of languages spoken in Assam, prototypes being Bodo and Naga), and Karenic (central and southern Burma, the status of which is not yet totally certain although it seems to be linked with both Burmic and Bodic). Most striking are the close relationships between the Bodic and Burmic divisions.

It has been assumed that the Bodic group was homogeneous and early scholars believed that all dialects were simply offshoots of Classical Tibetan. Recent research has shown that the situation is much more complex. Our present knowledge indicates that besides Tibetan (Bodic) proper there were a proto-eastern branch and a proto-western branch. The latter, in all probability, also includes "West Himalayish," as Robert Shafer calls it. Comparative work is difficult since in most cases the scholar is limited to comparing dialects recorded in modern times with archaic Classical Tibetan. Fortunately, languages have been found which are as old as Old Bodic: Zhang-zhung, the holy language of the Tibetan Bon-po, which is representative of archaic proto-West Bodic, is the key to the study of this group. It has been used as a written language since about the time of Classical Tibetan (seventh or eighth century); and its vocabulary shows a striking resemblance to several isolated languages of the eastern Himalayas (Dhimal and Toto). We also have ancient documents of the still insufficiently studied Nam language of the Nan-shan and adjacent areas, fragments of which were found in Chinese Turkestan. This language was probably representative of proto-East Bodic. We should also note that the shibboleth of Old West Bodic and Old East Bodic and their derivative dialects is the numeral "seven," *snis,* which is the word common to the Tibeto-Burmic group, whereas Old Central Bodic uses the word *bdun.* A tentative diagram of Bodic follows on p. 8.

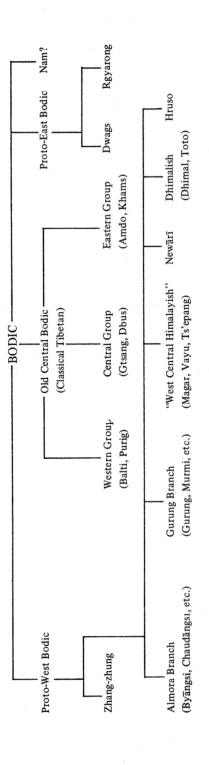

BIBLIOGRAPHY

LEXICOGRAPHY

Classical Tibetan

Alexander Csoma de Körös, *Essay towards a Dictionary, Tibetan and English*, Calcutta 1834; I. J. Schmidt, *Tibetisch-Deutsches Wörterbuch*, St. Petersburg 1841; H. A. Jäschke, *A Tibetan-English Dictionary*, 2nd ed., London 1934; Sarat Chandra Das, *A Tibetan-English Dictionary, with Sanskrit Synonyms*, rev. by Graham Sandberg and A. William Heyde, Calcutta 1902 (reprint 1960); Auguste Desgodins, *Dictionnaire thibétain-latin-français*, Hong Kong 1899; Lokesh Chandra, *Tibetan-Sanskrit Dictionary*, Śatapitaka Series on Indo-Asian Literature, New Delhi 1959; Chos-grags, *Dge bai bshes chos kyi grags pas brtsams pai brda dag ming tshig gsal ba* (Tibetan-Tibetan Dictionary), Peking 1957; L. S. Dagyab, *Tibetan Dictionary* (Tibetan-Tibetan), Dharmsala 1966.

Special glossaries: Alexander Csoma de Körös, *Sanskrit-Tibetan-English Vocabulary*, an edition and translation of the Mahāvyutpatti, ed. by E. Denison Ross and Satis Chandra Vidyabhusana, 2 parts, *MASB IV*, nos. 1 and 2, Calcutta 1910; Ryōzaburō Sakaki, *Compendium of Translation of Names and Terms of the Mahāvyutpatti* (with a Sanskrit Index), Tokyo 1916; Kyoo Nishio, *A Tibetan Index to the Mahāvyutpatti (Sakaki Edition)*, Kyoto 1936; Jacques Bacot, *Dictionnaire tibétain-sanskrit par Tse-ring-ouang-gyal* (phototype reproduction), Buddhica, 2nd series, vol. 2, Paris 1930; E. Obermiller, *Index verborum Sanskrit-Tibetan and Tibetan-Sanskrit to the Nyāyabindu of Dharmakirti and the Nyāyabindutīkā of Dharmottara*, Bibliotheca Buddhica 24, 25, Leningrad 1927/28; J. Rahder, *Glossary of the Sanskrit, Tibetan, Mongolian and Chinese Versions of the Daśabhūmika Sūtra*, Paris 1928; Johannes Nobel, *Suvarnaprabhāsottama-Sūtra*, Die tibetischen Übersetzungen mit einem Wörterbuch herausgegeben, vol. 2, Leiden-Stuttgart 1950; Johannes Nobel, *Udrāyaṇa, König von Roruka*, Die tibetische Übersetzung des Sanskrittextes, 2 vols. (vol. 2: Wörterbuch), Wiesbaden 1955; Friedrich Weller, *Tibetisch-Sanskritischer Index zum Bodhicaryāvatāra*, Abh. d. Leipziger Akademie d. Wissenschaften, 46 no. 3 and 47 no. 3, 2 vols., Leipzig 1953 and 1955; Edward Conze, *Sanskrit-Tibetan-English Index to the Prajñāpāramitā-ratnaguna-samcaya-gāthāh*, Bibliotheca Buddhica, Leningrad 1937 (reprint: s'Gravenhage 1960).

Colloquial Tibetan

H. Ramsey, *Western Tibet, A Practical Dictionary of the Language and Customs of the Districts Included in the Ladak Wazarat*, Lahore 1890; A. v. Rosthorn, "Vokabularfragmente ost-tibetischer Dialekte," *ZDMG* 51 (1897): 524-33; E. H. C. Walsh, *A Vocabulary of the Tromowa Dialect of Tibetan Spoken in the Chumbi Valley*, Calcutta 1905; Dawasamdup Kazi, *An English-Tibetan Dictionary*, Calcutta 1919; Sir Charles Bell, *English-Tibetan Colloquial Dictionary*, 2nd ed., Calcutta 1920; J. H. Edgar, "An English-Giarung Vocabulary," *JWCBRS* 5 (1932), supplement; Basil Gould and Hugh E. Richardson, *Tibetan Word Book*, London 1943; Pierre Philippe Giraudeau and Francis Goré, *Dictionnaire français-tibétain, Tibet Oriental*, Paris 1956.

GRAMMAR

Classical Tibetan

Alexander Csoma de Körös, *A Grammar of the Tibetan Language in English*, Calcutta 1834; I. J. Schmidt, *Grammatik der Tibetischen Sprache*, St. Petersburg 1839; H. A. Jäschke, *Tibetan Grammar*, 3d ed., addenda by A. H. Francke assisted by W. Simon, Berlin 1929; Philippe E. Foucaux, *Grammaire de la langue tibétaine*, Paris 1858; Palmyr Cordier, *Cours de tibétain classique*, Hanoi 1908; H. B. Hannah, *Grammar of the Tibetan Language*, Calcutta 1912; Vidhushekhara Bhattacharya, *Bhota Prakāśa*, A Tibetan Chrestomathy with Introduction, Skeleton Grammar, Notes, Texts, and Vocabularies, University of Calcutta 1939; Jacques Bacot, *Grammaire du tibétain littéraire*, 2 vols., Paris 1948 (a valuable book which follows the indigenous grammars although not suitable for beginners); Marcelle Lalou, *Manuel élémentaire de tibétain classique: méthode empirique*, Paris 1950; Shōjō Inaba, *Grammar of Classical Tibetan*, Kyoto 1954 (in Japanese); Roy Andrew Miller, "A Grammatical Sketch of Classical Tibetan," *JAOS* 90 (1970): 74-96 (phonematic approach); Michael Hahn, *Lehrbuch der Klassischen Tibetischen Schriftsprache*, Hamburg 1971.

Colloquial Tibetan

Graham Sandberg, *Handbook of Colloquial Tibetan*, Calcutta 1894; Sir Charles Bell, *Grammar of Colloquial Tibetan*, 2nd ed., Calcutta 1919; George N. Roerich and Tsetrung Lopsang Puntshok, *Textbook of Colloquial Tibetan*, Calcutta 1957; Eberhardt Richter, *Grundlagen der Phonetik des Lhasa-Dialektes*, 2 vols., Ph.D. diss., Berlin 1959; Chang Kun and Betty Shefts, *A Manual of Spoken Tibetan*, University of Washington Press, Seattle 1964; Melvyn C. Goldstein and Nawang Nornang, *Modern Spoken Tibetan: Lhasa Dialect*, Seattle and London 1971; A. F. C. Read, *Balti Grammar*, London 1934; A. H. Francke, "Sketch of Ladakhi Grammar," *JASB* 70 (1900): pt. 1, extra no. 2; George N. Roerich, "The Tibetan Dialect of Lahul," *Urusvati Journal* 3 (1933): 83-189; George N. Roerich, *Le parler de l'Amdo*, Serie Orientale Roma vol. 18, Roma 1958; August Desgodin, *Essai de grammaire thibétaine pour le langage parlé*, Hong Kong 1899 (eastern dialect).

SPECIALIZED GRAMMATICAL STUDIES

H. A. Jäschke, "Über das tibetanische Lautsystem," *Monatsberichte der Preussischen Akademie der Wissenschaften*, 1860, Nachtrag, pp. 257-78; H. A. Jäschke, "Über die östliche Aussprache des Tibetischen im Vergleich zu der früher behandelten westlichen," *ibidem*, 1865, pp. 441-54, H. A. Jäschke, "Über die Phonetik der tibetischen Sprache," *ibidem*, 1867, pp. 148-82; George N. Roerich, "Modern Tibetan Phonetics, with Special Reference to the Dialect of Central Tibet," *JASB*, N. S. 27 (1931): 285-312; Jacques Bacot, "La structure du tibétain," *Conférences Inst. Ling. Univ. Paris* 2 (1953): 115-35; Roy Andrew

Miller, "Notes on the Lhasa Dialect of the Early Ninth Century," *Oriens* 8 (1955): 284-91; Roy Andrew Miller, "The Independent Status of the Lhasa Dialect in Spoken Tibetan," *Tōhōgaku* 10 (1955): 144-58; André Migot, "Recherches sur les dialectes tibétains du Si-K'ang (province de Khams)," *BEFEO* 48 (1957): 417-562; Edward Stack, *Some Tsangla-Bhutanese Sentences*, Shillong 1897; Stuart N. Wolfenden, "Notes on the Jyarung Dialect of Eastern Tibet," *TP*, series 2, vol. 32 (1936): pp. 167-204; Yu Wên, "Verbal Directive Prefixes in the Jyarung Language and their Ch'iang Equivalents," *Studia Serica* 3 (1943): 11-20; P'êng Kin, "Étude sur le Jyarung, dialecte de Tsa-Kou-na," *Han Hiue* 3 (Peking, 1949): 211-310; Yu Wên, "On the languages of Li Fan," *JWCBRS* 14 (1942): 31-34; Yu Wên, "Studies in Tibetan Phonetics, Sde-dge Dialect," *Studia Serica* 7 (1948): 63-78; G. Uray, *Kelet-Tibet Nyelujárásainak osztályozása* [Classification of the dialects of eastern Tibet. With English summary], Dissertationes Sodalium Instituti Asiae Interioris, fasc. 4, 1949; Robert Shafer, "The Linguistic Position of Dwags," *Oriens* 7 (1954): 348-56; Roy Andrew Miller, "Segmental Phonology of the Ladakhi Dialect," *ZDMG* 106 (1956): 345-62.

Berthold Laufer, "Loan Words in Tibetan," *TP*, series 2, vol. 17 (1916): 403-552; George N. Roerich, "Tibetan Loan-words in Mongolian," *Sino-Tibetan Studies V (Festschrift Liebenthal)*, pp. 247-54; A. Róna-Tas, "Remarks on the Phonology of the Monguor Language (preservation of Tibetan prefixes)," *AOH* 6 (1956): 263-67; A. Róna-Tas, "Tibetan Loan-words in the Shera Yögur Language," *AOH* 15 (1962): 259-71.

A. H. Francke, "Kleine Beiträge zur Phonetik und Grammatik des Tibetischen," *ZDMG* 57 (1903): 285-98; Berthold Laufer, "Bird Divination among the Tibetans" (including: "On the Tibetan Phonology of the 9th century"), *TP*, series 2, vol. 17 (1916): 403-552; Hans-Nordewin von Koerber, *Morphology of the Tibetan Language*, Los Angeles and San Francisco 1935; Constantin Régamey, "Considérations sur le système morphologique du tibétain littéraire," *Cahiers Ferdinand de Saussure* 6 (1947): 22-46; Sir Basil Gould and Hugh E. Richardson, *Tibetan Verb Roots*, Kalimpong 1949; Jacques A. Durr, *Morphologie du verbe tibétain*, Heidelberg 1950; Robert Shafer, "Studies in the Morphology of Bodic Verbs," *BSOAS* 13 (1951): 702-24, 1017-31; G. Uray, "Some Problems of the Ancient Tibetan Verbal Morphology", *Acta Linguistica Academiae Scientiarum Hungaricae* 3 (1953): 37-60; Jacques A. Durr, "Wie übersetze ich Tibetisch," *Asiatica. Festschrift Friedrich Weller*, pp. 53-77, Leipzig 1954; R. K. Sprigg, "Verbal Phrases in Lhasa Tibetan," *BSOAS* 16 (1954): 134-50, 320-50; Kamil Sedláček, "On Some Problems of Using Auxiliary Verbs in Tibetan," *MIO* 7 (1959): 79-122; Stuart N. Wolfenden, "The Prefixed *m*- with Certain Substantives in Tibetan," *Language* 4 (1928): 277-80; Fang-Kuei Li, "Certain Phonetic Influences of the Tibetan Prefixes upon the Root Initials," *Academia Sinica* 4 (1933): 135-57; Robert Shafer, "Prefixed *n*-, *ng*- in Tibetan," *Sino-Tibetica*, no. 1 (1938): 11-28; Walter Simon, "Certain Tibetan Suffixes and Their Combinations," *HJAS* (1940): 372-91.

J. H. Edgar, "The Tibetan Tonal System," *JWCBRS* 5 (1932): 66-67; R. K. Sprigg, "The Tonal System of Tibetan [Lhasa dialect] and the Nominal

Phrase," *BSOAS* 17 (1955): 133-53; Kamil Sedláček, "The Tonal System of Tibetan (Lhasa Dialect)," *TP* 47 (1959): 181-250.
R. K. Sprigg, "Vowel Harmony in Lhasa Tibetan," *BSOAS* 24 (1961): 116-38; R. A. Miller, "Early Evidence for Vowel Harmony in Tibetan," *Language* 42 (1966): 252-77.
Anton Schiefner, "Tibetische Studien," *Bulletin de l'Académie des sciences de St. Pétersbourg* 8 (1851): 211-22, 259-71, 291-303, 334, 336-51; Anton Schiefner, "Über Pluralbezeichnungen im Tibetischen," *MASP* 25, no. 1 (1877); F. B. Shawe, "On the Relationship between Tibetan Orthography and the Original Pronunciation of the Language," *JASB* 63 (1894): 4-19; Berthold Laufer, "Über das *va zur,* ein Beitrag zur Phonetik der tibetischen Sprache," *WZKM* 12 (1898): 289-307 and 13 (1899): 95-109, 199-226; A. H. Francke, "Das tibetische Pronominalsystem," *ZDMG* 61 (1907): 439-40, 950; Max Walleser, *Zur Aussprache des Sanskrit und Tibetischen*, Heidelberg 1926; Stuart N. Wolfenden, "Significance of Early Tibetan Word Forms (*on gñi* "sun")," *JRAS* (1928): 896-99; Walter Simon, "Tibetan *daṅ, ciṅ, kyin, yin* and *ham,*" *BSOAS* 10 (1942): 954-75; Walter Simon, "The Range of Sound Alternations in Tibetan Word Families," *AM*, series 2, vol. 1 (1949): 3-15; Roy Andrew Miller, "The Phonemes of Tibetan [U-Tsang dialect] with Practical Romanized Orthography for Tibetan-speaking Readers," *Journal of the Asiatic Society, Letters* 17, no. 3 (1951): 191-216; G. Uray, "A Tibetan Diminutive Suffix," *AOH* 2 (1952): 183-219; G. Uray, "The Suffix *-e* in Tibetan," *AOH* 3 (1953): 229-44; G. Uray, "Duplication, Gemination and Triplication in Tibetan," *AOH* 4 (1954): 177-241; G. Uray, "The Tibetan Letters *Ba* and *Wa,*" *AOH* 5 (1955): 101-21; Helmut Hoffmann, "Über ein wenig beachtetes Hilfswort zur Bezeichnung der Zukunft im Tibetischen," *Corolla Linguistica, Festschrift Ferdinand Sommer*, Wiesbaden 1955, pp. 73-79; Roy Andrew Miller, "Morphologically Determined Allomorphs in Spoken Tibetan," *Language* 30 (1954): 458-60; Walter Simon, "Tibetan 'fifteen' and 'eighteen'," *ETML*, Paris 1971, pp. 472-78.

Max Walleser, "Subordinate Clauses in Tibetan," *Indian Linguistics* (1935): 309-22; Max Walleser, "Affirmative and Interrogative Sentences in Tibetan," *Indian Linguistics* (1935): 297-307.

INDIGENOUS TIBETAN GRAMMAR

Berthold Laufer, "Studien zur Sprachwissenschaft der Tibeter, Zamatog," *SMAW* (1898): 519-94; Sarat Chandra Das, *An Introduction to the Grammar of the Tibetan Language, with the Texts of Situi-sum-rtags, Dag-byed gsal bai me loṅ and Situi zhal-lung*, Darjeeling 1915; Johannes Schubert, Tibetische Nationalgrammatik, *MSOS* 31 (1928): 1-59 and 32 (1929): 1-54; Jacques Bacot, *Les slokas grammaticaux de Thonmi Sambhoṭa avec leurs commentaires,* Annales du Musée Guimet 37 (Paris 1928); Jean Przyluski and Marcelle Lalou, "Le da-drag tibétain," *BSOS* 7 (1933): 87-89; Johannes Schubert, *Tibetische*

Nationalgrammatik: Das sum cupa und Rtags Kyi ajug pa des Grosslamas von Peking Rol pai rdo rje. Mit Übersetzungen und Anmerkungen, *Artibus Asiae,* Supplementum Primum, Leipzig 1937; Jacques A. Durr, *Deux traités grammaticaux tibétains,* Heidelberg 1950; Roy Andrew Miller, "Thon-mỉ Sambhota and his Grammatical Treatises," *JAOS* 83 (1963): 485-502; Roy Andrew Miller, "Buddhist Hybrid Sanskrit *āli, kāli* as Grammatical Terms in Tibet," *HJAS* 26 (1966): 125-47.

COMPARATIVE LINGUISTICS

August Conrady, *Eine indochinesische Causativ-Denominativ-Bildung und ihr Zusammenhang mit den Tonaccenten,* Leipzig 1896; Walter Simon, "Tibetisch-Chinesische Wortgleichungen," *MSOS* 32, part 1 (1929): 157-228; B. Karlgren, "Tibetan and Chinese," *TP* 28 (1931): 25-70; Jean Przyluski and G. H. Luce, "The number 'a hundred' in Sino-Tibetan," *BSOS* 6 (1930/32): 667-68; Stuart N. Wolfenden, "Concerning the Origins of Tibetan brgi̯ad and Chinese pwât 'eight'," *TP,* series 2, vol. 34 (1939): 165-73; Robert Shafer, *Bibliography of Sino-Tibetan Languages,* 2 vols., Wiesbaden 1957 and 1963; Robert Shafer: *Introduction to Sino-Tibetan,* Wiesbaden 1966-71 (the basic work in the field); Kamil Sedláček, *Das Gemein-Sino-Tibetische,* Abhandlungen fur die Kunde des Morgenlandes 39, 2, Wiesbaden 1970. Paul K. Benedict, *Sino-Tibetan. A Conspectus,* Princeton-Cambridge Studies in Chinese Linguistics, Cambridge University Press, Cambridge 1972.

T. C. Hodson, "Note on the Numerical Systems of the Tibeto-Burman Dialects," *JRAS* (1913): 315-36; T. C. Hodson, "Note on the Word for 'water' in Tibeto-Burman Dialects," *JRAS* (1914): 143-50; Stuart N. Wolfenden, *Outlines of Tibeto-Burman Linguistic Morphology,* Prize Publication Fund, vol. 12, London 1929; B. H. Hodgson, *Essays on the Languages, Literature and Religion of Nepal and Tibet,* London 1874.

F. W. Thomas, "The Zhang-zhung Language," *JRAS* (1933): 405-10; Lajos Ligeti: "Tibeti források Közép-Ázsia történetéhez" [Tibetan sources on the history of Central Asia], (deals with the languages of Zhang-zhung, A-zha, Bru-zha, and Sum-pa), *Kőrösi Csoma Archivum* 1 (1936): 76-103; Helmut Hoffmann, "Žaṅ-žuṅ: the Holy Language of the Tibetan Bon-po," *ZDMG* (1967): 376-81; A. F. Thompson, "The Žaṅ-žuṅ Language," *A.M.,* N. S. 13 (1967): 211-17; Erik Haarh, *The Zhang-zhung Language. A Grammar and Dictionary of the Unexplored Language of the Tibetan Bonpos.* Acta Jutlandica 40, 1, Kφbenhavn 1968; Helmut Hoffmann, "Several Žaṅ-žuṅ Etymologies," *Oriens Extremus* (1972), 193-201.

Marcelle Lalou, "La Langue 'Nam'," *JA* 231 (1939): 453; F. W. Thomas, *Nam. An Ancient Language of the Sino-Tibetan Borderland,* London 1948.

Karl Bouda, "Jenisseisch-tibetische Wortgleichungen," *ZDMG* 90 (1936): 149-59; Karl Bouda, *Die Beziehungen des Sumerischen zum Baskischen, West-Kaukasischen und Tibetischen,* Mitteilungen der Altorientalischen Gesellschaft 12, part 3, Leipzig 1938; Helmut Hoffmann, "Gšen. Eine lexikographisch-religionswissenschaftliche Untersuchung," *ZDMG* 98 (1944): 340-58 (comparison of the word for "shaman" in Tibetan and Ket); Karl Bouda, "Die Sprache der Jenissejer, genealogische und morphologische Untersuchungen," *Anthropos* 52 (1957): 65-134 (comparison with Sino-Tibetan).

III. TIBETAN SCRIPT. SYSTEMS OF TRANSCRIPTION

At one time a great deal of controversy prevailed among the older Tibetologists over the origin of the Tibetan script. A. H. Francke's idea that in the first half of the seventh century Tibet had adopted the Khotanese form of writing was correctly discredited by Laufer and other scholars, and Jean Philippe Vogel had definitely proved (*Epigraphia Indica* XI: 266) that Tibetan writing originated in India and, more precisely, represents the northwestern variety of the Gupta script of the seventh century. Tibet thus owes her script to India while ink and paper were introduced from China.

The description of the introduction of writing as found in the Tibetan chronicles has been dealt with superficially by all early scholars including Laufer, as well as A. H. Francke, who relied only on western Tibetan sources. For a survey of the introduction of writing, four representative chronicles have been used (scholars in Tibetology have learned never to rely on a single source): the *Chronicle of the Fifth Dalai Lama*, the *rGyal-rabs gsal-bai me-long*, the *Histories of Buddhism* by Bu-ston and dPa-bo gtsug-lag 'phreng-ba. (These works will be referred to in this section by the following abbreviations: *CFD, G, B,* and *P,* respectively. For information on these works, see chapter V.)

After having consulted these sources, one can give the following synoptic description: the introduction of writing took place during the early years of the emperor Srong-btsan sgam-po (accession circa 620, died A.D. 649). No exact date exists, although 632 is generally accepted by older scholars. We cannot be certain of it, however, for it was calculated from a book, which was written very late, by the Mongolian historiographer Sagang Sechen. According to our sources a party of Tibetans was sent to India (*G* mentions seven and *P* sixteen members) by Srong-btsan sgam-po, but was unsuccessful. He then sent his famous minister whose name is generally given as Thon-mi A-nui bu Sambhota (although this was not his real name; *Thon-mi* means "man of the Thon tribe," *A-nui bu* "son of A-nu," [his mother] and *Sambhota* is Indian and means "the excellent Tibetan"). Only the *bKa'-thang sde-lnga* gives us his name hitherto overlooked by scholars: Thu 'Bring-to-re A-nu. *Thu* is a form of the tribal name *Thon, A-nu* the name of the minister's mother, but *'Bring-to-re* must be accepted as his personal name. He, too, travelled to India with a retinue, taking a considerable quantity of gold dust to please his prospective teachers. Concerning the details of his journey, *B* and *P*, the oldest sources, insert an interesting remark which has been overlooked by scholars. It is stated that he roamed throughout India, finally meeting in the south the Brahmin Li-byin, from whom he learned the Indian sounds and script. The problem of how to restore the original name of the Indian brahmin remains unsolved: neither Francke's interpretation "Glory of the Khotan Country," chosen because he connected the Tibetan script with the Khotanese, nor the other, *Lipikara*, "maker of writing," can be accepted. Laufer may well be right when he says that the second syllable suggests an Indian name formed with -*datta*, as in Devadatta ("given by the gods"). Mentioned among the Indian grammatical works which Thon-mi studied are the famous works of Pāṇini, the *Kalāpa Vyākaraṇa*, and the *Cāndra Vyākaraṇa*. This would seem to be an exaggeration; these texts probably came to Tibet much later.

According to our sources the minister also studied with Lhai-rig-pa-seng-ge (supposedly Sanskrit Devavidyāsiṃha) and other pandits, although according to *B* he studied with that scholar only; Li-byin was not mentioned in this source. After his return to Tibet, Thon-mi and the emperor went into seclusion together in the temple of Ma-ru (also written rMe-ru) and created the Tibetan alphabet using the Indian material as far as it suited the needs of the Tibetan language. Many letters in the Indian alphabet were of no use for the notation of Tibetan phonemes; and of the sixteen vowel-signs of the Sanskrit alphabet, only four (*i*, *u*, *e*, *o*) were chosen for Tibetan. It should be borne in mind that in Sanskrit as well as in Tibetan, unless otherwise specified, a consonantal sign stands for the ligature of a consonant followed by *a*. Old Tibetan writings found in East Turkestan and dating from the eighth and ninth centuries on occasion specifically indicate an interconsonantal *a*. The sign used for the purpose is the so-called '*a-chung*, "small *a*," rendered in transcription by the diacritical mark'. For instrance, in some old documents the clan name *Dbas* is written *Dba's*. The Tibetan script has thirty consonantal signs as compared to the thirty-four of the Indian alphabet.

As to the type of Indian script which Thon-mi used for his new alphabet, *B* and *P* state that the form of his letters was similar to the Kashmirian characters, which would be in accordance with J.Ph. Vogel's palaeographic research. But the more popular view represented by *P* and *CFD* that the minister constructed the capital letters (*dbu-can*, "provided with a head") on the basis of the Lāntsha script, and the cursive writing (*dbu-med*, "without head") from the Indian Vartula characters is subject to doubt; and although still accepted by present-day Tibetans this view should be rejected since the Lāntsha and Vartula characters are by far later than the seventh century, as is the Nāgāri script mentioned among others by *P*. If we consult the oldest extant specimens of writings excavated in eastern Turkestan we find that there is no strict separation of *Dbu-can* and *Dbu-med*, but that the latter developed from the former (which then differed somewhat from the *Dbu-can* of later centuries) and resulted from careless and hasty writings.

The letters *ca* (pron. *cha*), *cha*, *ja*, *ža*, *ža*, and '*a* (=a-chung) were added by Thon-mi "as they did not exist in Indian writing." Regarding the palatals this statement might seem surprising, but because the Tibetans represent the Indian palatals *ca*, etc., with the respective palatal sibilants *ts*, etc., they might call the adaptation of the palatals an addition. The pronunciation of Indian palatals as palatal sibilants was borrowed by the Tibetans from Nepal where this pronunciation still prevails. This indicates some Nepalese influence on the creation of the Tibetan script which is not mentioned in the chronicles. A related factor is the Tibetan use of the triangular *va (va-zur)* subscribed to several consonants, a practice also found in the Newārī script.

Owing to the primarily monosyllabic and isolating nature of the Tibetan language, it is understandable that each syllable stands by itself and is separated from the following by a dot called *tsheg.* This means that each Tibetan syllable may contain only one vowel or diphthong.

According to the Tibetan chronicles, Thon-mi, during his seclusion in the Ma-ru temple, also compiled eight books on Tibetan script and grammar, six of which have been lost. The remaining two, the *Sum-cu-pa (The Thirty Letters)* deals with the alphabet and the *rTags-kyi 'jug-pa (Description of the Distinction of Genders),* with phonemic problems, the consonants of the alphabet being classified into three groups: masculine *(pho),* feminine *(mo),* and neuter *(ma-ning).* This treatise indicates which prefix accords with which special base letter and which does not.

In the course of time several kinds of cursive script developed and were used for special and ornamental purposes. The most important of these are the *dPe-yig,* "book cursive," *Khyug-yig,* "running script" (used for letters and official documents such as passports, etc.), *'Bru-tsha* (used especially by the Tibetan Bon-po), and *'Bam-yig,* the large, regular style of cursive writing invented for the use of elementary writing schools.

As for the scientific transcriptions of Tibetan, it is not surprising that in a branch of philology as young as Tibetology no generally accepted system yet exists. Owing to Csoma's pioneering work in Indian Tibet the transliteration system for the northern Indian languages and Sanskrit was adopted also for Tibetan. Most of the scholars who wrote in English, such as H. A. Jaeschke, A. H. Francke, and F. W. Thomas used this transliteration system with slight variations and it is still in use. The system of transcription proposed in 1959 by Turrell Wylie was favorably recieved, principally in the United States.

Quite independently from their English-writing colleagues, French scholars developed a different system, certain particulars of which (e.g., the use of the letter *c*) may be explained by the application of the Latin alphabet to French writing. It is essential to know the French transliteration as scholars of outstanding stature such as Jacques Bacot, Marcelle Lalou, and R. A. Stein used this system of romanization.

A somewhat altered transliteration system has been developed by H. Hoffmann from the French one. The principle of this system implies the usage of a single letter in romanization for *one* Tibetan letter with the use of several diacritical marks if required. One letter should never be used for different purposes as is the case, for instance, in F. W. Thomas's Old English transcription where the letter *h* is used for three functions: the genuine *h*; the aspiration of *kh, th, ph;* and the so-called *'a-chung (ḥ),* not a very accurate system.

In 1971 the American Library Association agreed on a transcription system for use in all libraries. It remains to be seen whether this system will also be adopted for scientific publications by Tibetan scholars. For this book a simplified transcription system has been used which enables English-speaking people, even though not Tibetan scholars, to pronounce Tibetan words in an approximately correct way.

COMPARATIVE TABLE OF TRANSCRIPTIONS

Tibetan	Old English transcription F. W. Thomas	T. V. Wylie	French	H. Hoffmann	American Library Association
ཀ	ka	ka	ka	ka	ka
ཁ	kha	kha	kha	k'a	kha
ག	ga	ga	ga	ga	ga
ང	ṅa	nga	ṅa	ṅa	ṅa
ཅ	ca	ca	ča	ča	ca
ཆ	cha	ch	čha	č'a	cha
ཇ	ja	ja	ǰa	ǰa	ja
ཉ	ña	nya	ña	ña	ña
ཏ	ta	ta	ta	ta	ta
ཐ	tha	tha	tha	t'a	tha
ད	da	da	da	da	da
ན	na	na	na	na	na
པ	pa	pa	pa	pa	pa
ཕ	pha	pha	pha	p'a	pha
བ	ba	ba	ba	ba	ba
མ	ma	ma	ma	ma	ma
ཙ	tsa	tsa	ca	ca	tsa
ཚ	tsha	tsha	cha	c'a	tsha
ཛ	dza	dza	ja	ja	dza
ཝ	va	wa	va	va	wa
ཞ	źa	zha	ža	ža	źa
ཟ	za	za	za	za	za
འ	ḫa	'a	'a	'a	'a
ཡ	ya	ya	ya	ya	ya
ར	ra	ra	ra	ra	ra
ལ	la	la	la	la	la
ཤ	sha, śa	sha	śa	ša	śa
ས	sa	sa	sa	sa	sa
ཧ	ha	ha	ha	ha	ha
ཨ	'a	a	a	a	a

BIBLIOGRAPHY

Turrell Wylie, "A Standard System of Tibetan Transcription," *HJAS* 22 (1959): 261-67, can serve as an introduction to the practical sides of the problem.

For the different forms of the regular, cursive, and ornamental Tibetan scripts good material is available in Alexander Csoma de Körös, *A Grammar of the Tibetan Language*, Calcutta 1834, pp. 1-38; Sarat Chandra Das, "The Sacred and Ornamental Characters of Tibet," *JASB* 57 (1888): 41-49 with nine plates; and Jacques Bacot, *L'écriture cursive tibétaine*, Paris 1912.

For the introduction and history of the Tibetan script see A. H. Francke, "The Similarity of the Tibetan to the Kashgar-Brahmi Alphabet," *MASB* 1: 3 (1905): 43-45 with 5 plates; by the same author, "The Tibetan Alphabet," *Epigraphia Indica XI*, (1911/12): 226 seq. Both articles of Francke's have been severly criticized and are outdated; more informative are the following studies: I. J. Schmidt, "Über den Ursprung der tibetischen Schrift," *Mémoires de l'Académie Imp. de St. Pétersbourg*, 6th Series, 1 (1829): 41-52; Terrien de Lacouperie, *Beginnings of Writing in Central and Western Asia*, London 1894; Berthold Laufer, "Origin of Tibetan Writing," *JAOS* 38 (1918): 34-46; D. Diringer, *The Alphabet*, New York 1953, pp. 352-57.

IV. TIBETAN HISTORICAL SOURCES

Indigenous Sources

Tibet may be described as the "country between India and China" not only because of its geographical location but also because of its cultural relations with these two countries. Similarly, Tibetan historiography has points of contact with both Indian and Chinese historiography.

In religion, Tibet was Indian in its orientation and followed the Indian form of Buddhism, especially after the Chinese Ho-shang monks were defeated during the extremely important debate at bSam-yas between the Indian Pandit Kamalshīla and the Chinese monk Hva-shang Mahāyāna, after which the Chinese Buddhists were forced to withdraw from Tibet. The Tibetans adopted the Indian alphabet in the first half of the seventh century A.D., and Western science may be grateful that the Tibetans did this instead of creating a variant of the Chinese script as the Tanguts or Hsi-hsia of the Koko Nor region later did.

In their historiography, however, the Tibetans were and are nearer to the Chinese, since, generally speaking, the Indians have shown little interest in history. This is understandable if we realize that the Indians' concept of time is cyclic; they believe that the history of the world consists of four ages, beginning with a Golden Age *(Krit),* and deteriorating down to the present, the age we are now experiencing, which is the worst, the so-called *Kali Yuga.* When this age has ended, the whole cycle will start again. Hence they find the changing events of history of little interest since they always follow the eternal model. If we are aware of this, we need not be surprised that Indian literature, with very few exceptions, does not include works on history, since nothing really new can happen in relation to the events of past or future cycles. The only point in historiography which Tibetan and Indian literary activities have in common is genealogies. The very enigmatic genealogies of Indian dynasties in the *Manjushrīmūla Tantra* (Tib. *'Jam-dpal rtsa-rgyud*), which may be compared with the very old pre-Buddhist Bon-po genealogies of gods and kings, are similar to a genealogy found in the oldest Tibetan chronicle. This chronicle, which belongs to the first half of the ninth century and was discovered in the famous hidden library of Tun-huang in westernmost Kansu, is written in Chinese fashion on a scroll, not on a later-style Indian *pothi,* and gives the genealogy of the ancient, semimythical kings who came down to earth by a "sky-rope." This is followed by information on the petty chieftains who resided in the Yar-klungs and 'Phyong-rgyas valleys, the place of origin of the unifier of the Tibetan tribes and the founder of the great Tibetan empire, King gNam-ri srong-btsan (second half of the sixth century).

21

In addition to that chronicle we also have from the treasures of the library of Tun-huang a fragment of annals which covers the period from the death of Srong-btsan sgam-po to the reign of Mes-ag-tshoms, i.e., the years 649 to 747. The scroll is mutilated on both ends, and its content was compiled on the pattern of the Chinese dynastic annals. It gives a chronological outline of events in a very dry and schematic style. These Tibetan annals used the chronological system of the twelve animals, well-known in China and Inner Asia. They mostly indicate the locations of the summer and winter residences of the Tibetan emperors. On the basis of these data it is possible to form an idea of the territory then ruled by Tibetans. At its apogee the Tibetan empire included, besides Tibet proper, the state of the T'u-yü-hun, Kansu, Yunnan, and considerable parts of Szechwan in the east, Baltistan and Gilgit in the west, Nepal and parts of India in the south, the vast K'iang empire of the Yang-t'ung (Tib. Zhang-zhung), nearly the whole of Chinese Turkestan, and a part of the territory of the western Türks.

The annals also record military expeditions, victories, and defeats, since the official annalists of the Tibetan government accompanied the armies on their various expeditions. In addition, the annals mention the places where the summer and winter State Assemblies ('Dun-sa) were held, report births, marriages, and deaths in the imperial family, including the dates when an imperial corpse was embalmed in the special house of the dead (Tib. ring-khang), when it was buried, and when the special rituals in remembrance of the deceased took place. The annals also mention the affairs of the most powerful clans of the nobility, among whom the emperors before Khri-srong lde-brtsan (second half of the eighth century) had merely the status of primus inter pares. From the nobility were selected the ministers and generals, and sometimes, as the annals make evident, they played the role of major domo of the palace, and were even more powerful than the emperor himself.

From all these details it is evident that the value of these annals cannot be overestimated. They are the work of state annalists (Tib. yig-tshangs-pa) who, beginning with Srong-btsan sgam-po, were institutionalized after the Chinese model. This ancient period, the Imperial Age, is believed to have seen the compiling of an historical work of excerpts from Chinese historical books, The Records of China and Tibet (rGya bod yig-tsang), which was probably lost but known from some quotations preserved in later chronicles such as the Deb-ther-sngon-po and rGyal-rabs gsal-ba'i me-long.

Sources dating from the Imperial period are not restricted to the chronicle and annals. Thanks to the activities of Sir Aurel Stein, Paul Pelliot, and the four German Turfan expeditions, we have access to many other documents written on paper or on wood; most of them found in the Khotan, Mīrān, Tun-huang, and the Turfan areas. The majority of these documents have been translated by Sir Frederic William Thomas, Jacques Bacot, and Marcelle Lalou of Paris, and A. H. Francke. They give a vivid picture of the Tibetan colonial empire in eastern Turkestan.

Finally, another important source of Tibetan history are the inscriptions of the Tibetan emperors engraved on stone pillars or obelisks. The most famous inscription written in 764, is located at Zhol (south of the Potala, the winter residence of the Dalai Lamas). It preserves an account of Tibetan victories over the T'ang troops and also gives an appraisal of the Tibetan "Great Minister" *(blon-chen)* Ta-ra klu-khong. Another important inscription engraved on a *rDo-ring* was placed before the central Tibetan sanctuary at Lhasa, the so-called Jo-khang. This pillar was erected in memory of the 822 treaty between the Tibetans and Chinese terminating the constant state of warfare under the fervent Buddhist emperor Ral-pa-can (817-36) and the T'ang emperor Mu-tsung (820-24).

In addition to these inscriptions others have been discovered at bSam-yas, the oldest Tibetan monastery; at mTs'ur-p'u, a Karmapa monastery dating back to the times of Ral-pa-can; near the sKar-chung chapel; and at U-shang-rdo, a temple built by the emperor Sad-na-legs (804-17). These inscriptions were first edited by L. A. Waddell, and later by Sir Hugh Richardson, Professor Giuseppe Tucci, and Professor Li Fang-kuei.

After the breakdown of the empire following the assassination of the last emperor, gLang-dar-ma (middle of the ninth century), Buddhism declined, and with it all cultural and literary activities. Only after the reintroduction of Buddhism in about 1000 did the situation again improve in western Tibet. This was due to the zeal of the pious Tibetan translator Rin-chen bzang-po and the famous Indian teacher Atīsha of the monastic university of Vikramashīlā in the Pāla kingdom (present-day Bihār), as well as to the self-denial of the Tibetan monk-king of Gu-ge, Lha bla-ma Ye-shes-od. In addition to the old rNying-ma-pa, this period produced many new Tibetan schools of Buddhism, e.g., the bKa'-gdams-pa, the bKa'-brgyud-pa, the Zhi-byed-pa, and the famous Sa-skya-pa. The literary activities of these schools of Buddhism brought into existence a new monastic historiography. Some of the works produced were biographies of famous religious teachers (*rNam-thar*), one of the first of these being Atīsha's biography by his disciple 'Brom-ston. But there were also historical and chronological works devoted especially to the events of the Imperial period, such as the *Royal Lineages of Tibet (Bod-kyi rgyal-rabs)* by two famous Sa-skya Lamas, Grags-pa rgyal-mtshan (1147-1216) and ḥPhags-pa (1235-80).

With the weakening of the power of the Sino-Mongol Yüan emperors and the waning of Sa-skya power, a most important period began for Tibet as a result of the Tibetans' growing interest in their own history and the consequent compilation of several historical works. This occurred during the time of Byang-chub rgyal-mtshan (1302-64), who originally was only the chieftain of one of the Tibetan myriarchies *(khri-sde)* at sNe-gdong-rdzong in the Yar-klungs valley, the cradle of ancient Tibetan imperial power. This man, a sturdy and able personality, and the dynasty of Phag-mo gru-pa kings which he founded, restored consciousness of past Imperial glories, despite the fact that the Phag-mo gru-pa governed only central Tibet. This is strikingly symbolized by a custom that required high officials to wear the costumes of the early kings at New Year's celebrations, a practice which has prevailed down to our times.

During this period there arose a lively feeling for national antiquities, for historical research, and for the search for hidden historical documents of the Imperial period. This was certainly not mere antiquarianism but a true awakening of national consciousness. It was the time of the important *gTer-ston*, the "discoverers of hidden literary treasures." The Phag-mo gru-pa sponsored the famous rNying-ma-pa gTer-ston O-rgyan gling-pa, born in 1323, who was fortunate enough to discover a considerable number of old manuscripts written on scrolls (as was customary during the Imperial times), the ancient material of what is now the *Padma thang-yig (Biography of Saint Padmasambhava)* and the *bKa'-thang sde-lnga* (the five parts of orders, i.e., of Padmasambhava). Most of these materials are truly old and date back to the eighth and ninth centuries, although, naturally, both books contain a considerable amount of material added by the *gTer-ston* to propagate the rNying-ma-pa teachings and to insert certain prophecies concerning the time of the *Hor*, i.e., the period of Mongol power. As to textual criticism, we can state with almost total certainty that the portions of these books which describe the period prior to the death of the emperor Mu-ne btsan-po (798/99) are genuine, while those portions which deal with later events are probably additions made by the *gTer-ston*. Among the historical data found in the *bKa'-thang sde-lnga* are several old genealogies of the ancient kings and emperors which date back perhaps to an old pre-Buddhist Bon-po tradition, information on the administration and the military districts of the Tibetan empire, lists of the old castles and families of the powerful nobility who provided the state with ministers and generals, and lists of the Indian pandits and Tibetan translators who translated the Buddhist and Bon-po literature.

Turning to the monastic "Histories of Buddhism," we must mention as the oldest extant specimen of that literature the *Chos-'byung* of the "omniscient" teacher Bu-ston Rin-chen-grub, who wrote this work in A.D. 1347. Bu-ston was by no means the first to write on this subject; we know of several of his predecessors whose works have not yet been found but were quoted by Bu-ston and others, for instance, the famous Nel-pa Paṇḍi-ta. Bu-ston's work is not only a "history of Buddhism" but a comprehensive description and catalogue of the canonical Buddhist scriptures. In only one of the three sections which make up the work do we find a history of Buddhism in India followed by a fairly small but important and reliable chapter on Tibetan religious history.

To the best of our knowledge, the next important historical work was the *mKhas-pa'i dga'-ston, "A Festival for the Learned,"* completed in 1564 by dPa'-bo gtsug-lag 'phreng-ba, a monk of the Karma-pa school who, because of his own religious inclinations, devotes a considerable part of his work to the history of that special form of Buddhism. However, the book also contains valuable and rather rare information concerning the schools which preceded the dGe-lugs-pa or Yellow Church and a long and exceedingly valuable chapter on Tibet during the Imperial period. The author must have had access to the State Archives since he reproduces several original documents which are not known elsewhere, and we may gather from his book that there must have existed handwritten copies of the famous Sino-Tibetan treaties which were also engraved on the famous pillars (Tib. *rDo-ring*) erected below the Potala, in front of the Cathedral of Lhasa (Jo-khang), and near the burial ground of the old emperors in the 'Phyong-rgyas valley. According to the research of Professor Tucci of Rome, our text also reproduces inscriptions which have not yet been discovered.

The book is also important because dPa'-bo gtsug-lag 'phreng-ba quotes in full considerable portions of an old Tibetan chronicle, written in verse, which probably dates back to the Imperial Age. Traces of this metrical chronicle were first discovered by Berthold Laufer when he was researching the events connected with the foundation of the first Tibetan monastery of bSam-yas. The metrical chronicle was used also in a later book, the *rGyal-rabs gsal-ba'i me-long*. What gives dPa'-bo gtsug-lag 'phreng-ba's excerpts of the metrical chronicle their special value in his additional prose version, which does not always agree with the version in verse and sometimes even contradicts it. For Western historians, the fact that dPa'-bo stsug-lag 'phreng-ba does not harmonize his sources is extremely important since it enables us to compare the two versions and make some sort of critical evaluation of their validity.

In 1476 another work of considerable importance appeared: the *Blue Annals (Deb-ther sngon-po)*, compiled by the monk 'Gos lo-tsā-ba gZhon-nu-dpal. This author devoted his attention to the discussion of chronological problems, for which he became well known. In his valuable but short chapter on the Imperial Age, in which he gives only a skeletal account of events, he also uses Chinese sources such as the *T'ang-shu*, attempts to reconcile the data of the Chinese and Tibetan sources, and tries to show the exact contemporaneity of the respective Chinese and Tibetan emperors. The remaining and largest part of his work is devoted to the development of the different Tibetan schools of Buddhism and includes materials not available elsewhere.

It is not within the scope of this survey of Tibetan historical literature to enumerate all Tibetan historical works, only to point out the characteristics of the more important ones. However, it should be noted that the followers of the Bon religion also wrote histories, one of which has been dealt with by Berthold Laufer. Moreover, we should at least cite the *Lineage of Kings (rGyal-rabs gsal-ba'i me-long)* by Grags-pa rgyal-mtshan, written in 1508 at the ancient monastery of bSam-yas. Grags-pa rgyal-mtshan, too, uses the old metrical chronicle and excerpts from the Chinese sources entitled *rGya-bod yig-tshangs*.

Two other books which originally must have been of considerable age, but were later revised to their detriment, are the *Red Annals (Deb-dmar)* by Kun-dga' rdo-rje, and the *sBa-bzhed (The Statements of sBa)*. The second of these in its original form if attributed to sBa gSal-snang, one of the zealous Buddhist ministers of the emperor Khri-srong lde-brtsan. The fragment of the *Deb-dmar*, published by the Namgyal Institute at Gangtok, is by no means the original. There are two editions of the *sBa-bzhed*, a work which deals mainly with the events which took place during the period of the foundation of the bSam-yas monastery and with other religious activities of Khri-srong lde-brtsan: a "Pure sBa-bzhed" *(sBa-bzhed gtsang-ma)* and a *sBa-bzhed zhabs-btags-ma* (i.e., "with a supplement"). The text, edited by Professor R. A. Stein of Paris, is the latter since it covers the period of the emperors Ral-pa-can and gLang-dar-ma (ninth century). In the present writer's opinion, the book was rewritten as late as the period of the Yellow Church, since in its account of the murder of gLang-dar-ma by the hermit Lha-lung dpal-gyi rdo-rje, which took place near the *rDo-ring* in front of the Jo-khang, there is mention of a nearby stupa erected to house the relics of the Fourth Dalai Lama, Yon-tan rGya-mtsho, of Mongol descent.

Passing over Tāranātha's famous *History of Buddhism in India* (1608), for this deals with Indian, not Tibetan historical events, we must finally mention an exceedingly important contribution found in dGe-lugs-pa historiography: the *Lineage of Kings (rGyal-rabs)*, compiled by the celebrated Fifth Dalai Lama, Ngag-dbang blo-bzang rgya-mtsho (1617-82). This famous hierarch had access to the state archives; hence his work is a true mine of information, especially on the Tibetan Middle Ages. The Fifth Dalai Lama quotes the opinions of his predecessors more frequently than the above-mentioned authors and often takes sides against or in favor of opinions of the past historians. His style is that of Indian scholastic literature which usually gives the reasons for rejecting another writer's opinion. We know definitely that the "Great Fifth" *(lNga-pa chen-po)*, as he is usually called, was an eminent Sanskrit scholar who studied extensively the florid Indian *Kāvya* style. He not only wrote an important commentary to the *Kāvyādarśa (Mirror of Poetry)* by Daṇḍin, but imitated this style even in his historical work. To end this survey of Tibetan historiography, we shall attempt to reproduce an example of lNga-pa chen-po's language by quoting a passage which describes the accession of the apostate Emperor, gLang-dar-ma.

> At that time, when gLang-dar-ma U-dum-btsan was enthroned, the situation appeared as though the god of sensual lust *(Kāmadeva)* together with his army, after having completely conquered virtue, were shouting aloud, because the fresh sprout of the Buddha's doctrine, just being beyond the need of using the nourishment of her nurse, the spring season, namely good deeds (and that fresh sprout), was destroyed by the heavy hail storm of the shameless life of practicing the ten sins.

The difficulty of translating passages of this sort which make an abundant use of what Sanskrit poetics (Alankāra Shāstra) call "metaphorical karmadhāraya" is obvious.

Little scholarly attention has been given to the local chronicles in Tibetan historiography. Before 1968 we had only one specimen of these chronicles, the *La-dvags rgyal rabs (The Genealogy of the Kings of Ladakh)*, an important work published by A. H. Francke in 1926. Only in 1968 did Josef Kolmaš of Prague publish another interesting specimen of this literature, *The Genealogy of the Kings of Derge (sDe-dge'i rgyal-rabs)*, a small principality in eastern Tibet near the upper Yang-tse or 'Bri-chu. In 1969 another example of local historiography appeared, *The Annals of Kokonor* in Amdo, edited and translated by Yang Ho-chin of Seattle. The author of this small booklet was the famous Sum-pa mk'an-po (1704-77), a prolific writer of the Yellow Church and later abbot of the dGon-lung monastery in Amdo. To him we also owe the universal *History of Buddhism in India, Tibet and Mongolia*, which draws profusely on earlier writers.

The most comprehensive local history extant within the literature of Tibet is *The Religious History of Amdo (A-mdo chos-'byung)*, also called *Deb-ther rgya-mtsho*. It was completed in A.D. 1865. This is an especially valuable work for it provides a long catalogue of Tibetan historiographical literature and a detailed history of the monasteries of Amdo.

A final word may be said concerning the characteristics of the monastic chronicles we have discussed. Although they certainly do not furnish us with material which we would call "historical" in the strict sense of the word, the legendary material which these books contain is highly valuable as it provides scholars with much information of a secondary historical nature. A single instance may prove indicative, lest we become the victims of barren criticism. If the records of the Chinese marriage of the emperor Srong-btsan sgam-po were found in the Tibetan monastic chronicles alone, a supercritical historian might state, in view of legendary style in which this event is described, that it was mere fantasy. Fortunately, the sober Chinese *T'ang Annals* prove the reality of this event.

BIBLIOGRAPHY

GENERAL

A. I. Vostrikov, *Tibetskaya istoricheskaya literatura*, Bibliotheca Buddhica 32, Leningrad 1962. In English: *Tibetan Historical Literature*, Soviet Indology Series No. 4, Calcutta 1970; Helmut H. R. Hoffmann, "Tibetan Historiography and the Approach of the Tibetans to History," *JAH* 4 (1970): 169-77; Giuseppe

Tucci, "The Validity of Tibetan Historical Tradition," *India Antiqua, Commemoration Volume in Honor of J. Ph. Vogel*, Leiden 1947, pp. 309-22; Giuseppe Tucci, *Tibetan Painted Scrolls*, vol. 1, Rome 1949 (important data on Tibetan historiography pp. 139-70); Bunkyo Aoki, *Study of Early Tibetan Chronicles*, Tokyo 1955. J. Bacot, F. W. Thomas, Ch. Toussaint, *Documents de Touen-houang relatifs à l'histoire de Tibet*, Annales du Musée Guimet, vol. 51, Paris 1940/46; F. W. Thomas, *Tibetan Literary Texts and Documents Concerning Chinese Turkestan*, 4 vols., London, 1935-63; R. E. Emmerick, *Tibetan Texts Concerning Khotan*, London Oriental Series, vol. 19, London 1967; L. A. Waddell, "Ancient Historical Edicts at Lhasa," *JRAS* (1910): 1247-82; Giuseppe Tucci, *The Tombs of the Tibetan Kings*, Serie Orientale Roma 1, Rome 1950 (contains several old Tibetan inscriptions with translations); H. E. Richardson, *Ancient Historical Edicts at Lhasa and the Mu Tsung/Khri Gtsug Lde Brtsan Treaty of A.D. 821-822 from the Inscription at Lhasa*, Prize Publication Fund, vol. 19, London 1952; H. E. Richardson, "Three Ancient Inscriptions from Tibet," *JASB* (1949): 45-65; H. E. Richardson, "A Ninth Century Inscription from Rkoṅ-po," *JRAS* (1954): 157-73; H. E. Richardson, "Tibetan Inscriptions at Žvaḥi Lha Khang," *JRAS* (1952): 133-54, and (1953): 1-12; H. E. Richardson, "A New Inscription of Khri Srong Lde Brtsan," *JRAS* (1964): 1-13; H. E. Richardson, "A Tibetan Inscription from Rgyal Lha-Khang, and a Note on Tibetan Chronology from A.D. 841 to A.D. 1042," *JRAS* (1957): 57-78. Berthold Laufer, *Der Roman einer tibetischen Königin*, Leipzig 1911 (contains documents from the ninth century revised in the fourteenth century), Emil Schlagintweit, "Die Lebensbeschreibung von Padmasambhava," 1, *AKBAW* (1899): 417-44 and 2, *AKBAW* (1905): 517-76; G. Ch. Toussaint, *Le dict de Padma*, Paris 1933 (French translation of the biography of Padmasambhava); W. Y. Evans-Wentz, *The Tibetan Book of the Great Liberation*, London 1954 (contains an abstract of the biography of Padmasambhava on pp. 105-92).

MONASTIC CHRONICLES

E. Obermiller, *History of Buddhism by Bu-ston*, 2 vols. Materialien zur Kunde des Buddhismus, Heft 18/19, Heidelberg 1931/32 (translation of Bu-ston's *Chos-'byung*); *Mkhas paḥi dgaḥ ston by Dpaḥ-bo-gtsug-lag 'phreng-ba*, 4 vols. Satapitaka Series, Bhota Pitaka, vol. 4, ed. by Dr. Lokesh Chandra, New Delhi 1959-62; G. N. Roerich, *The Blue Annals of gZhon-nu-dpal*, Royal Asiatic Society of Bengal, Monograph Series, vol. 7, Calcutta 1949-53 (translation of the *Deb-ther sngon-po*); B. I. Kuznetsov, *Rgyal Rabs Gsal Ba'i Me Long* (Tibetan text in transliteration with an introduction in English), Scripta Tibetana 1, Leiden 1966; *The Red Annals*, part one (Tibetan text), with a foreword by Palden Thondup Namgyal, published by the Namgyal Institute of Tibetology, Gangtok (Sikkim) 1961; R. A. Stein, *Une chronique ancienne de bSam-yas: sBa-bžed*, édition du texte tibétain et résumé français, Publications de l'Institut des Hautes

Études Chinoises, Textes et Documents 1, Paris 1961; a version of the *Chronicle of the Fifth Dalai Lama* has been edited under the title *Early History of Tibet*, by Ngawang Gelek Demo, New Delhi 1967, while considerable portions of this chronicle have been translated by Giuseppe Tucci into English, *Tibetan Painted Scrolls*, vol. 2, Rome 1949, pp. 625-51; *Pag Sam Jon Zang* [A history of Buddhism in India, Tibet, and Mongolia] by Ye-shes dPal-'byor, generally called *Sum-pa mKhan-po*, 2 vols. (dealing with India and Tibet), ed. by Sarat Chandra Das, Calcutta 1908; the third part (*Mongolia*, and a *Chronological Table*) has been published by Lokesh Chandra, *Dpag-Bsam-Ljon-Bzaṅ*, part 3, Satapitaka Series, Bhota Pitaka, vol. 3, New Delhi 1959.

LOCAL CHRONICLES

The La-dvags rgyal-rabs [Chronicles of Ladakh] were first translated into German: Emil Schlagintweit, *Die Könige von Tibet*, Abhandlungen der K. Bayerischen Akademie der Wissenschaften, 1. Classe, vol. 10, Abteilung 3, München 1866; the standard edition and translation of this work was published by A. H. Francke, *Antiquities of Indian Tibet*, Part 2: *The Chronicles of Ladakh and Minor Chronicles*, Archaeological Survey of India, New Imperial Series, vol. 50, Calcutta 1926; this book should not be used without comparing the data given in Luciano Petech, *A Study on the Chronicles of Ladakh*, Calcutta 1939, and the following articles by the same author: "Notes on Ladakhi History," *IHQ* (1948): 213-35, and "The Tibetan-Ladakhi Moghul War," *IHQ* (1947): 169-99.

Josef Kolmaš, *A Genealogy of the Kings of Derge*, Tibetan text edited with historical introduction, Czechoslovak Academy of Sciences, Dissertationes Orientales, vol. 12, Prague 1968.

Ho-chin Yang, *The Annals of Kokonor*, Indiana University Publications, Uralic and Altaic Series, vol. 106, Bloomington 1969.

Muslim Sources

The word "Tibet" was borrowed from Muslim geographers and historiographers, where it occurs as *Tubbat*. Older occurrences may be found in Zoroastrian Middle Persian *Töpüt* (in the Bahman Yasht) attested also in the Turkic Orkhon inscriptions from the mid eighth century. The name has never been satisfactorily explained. The Tibetans themselves call their country *Bod* (sanskritized *Bhoṭa*).

The Muslim data on Tibet originated in three different sources, the first of which is the data collected by the Caliph al-Ma'mūn and handed down by later writers. Al-Ma'mūn, commander-in-chief in Khorasān at a time of clashes with the Tibetans (A.D. 809-18), was Caliph from 818-33 and greatly encouraged the study of the geography and history of foreign peoples. On Ma'mūn's data depend the works of Mas'ūdī al-Ḥuwārizmī (written about 817-26), of al-Ya'qūbī (about 891), and of al-Battānī (died 929). Legendary connection of Tubbat with the name of an old king of Yemen to whom was ascribed a campaign to the east is found in that literature, and the Tubbat were said to be the descendants of the army of the Yemen king called Tubba' al-Aqran. All this is, of course, mere fantasy.

Although the sources belonging to this group speak of Tibet, they denote by this name only the Tibetan colonial empire, the borders of which touched the Muslim zone of influence. It is not surprising, therefore, that Khotan was believed to be the capital of Tibet, whereas it was only the residence of an official with the title of Nang-rje-po. When the above-mentioned sources use the word "king of Tubbat," they refer only to the colonial districts of the Nang-rje-po of Khotan and include the western Himalayan countries, e.g., Ladakh, Baltistān, Gilgit, and Yāsīn.

The second independent group of Muslim works which describes Tibet goes back to Ǧaihānī, the wazīr of the Samanid kings (circa 914). His material was used in the famous anonymous geography *Ḥudūd al-'Ālam (The Regions of the World)*, 982-83, excellently translated into English by Minorsky. This work still mentions parts of the lost Tibetan colonial empire but is also acquainted with Tibet proper, i.e., central Tibet (Ü and Tsang). Gardīzī, who wrote about 1050, also depended on Ǧaihānī. He mentions the old prehistorical legend wherein the first Tibetan king came down from the sky, the abode of the old pre-Buddhist gods. There are also indications that he knew of the existence of Lhasa.

A third group of data is represented by random notes made by various Muslim travellers, among whom were Abū Dulaf (circa 942) and the famous scholar al-Bīrūnī (died 1048). The latter describes the itinerary from Kanauj on the Ganges via Nepal to Lhasa, and distinguishes inner Tibet (Yāsīn and Gilgit) from outer Tibet and Lhasa. Mahmūd al-Kāsgharī (circa 1074), who was famous for his information on the Turks, also makes brief mention of Tibet, which he considers a nation dwelling among the Turks. He also mentions the Tibetan export of musk, and reports the old legend wherein the Tibetans descended from the Arabs as shown by their reputed use of the Arabic words for "mother" (*umm*) and "father" (*ab*), *a-ma* and *a-pha* in Tibetan. This is, of course just a folk etymology. Because later writers only reproduced the material of the older ones, they need not be mentioned here.

From the tenth century western Tibet was separated from Ü and gTsang and had its own independent historiography. The principal source for the invasions of the Chagatay sultan Sa'id of Ladakh is the work of the general Mirza Haidar, who invaded Ladakh in 1517 and again in 1533. After the death of the sultan in 1533, Mirza Haidar acted on his own. In 1536 he was obliged to withdraw from Ladakh, as the majority of his soldiers had perished from the extreme cold of that high country. Mirza Haidar wrote of his activities in his *Tarīkh-i Rashīdī* (Rashīd was the successor of Sultan Sa'id of Yarkand). He was not only a brilliant soldier and fanatic Muslim but a magnificent writer who, in addition to describing his own military experiences, also collected a large mass of other information on Ladakh, its customs, and religion.

For the period of the conquest of Ladakh by the Moghuls of India we have the *Tarīkh-i Kashmīrī*, written by Muhammed Azam in 1736. This work has still not been edited although it has been used by Professor Petech in a book and in several articles. The work describes, among other things, the emperor Aurangzeb's reception of a Ladakhi embassy in 1665 and the final defeat of western Tibet by the Moghul troops in 1683. The consequences of this defeat were disastrous for the Tibetan population of Ladakh, and included high levies for the Moghul governor of Kashmir, the use of coins of the Moghul type minted in Kashmir, and the coercion of the Ladakhi king to embrace Islam at least nominally. Islam had been accepted by the Balti king of Skar-rdo in the Indus valley in 1637.

With the waning of Muslim power which followed the breakdown of the Moghuls, Ladakh was invaded in 1683 by the troops of the kings of the Dogra dynasty of Kashmir.

REFERENCES

An excellent description of the Muslim (Arabic and Persian) sources of Tibetan History can be found in Luciano Petech, "Il Tibet nella geografia musulmana," *ANL*, Classe di Scienze morali, storiche e filologiche 8 (1947): 55-70. The majority of these sources have not been translated into any Western language. We may just quote the following: *Hudūd al-'Ālam, "The Regions of the World"*, A Persian Geography 372 A. H.–Ă.D. 982, translated and explained by V. Minorsky, E. J. W. Gibb Memorial Series, New Series 11, London 1937, V.

Minorsky, *Une nouvelle source musulmane sur l'Asie Centrale au XIe siècle,* Comptes Rendus, Académie des Inscriptions et Belles-Lettres, 1937, pp. 318-19 (concerning ibn-Ḥordaḏbeh); and *Sharaf ez-Zaman Tāhir Marwazī on China, the Turks, and India,* James G. Forlong Fund, vol. 22, London 1942; A. von Rohr-Sauer, *Des Abū Dulaf's Bericht über seine Reise nach Turkestan, China und Indien,* Bonner Orientalistische Studien 26, Leipzig 1939; E. Sachau, *Alberuni's India,* 2 vols., London 1910; A. Jaubert, *Géographie d'Edrisi* (French translation), Paris 1836-40; N. Elias–E. Denison Ross, *A History of the Moghuls of Central Asia, being the Tarīkh-i-Rashīdī of Mirza Muhammad Haidar, Dughlát,* London 1898; reprint: New York, Praeger 1970, with an introduction by Denis Sinor.

Chinese Sources

The Chinese sources are by far more important for Tibetan history than are the Muslim writings, for they cover the entire period from the pre-historic Proto-Tibetan Ch'iang down to the present. We shall discuss these sources only briefly since good histories of Chinese literature exist, while relatively little information about Tibetan historiography and the lesser known data of Muslim writers is available.

Reliable information on the ancestors of the Tibetans, the so-called "Ch'iang of the West," is to be found in the official Chinese dynastic histories of the Later Han dynasty. The annals of the short-lived Sui dynasty give a vivid picture of the Ch'iang states which existed during the time of the formation of the Tibetan empire (seventh century), and contain data on an earlier Inner Asian empire called Zhang-zhung in Tibetan and Yang-t'ung in Chinese. But the most important sources for ancient Tibetan history are the two *T'ang-shu,* the Old and the New Annals of the T'ang dynasty (618-906), which cover nearly the whole period of the Tibetan empire. These annals, composed in a similar style, contain three sections: 1) the "Imperial Records," which give a short description of events during the reign of the respective emperors; 2) the "Memoirs," which are monographs on chronology, rites, music, jurisprudence, political affairs, economy, official sacrifices, astronomy, influences of the elements, geography, government offices, material culture, literature, and bibliography; and 3) biographies of outstanding personages who lived during the time of the dynasty. The Old *T'ang-shu* devotes chapter 196 A and B to Tibetan subjects, while the New *T'ang-shu* contains a monograph on Tibet in chapter 216 A and B. Concerning the chronological discrepancies between Chinese and Tibetan sources it must be borne in mind, for example, that the death of a Tibetan emperor during peace time was announced at the Chinese court by an embassy at the end of a journey, which from Lhasa to Ch'ang-an took at least one year. Consequently, events in Tibet generally were recorded by the two *T'ang-shu* a year later than in Tibet proper.

Most important among the later Chinese annals are those of the Mongol Yuan and the Manchu Ch'ing dynasty, the first because of the so-called first conversion of the Mongols to Buddhism and the second because they describe the gradual Chinese penetration into Tibet. There was a considerable difference between the two dynasties as regards Tibet. The Mongol attitude simply implied patronage of the Buddhist church and hierarchy, whereas the Manchus, by degrees, established a protectorate which ceased only after the breakdown of that dynasty in 1911.

In addition to the official dynastic annals there are two especially important encyclopaedias: the *T'ung-tien,* which goes back to T'ang times and was completed in 801, and the later *Wen-hsien t'ung-kao* by Ma Tuan-lin, completed during the thirteenth century. During Manchu times several historico-geographical works were compiled including the *Wei-ts'ang t'u-chih*, a source of valuable information on events during the reign of the Ch'ing dynasty.

REFERENCES

S. W. Bushell, "The Early History of Tibet. From Chinese Sources," *JRAS*, N.S. 12 (1880): 435-541; this publication has been superseded by Paul Pelliot, *Histoire ancienne du Tibet,* Oeuvres posthumes de Paul Pelliot, vol. 5, Paris 1961 (translation of the chapters on Tibet in the Old and New T'ang Annals).

W. Woodville Rockhill, *Tibet. A Geographical, Ethnographical, and Historical Sketch, Derived from Chinese Sources,* first published London 1891, reprint Peking 1939.

Valuable data on Tibetan History during T'ang times is also found in Édouard Chavannes, *Documents sur les Tou-kiue (Turcs) occidentaux,* recueillis et commentés suivi de notes additionelles, reprint Paris, n.d. (original edition St. Pétersbourg 1903).

Information on Tibet from Classical Antiquity

The oldest extant data on India and the adjacent Himalayan regions are to be found in Herodotus, book three, paragraphs 102-5. This subject is again mentioned in the fragments of Megasthenes, who about 300 B.C. was ambassador of Seleukus I, one of the diadochs after the death of Alexander the Great, to the court of the Indian Maurya Emperor Candragupta.

Herodotus liked to collect ethnographic data on foreign peoples, especially curious and legendary things. His information on western Tibet, too, seems to be quite legendary, but there are interesting facts behind his story. He comments on the origin of the wealth of the Indians and is the first to mention the strange story of the "gold-digging ants." This can be summarized as follows: in the western Himalayas near the Dard people (Daradai), on a sandy mountain plain by the upper Indus, exist huge ants which dig the earth and bring out sand mixed with gold dust. These ants have a skin like the panther, run very fast, and present a danger to humans who wish to seize the gold. In this form, of course, the story is legendary, but the substance seems to be historical and the geographical data are quite exact. Many scholars, such as Schiern, Laufer, and W. W. Tarn, have dealt with this subject but the most credible explanation is that proposed by A. Herrmann. The Dards still live near the western Tibetans, and at Kargil (dKar-skyil), a place in the valley of a tributary of the river Indus, there is a sandy plain where until recent times gold has been found. Some very large ants can be found in the region. The animals attacking the gold collectors probably were large predators such as panthers, which confused Herodotus' Persian informants. Later Buddhist sources also mention the existence of a "Gold Country" in this part of the world (Suvarṇagotra or Rukmadesha) which seems to have belonged to the Zhang-zhung empire, the predecessor of the Tibetans in this region. Even western Tibetan folklore has kept the memory of the gold-digging ants. Two stories about them were published by A. H. Francke in 1924.

The Hellenistic geographer and astronomer Claudius Ptolemaeus also knew about the Tibetans. In his book written in approximately A.D. 177 he calls them *Bautai*, a name certainly borrowed from *Bhota*.

REFERENCES

Albert Herrmann, *Das Land der Seide und Tibet im Lichte der Antike*. Quellen und Forschungen zur Geschichte der Geographie und Völkerkunde, Band 1, Leipzig 1939.

Concerning the "gold-digging ants": Frederik Schiern, *Über den Ursprung der Sage von den goldgrabenden Ameisen*, Kopenhagen und Leipzig 1873; Berthold Laufer, "Die Sage von den goldgrabenden Ameisen," *TP* (1908): 429-52; A. H. Francke, "Two Ant Stories from the Territory of the Ancient Kingdom of Western Tibet," *AM* (1924): 67-75; Albert Hermann, loc. cit., pp. 10-16.

European Travellers to Inner Asia
Since Marco Polo

The Venetian merchant Marco Polo who travelled from 1271 to 1292 to Peking and the court of the Mongol Great Khan did not enter Tibet, nor did the Franciscan monk Odorico de Pordenone, whose travels spanned the years 1325 to 1330; their records on Tibet were consequently compiled from hearsay. Since the seventeenth century, however, the Western world has obtained valuable information about the roof of the world from the brave and daring Christian missionaries, whose missionary work proved unsuccessful. The first to institute a short-lived Christian mission on Tibetan soil were the Jesuits who stayed at Gu-ge in western Tibet (1624-32), and Tsang, in west-central Tibet. In 1661 Johann Grueber from Austria and the Belgian Albert d'Orville resided for two months in Lhasa during the reign of the great Fifth Dalai Lama, thus claiming with justification to have been the first Christian missionaries in the Tibetan capital. Grueber's interesting account of his experience was used by Athanasius Kircher in his work *China Illustrata*, published in Amsterdam in 1667.

Italian Capuchins first arrived in Lhasa in 1707 but had to leave in 1711 because of a lack of funds. They witnessed the troubles which followed the death of the "Great Fifth" and the fighting between the Chinese and the Mongolian Khoshot Khan Lha-bzang. In 1716 Ippolito Desideri, Jesuit and scholar, went to Lhasa where he stayed until 1721. He wrote a highly interesting book on his experiences. By late 1716 the indefatigable Capuchins had instituted another mission which functioned until 1733. They were much appreciated as physicians but failed in their missionary activities.

Two French Lazarist Fathers, E. Huc and J. Gabet, arrived in Lhasa in 1846 through Mongolia and Amdo. They built a small Christian chapel but were expelled the same year, not by the Tibetan government but by the suspicious Chinese *ambans* (residents). The religious minister of Tibet, the bKa'-blon Lama, showed much kindness to the travellers, and when the *amban* told him that the Frenchmen might be dangerous spies, he answered: "If the religious teaching of these people is wrong, the Tibetans will not accept it. If it is true, then there is nothing to fear. Truth cannot cause any damage. We cannot deprive them of their liberty and our protection, which they should share with all aliens and especially with all pious people." The bKa'-blon Lama's words were in vain, although he was right, for Christianity could never have been a danger to the highly sophisticated Buddhist religion. Huc wrote a valuable report on his Tibetan experiences.

REFERENCES

A good general introduction written in a popular vein: John MacGregor, *Tibet. A Chronicle of Exploration*, New York and London 1970. Carlo Puini, *Il Tibet* (Geografia, Storia, Religione, Costumi) secondo la relazione del viaggio del P. Ippolito Desideri (1715-21), Memorie della Soc. Geogr. Ital., vol. 10, Rome 1904; Filippo de Filippi, *An Account of Tibet. The Travels of Ippolito Desideri of Pistoia, S. J., 1712-1727*, London 1937; C. Wessels, *Early Jesuit Travellers in Central Asia, 1603-1721*, The Hague 1924; Agostino Antonio Giorgi, *Alphabetum Tibetanum, missionum apostalicarum commodo editum*, Romae 1762 (the oldest European book on Tibet which describes the experiences of the missionaries); Athanasius Kircher, *China Monumentis qua sacris, qua profanis, nec non variis naturae et artis spectaculis, aliarumqua rerum memorabilium argumentis illustrata*, Amsterdam 1667 (also contains data on Tibet); the entire material collected by the Capuchin and Jesuit missionaries has been edited and commented on by Luciano Petech, *I missionari Italiani nel Tibet e nel Nepal*, Il Nuovo Ramusio 2, Rome 1952-56, 7 vols.

Clements R. Markham, *Narratives of the Mission of George Bogle, and of the Journey of Thomas Manning to Lhasa*, London 1876; M. Huc, *Souvenirs d'un voyage dans la Tartarie et le Tibet* 1844-46, 2 vols., Paris 1878. An English translation by W. Hazlitt appeared under the title *Travels in Tartary, Tibet and China*, London n.d.

V. THE HISTORY OF TIBET

The Age of Imperial Unity
and Expansion (600-860)

As far back as the time of the oracle bones of the Chinese Shang dynasty we have records of a large group of nomadic tribes called the Ch'iang believed to have been the ancestors and precursors of the Tibetans. The Ch'iang were nomads who wandered as far as the northwestern border of China about the highlands of what is now northern Tibet. Their economy depended almost entirely upon their flocks of sheep, goats, yaks, and horses. Only those few tribes which penetrated as far south as the upper valley of the great Yangtze ('Bri-chu), Ya-lung (Nyag-chu), Mekong (Dza-chu), and Salween (Nag-chu) rivers combined cattle-breeding with farming. The Ch'iang lived in tents of felt and hide and used the same materials for clothing. Their food consisted of tsam-pa (roast barley), buttered tea, beer, and meat. The easternmost Ch'iang who dwelt in the deep, damp valleys regarded the monkey as their totem. Some evidence points to the existence of matriarchy. The Ch'iang had no script but are believed to have had an oral literature. Their languages were not identical with Tibetan although they belonged to the same linguistic family—Tibeto-Burmese.

The Chinese frequently mention raids by the Ch'iang against the western frontier of the Celestial Empire. One outstanding event of this kind took place as early as 63 B.C. when the Ch'iang joined the invasions of the Hsiung-nu and caused a great deal of trouble in the western provinces of China. At the time when the real Tibetans were beginning to form a nation, the most important of the Ch'iang tribes were the Tang-hsiang, who lived at the large bend of the rMa-chu (upper Huang-ho); and the Su-p'i (Tibetan Sum-pa), who lived in the rGyal-mo-rong country (present day Chin-ch'uan). For a time the latter also lived in the far north, and as far west as the 'Bri-chu (upper Yang-tse) where the Su-p'i state bordered the Ch'iang empire of the Zhang-zhung (Chin. Yang-t'ung), about which we still have little information. We do know, however, that the Zhang-zhung empire included the whole area now known as western Tibet, that its center was in the upper Sutlej valley, and that it extended as far north as the frontier of the kingdom of Khotan and in the east included the whole lake country of Tibet, whose center was in the Dangra Yumtsho area. Zhang-zhung was the most important military power among the Ch'iang.

To understand the formation of the Tibetan nation we must bear in mind the constant migration of the great clan leaders and their subjects from the far northeast to the southwest, where there was soil conducive to a settled way of life. According to Chinese sources the unifier of these Ch'iang tribes in the fifth

39

century A.D. was a prince of the Sien-pi, an Altaic nomad people. To this aristocracy of steppe warriors is ascribed the dog totem, found also among the Tibetans of Imperial times. Apparently the new nation first settled in the gorge and wood country of Kong-po near the big bend of the river Tsang-po and then proceeded to the west to take possession of what was later to become the province of Ü (Dbus), especially the Yar-klungs and Skyid-chu valleys. In the ancestral legends memories still survive of the time when the Tibetans lived in the Kong-po region.

Unfortunately very little is known of the earliest period of this settlement for excavations were never permitted. The oldest records in the Tibetan chronicles contain so many legendary elements that it is difficult to disentangle the small amount of genuine historical information they may contain. The list of alleged twenty-seven predecessors of the emperor Srong-btsan sgam-po (seventh century) was shown to be a product of repeated manipulation. Thus the first ancestor, O-lde spu-rgyal, also mentioned in the *T'ang-shu,* is listed as the eighth in later Buddhist revisions, because of his close association with the pre-Buddhist religion. Nevertheless, the four immediate predecessors of Srong-btsan sgam-po would seem to be historical. With the exception of Khri-slon-brtsan (in later texts written gNam-ri srong-btsan), father of Srong-btsan sgam-po, these were princelings in the Yar-klungs and 'Phyong-rgyas valleys. Khri-slon-brtsan battled the other princelings who lived in various castles in central Tibet and eventually succeeded in overthrowing them. He was supported by other clans, mainly the dBas and 'Bro, and the minister Khyung-po sPung-sad zu-tse (an obvious Zhang-zhung name) through whom Khri-slon-brtsan gained supremacy over gTsang-bod (the present province of gTsang). This king must be regarded as the unifier of Tibet since it was he who laid the foundation of the empire which was to play an important role in Inner Asia and beyond. The first impact of the new state was felt by the powerful Zhang-zhung confederation, whose leader, known by the title of Lig gnya-zhur or Lig-mi-rgya (these are not personal names but titles of the Zhang-zhung kings), became a vassal of the Tibetans who killed him following an insurrection.

The new dynasty of Tibetan emperors was far from being an absolute monarchy. The heads of the clans which formed the new nobility were very powerful and it was from among them that the great ministers (*blon-chen*) were selected. The power of these ministers was only slightly less than that of the monarch. During the minority of the emperors the *blon-chen* acted as de facto heads of state, and only a few emperors such as Srong-btsan sgam-po and Khri-srong lde-brtsan were able to surmount the status of *primus inter pares.* Moreover, the Tibetan rulers were subject to the law of sacral kingship and might be deposed by ritual murder, although in most instances the predecessors simply retired when the heir apparent reached the age of thirteen, when, as it is stated, he was able to ride a horse, hunt, and wage war. gNam-ri srong-btsan was poisoned about A.D. 620, but it seems that this was the result of a rebellion rather than a ritual murder.

He was succeeded by Khri-srong-btsan, in later sources usually known as Srong-btsan sgam-po (circa 620-49), who as emperor or *bTsan-po* of the new Tibetan state was even more successful than his father. Tibetan imperial glory began with him. At first, the new sovereign had to suppress rebellions in several parts of his state and crush the intrigues of those nobles unwilling to relinquish their independence. sPung-sad zu-tse, the aide and favorite of the emperor's father, had slandered the father's old minister, who belonged to the king-making clan of Myang; and both the old noble and his successor were banished. sPung-sad himself then became "Great Minister" but plotted against the emperor, who was warned of this by mGar sTong-brtsan yul-bzung. The emperor deposed the ambitious and powerful sPung-sad and appointed mGar in his place, thus gaining for the state an able and loyal minister. These details are typical of the usual disturbances which followed practically every change of sovereign.

Having crushed the rebellions and intrigues, Srong-btsan sgam-po was now free to employ the formidable might of the new state even beyond its frontiers. He subdued most of the Ch'iang peoples on the western and northwestern borders of China, and even the A-zha (Chin. T'u-yü-hun) in the Koko Nor regions, whose kingdom had also included the old Shan-shan state in the Lop Nor region. The A-zha king became a vassal of the Tibetans and was linked to the Tibetan dynasty by a matrimonial alliance. Similar arrangements were made with the western Turks, Nepal, and the country of Bru-zha (Gilgit), the latter highly important for strategic reasons. Marriages were also arranged between Tibet and its tributary empire of Zhang-zhung. The Tibetan sovereign married the Zhang-zhung princess, Li thig-dman, while the sister of Srong-btsan sgam-po, known only by her Zhang-zhung name, Sad-mar-kar, married the Zhang-zhung king, Lig Myi-rhya. This however did not prevent Lig Myi-rhya from rebelling against his Tibetan overlord. The uprising was suppressed within the course of a year, and the Tibetan princess who, according to the Tun-huang chronicles, was unhappy in the Zhang-zhung capital, played an important role in the overthrow of Zhang-zhung. Lig Myi-rhya was eventually killed by the Tibetans while on his way to an assembly in the Sum-pa country, originally a part of the Zhang-zhung confederation. According to a Bon-po source, the murder took place in "lower Zhang-zhung" in the Dangra Yumtso area in the so-called Conch-shell Cave to the northeast of the great lake. In 653, shortly after the death of the emperor, the Tibetan administration of Zhang-zhung was consolidated and the Lig dynasty of that country deposed.

Marital ties linked the emperor not only to the rulers of the countries mentioned above but also to several important clans of his nobility. Ru-yong-bza rGyal-mo-btsun, daughter of the king of Mi-ñag (in the Minya Konkar mountain district in Kham) is believed to have been Tibetan or at least part Tibetan. It was one of his Tibetan wives, Mong-bza Khri-mo mnyen-ldong-steng from the sTod-lung district in Dbu-ru, who bore him his heir apparent, Gung-srong gung-btsan.

The emperor's two most important marriages were with the Chinese T'ang princess Wen-ch'eng, and with the daughter of the Nepalese king. Because of the merely legendary accounts of the event, the Nepalese marriage is believed by some scholars to be unhistorical, although this attitude would seem to be hypercritical since accounts of the Chinese marriage are also mostly legendary. Relations with Nepal at this time seem quite probable. When Tibet was making its power felt in the south, Nepal appears to have acted as its vassal. Nepalese soldiers joined Tibetan troops in protecting ambassador Wang Hsüan-ts'ê (648), who had been ill-treated by the Indian Rāja of Tīrabhukti.

Prior to Srong-btsan sgam-po's marriage to the Chinese princess military clashes with China occurred because of the Tibetan victory over the Tu-yü-hun, dependents of China. The ensuing military expedition into China proper proved the Tibetans, known as "Red Faces," to be formidable adversaries, and the T'ang emperor T'ai-tsung, wiser than his successors, found it expedient to remain on friendly terms with the new Inner Asian power. During the lifetime of the two great monarchs the frontier remained quiet.

These peaceful relations strengthened Chinese cultural influence on Tibet. The state chancellery was patterned after the Chinese model, and for the convenience of the Chinese consort and also to centralize the government, the first Chinese-style walled city was built in the sKyid-chu valley. It was called Ra-sa ("walled city," not, as sometimes suggested, "place of the goats"), and later Lhasa ("place of the gods"). Contacts with China and Nepal brought about the first acquaintance with Buddhism, although this religion was not actually introduced until the eighth century. According to certain ancient traditions, the emperor built several Buddhist chapels, among which was the nucleus for the Jo-khang, regarded as the *axis mundi* ("central point of the world"). For the expanding empire the acquisition of a system of writing was indispensable, and a minister, Thon-mi Sambhoṭa, was sent to India for this purpose. He created a Tibetan alphabet of thirty letters based on the late Gupta script. According to Chinese sources the Tibetans had formerly used knotted cords and notched tally-sticks.

The crown prince, Gung-srong gung-btsan, was enthroned at the age of thirteen, but the old emperor did not abdicate. After five years of nominal reign the young monarch died and Srong-btsan sgam-po resumed all responsibilities until his death.

The time of the three following emperors, the grandson of Srong-btsan sgam-po, Mang-slon mang-brtsan (649-76), Khri-'du-srong-brtsan (676-704), and Khri-lde gtsug-brtsan Mes-ag-tshoms (704-55) might be called the period of the regency, since all these rulers were minors when their respective fathers died. When Srong-btsan sgam-po died the minister mGar stong-btsan retained the title of "Great Minister" until his death in 667, when he was succeeded by his son mGar btsan-snya ldem-bu. Thus before the end of the seventh century a hereditary major domo dynasty had arisen, which ruled on behalf of the emperors who, left without real power, remained on the throne because of the divine nature of their office. Only Khri-'du-srong-brtsan succeeded in assuming command of the army and in overthrowing this dynasty. His military campaigns, however, were unsuccessful. The Chinese defeated him, and he died a premature death fighting the Mo-so kingdom of 'Jang (present-day Yunnan). The overthrow of the mGar clan was possible only because the other powerful clans had grown weary of the unrestricted power of the hereditary prime ministers. The clans exerted considerable influence on state affairs, especially those who had married into the imperial family, the so-called *Zhang-blon* ("uncle ministers"), who during the minority of an emperor had the privilege of acting as regents.

During the period of regency Tibet's political horizon widened considerably. Because the successors of T'ang T'ai-tsung lacked the foresight of that great leader, war was again incurred with China. The Tibetans totally destroyed the T'u-yü-hun state in A.D. 663, and the A-zha king who bore the title of Maga Toghon Khagan was accepted into the Tibetan feudal hierarchy on the same level as the princes of rKong-po and Myang and even held higher rank than the "Great Minister" (blon-po chen-po). Immediately after the fall of the A-zha the Tibetan armies invaded the Chinese protectorate in the Tarim basin, advancing on Kashgar in A.D. 662 and Khotan in 665. A Chinese relief army was defeated at Zi-ma-khol (in the Ta-fei valley), and in 670 the Tibetans took eastern Turkestan. After having established friendly relations with the western Türks (Tib. Dru-gu) in 674, the Tibetans attacked China proper (676).

During the minority of Mes-ag-tshoms, his grandmother, Khri-ma-lod of the (originally Zhang-zhung) clan of 'Bro, became very influential. The young king married a Chinese princess, Chin-ch'eng (710), but, owing to the behavior of the Chinese frontier officials, the Tibeto-Chinese peace did not long endure. China tried in vain to drive a wedge between Tibet and the rising power of the Arabs in the west and to prevent the Tibetans from taking the strategically important country of Bru-zha (Gilgit) in the west. After some initial successes of the Chinese army under the command of Kao Hsien-chih, the Chinese were defeated by the Arabs and their Qarluq Turk allies in 751 near the Talas river. This defeat opened the way into China for the Tibetan armies. Tibet was now one of the great powers of Asia, in the north bordering the territory of the Türks, and in the south, India. The year of the Talas battle the independent Moso state of Nan-chao (Tib. 'Jang) (present-day Yunnan), under its king Kag-la-bong (Chin. K'o-lo-feng), submitted to the Tibetans (751), following the example of Gilgit (740).

At this time growing Buddhist influence made itself felt. Monks expelled from Turkestan were favorably received by the Chinese consort and found asylum in Tibet. The jealous nobility, however, which followed the old Tibetan religion mixed with the Bon religion of Zhang-zhung, feared the political ambitions of the clergy and finally had the monks expelled from Tibet. Nevertheless, the dynasty favored Buddhism and Mes-ag-tshoms erected several Buddhist chapels.

Tibetan power reached its apogee during the reign of the greatest Tibetan emperor, Khri-srong lde-brtsan (755-97). Tibetan armies penetrated deeply into China proper, took the capital, Ch'ang-an (763), and installed a puppet emperor who, however, ruled for only three weeks. Gradually the Tibetans conquered the whole of Kansu and the adjacent regions and a considerable part of Sze-chwan. The T'ang dynasty was saved only by the intervention of the new power of the Turkic Uighurs, which had replaced the old Turkish empire. The Tibetan domination of eastern Turkestan came to an end in 692, became re-established in 790, and lasted until about 860. In the Sino-Tibetan treaty of 783 the Chinese acknowledged Tibetan dominion over the conquered Chinese territory including the Tarim basin. China was in no position to reconquer its lost territory due, among other things, to the disastrous rebellion of An Lu-shan which had begun in 755.

In the south, the Dharmapâla king of Bihar and Bengal became a vassal of the Tibetans; this is why the Muslim writers call the Bay of Bengal the "Tibetan Sea." By now thinly populated Tibet had reached the limits of its possibilities although it was still able to defeat, with the help of its ally the Turkic Qarluq, the combined Chinese and Uighur forces at Bishbalik. During the last years of Khri-srong lde-brtsan the Tibetans were faced with considerable difficulties: the end of the Tibeto-Arab alliance (789) terminated by Harūn ar-Rashīd, and the secession of 'Jang (788).

The most threatening danger, however, was the internal situation in Tibet itself. During the minority of Khri-srong lde-brtsan a Bon reaction flared up among the powerful nobility. The monarch had shown early sympathy for Indian Buddhism, probably because of its cultural values and also because he saw in the clergy a welcome counterbalance to the powerful Bon nobility. However, he never went so far as to question the office of the divine kingship which was rooted in the soil of the Bon religion. Even the most ardent supporter of Buddhism, the emperor Ral-pa-can, was buried according to ancestral Bon custom in the compound of the imperial tombs at 'Phyong-rgyas. When he came of age, Khri-srong lde-brtsan invited to Tibet the famous Indian teachers Shāntirakshita, Kamalashīla, and the tantric sage Padmasambhava, singularly well qualified to neutralize the hostile Bon-po. The first Tibetan monastery, bSam-yas, was founded about 775; and in 779 Buddhism became the state religion. Consequently, the Bon priests were exiled to the borders of Tibet.

Khri-srong lde-brtsan also decided in favor of Indian Buddhism in place of the Chinese Ch'an school (following the debate at bSam-yas, circa 792-94) and ordered the canonical scriptures of Indian Buddhism translated into Tibetan.

The Bon-po and the nobility remained in the background while the monarch was strong, but after the setbacks of the last years of his reign they regained strength, with the help of one of the empresses who belonged to the Tshe-spong clan. She played a rather sinister role in Tibetan politics, and was probably responsible for the death of Khri-srong lde-brtsan.

Mu-ne btsan-po (797-99), the son of Khri-srong lde-brtsan, succeeded his father and followed the paternal pattern of policy. According to legend he thrice redistributed the wealth of the Tibetan people. The reality behind this is probably an experiment intended to destroy the dangerous feudal nobility. Mu-ne btsan-po was poisoned by his mother, Tshe-spong-bza, after a reign of only a year and a half. The empress enthroned the youngest son, Khri-lde srong-brtsan Sad-na-legs (799-815), but the real ruler seems to have been his elder brother, Mu-rug btsan-po, a protégé of Bon-po nobility and most influential until he was murdered in 804 by a member of the sNa-nam clan.

It was under Sad-na-legs that Buddhism first emerged as a real political power. Of great importance was the monk (ban-de) of Bran-ka dPal-gyi yon-tan, whose rank eventually was higher than that of the "Great Minister"; Myang Ting-nge-'dzin was also very influential. In the proximity of one of the sanctuaries founded by Sad-na-legs an inscription on a pillar (rDo-ring) gives information concerning the religious attitude of this pious emperor, while, very typically, the inscription near his tomb uses the traditional Bon-po terminology.

Even more devoted to Buddhism was his son, Khri-gtsug lde-brtsan Ral-pa-can (817-36), who favored a strong clerical bureaucracy capable of counterbalancing the unruly nobility. Politically this reign as well as the previous one must be seen as a period of increasingly deteriorating conditions. The Caliphate during the period of al-Amîn (809-13) and al-Ma'mûn (813-33) enabled the tottering T'ang empire to rebuff Tibetan invasions, but Tibet was still able to maintain her rule over the Tarim basin although the fighting on different fronts against the Arabs, the Chinese, the Uighurs, and the 'Jang (Nan-chao) had become increasingly difficult. On the Chinese border the exhaustion of the Tibetan and Chinese combatants led to the treaty of 822, more or less the work of of the monk-minister, dPal-gyi yon-tan. This treaty, confirmed Tibetan domination of eastern Turkestan, practically all of Kansu, and the western part of Sze-chwan. During the oath ceremony an animal sacrifice was performed, and the participants smeared their lips with the blood of the victims. Only the Buddhist minister abstained from this archaic blood ceremony and took his oath by invocation of the Buddha. With the decline of the Abbasid Caliphate at about this time, hostilities on the Arab border ceased. Tibet, however, was having internal problems. Tensions increased between the

nobility and the dynasty, especially since the emperor had decreed that seven
households were to assume responsibility for the maintenance of one monk.
According to Chinese sources the emperor was a weak personality and totally
under the influence of the Buddhist clergy. Eventually the nobles revolted.
Through a slander campaign the Bon-po nobility first plotted against the
religious ministers with the result that the deluded emperor put the chief
minister to death. The nobles also exiled Ral-pa-can's elder brother to the
southern frontier. Eventually two nobles of respectively the dBas and Cog-ro
clans assassinated the emperor.

    After this spectacular event the nobility enthroned Khri-u-dum-brtsan
gLang-dar-ma (838-42), a brother of the murdered emperor, and a mere puppet
of the new "Great Minister," dBas rGyal-to-re, an exponent of the anticlerical
faction. A strong reaction, religious as well as political, set in. The foreign monks
were obliged to leave the country while Tibetan monks were forced to become
laymen again. The doors of the Buddhist sanctuaries were walled in, and there
was a general suppression of Buddhism and a restoration of the Bon religion.

    After the emperor was killed by a tantric Buddhist monk called dPal-gyi
rdo-rje, gLang-dar-ma's descendants were not universally recognized. The assassination of several emperors before him (Khri-srong lde-brtsan, Mu-ne btsan-po,
Ral-pa-can, gLang-dar-ma) had dealt a severe blow to the dynasty. Thus Tibet
was plunged into feudal anarchy, while in the central part of the empire
Buddhism became almost extinct. Tibetan possessions in China and the Tarim
basin were lost, although a certain degree of Tibetan sovereignty seems to have
existed for several decades in western Kansu. In 866 the last "Great Minister,"
dBas Kong-bzher, was killed in a battle near the Chinese border. The western
portion of eastern Turkestan was seized by the Turkic Qarluq, and the eastern
portion by the Uighur kingdom of Khocho. During the tenth century the
kingdom of Hsi-hsia arose in northeastern Tibet, a kingdom ruled by a family of
one of the old Ch'iang tribes, the Tang-hsiang or Tangut.

    The Tibetan state's ability to withstand the great powers of that time, i.e.,
China, the Arabs, and the Turks, can be explained only by the strictness of its
organization and the outstanding leadership of several of its emperors (Srong-
btsan sgam-po, Khri-srong lde-brtsan) who supported the magical prestige of
sacral kingship. Unfortunately, the organization of the Tibetan empire has not
yet been sufficiently studied and only its most salient features can be described.
In the beginning Tibet was divided into three military districts (ru, "horns"); a
fourth was added shortly before 733. Their names are given as dbU-ru ("main
horn," in the center), gYon-ru ("left horn," the eastern district), gYas-ru ("right
horn," that part of present gTsang which borders upon the Lha-sa province), and
later Ru-lag (the southwestern part of gTsang inherited from Zhang-zhung). The
horns were subdivided into the "ten thousand districts" and the "thousand dis-

tricts" which also functioned as administrative units. The head of the state was, of course, the *bTsan-po* ("emperor"), who generally made his decisions in consultation with the state council (*'dun-sa*). This council, which convened every summer and winter, consisted of members of the feudal nobility, who owned practically all the land. To the previously independent princes of the A-zha, rKong-po, and Myang were given honorary ranks directly under the bTsan-po. Next in rank was the most important "Great Minister" (*blon-chen*), who often belonged to a clan connected with the emperor by marriage. According to their position in the imperial palace the other officials were classified as "inner" and "outer" ministers (*nang-blon* and *phyi-blon*, respectively). The Tarim basin, a colonial possession, was entrusted to a governor general (*nang-rje-po*) whose residence seems to have been in the Khotan (Tib. U-ten) region. The various local kings were allowed to administer their own districts.

BIBLIOGRAPHY

Information on Tibetan prehistory is meager: George N. Roerich, *The Animal Style among the Nomad Tribes of Northern Tibet,* Seminarium Kondakovianum, Prague 1930; by the same author: "Problems of Tibetan Archaeology," *Urusvati Journal* 1 (1931): 27-34. Peter Aufschnaiter, "Prehistoric Sites Discovered in Inhabited Regions of Tibet,"*EW* 7 (1956-57):74-95.

There is only one synoptic history of Tibet for the Imperial period. Erik Haarh: *The Yar-luṅ Dynasty,* Kφbenhavn 1969 (this covers the entire imperial age, discusses the whole prehistorical tradition of the mythical kings, and suggests further study in this most important field); Luciano Petech, *A Study of the Chronicles of Ladakh,* Calcutta 1939. Since the publication of this book a considerable amount of new material has been published. See Sir Charles Bell, *Tibet Past and Present,* Oxford 1968, and Tsepon W. D. Shakabpa, *Tibet. A Political History,* New Haven and London, Yale University Press 1967. Both are rather abridged. A good description of the cultural aspects of this period has been given by David Snellgrove and Hugh Richardson, *A Cultural History of Tibet,* New York 1968, pp. 19-110, and by R. A. Stein, *Tibetan Civilization,* Stanford University Press 1972. Summaries are given in Jacques Bacot, *Introduction à l'histoire du Tibet,* Paris 1962; Helmut Hoffmann, *Geschichte Tibets,* Oldenbourg's Abriss der Weltgeschichte IIB, München 1954, and Luciano Petech, "Tibet," in *Handbuch der Orientalistik,* vol. V.5: *Geschichte Mittelasiens,* pp. 311-47.

Because of the complexities of Tibetan history during the Imperial Age the student must deal with a number of important specialized books and articles: Giuseppe Tucci, "The Validity of Tibetan Historical Tradition," *India Antiqua, Commemoration Volume in honor of J. Ph. Vogel,* Leiden 1947, pp. 309-22; *The Tombs of the Tibetan Kings,* Roma 1950; "The Sacred Character of the Kings of Ancient Tibet," *EW* 6 (1955): 197-205; *Preliminary Report on Two Scientific Expeditions in Nepal,* Roma 1956 (with accents on the ancient history of Tibet); "The Wives of Sroṅ btsan sgam po," *OE* 9 (1962): 121-26.

Luciano Petech, "Glosse agli annali di Tun-huang," *RSO* 42 (1955): 241-79; "Nota su Mabd e TWSMT," *RSO* 24 (1949): 1-3; "Nugae Tibeticae," *RSO* 31 (1957): 291-94; "La struttura del Ms. Tib. Pelliot 1287," *RSO* 43 (1956): 253-56; "Alcuni nomi geografici nel La-dvags-rgyal-rabs," *RSO* 22 (1947): 1-10.

Hugh E. Richardson, "Early Burial Grounds in Tibet and Tibetan Decorative Art of the VIII and IX Centuries," *CAJ* 8 (1963): 73-92; "A Fragment from Tun-huang," *BT* (Gangtok) 3 (1965): 73-83; "Names and titles in Early Tibetan Records," *BT* (Gangtok) 4 (1967): 5-20; "A Note on Tibetan Chronology from A.D. 841 to A.D. 1042," *JRAS* (1957): 57-62.

Eric Haarh, "The Identity of Tsu-chi-chien, the Tibetan 'King' who died in 804 A.D.," *AO* 25, 121-70 (deals with the difficult chronological problem of the successors of Khri-srong lde-brtsan).

Wolfram Eberhard, *Kultur und Siedlung der Randvölker Chinas*, Leiden 1942 (pp. 69-97) give important data on the Ch'iang peoples from Chinese sources).

Jacques Bacot, "Le mariage chinois du roi tibétain Sron bcan sgan po," *MCB* (1935): 1-60 (although this study deals mostly with legendary matter it gives a vivid impression of the importance the Tibetans attached to matrimonial alliances with the ruling dynasty of China).

Marcelle Lalou, "Fiefs, poisons et guérisseurs," *JA* (1958): 157-201; "Revendications des fonctionnaires du Grand Tibet au VIIIᵉ siècle," *JA* (1955): 171-212.

Rolf A. Stein, *Les K'iang des marches sino-tibétaines, exemple de continuité de la tradition*, Paris 1957.

Helmut H. R. Hoffmann, "Tibets Eintritt in die Weltgeschichte," *Saeculum*, 1950, pp. 258-79; "Die Gräber der tibetischen Könige im Distrikt 'Phyoṅs-rgyas," *Nachrichten der Akademie der Wissenschaften in Göttingen*, Phil.-hist. Klasse 1950, pp. 1-14; "Die Qarluq in der tibetischen Literatur," *Oriens* 3 (1950): 190-203; "The Tibetan names of the Saka and Sogdians," *AS* (1971): 440-55 (the latter two articles deal with records of foreign peoples in the Tibetan historical tradition).

Fang-Kuei Li, "On Tibetan Sog," *CAJ* 3 (1958): 39-142.

Géza Uray, "The Four Horns of Tibet According to the Royal Annals," *AOH* 10 (1960): 3-57; " 'Greṅ, the Alleged Old Tibetan Equivalent of the Ethnic Name Ch'iang," *AOH* 19 (1966): 245-56; "Notes on a Chronological Problem in the Old Tibetan Chronicle," *AOH* 21 (1968): 289-99; "Notes on a Tibetan Military Document from Tun-huang," *AOH* 12 (1961): 223-30; "The Offices of the bruṅ-pas and Great mṅans and the Territorial Division of Central Tibet in the Early 8th Century," *AOH* 15 (1962): 353-60.

A. Róna-Tas, "Social Terms in the List of Grants of the Tibetan Tun-huang Chronicle," *AOH* 5 (1955): 249-70.

L. A. Waddell, "Tibetan Invasion of India in 647 A.D. and its Results," *Asiatic Quarterly Review* (1911): 37-65.

Sylvain Lévy, "Les Missions de Wang Hiuen-tzê dans l'Inde," *JA* (1900): 297-341, 401-68.

Jacques Bacot, "Reconnaissance en haute Asie septentrionale par cinq envoyés Ouigours au VIII^c siècle," *JA* (1956): 137-53 (with reproduction of the entire document, which is of great importance as it gives an idea of Tibetan knowledge of other Central Asian peoples). L. Ligeti, "À propos du 'Rapport sur les rois demeurant dans le Nord'," *ETML*, (Paris 1971): 166-89 (important comments on the preceding publication).

The Age of Feudal Disintegration
and the Development of Monastic Power (900-1200)

After the murder of gLang-dar-ma the Tibetan empire collapsed. The last emperor left no heir although one of his queens produced a son of doubtful legitimacy who was recognized by some of the Bon-po nobility. He was enthroned at Lhasa and bore the dynastic title of Khri-lde. Later generations called him, significantly, Yum-brtsan ("dependent on his mother"). A son by another queen was called gNam-lde Od-srungs and seems to have been the candidate of the Buddhist party. Disorder and civil war erupted as neither candidate was able to obtain universal recognition. Od-srungs's son, dPal-'khor-btsan, was murdered by his subjects. Soon Tibet was broken up into many small principalities, which were governed both by the descendants of Yum-brtsan and Od-srungs and by representatives of the nobility. The disintegration of the imperial system was now complete. A scion of the Od-srungs lineage went to western Tibet where his descendants founded a new kingdom in Ladakh (La-dvags) and Gu-ge (the old center of the Zhang-zhung empire).

The destruction of the monarchy proved to be of no advantage to the famous old clans, since during the universal struggle the ancient clans of Cog-ro, Myang, dBas, sNa-nam, mC'ims, and 'Bro were replaced by a new feudal nobility. Because of the atomization of Tibetan political life, the history of the following period can only be characterized as religious history. By the time of the political debacle no Bon organization of any kind had emerged from the general turmoil. Although laymen followed to some extent the Buddhist way of life, there was no ordination of monks in the Lhasa province. Idealists fled to Amdo in the northeast where the impact of the Lhasa government was no longer felt and where it was still possible to become a Buddhist monk. Most important among these Buddhist were bLa-chen dGongs-pa rab-gsal (circa. 832-915) and his disciple kLu-mes, who, after the religious persecutions in dbUs, reintroduced Buddhism there in the form of the old teaching which dated back to the time of Padmasambhava. Later, when other Buddhist schools arose, they were known as the rNying-ma-pa, "Holders of the old [tantric] Tradition."

The greatest impetus to the revival of Buddhism originated in the western Tibetan kingdom of Gu-ge founded by the descendants of Od-srungs. Tibetan historiography calls this period the "second propagation of the doctrine" (*phyi dar*). (See page 138.) In 1042 the famous Indian master Atīsha arrived in Gu-ge, and with his help it was possible to reform and to disseminate Buddhism. (On Atīsha's activity in Tibet see below, pp. 140-42.)

Evidence of the revival of Buddhism in Gu-ge is the great synod of Tabo (1076), attended not only by monks from the west but from central and eastern Tibet as well. It was also a demonstration of the political power of the western

Tibetan kingdom. Today the deserted capital of rTsa-brang (Tsaparang) and the temples of mTho-gling, even in their deplorable state of desolation and decay, are mighty witnesses to the religious and artistic magnificence of that period.

The pioneering activities of Atīsha and Rin-chen bzang-po opened the way for further direct contacts with the ancient Buddhist monasteries in Magadha (Bihār). The "translator" Mar-pa of Lho-brag (1012-98) travelled to India three times for initiations and to obtain sacred books which he translated into Tibetan. His new school, the bKa-brgyud-pa (see below pp. 152-157), which originated with the tantric saints Ti-lo-pā, Nā-ro-pā, and Maitri-pā, later split into several branches: the 'Bri-gung-pa, sTag-lung-pa, 'Brug-pa (now predominant in Bhutan), and the Karma-pa. Later, several of those subschools were to become politically important. Only the Zhi-byed-pa with its center at Ding-ri, founded by the Indian sage Pha-dam-pa Sangs-rgyas (died 1117) who visited Tibet seven or perhaps three times, was of no political importance. The school to attain great political power was the Sa-skya-pa (see below pp. 149-151). Its doctrines were based on the teachings of 'Brog mi lo-tsā-ba, and its chief monastery was founded in 1073 by dKon-mchog rgyal-po of the 'Khon family. This family was of Bru-sha (Gilgit) Bon-po descent, and we know that Sa-skya Paṇḍita Kun-dga rgyal-mtshan (1182-1251) still had some knowledge of the Bru-sha language and script. Like the bKa-brgyud-pa, the Sa-skya-pa had several offshoots: the Ngor-pa, sTag-tshang-pa, and Zhva-lu-pa, to which the famous teacher Bu-ston Rin-chen-grub (1290-1364) belonged.

Beginning with the "second propagation" of Buddhism (*phyi-dar*) the interest of the Tibetans turned away from political and military exploits and produced that strong feeling for religious and spiritual life which, henceforth, totally permeated the life of the people. The place of the old feudal nobility was taken over by the religious leaders, who also became prominent in worldly affairs. The monasteries became centers not only of learning and religious life, but also of economic power, thus creating a new monastic aristocracy which eventually was to become a theocracy.

BIBLIOGRAPHY

In contrast to the early period of Tibetan history, the period from 900 to 1200 has been neglected by scholars and there are only a few books and articles which deal with this period. There is no detailed monograph on the revival of Buddhism in eastern Tibet—only the article by Hugh E. Richardson, "A Note on Tibetan Chronology from A.D. 841 to A.D. 1042," *JRAS* (1957): 57-62. Concerning the revival of Buddhism which began in Gu-ge we have two monographs: Giuseppe Tucci, *Indo-Tibetica II. Rin c'en bzañ po e la rinascità del Buddhismo nel Tibet intorno al mille,* Roma 1933; and Sarat Chandra Das,

Indian Pandits in the Land of Snow, 2nd ed., Calcutta 1965 (which mainly describes the activities of Atīsha). Alaka Chattopadhyaya, *Atîsha and Tibet,* Calcutta 1967.

No works deal specifically with the new Buddhist schools which emerged in the eleventh century. For the development of the bKa-brgyud-pa: Jacques Bacot, *Marpa le traducteur,* Paris, 1937; An-che Li, "bKa-brgyud Sect of Lamaism," *JAOS* 69 II, (1949): 51-59; Hugh E. Richardson, "The Karmapa Sect," *JRAS* (1958): 139-64, and (1959): 1-17.

For Sa-skya-pa developments: Tucci's work, *Tibetan Painted Scrolls,* Roma 1949; An-che Li, "The Sakya Sect of Lamaism," *JWCRS* 16 (1945): 72-86; C. W. Cassinelli and Robert B. Ekvall, *A Tibetan Principality, the Political System of Saskya,* Cornell University, Ithaca, New York 1'69.

For the history of the rNying-na-pa: An-che Li, "rNying-ma-pa, the Early Form of Lamaism," *JRAS* (1948): 142-63.

For a general survey of the development of Tibetan Buddhist schools: Giuseppe Tucci, *Tibetan Painted Scrolls,* Rome 1949; Helmut Hoffmann, *The Religions of Tibet,* London 1961.

Tibet and the Mongols (1200-1600)

The meteor-like rise of Mongol power was quick to make itself felt in disintegrated Tibet. Following the defeat of the Hsi-hsia state by the troops of Chingis khan (1207) and the threat of imminent invasion, the Tibetan clergy and nobles met for a conference and sent a legation to the formidable emperor to offer submission. For a time this event was without consequence, as Chingis khan was leading his armies against the Chin empire of northern China and the Muslim state of Khwarezm to the west. The Tibetans consequently ceased to submit the prescribed tribute, with the result that in 1240, during the time of the Great Khan Ögödei, the commander of the Mongol forces in the Koko Nor area, Prince Godan, sent a military detachment under the command of rDo-rta-nag into Tibet proper. The troops sacked and burned the sanctuaries of Rva-sgreng and rGyal-lha-khang and penetrated as far as the valley of the 'Phan-po-chu to the north of Lhasa. The frightened Tibetans sent the most respected religious man of that time, the abbot of Sa-skya, Kun-dga' rgyal-mtshan (1182-1251), generally known by the title of Sa-skya Paṇḍita, to the camp of the Mongol prince for negotiations. Owing to the realistic policy of this shrewd hierarch, the parties reached an agreement whereby Tibet would acknowledge Mongolian suzerainty and agree to a fixed tribute. The Sa-skya hierarch himself became the Mongol representative (*darugachi*), and thus wielded power throughout Tibet. Mongol secretaries and treasurers entered the country to supervise the collection and payment of tribute. Sa-skya Paṇḍita remained for years in the Mongol camp and sent a famous letter to his countrymen pointing out that resistance would be both impossible and disastrous. As could be expected, the unruly Tibetan nobility, unwilling to accept the overlordship of the Sa-skya abbot, revolted. The insurrection was suppressed by Mongol troops in 1251. The Tibetans urged Sa-skya Paṇḍita to return to his monastery, but he refused as he felt that his presence was more needed at the Mongol camp at Lan-chou. As his representative he sent to Sa-skya his nephew, 'Phags-pa Blo-gros (1235-80), a former member of the delegation that negotiated with the Mongols. Sa-skya Paṇḍita attempted in vain to convert Godan and his Mongols to Buddhism.

With Godan's death in 1221, Khubilai Sechen, the future great khan, assumed command at Lan-chou. When Saskya Paṇḍita died, his place as abbot of Sa-skya was taken by 'Phags-pa. The new hierarch became the spiritual teacher of Khubilai and as such refused to prostrate himself before the prince. The dispute was settled in the following way: 'Phags-pa was entitled to occupy a higher seat when acting as religious preceptor, but in public was obliged to relinquish this privilege to Khubilai. At a later period Khubilai, as well as some of his ministers, were initiated into certain of the Vajrayāna mysteries. In 1275

Khubilai bestowed upon 'Phags-pa the hereditary donation of the thirty-three districts of dbUs and gTsang, and later, when Khubilai became emperor of China, his spiritual friend was given the title of "Imperial Preceptor," *Tishri* (Chin. *Ti-shih*).

The relationship between Mongol China of the Yuan dynasty and Tibet was one of patronage by the emperor toward his spiritual teacher, who had been given temporary dominion over the three Chol-kha regions of Tibet: dBus-gTsang, Khams, and Amdo. The emperor even offered to order all the Buddhists of Tibet to follow the special doctrine of the Sa-skya school, but 'Phags-pa insisted that every Buddhist be allowed to practice Buddhism according to his own tradition. This principle had always been followed by the Tibetans, and a different attitude could have led to disastrous developments. Sa-skya supremacy did not remain undisputed. There was, for instance, a rebellion of the powerful and wealthy 'Bri-gung monastery, put down in 1290 with the help of Mongol troops. The monastery itself was burned down. The Sa-skya always showed loyalty to the Mongols, and their dominion was more or less dependent on the backing of the Yuan emperors. However, all internal affairs were left to the Tibetans themselves to settle. 'Phags-pa spent a considerable part of his time at the Mongol court and created for his patron the so-called *Dörbeljin* or square script, which was used in official documents until the end of the Yuan dynasty. During the numerous absences of the Grand Lama, Tibetan governmental affairs were supervised by a regent called the *dPon-chen* or "Great Master."

With the gradual weakening of the Yuan dynasty following the death of Khubilai khan, reaction arose in Tibet both against foreign rule and the clerical domination of the Sa-skya, a domination which had depended totally upon the Mongols. There was also ill feeling on the part of the dbUs feudal nobility because of the gTsang prerogative. These developments found an exponent in the person of the myriarch (*khri-dpon*) Byang-chub rgyal-mtshan (1302-73). This courageous and able man was himself a monk and belonged to the Phag-mo-gru-pa branch of the bKa-brgyud-pa, which had its headquarters at gDan-sa-mthil, although he acted especially as an exponent of the rLangs family. From his headquarters at sNe-gdong-rdzong in the Yar-klungs valley, the cradle of the dynasty of the old Tibetan emperors, he fought not only against the Sa-skya-pa but also against the 'Bri-gung-pa and the still powerful nobility. His main goal seems to have been the restoration of the ancient imperial glory of Tibet, and although he was unable to realize this goal completely, he did succeed in gaining undisputed overlordship over all of dbUs and gTsang and in acquiring the title of *sDe-srid* ("regent"). The Yuan government, unable to interfere, was obliged to appoint him *darugachi* in place of the Sa-skya lamas.

Several measures taken by him may be interpreted as symbols of the restoration of imperial times: he reintroduced the old laws of Srong-btsan sgam-po and extended them to serve as a comprehensive code of law. He also sponsored to some extent the rNying-ma-pa, "discoverers of hidden literary treasures," e.g., O-rgyan gling-pa (born 1323), who found a considerable number of old scrolls from Imperial times. These he edited with quite a few additions under the title *Biography of Padmasambhava (Padma thang-yig)*, and *Five Groups of Scrolls* [of Padmasambhava], i.e., the important *bKa-thang sde-Inga*. During the entire Phag-mo-gru-pa period there was a strong feeling for national antiquities and the historical past of the Imperial period. In the field of administration the system of "myriarchs" was abolished and Byang-chub rgyal-mtshan and his successors governed the country through a system of fortresses (*rdzong*) which controlled the smaller administrative units of the country. The new system, efficient under an able king like Byang-chub rgyal-mtshan, became a danger to the central government under weak kings once the office of the prefect (*rdzong-dpon*) had become hereditary. This created a new feudal nobility which struggled for its indepndence. Thus the overlordship of the Phag-mo-gru-pa outlived its founder only a short time, although the rulers assumed exalted titles such as *Lha-btsun* ("Divine Lord") and later even *Gong-ma* ("Most High One"), an imperial title subsequently given to the Manchu emperors. The Ming dynasty of China (1368) automatically confirmed the titles and privileges of the Phag-mo-gru-pa and bestowed high ranks upon the Lamas of other important sects, e.g., the Karma-pa hierarch who was invited to China in 1406 and was made "Prince of the Holy Law" (*Ta-pao-fa-wang*). It must be emphasized, however, that the Ming never exercised overlordship in Tibet and no Chinese officials or military commanders ever entered the country, for the Ming were totally unable to inaugurate such a policy. Tibet again became divided during this period as a result of the ancient and disastrous rivalry between dbUs and gTsang. The *rDzong-dpon* of Rin-spungs became practically independent and was in a position to control the whole of gTsang. From 1434 he resided at bSam-grub-rtse and sponsored the Karma-pa school which competed with the Phag-mo-gru-pa.

This period was also characterized by the emergence of a new factor of utmost historical importance: the reformation by bTsong-kha-pa bLo-bzang grags-pa (1357-1419), who was obliged to repeat the work of Atīsha since the majority of the monasteries no longer observed the Buddhist monastic laws of discipline and celibacy. As a result of bTsong-Kha-pa's reluctance to visit China to receive an imperial diploma, the official Chinese records give incorrect dates for his life: 1417-78. *Quod non est in actis non est in mundo!*

Most of the monasteries of the new dGe-lugs-pa order were founded in dbUs: dGa-ldan in 1409, 'Bras-spungs in 1416, and Se-ra theg-che-gling in 1419; only bKra-shis lhun-po, founded in 1447, is located in gTsang. The dGe-lugs-pa actually adopted the regulations of Atīsha and his bKa-gdams-pa sect, and this older school was absorbed by the school founded by bTsong-kha-pa. Since, unlike all the older schools, the dGe-lugs-pa did not use the red monastic hats but used yellow ones, they are often called the "Yellow Hat Sect" or "The Yellow Church." One innovation which would be of great importance for the future was the introduction of the *Tulku (sPrul-sku)* system in which the hierarch-successors of bTsong-kha-pa reincarnated into another body after death. That new incarnation was discovered by following special regulations.

The strict organization of the new dGe-lugs-pa order seems to have been primarily the work of bTsong-kha-pa's first successor, the abbot of dGa-ldan, dGe-'dun grub-pa' (1391-1475). He was an incarnation of the patron of Tibet, Avalokiteshvara, and bore the title rGyal-ba rin-po-che. His reincarnation was dGe-'dun rgya-mtsho (1475-1542), during whose reign a difficult period started lasting from 1498 to 1517 because the dGe-lugs-pa were forbidden to participate in the New Year celebration and the great *sMon-lam* ("Wish Prayer") ceremony institutionalized by bTsong-kha-pa because the King of gTsang governed Lhasa at that time. The Yellow Church did not openly interfere in politics but worked indirectly through the dbUs nobility, especially the Phag-mo-gru-pa, although the latter were rather weak and internally at odds during this period. Consequently, bSod-nams rgya-mtsho, the third rGyal-ba rin-po-che, sought powerful allies, which he hoped to have found in the Mongolian tribes of Altan khan of the Tumet. His journey to Mongolia (1528) at the invitation of Altan khan was motivated by missionary zeal, of course, but it was also unquestionably dictated by political motives. This "second conversion" of the Mongols, which repeated the work of Sa-skya Paṇḍita and 'Phags-pa, must be viewed as an important event in world history for the Mongols became the most faithful adherents of the Yellow Church for many centuries. This event must not be minimized just because of the total interruption of contacts between Tibet and the Mongols after the fall of the Yuan dynasty in China. Such a theory is untenable for there is sufficient evidence to show a continuous link between the Karma-pa and the other red sects and the Mongols during the entire preceding period. It was Altan khan who bestowed on bSod-nams rgya-mtsho the title of *Dalai Lama* ("Ocean Teacher") by which the dGe-lugs-pa hierarchs later became known in the West. To strengthen the new ties with the Mongols, the third rGyal-ba visited Mongolia once more and died in that country in 1588.

His reincarnation appeared within the family of Altan khan; hence the bonds between the dGe-lugs-pa hierarchy and the powerful Mongols became unbreakable. The new Dalai Lama, Yon-tan rgya-mtsho (1589-1617), was soon sent to be educated in Tibet. The increase of the power of the Yellow Hats and of dbUs understandably led to a reaction on the part of the gTsang-pa king, Phun-tshogs rnam-rgyal, and dbUs was invaded by gTsang troops who violently attacked the 'Bras-spungs and Se-ra monasteries; consequently, the Dalai Lama had to take flight. He died at the early age of twenty-five. Now the policy of the third rGyal-ba produced results. Mongolian armies pushed into dbUs (1621 and 1635) and conquered the gTsang troops. At the same time the gTsang-pa ruler faced attacks on another front as the whole of western Tibet, which had been unified by the Ladakhi king Seng-ge rnam-rgyal (circa 1600-45), and had become strong enough by 1640 to trouble the western frontier of the Tsang kingdom.

The situation was settled only through the unusual personality of the new dGe-lugs-pa incarnation, the famous Fifth Dalai Lama Ngag-dbang blo-bzang rgya-mtsho (1617-82), who was not only an outstanding cleric and scholar but also a very able and shrewd politician. It was he who established the dGe-lugs-pa state with the help of the Mongols. As early as 1621 a large Mongol army had invaded Tibet to protect the Yellow Church. But now a truce could be mediated between dbUs and gTsang. Of a more serious nature was the interference of the western Mongols under Gushri khan of the Khoshot, who in 1641 set out from the Koko Nor area which he had conquered earlier. He subjugated the king of Beri in eastern Tibet who favored the Bon religion and persecuted Buddhist lamas of all schools. Gushri khan then defeated the king of gTsang, took him prisoner, and later put him to death. A typical nomad, Gushri khan, disliked living in Tibet and presented the whole of that country (dbUs, gTsang, and a considerable part of eastern Tibet) to the Dalai Lama. The year 1642 is consequently the date of the establishment of the theocracy of the Yellow Church. Fighting continued for a while in the province of Kong-po where the Red Sect refused to accept defeat. With the victory of the Yellow Church secure, both the Red Sect and the feudal nobility were stripped of all political influence. As the Khoshot khan had reserved for himself only a kind of military overlordship and protectorate of the dGe-lugs-pa state, the "Great Fifth" delegated the civil administration to a lay regent. Following the death of Gushri khan (1655), his younger son administered the Koko Nor area while the elder son remained with his troops south of the gNam-mtsho (Tengri Nor) and inherited the protectorate of Tibet. His influence decreased gradually. Tibetan relations with the newly-established dynasty of the Manchus (Ch'ing, 1644) were friendly in the beginning. The first contact was a Tibetan embassy to Mukden in 1642. Later the Dalai Lama received and accepted an invitation to visit the imperial court at Peking (1651-53) where honors of all kinds were showered upon him. He left Peking with a golden seal and a new title, but there was not the slightest indication of any Manchu overlordship of Tibet.

As part of the domestic policy of the Fifth rGyal-ba, quite a few monasteries were confiscated from the Red Cap schools, especially those which had politically opposed the hierarch. There was total suppression of the Jo-nang-pa, an offshoot of the Sa-skya-pa, whereas the rNying-ma-pa were treated rather gently, certainly because several rNying-ma-pa lamas had been the personal teachers of the Dalai Lama. Moreover, the Dalai Lama retained a vivid interest in the teachings of that school throughout his lifetime. As a symbol of his new rule over all Tibet, the Dalai Lama began the construction of a new residence, the Potala, on the same hill where during imperial times the emperor Srong-brtsan sgam-po, himself an incarnation of Avalokiteshvara, had his residence. To show his gratitude to his old teacher bLo-bzang chos-kyi rgyal-mtshan, the Great Fifth bestowed on him the title of *Paṇ-chen Rin-po-che* ("Precious Great Scholar"). The Paṇ-chen Rin-po-che, abbots of bKra-shis lhun-po near gZhis-ka-rtse, succeed each other according to the same principle of reincarnation as the rGyal-ba Rin-po-che, and are incarnations of Od-dpag-med (Amitābha) Buddha.

Throughout this entire period Tibet was in no sense a "forbidden land." As we have seen (pp. 36-37), Jesuit missionaries as well as Capuchins visited Gu-ge (Antonio de Andrade) and central Tibet (Cacella, Cabral, Grueber, and d'Orville), and a short-lived Catholic mission operated in Tsang between 1626 and 1632. Factories of wealthy Muslim, Mongol, Indian, and even Armenian and Russian merchants grew up at Lhasa.

BIBLIOGRAPHY

The most authoritative work on this period is Giuseppe Tucci, *Tibetan Painted Scrolls,* vol. 1, Roma 1949, pp. 6-80. This work also contains data on the Saskya-pa (pp. 625-29), Phag-mo-gru-pa (632-41) and Rin-spungs-pa (pp. 641-42). Also useful is Tsepon W. Shakabpa, *Tibet. A Political History,* New Haven, Yale University Press 1967, pp. 61-124. Special mention should be made of the detailed description of the Byang-chub rgyal-mtshan period according to the rLangs Po-ti bse-ru (pp. 74-83). Tieh-tseng Li, *Tibet Today and Yesterday,* New York 1960, pp. 18-37 (2nd ed. of *The Historical Status of Tibet,* New York 1956), should be used with utmost caution as it is strongly biased in favor of the Chinese. There also exists a special monograph on the Sa-skya: C. W. Cassinelli and Robert B. Ekvall, *A Tibetan Principality, the Political System of Sa-skya,* Cornell University, Ithaca, New York 1969. For the events in western Tibet, see Luciano Petech, *A Study on the Chronicles of Ladakh (Indian Tibet),* Calcutta 1939, as well as the same author's "Notes on Ladakhi History," *IHQ* (1948): 213-35, and "The Tibetan Ladakhi Moghul War," *IHQ* (1947): 169-99. See also A. H. Francke, *A History of Western Tibet,* London 1907.

Useful, but not always reliable, are the following articles by Sarat Chandra Das: "Contributions on the Religion, History, etc., of Tibet," *JASB* L (1881): 187-251; *JASB* 51 (1882): 1-75, 87-128; "A Short History of the House of Phagdu," *JASB* (1905): 202-7; "Tibet a Dependency of Mongolia, 1643-1716," *JASB* (1905); "Tibet and Her Last Kings," *JASB* (1905): 165-67.

On the Christian missions in Tibet, see the bibliography of chapter 4, p. 37.

The Government by the Yellow Church
and the Manchus (1650-1912)

During the last years of the "Great Fifth" the office of Regent was held from 1679 on by Sangs-rgyas rgya-mtsho, an able man and an important author. The Dalai Lama was thus able to realize his desire to retire and meditate. When the great hierarch died in 1682, Sangs-rgyas rgya-mtsho, fearing possible disturbances during the interregnum, concealed his death and pretended that the Dalai Lama was living in strict seclusion. Secretly, however, he searched for and found the new incarnation, Tshangs-dbyangs rgya-mtsho (1683-1706), who was consecrated and educated without knowledge of the people or the political powers, i.e., the Mongols and the Manchus. During this period Sangs-rgyas rgya-mtsho completed the Potala Palace and sent an army against Ladakh which ran into resistance from the Moghul Emperor Aurangzeb. The peace of 1683, however, guaranteed Tibet the possession of Gu-ge and other western districts which have continued to be part of Tibet until the present time.

In the north and east, however, the political situation had changed because of the formation of the powerful Dzungarian empire which challenged Manchu supremacy in Mongolia and led to dangerous tensions. The Khoshot khan of that time, Lha-bzang, who came to rule by murdering his elder brother (1697), tried to change the nominal overlordship of Tibet inherited from Gushri khan's time to an effective one, and to rule over Tibet as king. This ambition, of course, set him at odds with Sangs-rgyas rgya-mtsho who sympathized with the Buddhist Dzungars, ruled by dGa-ldan since 1676. Although the troops of the K'ang-hsi emperor of China defeated the Dzungars in 1695, Tshe-dbang rab-brtan, who succeeded his uncle dGa-ldan in 1697, continued to be a dangerous enemy of the Manchus. Sangs-rgyas rgya-mtsho's involvement with the Dzungars and his deliberate concealment of the Dalai Lama's death, which of course eventually became known, caused hostility on the part of the Manchus as well as the Dzungars. In 1697 Tshangs-dbyangs rgya-mtsho was enthroned. He showed little interest in his high spiritual and secular position and indulged in sexual adventures. A collection of beautiful erotic poems has been ascribed to him, but judging from a letter of the Dzungar khan to the K'ang-hsi emperor, it seems more probable that his behavior was due less to libertinism than to involvement in heretical tantric cults based on sexual rituals. Logically, he renounced his monastic vows before the Paṇ-chen Rin-po-che who had ordained him, but still maintained his political position, a necessity in view of the incarnation system. A *sPrul-sku,* even if doing wrong, must remain an incarnation. In 1705 the Khoshot khan, pretending offense at the scandal and backed by the Chinese, attacked and took Lhasa by surprise, putting the regent to death. Now formally recognized by K'ang-hsi as governor of Tibet, Lha-bzang also captured the young Dalai Lama,

deposed him, and tried—of course with little success—to persuade the leading
dGe-lugs-pa authorities to renounce him as a true incarnation and to accept his
own candidate, Ye-shes rgya-mtsho, as the true successor of the Fifth Dalai
Lama. In spite of his popularity, Tshangs-dbyangs rgya-mtsho did not take
advantage of the Tibetans' devotion to him but voluntarily set out for China. En
route he either died a natural death or was murdered.

Lha-bzangs's government was totally unsuccessful. His troops suffered
defeat at the hands of the Bhutanese, and the Dalai Lama whom he had installed
was ignored by the Tibetans. They were searching for the reincarnation of
Tshangs-dbyangs rgya-mtsho which, according to prophecy, was to be found at
Li-thang in the east. The prophecy actually did prove to be correct, and the new
incarnation, bsKal-bzang rgya-mtsho, the Seventh Dalai Lama (1708-57), was
brought to sKu-'bum monastery to be educated.

Tibet's position was now considerably weakened by the unsuccessful and
detested rule of Lha-bzang, and the country became a source of discord between
two great powers, the Dzungars and the Manchus. Lha-bzang's main support
proved to be an envoy sent by K'ang-hsi and two Tibetan noblemen,
Khang-chen-nas and Pho-lha-nas bSod-nams stobs rgyas (1689-1747). In 1717
the Dzungars invaded Tibet, killed Lha-bzang, captured Lhasa, and inflicted on
that unhappy city a terrible disaster which in fact might be called a *sacco di
Lhasa*. The marauding Dzungars remained in Tibet three years, especially
harassing the rNying-ma-pa institutions. Eventually they were expelled by
Pho-lha-nas. In 1720 a large Manchu army arrived and occupied Lhasa, where it
remained until 1723 establishing thereby a de facto Manchu protectorate over
Tibet.

Because of these circumstances, the Chinese arrived as friends, especially
since they brought with them from sKu-'bum the seventh rGyal-ba rin-po-che,
bsKal-bzang rgya-mtsho, who was welcomed with frenetic rapture by the
Tibetans. Totally ignoring the donation that had been made by Gushri khan to
the Dalai Lama, the Chinese manipulated the installation of a secular
government headed by Khang-chen-nas. But the new aristocrat-officials were
jealous, and their internecine struggles ended with the murder of Khang-
chen-nas. Pho-lha-nas emerged from the ensuing civil war as the undisputed ruler
of Tibet and was confirmed by the Chinese who bestowed on him the title of
"king" *(wang)* of Tibet. Since by the K'ang-hsi Edict of 1721 a new
Sino-Tibetan relationship was thus established, incorrectly based on the
assumption that Tibet had been a tributary state for eighty years, a new and
dangerous status for Tibet was created by a unilateral move on the part of the
Chinese. There was no written treaty, however, and the Tibetans continued to
regard their relations with China in terms of the traditional patronage of the
emperor which dated back to Yuan times.

The reign of Pho-lha-nas, overtly pro-Chinese, brought the Tibetans an era of peace which lasted until their ruler's death in 1747. His son, 'Gyur-med rnam-rgyal, was less wise and successful and formed a new conspiracy with the Dzungars. In 1750 the two Manchu *ambans* ("residents") who had been appointed by the Chinese emperor in 1721 murdered 'Gyur-med rnam-rgyal, and were in turn put to death by an infuriated Tibetan mob. The Dalai Lama himself restored order within one day, and when Chinese representatives arrived in Lhasa they found him the only undisputed authority. The secular government was consequently abolished and the Dalai Lama recognized as ruler of Tibet by the Chinese. The actual administration was taken over by a state council (*bKa-shag*) which consisted of four ministers. Two *ambans* who enjoyed the protection of a small Chinese garrison were appointed to control the council.

One other feature of this period which began during the reign of the Fifth Dalai Lama was Tibetan colonization and missionary activities in the Himalayan countries of Bhutan, Sikkim, Nepal, and Ladakh. The majority of the peoples living on the southern slopes of the Himalayas were primitive tribes to whom Tibetan Buddhism brought the light of a higher civilization. The definite opening and conversion of 'Brug-yul (Bhutan) did not take place until the sixteenth century and was achieved through the activities of the 'Brug-pa sub-sect of the bKa-brgyud-pa, which had its headquarters at Rva-lung in gTsang. Because of the persecution of several of the Red-Cap schools by the Fifth Dalai Lama, 'Brug-pa monks, including the famous Zhabs-drung Ngag-dbang rNam-rgyal, went to Bhutan where they established a new theocracy of the 'Brug-pa school. They founded several monasteries and castles in the country and the ruler assumed the title of a Chos-rgyal ("king of the Buddhist Law"). The succession of these hierarchs became institutionalized according to the incarnation system. The first Chos-rgyal also established relations with Ladakh, where the monastery of He-mis was founded in 1604.

Tibetan Buddhism was brought to Sikkim ('Bras-ljongs) primarily by the Karma-pa and rNying-ma-pa monks. To the latter school belonged Lha-btsun chen-po Kun-bzang rnam-rgyal, who met two other missionaries at Jo-gsum and founded the first religious institution of Sgrub-sde for the conversion of the animistic Lepchas. This was followed by the erection of gSang-sngags chos-gling (1697), the state monastery Pad-ma gyang-rtse (1704), and bKra-shis-lding. The year 1604 saw the enthronement of Phun-tshogs rnam-rgyal, the founder of the Tibetan dynasty of Sikkim.

During the years 1753-57 the Dzungar state was destroyed by the Manchus and warfare in Central Asia ceased. The following period of a century and a half was for Tibet a period of colonialization and dependence on China. Because the Seventh, and his successor the Eighth Dalai Lama ('Jam-dpal rgya-mtsho, 1758-1804), abstained from politics, the administration was controlled by the regents, who were mere puppets in the hands of the two Chinese residents. The whole period may be characterized as one of indolence, gradual economic decline, and cultural stagnation. Typically, De-mo Khutukhtu, the regent of the Seventh Dalai Lama, was confirmed in office by the Chinese emperor. When the Eighth Dalai Lama assumed his place, the regent remained in office until his death in 1777. Following the regent's death, another monk was sent by the Peking government to fill the vacancy. For the Tibetans, however, the regents lacked the aura of the Dalai Lama; and they were therefore more interested in the Paṇ-chen Rin-po-che, dPal-ldan Ye-shes (1737-80), who was a more vivid personality. In fact, it was to the Paṇ-chen Lama that the British East India Company, interested in commercial relations with Tibet, sent their emissary, George Bogle. Bogle stayed in Tashilhumpo at the court of the hierarch from 1774 to 1775 and described the hospitality, intelligence, and humor of the Paṇ-chen. He also noted the rivalry between the Paṇ-chen's officials and the Lhasa administration. The importance of the Paṇ-chen's office was connected with the personality of dPal-ldan Ye-shes, who died in Peking in 1780 during a visit there. He had been given a lavish reception by the Ch'ien-lung emperor. His successor, a minor, was unable to maintain the position of his predecessor.

During the second half of the eighteenth century trouble arose for Tibet as a result of the rise of the new Gurkha state in Nepal. The Gurkhas, descendants of the Rajputs of India, conquered the entire Nepal valley in 1768-69, expanded to the northwest and east; and the old Tibetan districts of Dol-po and Blo-bo (the Mustang of the maps) fell into their hands. Eventually, in 1788, they invaded Tibet proper and looted the Paṇ-chen's own monastery of bKra-shis lhun-po. To avoid the complete capitulation of Tibet, the Manchu Ch'ien-lung emperor sent a costly and successful expedition under the Manchu general Fukanggan across Tibet to drive the fierce Gurkhas back to their own country. The Gurkhas were defeated several times and in 1792 the Manchus were able to dictate peace before the very gates of the Nepalese capital, Kathmandu. Tibet now enjoyed security but had lost her commercial relations with the Newar kingdoms of Nepal. What is worse, for the whole of the nineteenth century Tibet was subjected to the Manchu "forbidden land" policy. The Tibetans were led to become xenophobes, and were convinced by the Chinese that Tibet would be endangered if foreigners were allowed into it, particularly, of course, the British and Russians. Hence, as we have seen, even the two French Lazarist missionaries, Huc and Gabet, had to cut short their stay at Lhasa. They were clearly able to distinguish between the open and kindly attitude of a member of the Tibetan government, the bKa-blon Lama, and the suspicious behavior of the Chinese *amban.*

The Ninth, Tenth, Eleventh, and Twelfth Dalai Lamas (1805-75) either did not reach the age of majority (perhaps murdered by the regents who acted for the Chinese) or enjoyed a reign of a few short years. The only remarkable personage among the regents was the mTs'o-smon-gling Rin-po-che (1819-44), who was able to avert serious dangers from the west. He could no longer depend upon Chinese troops for the Manchu dynasty was by then in full decline. The Indian Rajah, Gulab Singh, had in 1842 defeated the already tottering kingdom of Ladakh, which since that time had been part of the kingdom of Jammu and Kashmir. Zorawar Singh, Gulab Singh's general, pushed further into central Tibet where he was defeated in 1841. However, when the Tibetans ventured too far into Ladakh, the Jammu army successfully counterattacked and drove them back. Another conflict ensued with Nepal (1854-56); and Tibet, unaided by her Chinese protector, could persuade the Gurkhas to leave only in return for a long-term indemnity.

Tibet's period as a "forbidden land" and as Chinese protectorate ended during the reign of the Thirteenth Dalai Lama, T'ub-bstan rGya-mtsho (1876-1933), who was the first to survive an attempted assassination, for which the regent then in power was condemned.

BIBLIOGRAPHY

The two comprehensive works on the Yellow Church are in German: Robert Bleichsteiner, *Die gelbe Kirche,* Wien 1937; Günther Schulemann, *Geschichte der Dalai-Lamas,* Leipzig 1958. On Manchu-Tibetan relations we have W. W. Rockhill, "The Dalai Lamas of Lhasa and their Relations with the Manchu Emperors of China," *TP* 11 (1910):1-104. This study is superseded by several publications of Luciano Petech: *China and Tibet in the Early 18th Century,* Leiden 1950 (a classic); "The Dalai Lamas and Regents of Tibet: A Chronological Study," *TP* 47 (1960): 368-94; "Notes on Tibetan History of the 18th Century," *TP* 52 (1966): 261-92. For the earlier periods we have Zahiruddin Ahmad, *Sino-Tibetan Relations in the Seventeenth Century,* Serie Orientale Roma 40, Roma 1970. For British-Tibetan relations there are useful studies by Alastair Lamb: *Britain and Chinese Central Asia. The Road to Lhasa,* London 1960; *The McMahon Line,* 2 vols., London-Toronto 1966; "Some Notes on Russian Intrigue in Tibet," *RCAJ* (1959); 46-65. On the war against the Gurkhas: Erich Haenisch, "Zwei kaiserliche Erlasse vom Ausgange der Regierung Kienlung, die Gorkha betreffend," *HJAS* 3 (1938): 17-39, and "Dokumente aus dem Jahre 1788 zur Vorgeschichte des Gorkha-Krieges," *AKBAW* (1959): Heft 49. On George Bogle and his relations with the third Pan-chen Rin-po-che, see Sir Clement Markham, *Narratives of the Mission of George Bogle to Tibet and of the Journey of Thomas Manning to Lhasa,* London 1876, and the relevant chapters of John MacGregor, *Tibet. A Chronicle of Exploration,* New York 1970. Also, Luciano Petech, "The Missions of Bogle and Turner According to Tibetan Texts," *TP* (1950): 330-46. On Gulab Singh: Robert A. Huttenback, "Kashmir as an Imperial Factor During the Reign of Gulab Singh (1846-1857)," *JAH* 2 (1968): 77-108. As to the Dzungar War, compare Eva S. Kraft, *Zum Dsungaren Krieg im 18. Jahrhundert. Berichte des General Funingga.* Leipzig 1953.

The Period of De facto Independence
and the Chinese Communist Occupation (1912-69)
Tibet: a Pawn of Great Britain, Russia, and China

The period of the Thirteenth Dalai Lama (1876-1933) may be characterized as one of persistent attempts at interference by the great, imperialistic foreign powers: China, British India, and Russia. Before considering these momentous developments, a few remarks on the personal life of this Dalai Lama should be made, both because he was the most remarkable hierarch after the "Great Fifth," and because we have especially good material in the form of his official biography, which describes the functioning of the incarnation system.

Like his predecessors, the Twelfth Dalai Lama did not live long (1856-75). Two government officials, perhaps encouraged by the Chinese *ambans,* were instrumental in his illness and were consequently imprisoned after the death of the young hierarch. The *Kashag,* or "cabinet," took charge of day-to-day affairs for some months until the "National Assembly" nominated a regent, Tatsa Rinpoche, of the Kundeling monastery. To him fell the duty of governing the country until the reincarnation of the Dalai Lama could be found and until he was mature enough to assume ruling power.

To find the incarnation the responsible authorities analyzed inspirations and visions and consulted oracles to obtain guidance regarding the whereabouts of the new Dalai Lama. While meditating, the Eighth Paṇ-chen Rinpoche of Tashilhunpo received an inspiration which indicated that the new incarnation would be found to the southeast of Lhaṣa. Simultaneously the State Oracles of gNas-chung and Samye unanimously announced that the next Dalai Lama would be born in southeastern Tibet. Another clue for finding the new Dalai Lama came from a holy lake, not far from the house which was to become the birthplace of the incarnation. While the officials were visiting the lake, a strong gale blew on the snow-covered surface, scattered the snow, and broke the ice. Visions of a nursing baby and images of the Potala Palace and of a peasant's house appeared in the waters. When one member of the committee visited this house, he saw a baby whom he believed to be the reincarnation of the Twelfth Dalai Lama. As predicted, the small farmhouse at the foot of a holy mountain was situated in the Dvags-po region southeast of Lhasa. The next phase of the procedure involved the dispatch of an investigating commission of the Tibetan government to the house to confirm whether this was really the holy baby. When the child was shown two sets of clothing and belongings, one of which had actually belonged to the late Dalai Lama, and another set which had not, he was able to indicate the authentic ones. His way of speaking and his gestures also resembled those of the former Dalai Lama. It was consequently affirmed that this was the true reincarnation.

The Panchen Rinpoche, the regent, the ministers, and the high officials of the three great dGe-lugs-pa institutions of Gandan, 'Bras-spungs, and Sera unanimously invited the boy to come to the Potala Palace to become Tibet's religious and temporal ruler. The urn presented in 1792 by the Ch'ien-lung emperor, which was normally used as an aid in the selection of the Dalai Lama by lot (a device which enabled the Chinese to interfere), was not used. The *amban* could do nothing but confirm the newly-discovered Dalai Lama by proclamation.

In October 1877 an elaborate ceremony was celebrated at the home of the Dalai Lama's parents, and government officials presented to the new hierarch religious objects: a *maṇḍala,* a Buddha image, holy scriptures, and a *stūpa* (Tib. *mchod-rten*). The ceremony of departure then ensued; and the long, solemn journey to the Potala began. This was to give the young hierarch the opportunity of being instructed in the duties of his new life. At the Dechen temple Tatsa Rinpoche, the regent, paid homage for the first time. At a certain place on the sKyid-chu river just opposite Lhasa, high lamas welcomed the holy child; and in February 1878 the Panchen Rinpoche performed there the Buddhist ceremony of tonsure and naming of the Dalai Lama, who was now known by his official name, Thubtan Gyamtsho, and henceforth wore the monastic robe. After crossing the river the royal party partook in another sojourn—lasting more than a year—so that the preceptor of the former Dalai Lama might teach the child to perform the daily activities of a Buddhist priest, to chant the holy texts, and, especially, to behave as a Dalai Lama. In August 1879, at age four, the child entered the Potala and ascended the Lion's Throne. The solemn enthronement took place on an auspicious day, 31 July 1879, in the presence of many Tibetan officials, religious and secular, as well as the ambassadors of Nepal, Kashmir, and other outlying regions, not to mention, of course, the Chinese *amban* and his entourage. There followed a visit to the Jo-khang, the Lhasa Cathedral, the holiest of the holy places of Tibet.

During the following years the child received a strict Buddhist education under monk-teachers, whose head was the teacher of the former Dalai Lama. Ten other teachers were selected from the three great dGe-lugs-pa monasteries, among whom was the Buriat lama Dorjeev from the Baikal region, who was later to play an important role in international politics.

Unfortunately, the Dalai Lama lost, through death, several trustworthy and helpful advisors: in 1886 the regent, Tatsa Rinpoche; in 1881 the Panchen Rinpoche, who would have ordained the Dalai Lama to full monkhood; and in 1887 his own father. The Dalai Lama was consequently obliged to rely more upon his teacher, who continued to direct his education and who allowed him to be admitted to congregational debate in the three great dGe-lugs-pa monasteries.

With the approval of the Chinese, Demo Rinpoche of the Tengyeling monastery had been appointed as the new regent. This man was later to play a sinister role in the life of the young Dalai Lama. When at twenty the Dalai Lama had completed his studies, he received the 371 precepts of the "full monk" (*Gelong*) during a ceremony before the Buddha image in the Lhasa Cathedral.

Now that the Dalai Lama had been fully ordained, the transfer of power from the regent should have taken place. Although according to custom this event normally occurred when a Dalai Lama was eighteen, the accession was postponed following the wishes of the regent, who seems to have been a partisan of the Chinese *amban* and had no desire to relinquish his political authority, at least for the time being. Because of the early deaths of the last four Dalai Lamas the Thirteenth, an energetic man, was on his guard. When he learned that the nephew and secretary of the regent, Nor-bu Tshe-ring, was plotting against him, and that Demo was also involved, he immediately ordered an interrogation of the suspects. It became evident that the Demo party had intended to act against the young hierarch with the help of a certain lama from Nyarong. Accordingly, the Dalai Lama ordered the arrest of the ex-regent and his relatives.

Having overcome this internal difficulty, the Dalai Lama turned his attention to foreign affairs, inasmuch as dark clouds were gathering beyond the Tibetan borders. By means of a series of treaties and annexations, the British Indian government had been strengthening its borders across the entire northern frontier, creating along the Himalayas a *cordon sanitaire* as protection against intrusions from Central Asia.

After the travels of Bogle and Turner in the second half of the eighteenth century, Tibetan relations with the British had practically ceased. The development of trade was the principal British-Indian interest in Tibet. Trade regulations were one-sided at this time because Tibetan merchants were permitted to enter India, although no British trade was permitted in Tibet. The Tibetans had no interest in the outside world, an attitude which greatly pleased the Chinese.

When in 1846 China was approached by British diplomats in Peking, it was evident that the former disliked any, even harmless, British activities, and it was not until the Sino-British Chefoo Conference of 1876 that a paragraph was agreed upon wherein the Chinese promised to provide facilities for a British exploratory mission in Tibet. In 1885 the British Indian government made preparations for mission to Tibet, but was met with strong Tibetan opposition. It could no longer be concealed that Chinese influence had waned enormously after the accession of the Thirteenth Dalai Lama, and that, owing to the disaster of the Sino-Japanese war of 1894/95, effective Chinese control in Tibet had come to an end. This pleased the British, but they nonetheless recognized that insurmountable distrust toward them on the part of the Tibetans still existed. The British mission attempted to enter Tibet via Sikkim but was met by Tibetan armed resistance near Natong, well within Sikkim. Although surprised, the British at first only sent a request to Peking for a Tibetan withdrawal which understandably produced no results. Two other requests for withdrawal had equally little result and finally the British used armed force to drive out the Tibetans.

Mutual ignorance which, as far as the Tibetans were concerned, had been fostered by the Chinese, can be blamed for this first hostility. Worried over being preempted by the British, the Chinese were now ready to open trade negotiations in India and to settle the status of Sikkim. This agreement might have been signed in 1890, but it was three years before the signatures for the Tibetan Trade Regulations were forthcoming. However, since no Tibetan representative attended the negotiations or signed the agreement, the regulations were never really enforceable. That the Tibetans refused to cooperate was due to the policy of the Thirteenth Dalai Lama, who had always considered Tibet to be an autonomous country which acknowledged the Chinese emperor only as patron in accordance with the tradition of Ming and early Manchu times.

After the appointment of Curzon as viceroy of India in 1898, Tibeto-British relations became a matter of increasing importance, but now the desire to initiate active trade had been replaced by concern over Russian expansion into Central Asia, which proved to be a serious challenge to the defense policy of the British government in India. The danger seemed the more threatening because the Torgut Kalmucks and Buriats, fervent adherents of the dGe-lugs-pa church, were subjects of the czar and, like other Mongols from the time of the Third Dalai Lama, had experienced no difficulties travelling in Tibet. In 1898 Curzon was perturbed by the news that a Russian mission headed by a certain Baranov had been to Lhasa. Even more alarming for the British was the activity of the Buriat monk, Dorjeev, who had been a member of the group of lamas which supervised the education of the young Dalai Lama. After the accession of the Thirteenth Dalai Lama, Dorjeev's influence continued to be strong. He succeeded in making the hierarch believe that the mysterious country of Shambhala, where, in accordance with Buddhist apocalyptic doctrine, pure Buddhism will be preserved until the end of the present world period and from where the debased world will be converted again after a terrible apocalyptic battle, was actually the Russian empire and that the czar was to be regarded as the "Religious King" (*Kalki*). Dorjeev travelled to Russia several times with letters from the Dalai Lama and returned with imperial gifts for the hierarch. He also made the Dalai Lama believe that the czar was a fervent Buddhist, compelled to behave like a Christian. Eventually the Dalai Lama even made preparations to meet the czar at the latter's invitation, but the xenophobia of the National Assembly prevented him from this dangerous undertaking. Talk ensued of a Russian prince coming to Lhasa as a Russian envoy, and the Russian newspapers enflamed the situation even more by overtly writing about what they termed "our mission to Tibet." Curzon felt there was danger ahead, and the additional fact of British ignorance of Tibetan thought patterns could only lead to imminent trouble. Rumors, substantiated by eyewitness reports, that arms were sent to Lhasa by the Russians did nothing to relieve Curzon's suspicions. He decided in favor of direct action. This was delayed by the British Foreign Office, which strongly felt that the Tibetan question might involve the United Kingdom in international difficulties. However, in July 1903 a British party accompanied by an important armed escort penetrated into Tibet as far as Khampa Dzong, where the head of the mission Major Francis Younghusband, halted for negotiations. These did not take place since the Tibetans saw no reason to negotiate. Nothing happened either from the side of the Chinese. After a delay of five months, winter was approaching and military concentrations had been reported between Phari Dzong and Shigatse. In view of this development London allowed the mission to advance as far as Gyantse.

Near Tuna the expedition met with the poorly armed Tibetans who took cover behind a stone wall. Younghusband made it known to the Tibetan general that he would not order fire unless fired upon. When the British began to tear down the wall, a shot was fired by the Tibetans and general fighting broke out, from which the British emerged victorious, killing more than three hundred and wounding many more. Younghusband moved on to Gyantse and found that the Tibetan government was still not ready for negotiations. By now he had learned something of Tibetan mentality and so knew that negotiations would have to take place at Lhasa. He pushed on, but on reaching the capital was disappointed to find that the Dalai Lama, together with his counsellor Dorjeev, had departed for Mongolia and left his ministers behind with no real power to act. The Chinese *amban* was the first to meet the British, but it was immediately evident that he held practically no authority. It was the Khri Rinpoche of Gandan, who had been appointed regent before the Dalai Lama's escape from his capital and who had been given plenipotentiary powers by the National Assembly, who opened negotiations and who on 7 September 1904 signed the Anglo-Tibetan Convention.

The convention stipulated the payment of an indemnity. Until it had been paid, the British would continue to occupy the Chumbi Valley, held as a security. The principal and positive clauses of the convention resulted in a definitive settlement of the Tibeto-Sikkimese boundary, provisions for renewed Trade Regulations, and, finally, clauses excluding any foreign power from political influence in Tibet. The Chinese *amban* was present during the signing ceremony but did not, of course, himself sign. After the usual period of protest and delay, an Anglo-Chinese Convention of 1906 endorsed the validity of the Anglo-Tibetan Convention. It did not recognize Chinese "sovereignty" over Tibet, but provided for what is known in diplomatic language as "suzerainty." This rather unclear concept was to be a source of constant trouble for the Tibetans.

Meanwhile the Dalai Lama had been received with great honors in Outer Mongolia where he was visited not only by a local Chinese *amban* but even by the Russian Ambassador, a fact which speaks for itself: Dorjeev was still operating in the background. In 1906 the Dalai Lama visited the Kumbum monastery in Amdo, a most holy sanctuary of the dGe-lugs-pa school. Although he intended to leave Kumbum and return to Lhasa when the British troops had left his capital, a Chinese imperial messenger thwarted these plans by informing him that it was the emperor's urgent wish to receive a visit from the Dalai Lama in Peking. This invitation was signed both by the emperor and the empress dowager, but it was the latter who at this time represented the actual power in China. The Dalai Lama reluctantly changed his plans and arrived in Peking in September 1908. Although received as an illustrious guest in the emperor's palace and permitted to initiate a great religious ceremony, he learned that he had been deposed by the Chinese, who were already seeking a new incarnation and preparing for an invasion of eastern Tibet. Later, when the Chinese government learned of the uprisings in Lhasa which had resulted from the "deposition" of the popular Dalai Lama, it altered its policy and allowed the hierarch to maintain his religious rank and return to Lhasa. At the same time, it insulted its guest by giving him the title of "Most Faithfully Obedient and Enlightened Buddha of no Restraint in the Western Paradise," from which it was obvious that it looked upon the Dalai Lama as a vassal of China, although it had signed away sovereignty over Tibet in the Anglo-Chinese Treaty of 1906. For the Dalai Lama this visit meant nothing more than a meeting of "priest and patron" as had been customary from the time of Khubilai Khan and 'Phags-pa. Because of his unfriendly treatment in China the Dalai Lama was exasperated and harbored hostile feelings toward the Chinese. It was in this state of mind that he left Peking, and in July 1909 again reached his residence in Lhasa.

During the Dalai Lama's stay in Peking the Chinese had taken steps to enforce their authority over Tibet, thus provoking an uprising on the eastern border. At the end of 1905 the situation deteriorated further when the Manchu general Chao Erh-feng, governor of Szechwan, arrived and assumed control of eastern Tibet, a situation which had never existed before. The Szechwan army's looting, killing, and destruction were so atrocious that the Younghusband expedition seemed quite harmless in comparison with the events now occurring in Khams and those which were later to occur in central Tibet. Chao Erh-feng made great efforts to annex small portions of Szechwan to the whole of Khams as far as Giamda in Kong-po (only sixty miles from Lhasa), which included districts always ruled by the Lhasa government, and to create a new Chinese province which he called Hsi-k'ang. In doing this, he followed an ancient Chinese pattern: the setting up of a Chinese administration in a so-called barbarian border country, followed by the advent of Chinese settlers and merchants. By this method the original inhabitants, after some decades, became a minority in their own country and were later destined to be swallowed by the Chinese.

Another move made to demonstrate Chinese overlordship in central Tibet was the announcement by China that it would pay the Tibetan indemnity imposed by the 1904 Anglo-Tibetan Convention. Most important, Chang Yin-tang was sent to Lhasa as High Commissioner. Because of continuing disturbances in eastern Tibet he was forced to travel through India.

In 1909 the Tibetan government, notwithstanding the memories of the Younghusband mission, made a desperate plea to the British and other nations for assistance. British formal protests had no effect, and in February 1910 Chao's troops entered Lhasa under General Chung Yin. The Dalai Lama managed to escape and took refuge in India, where he formally renounced the Manchu-Chinese government's claim to overlordship of Tibet.

While the Lhasa population was being harrassed by the Chinese soldiery, the British government, strongly involved in international affairs, reacted only by issuing repeated formal protests, which the Chinese answered with non-committal statements. In any case, the Chinese invasion of 1910 brought a radical change in Sino-Tibetan relations. For the first time in history a Chinese army had occupied Lhasa despite unanimous opposition by its citizens.

The Chinese did not achieve their political goals in Tibet; those members of the government who had not fled to India with the Dalai Lama were unwilling to assist them. Chinese attempts to persuade the Panchen Rinpoche to act as head of a provisional administration failed, and they realized that it had been an error to depose the Dalai Lama for the second time. They tried to persuade him to return, understandably without success. From his exile in India the Dalai Lama declared void any political links between his country and China.

In 1911 the Chinese republic was established under the presidency of Yüan Shih-k'ai. In Tibet, Chinese troops mutinied, and in some parts of the country attacks were made on Chinese garrisons. Through mediation of the Nepalese government, an agreement was reached which resulted in complete withdrawal of the Chinese troops by the end of 1912, and in January 1913 the Dalai Lama returned to Lhasa.

That same year the Dalai Lama stressed the independent status of Tibet in a solemn proclamation and blamed the Chinese for having willfully misinterpreted the priest-patron relationship which had "never been one of subordination of one to the other." The Dalai Lama announced that "under my orders the remnants of the Chinese troops are now being pushed back from DoKham" (i.e., Amdo and Khams). In fact, when the Manchu regime was overthrown, eastern Tibet had arisen and attacked the centers and garrisons of Chao Erh-feng's newly-established Hsi-k'ang province. The newly-established republic was as nationalistic as the Manchus had been, and Tibet was menaced by a new Chinese invasion.

The Dalai Lama's statement concerning Tibetan independence was disregarded by the British, who in the earlier conventions had acknowledged

Chinese suzerainty, although not sovereignty, over Tibet. Internal disorders notwithstanding, China refused to make any concession on Tibet. Yüan Shih-k'ai voiced regrets for the treatment of Tibet by the Manchu regime and offered to restore "the Dalai Lama's official rank." The latter refused to accept a Chinese charge and proceeded with consolidating his position in the east, along the Mekong-Salween watershed.

As a result of the Chinese revolution, the situation became chaotic in Mongolia—another semiautonomous part of the former Manchu empire—and led to the strengthening there of Russian influence. On 11 January 1913 a Mongol-Tibetan treaty was signed in Urga, a clear affirmation by the contracting parties of their respective national independence.

The Chinese, anxious to prevent direct contacts between Britain and Tibet, accepted to enter negotiations on the basis of the British note of 1912. After some haggling concerning the place of the conference, the three plenipotentiaries met in Simla on 6 October 1913. Great Britain was represented by Henry McMahon, assisted by Charles Bell; China, by Ivan Chen; and Tibet, by Lonchen Shatra.

The Tibetans, of course, pleaded for complete home rule which they had received de facto. They also urged the other participants to accept a Tibeto-Chinese boundary which would unite all the Tibetan-speaking peoples in the east as far as Dartsendo (Ta-chien-lu) and Koko Nor. They supported their case with careful documentation. The Chinese—using historical arguments—pressed for sovereignty over Tibet. Thus they invoked the 1207 conquest by the Mongol Chingis khan, an absurd argument which would make as much sense as a German claim to sovereignty over Italy based upon conditions in the Holy Roman Empire during medieval times. This and other fallacious arguments were used to support their claim that Tibet was an integral part of China. They wanted the same frontiers claimed earlier by Chao Erh-feng, which would bring them to within sixty miles east of Lhasa.

McMahon attempted to save Tibetan autonomy while leaving the Chinese in a position which would allow them to save face. He suggested the concept of an "Outer" and an "Inner" Tibet: the former, to the west of the Yangtze, would be independent, while Inner Tibet would, to a limited degree, remain under Chinese jurisdiction.

The Chinese representative refused to accept the terms of the convention for a long time, but finally, when it became evident that he could gain no additional concessions, he initialled the draft along with his British and Tibetan colleagues. However, the Chinese government refused to ratify the Simla Convention, which then was signed on 3 July 1914 by McMahon and the Tibetan minister Shatra. A codicil was appended to the convention making it binding on the signatories and insuring that China would not enjoy the advantages of the agreement unless its government also signed the convention.

The Tibetans were temporarily relieved of the concessions to the Chinese to which they had earlier been coerced to agree. In addition, the Tibetans could count on British support, both diplomatic and military. The way was now open for additional British-Tibetan agreements on trade regulations, for a guarantee that the British might send a representative to Lhasa, and for an adjustment of the British Indian-Tibetan border, which later became known as the "McMahon Line." Special care was taken to guarantee the unrestricted communications of the Tibetans with the Tibetan monasteries and settlements south of the line.

The Dalai Lama now exercised unrestricted authority over the whole of Tibet, though Sino-Tibetan relations were strained and erupted into occasional fighting at the de facto frontier. The Chinese attempted to persuade the Tibetans to come to an agreement with them. The Dalai Lama always met these overtures by pointing out that the Chinese Revolution had totally changed the situation. After the fall of Yüan Shih-k'ai, Szechwan and Yünnan seceded from the central Chinese government; and the Tibetans were obliged to deal with the local Chinese generals, particularly with P'eng Jih-sheng, governor of Szechwan. With Tibetan troops advancing, the line on the upper Yangtze again became the de facto frontier. In August 1918 an armistice agreement was signed at Rongbatsa near Kanzé. The Tibetan government hoped for new definitive negotiations, but the general confusion in China and the weakness of the Kuomintang regime, much criticized by its own citizens, prevented the two parties from entering even preparatory discussions. The truce lasted for more than twelve years.

Because the Dalai Lama quite understandably felt great concern for a definite solution to the eastern frontier problems, he was deeply disappointed with the failure of the Simla Conference. To improve relations, in 1920 Charles Bell, a close friend of the Dalai Lama, was sent to Lhasa where he stayed for nearly a year. The results of their confidential talks were, of course, meager because of the situation in general. A British overture to the new Peking government was answered evasively. The Chinese hinted at an imminent 1921 Washington conference and negotiations were promised only after that event. All the British were able to do to please the Dalai Lama was to supply Tibet with arms and ammunition and to construct a telegraph line connecting Tibet with India.

As regards Tibet, the Washington conference brought no tangible results. Because of internal problems the Chinese were not able to deal effectively with matters of foreign policy. Within Tibet the situation deteriorated considerably owing to the flight to China of the Panchen Rinpoche in 1923, who was motivated by his reluctance to contribute to the maintenance of the Dalai Lama's army. His presence in China proved to be a continuing threat to the government of the Dalai Lama for it was feared that the hierarch might return only with a strong Chinese escort. It had never been forgotten that during the K'ang-hsi era the Chinese had used the Panchen to weaken the authority of the

Dalai Lama, a stratagem which was to be later revived by Communist China. This time, of course, the Panchen Rinpoche was warmly welcomed by the Chinese. Trouble was also in the offing because of the modernizing tendencies of the Dalai Lama, which caused the powerful clergy to be apprehensive lest lay generals and technicians take away the influence of the high monastic officials. The forces of opposition rallied round a young lay official called Lungshar. The reactionary forces were able to close the popular British school at Gyantse, to sabotage the new army and police force, and to do away with the new motor mail service of the British trade agencies in Tibet. It would seem that the Dalai Lama had made too many innovations too quickly for the traditional mentality of the Tibetans. The consequences of the setback were disastrous, for both the Russians and the Chinese used it for propaganda purposes, characterising the events as "the crash of British influence" and "a turning strongly towards China." The Chinese did not hesitate to send a mission to Lhasa in 1930 which, headed by the abbot of the Tibetan temple in Peking, was received courteously. The Dalai Lama's answer to the mission, however, was unconditional Tibetan independence.

Because of a monastic dispute, the armistice in the east was broken and the independent governor of Szechwan, Liu Wen-hui, interested in reviving Chao Erh-feng's Hsi-k'ang project, took advantage of the situation. Ignoring the telegrams exchanged between Chiang K'ai-shek and the Dalai Lama, Liu's troops drove the Tibetans back and even threatened Chamdo. In panic the Dalai Lama telegraphed the British-Indian government; but when a British political officer reached Lhasa in September 1932, conditions were better than he had been led to believe, especially since the Tibetans had again been able to move up to the Yangtze line because of a civil war between Liu Wen-hui and his nephew. A new armistice was signed early in 1933 and another with Governor Ma Pu-fang, who was virtually the independent ruler of the Koko Nor area. Without participation of the Nanking government, the upper Yangtze was agreed upon as the new boundary.

The death of the Thirteenth Dalai Lama in December 1933 spelled real disaster for Tibet; the late hierarch had been an able politician despite his failure—the result of unfavorable political circumstances—to achieve his main goal: the definite tripartite agreement on Tibet's eastern border. Now, during one of the most precarious periods in its history, Tibet became the victim of all the uncertainties of a *sedis vacantia,* the Tibetan government finding itself in a state of confusion following the disappearance of the strong hand of the Dalai Lama.

Only as a result of the usual conditions following the death of a Dalai Lama was the short interlude by the ambitious Lungshar possible. At odds with the *Kashag,* which normally conducts the interim administration, Lungshar worked through the Tibetan National Assembly, which he believed to be a suitable instrument to further his own plans. According to custom and certainly because of the influence of Lungshar, Reting Rinpoche, a very young man with no experience in politics, was appointed regent; although again because of Lungshar's influence there was little chance that he would ever exercise much power. Lungshar wanted Tibet to become a republic and the National Assembly, under his guidance, to become the supreme political body of the country, an incredible thing within the framework of the Tibetan theocracy. It soon became obvious to the clergy that the layman Lungshar was not the person to rule a monastic state like Tibet. Eventually the *Kashag* arrested him, tried him, and sentenced him to life imprisonment. The *Kashag*, in power once again, ruled to a large extent by adhering to the policies set forth in the testament of the Thirteenth Dalai Lama.

Accustomed to the strong hand of the Thirteenth Dalai Lama, the *Kashag* was soon forced to deal with a challenging problem of diplomacy. The Chinese, who had been expelled from Lhasa in 1912, took advantage of the situation, as they traditionally did even during periods of their own weakness, and managed a reappearance on the diplomatic scene by sending a large delegation to offer condolences on the death of the Dalai Lama. Their leader was General Huang Mu-sung, a member of the National Military Council of the Republic of China. The delegation reached Lhasa in the spring of 1934 and brought a radio transmitter with them. Although General Huang announced that his visit was solely for the purpose of participating in the ceremonies of condolence, the Tibetans were perfectly aware of the fact that the Chinese had come to ascertain whether, following the death of the uncompromising Dalai Lama, the Tibetan government might not be persuaded to accept a status of dependence. The *Kashag* agreed to discussions in hopes of resolving the lingering border dispute. When Huang insisted upon Tibet's status as an integral part of China and the termination of direct relations with foreign countries, i.e., Britain, Tibet insisted on continuing the late Dalai Lama's policy of independence, although there was no objection to a resumption of relations with China on principle. The Tibetans also informed the Chinese emissary that they would agree to the return of the Panchen Rinpoche provided he came alone and without Chinese escort. The *Kashag* knew that the Panchen, who had been made a member of the Chinese Supreme Council in February 1934, was destined to become the Kuomintang's puppet in Tibet. General Huang later became Chairman of the Commission for the Western Regions and did everything possible to carry through his own recommendations, which included the Panchen's return to Tibet. In 1937 the unfortunate hierarch died at Jyekundo and the Chinese immediately selected a boy to succeed him. Tibet, however, refused to recognize him, for the traditional manner of finding a new incarnation had not been employed. Although Huang returned to China, he left behind at Lhasa the radio transmitter and two officers who formed the nucleus of what gradually became a regular mission.

The British Indian government, concerned over the Chinese activities, in turn sent a British mission to Tibet headed by Basil Gould, political officer for Sikkim, along with Brigadier Philip Neame. The purpose of the mission was to learn whether Tibetan independence was endangered or not and to offer material aid if necessary. Brigadier Neame was in charge of military affairs, which implied a strengthening of the Tibetan army to prevent the Chinese from imposing their will in Tibet. The supply of arms continued. Like the Chinese, the British left behind a representative with a radio transmitter. The government of Tibet greatly welcomed the presence of a British representative in Lhasa and seemed to regard it as insurance against Chinese encroachments.

The most urgent task for the *Kashag* was, of course, finding the new incarnation of the Dalai Lama. The usual procedures led to the conviction that the new incarnation would be born in the east, and a mission headed by a high religious dignitary from the Sera monastery proceeded to the northeast where the incarnation was found near Kumbum monastery. The boy passed all tests satisfactorily. Great difficulties were caused by the independent Chinese Muslim governor of Ch'inghai (Koko Nor), Ma Pu-fang, who refused to allow the boy to travel to Lhasa until he was paid the exorbitant sum of 300,000 Chinese dollars. Eventually the Tibetans were able to raise the necessary money and brought the holy boy to Lhasa in 1939, where he was enthroned early in 1940. China was represented at the enthronement ceremonies by Wu Chung-hsin, chairman of the Commission for Mongolian and Tibetan Affairs. He announced that the Chinese office at Lhasa would henceforth be a branch of the Commission for Mongolian and Tibetan Affairs, and that the Chinese officials at Lhasa would be known as "resident officers." This change in nomenclature in no way caused the Tibetans to modify their attitude toward the Chinese, and all their attempts to interfere in Tibetan domestic affairs were rebuffed. The mission of Shen Tsung-lien in 1944, which pretended to have the solution to the Sino-Tibetan problem, was also unsuccessful. This official was at least sincere enough to later admit that "the patron-chaplain partnership endured as long as the patron was capable of being a patron, and the chaplain willing to remain a chaplain." Shen also conceded that Tibet had enjoyed full independence since 1911.

In 1949 the Tibetan government sent home the Kuomintang mission, which had been in Lhasa for fifteen years. The formal ejection order was intended to stress Tibet's independence from China and to emphasize her neutrality in the Chinese domestic struggle. The Tibetans, of course, were unhappy with the Sino-British alliance which followed the entry of Japan into the Second World War; and although not unsympathetic to the cause of the Allies, they remained, after careful consideration, totally neutral. When, following the Japanese invasion of Burma, the "Burma Road" to China was cut off, the Tibetans firmly rejected a Chinese request for permission to construct a road through southeastern Tibet into India. When the Chinese government sent a surveying party to begin construction of the road, Tibetan troops stopped them. Pressed by Chiang K'ai-shek, the British sought an alternative for the organization of pack transport along existing routes in Tibet, but the Tibetan government stressed its neutrality and refused even to consider the proposal. Eventually, however, it yielded to British persuasion and agreed to grant transit rights limited to goods which did not include war materials. In 1942 two Americans, Captain Tolstoy and Lieutenant Dolan, conferred directly with the Foreign Department of the Tibetan government and attempted to establish a supply route through Tibet into China which would replace the dangerous and costly airlift of war supplies. Although this did not produce the desired results, the tone of U.S. official correspondence with the Tibetan government left no doubt that it dealt with the Tibetan government in a manner consistent with de facto independence and neutrality.

Two German, or rather Austrian, prisoners of war who escaped from a detention camp in India to Tibet were given asylum at Lhasa. One of them, Heinrich Harrer, became a close companion of the young Dalai Lama. These events show the success of the Tibetan government in obtaining recognition of its independent and neutral status. Tibetan goodwill missions were sent to India and China during the spring of 1946 to offer congratulations on the Allied victory, and a Tibetan delegation to the Asian Relations Conference at New Delhi in 1947 emphasized Tibetan independence.

The solution of the Outer Mongolian question at the Yalta Conference without China's participation or knowledge caused the Tibetans to wonder whether they might not be able to follow the same course. They felt certain the British would give them the necessary support and were consequently surprised and bewildered by the emergence of India as an independent nation on 15 August 1947. Formal assurance was given the Tibetan government by the British that India would continue to occupy the position held by Britain. The government of India agreed to maintain the status quo as an interim arrangement and thus found itself bound by the Simla Convention of 1914 and by other Tibeto-British agreements. India declared that relations between the two countries would be maintained on the same basis as prior to 1947. In 1949 the first Indian political officer in Sikkim, Harishvar Dayal, according to British custom visited Lhasa and upon that occasion agreed to provide Tibet with some arms. It is thus evident that the government of India consistently treated Tibet as an autonomous state even on the very eve of the emergence of the People's Republic of China.

While engaged in these external political affairs, Tibet was experiencing internal problems. Reting Rinpoche had resigned from the regency as early as 1941, having failed to convince the leaders of Tibet of his integrity and loyalty. He was replaced by Taktra Rinpoche, who ruled until the communist invasion. Unquestionably devoted to his lord, the young Dalai Lama, and supervising his education, the new regent was overtaxed by the requirements of a shrewd and firm way of ruling in these extremely dangerous times. In 1947 a conspiracy was detected in which the former regent, Reting Rinpoche, had become involved. Its center was the great Sera monastery which seems to have been a partisan of the Chinese during this time. The ex-regent was tried and sentenced to prison, where he died on May 8 of the same year.

Soon after the expulsion of the Kuomintang mission from Lhasa the new communist regime made itself felt in Tibet. The Tibetans had expelled the Chinese officials in order to free themselves from Chinese control, but the government of the People's Republic of China charged that the Tibetans had acted at the instigation of foreign agents. It asserted its claim to Tibet in the strongest terms and announced its program of "liberation" of Tibet as early as January 1950.

The Tibetans were naturally greatly worried as they had neither the manpower nor the armament sufficient to resist a Chinese attack. They made some attempts to secure outside help, but received little sympathy. Nehru advised the Tibetans not to meet the Chinese challenge with military resistance but to negotiate a peace treaty on the basis of the Simla Convention, although he was perfectly aware that the Chinese would never accept such an arrangement. The Indian Union was in no position to match the Chinese in the military field, but in view of Nehru's worldwide prestige a firmer attitude at an early date might have prevented the terrible events which were to take place in Tibet. Nepal, also concerned, was bound by the Indo-Nepalese Treaty of Friendship of 1950, by which it was obliged to cooperate with India in foreign policy. The Tibetan government's last hope was an appeal to the United Nations to request international help. But here, too, it was handicapped for it was not a member of that organization and even India declined to sponsor Tibet's case. Eventually the Tibetan minister, Tsepon W. Shakabpa, went to New York and found a sponsor in El Salvador, a palpable symbol of the lack of interest on the part of the great powers. The decision of the U. N. General Assembly (24 November 1950), which at that time was seriously involved in the Korean question, was unfavorable and left Tibet in disappointment and despair.

Nevertheless, India was greatly upset by China's invasion of Tibet in the winter of 1950, although it was not Nehru but the Indian deputy prime minister, Vallabhai Patel, who stated in the Parliament in New Delhi: "To use the sword against the traditionally peace-loving Tibetan people was unjustified. . . . The Chinese government did not follow India's advice of settling the Tibetan issue peacefully. They marched their armies into Tibet and have explained this action by talking of foreign interests intriguing in Tibet against China. But this fear is unfounded."

It was against this dark background that in the winter of 1950 at the request of the *Kashag*–urged on by the crowds in the Tibetan capital–the Fourteenth Dalai Lama, barely sixteen, assumed power.

Even while China was attempting to persuade the Dalai Lama to abandon the idea of Tibetan independence, on 7 October 1950 Chinese troops invaded eastern Tibet. They soon took the important center of Chamdo where they captured a Tibetan minister, Ngawang Jigme Ngabo, who was to become the Quisling of Tibet although he had been sent to the east to defend the country. After being released by the "liberation" generals, he was encouraged to keep in touch with the Lhasa government and to persuade it to capitulate. Alarmed by events, the counselors of the Dalai Lama urged him to leave Lhasa immediately and to go to Yatung near the Sikkimese border, where he could make his way to India in the event of the capture of Lhasa by the Chinese. Reluctantly, the Dalai Lama accepted this proposal, and on 19 December 1950, he started for Yatung, leaving behind two prime ministers to manage the government during his absence. He sent a small portion of the Tibetan State Treasure to India in case he was obliged to seek asylum there. The first official act carried out at Yatung was the dispatch of a peace delegation to China; but this delegation was headed by Ngabo, a secret partisan of the Chinese. On 23 May 1951 he concluded, as representative of the Tibetan government, a seventeen-point agreement concerning what was styled "measures for the peaceful liberation of Tibet."

A consideration of this agreement makes it clear that it was a Trojan horse intended to serve the interests of the Chinese. Regional autonomy, it is true, was promised although "the Tibetan people shall return to the great family of the motherland—the People's Republic of China"—a statement based on wrong suppositions. The central authorities, i.e., the government of China, "will not alter the established status, functions and powers of the Dalai Lama." But the fact that the status, functions, and powers of the Panchen were to be maintained hints at the traditional Chinese policy of playing the Panchen against the government of the Dalai Lama. Freedom of religion was guaranteed. Tibetan troops were to be reorganized as a part of the "People's Liberation Army." Tibetan agriculture would be developed. Concerning various reforms, "there will be no compulsion on the part of the Central Authorities." Foreign affairs were to be surrendered to the Central Chinese government, i.e., Tibetan independence would no longer exist. Above all, the Tibetan people were to drive from Tibet the "imperialistic aggressive forces," meaning the British and possibly the Kuomintang Chinese. This agreement was a heavy burden for the Tibetans to bear, for it meant acknowledgment of Chinese sovereignty. Promised local autonomy was also more than doubtful.

In July 1952 Chang Ching-wu, representative of the Central People's government in Tibet, went to Yatung and persuaded the Dalai Lama to return to Lhasa. In September the Chinese army advanced and occupied all strategic positions in the country. Ngabo became the most influential man in the *Kashag*, and in reality was something of a liaison officer for the Chinese. In February 1952 the Chinese Communists established the "Military District of Tibet" and experimented with agrarian reform which met with Tibetan resistance, especially in Khams. The deposition and arrest of the most important councilor of the Dalai Lama, Lu-Khang-ba, was an event which proved that even the few concessions made in the seventeen-point agreement were mere words.

The government of India signed away not only Tibet's independence, but also the rights and responsibilities it had inherited from the British. The Indian mission at Lhasa was converted into a Consulate-General (under the jurisdiction of the Indian Embassy in Peking), and in addition the Indians were obliged to accept the establishment of a Chinese Consulate in Bombay. All Indo-Tibetan conventions and treaties lapsed, and the Indians were allowed to maintain trade agencies only at Yatung, Gyantse, and Gartok. All Indian property in Tibet, including the telegraph installations and the government bungalows, were confiscated by the Chinese. Prime Minister Nehru, who had relied on his agreement with Chou En-lai, the so-called *Panch Shila* or "Five Principles of Peaceful Coexistence," met with strong criticism not only in the Parliament but also from the population of India. He was thought to have been naive in dealing with the Chinese, and future developments were to prove that his naiveté was indeed real. Following the Sino-Indian agreement of 29 April 1954 there was at any rate no longer any contact between India and Tibet.

It was by mere chance that Pandit Nehru happened to be in Peking when the Dalai Lama and the Panchen were ordered to attend the 7th Plenary Meeting of the Chinese State Council in 1955, although there was no opportunity for private talks. The two high incarnations received an Indian invitation to attend the 2,500th Buddha Jayanti ("birthday") Celebrations in 1956.

After his return from the Peking meetings in March 1955, the Dalai Lama entered Tibet via Szechwan and learned that the resistance to Chinese rule in eastern Tibet had assumed serious proportions. For the warlike, freedom-loving Goloks, Amdo-pa, and Kham-pa, conditions under the occupation had become intolerable, especially because of the large-scale Chinese immigration and colonization and the policy of collective farming, but also because of their opposition to Chinese construction of strategic roads from the border of China to Lhasa in 1951-54. A major revolt broke out in eastern Tibet in the spring of 1956, in which tens of thousands of guerillas battled the Chinese. India was scarcely aware of the overwhelming discontent in Tibet until the number of Tibetan refugees who came to India, ostensibly as pilgrims, had greatly increased.

In November 1956, in the course of the Buddha Jayanti Celebrations in New Delhi (a powerful demonstration of Buddhist unity), it was evident that the Dalai Lama was acutely unhappy over the situation in Tibet. He felt that he could do very little for his people, and he considered not returning to his country unless there were actual signs of improvement. Prime Minister Nehru, appeased by Chinese Premier Chou En-lai, who promised full implementation of the 1951 agreement, advised the Dalai Lama to return to Tibet early in 1957. The Chinese promises, however, proved to be merely verbal. Ruthless Chinese armed intervention continued, and the final period before the Dalai Lama's flight to India in the spring of 1959 was heavy with tension. Failing to transform the Tibetans into Chinese, the communist invasion turned to sheer brutality, worse than the Tibetans had ever experienced. This led to the spontaneous national uprising which began at Lhasa on 10 March 1959, and was the final Tibetan endeavor to live in absolute freedom and to maintain the political and religious institutions peculiar to their traditions and history.

At that time the Dalai Lama and the majority of the *Kashag,* not including Ngabo, were residing at his summer palace, the Norbu Lingka. Lhasa and the adjacent regions were filled with Khampa rebels, and when rumor spread that the Chinese would escort the Dalai Lama to China, huge crowds of Lhasa citizens and Khampas blocked the area surrounding the palace. Meanwhile, following the explosion of two Chinese grenades on the grounds of Norbu Lingka, the *Kashag* and the loyal lord chamberlain, Phala, decided that the Dalai Lama had better escape. Under the pressure of these events, the Dalai Lama reluctantly agreed to leave his capital in the disguise of a simple, poor Tibetan. His escape and that of several of his ministers under protection of a Khampa bodyguard remained at first undetected, for one of the terrible Tibetan sandstorms had darkened the entire Lhasa area. The party succeeded in evading Chinese detection. Eventually, when the Chinese guards on the main road to China (which the Dalai Lama was obliged to cross) became suspicious, a Khampa detachment led the Chinese astray and sacrificed itself to allow the hierarch to escape. The party did not take the usual way to India via Sikkim; instead it followed an eastern track through Lhokha and Tawang monastery, which led through the Khampa-controlled area to Tezpur in Assam. The Dalai Lama and his entourage were immediately given asylum by Prime Minister Nehru, and it was at Tezpur, before his departure to Mussoorie, that the Dalai Lama made an important statement in which he informed the world that the Chinese had broken the seventeen-point agreement, that so-called local autonomy and religious freedom were a farce, that the Chinese had turned to violence and oppression, and that a large number of monasteries had been destroyed and many Lamas killed or employed on the construction of roads in China. The Dalai Lama also stressed that fact that he had left Tibet voluntarily, whereas the Chinese charged that he had been kidnapped by a reactionary clique.

On his way to Mussoorie in a special train, the Dalai Lama, who was very popular with the Indian population, was cheered by huge crowds. He first stayed for a year at Mussoorie, then moved to Dharamsala which became his headquarters in India. Among his first political acts, was his denunciation of the agreement of 1951 for it had been violated by the Chinese. In 1959 and 1960 the International Commission of Jurists published the results of its careful investigation of the Tibetan question wherein the Chinese were accused of violating international law and committing atrocities such as flogging to death, crucifixion, burying of living people, intentional death by starvation, drowning, and burning.

After the revolt and the flight of the Dalai Lama the situation worsened enormously. The Chinese continued to force the Tibetans to become Chinese by taking children away from their families for education and indoctrination in China and through forced Sino-Tibetan intermarriage. The Paṇchen Rinpoche was installed as successor to the Dalai Lama, but after trying for some time to alleviate the conditions of the harassed people, in 1962 he officially declined to assume the office of the Dalai Lama. The Great Proletarian Cultural Revolution and the intrusion of the Red Guards into Tibet in 1966 brought further hardships to the Tibetans and a violent persecution of the Buddhist religion. The Central Sanctuary of Lhasa, the Jo-khang, was desecrated, dismantled, and destroyed. As a consequence of these generally unbearable conditions, increasing masses of refugees poured into India. The main concern of the Dalai Lama in exile (see below chapter 11) has been to help his people and to rehabilitate them in every possible way. With the end of Tibet as an independent state, the Dalai Lama remains the symbol of Tibetan political and religious unity, and his efforts to perform this extraordinarily difficult mission are nothing less than heroic.

BIBLIOGRAPHY

A complete description of this period will be found in: Tsepon W. Shakabpa, *Tibet. A Political History*, Yale University Press, New Haven and London 1967; Hugh E. Richardson, *Tibet and its History*, London 1962; Günther Schulemann, *Geschichte der Dalai-Lamas*, Leipzig, 1958 (the last chapter on the Chinese occupation should be perused with caution); Tieh-tseng Li, *Tibet Today and Yesterday* (2nd ed. of *The Historical Status of Tibet*), New York 1960 (written from a decidedly Chinese partisan standpoint, even in the portions dealing with the older periods); T. L. Shen and S. C. Liu, *Tibet and the Tibetans*, Stanford and London 1952 (also written from the Chinese viewpoint but more objective); Zahiruddin Ahmad, *China and Tibet 1708-1959*, London 1960 (contains copious material).

Much useful information can be culled from Dorothy Woodman, *Himalayan Frontiers. A Political Review of British, Chinese, Indian, and Russian Rivalries*, New York 1969, which contains a very good description of the Simla Conference.

Special studies of Sino-Tibetan relations are provided by Josef Kolmaš, *Tibet and Imperial China*, Australian National University, Centre of Oriental Studies, Occasional Papers 7, Canberra 1967; Anon, *The Boundary Question between China and Tibet*, Peking 1940.

Sources for the period of the Thirteenth Dalai Lama: Sir Charles Bell, *Portrait of the Dalai Lama,* London 1946; Tokan Tada, *The Thirteenth Dalai Lama,* Tokyo 1965; Taraknath Das, *British Expansion in Tibet,* Calcutta 1927; Sir Francis Younghusband, *India and Tibet,* London 1910; Parshotam Mehra, *The Younghusband Expedition,* London 1968, and "The Mongol-Tibetan Treaty of January 11, 1913," *JAH* 3 (1969): 1-22; L. A. Waddell, *Lhasa and its Mysteries,* London 1906; P. Fleming, *Bayonets to Lhasa,* London 1961; Alastair Lamb, *Britain and Chinese Central Asia. The Road to Lhasa,* London 1960; same author, *The McMahon Line,* 2 vols., London and Toronto 1966 (deals in full with the period of the Simla Convention and following events); two articles by A. Lamb should also be mentioned: "Tibet in Anglo-Chinese Relations," *JRCAS* (1957/58); "Some Notes on Russian Intrigue in Tibet," *JRAS* (1959): 46-65; Ram Rahul, *The Government and Politics of Tibet,* Delhi 1969 (probably the best book on Anglo-Tibetan and Sino-Tibetan relations).

Concerning the period of the Fourteenth Dalai Lama and the Chinese Communist occupation: Fourteenth Dalai Lama, *My Land and My People,* London 1962; Thubten Jigme Norbu, *Tibet is my Country,* London 1960; Heinrich Harrer, *Seven Years in Tibet,* London 1952 (a useful book by an eyewitness); Noel Barber, *The Flight of the Dalai Lama,* London 1960; F. Moraes, *The Revolt in Tibet,* New York 1960; International Commission of Jurists, *The Question of Tibet and the Rule of Law,* Geneva 1959; International Commission of Jurists, *Tibet and the People's Republic of China,* Geneva 1960; *Tibet 1950-1967,* Union Research Institute, Hong Kong 1968 (an important collection of all declarations, treaties, and conventions).

VI.   THE PRESENT POLITICAL FRAMEWORK OF TIBET

Introduction

By the "Order of the State Council of the People's Republic of China," issued on 28 March 1959, the Tibet Local Government was ordered dissolved, just eleven days after the Dalai Lama had fled Lhasa for India. To replace the Tibet Local Government system, the Chinese Communist Central Government eventually established Tibet as an Autonomous Region, which was officially inaugurated on 9 September 1965. By this time, throughout the Region, five special districts (*chuan-ch'ü*), one municipality (Lhasa), and seventy counties (*hsien*) were set up, in addition to some 283 administrative organs of the *ch'ü* level and some 2,100 of the *hsiang* level. The *hsiang,* or township, was the basic unit of state power comprising several villages.[1]

Before 28 March 1959, the traditional political organization and functions of the former Tibetan government, headed by the Dalai Lama, had been protected by law. This was established in the Agreement between the Peking government and the Tibet Local Government on the "Peaceful Liberation" of Tibet, *Article 4*: "The Central Authorities will not alter the existing political system in Tibet. The Central Authorities also will not alter the established status, functions and powers of the Dalai Lama. Officials of various ranks will hold office as usual."[2] According to the same Agreement, the communists also set up a Military Region Headquarters in Lhasa, in addition to the Preparatory Committee for the Tibet Autonomous Region.

The following articles of the "General Program of the People's Republic of China for the Implementation of Regional Autonomy for Minorities," issued on 8 August 1952, were the fundamental principles for the establishment of the Tibet Autonomous Region:

> *Article 2*: Each autonomous region is an integral part of the territory of the People's Republic of China. The autonomous organ of each autonomous region is a local government led by the government of the next higher level, under the unified leadership of the central government. ... *Article 7*: The administrative status of an autonomous region shall correspond to that of a township (*hsiang*), division (*ch'ü*), county (*hsien*), special district (*chuan-ch'ü*) or a higher level, depending on the size of its population, its area and other factors. ... *Article 11*: Autonomous organs shall be set up according to the basic principles of democratic centralism and of the system of people's congresses. ... *Article 33*: Governments of higher levels shall assist autonomous areas in their political, economic, cultural, and educational development.[3]

83

The Preparatory Committee for the Tibet Autonomous Region

With the approval of the State Council of the People's Republic of China, the Preparatory Committee for the Tibet Autonomous Region was formally established on 22 April 1956. The committee was composed of representatives from the Tibet Local Government, the Panchen Lama's Council of *mkhan-po*, the People's Liberation Committee in the Chamdo area, leading monasteries, principal religious sects, social circles, the local Tibetan officialdom, and from other groups, as well as from the cadres sent to Tibet by the Central People's Government.[4] Those cadres included Chang Ching-wu, representative of the Central People's Government in Tibet, and secretary of the Work Committee of the Chinese Communist Party for the Tibet Area; Chang Kuo-hua, commander of the Tibet Military Region of the People's Liberation Army; T'an Kuan-san, political commissar of the Tibet Military Region; and some other personnel from China proper.

The committee consisted of fifty-five members.[5] For the purpose of supervising routine work, a Standing Committee was established. The Dalai Lama and the Panchen Rin-po-che were appointed by the State Council as chairman, and vice-chairman respectively. Chang Kuo-hua has the Second-Vice-Chairman, and Nga-phod Ngag-dbang 'Jigs-med (A-p'ei A-wang Chin-mei) was the secretary-general. Under the committee were one general administrative office, two commissions (Religious Affairs, and Finance and Economics), and eleven departments, including those of Civil Affairs, Finance, Construction, Culture and Education, Public Health, Public Security, Agriculture and Forestry, Animal Husbandry, Industry and Commerce, Communications, and Justice.[6]

In August 1957, together with the abolition of the Finance and Economics Commission, the existing eleven departments were also reorganized into four. On 8 April 1959, after the flight of the Dalai Lama, the Preparatory Committee for the Tibet Autonomous Region began to exercise the functions of the Tibet Local Government, and the four departments were also reorganized into the former structure with only a little change. The newly strengthened administrative departments now included the six then operative subordinate bureaus: the Administrative Office, the Religious Affairs Commission, and the departments of Civil Affairs, Finance, Culture and Education, and Construction, and the six new ones: the departments of Public Health, Industry and Commerce, Communications, Agriculture and Animal Husbandry, Public Security; and the Counsellor's Office.[7] These political organs have been functioning within the administrative system of the Tibet Autonomous Region up to the present.

After the Tibet Local Government on 28 March 1959 was officially dissolved, the leadership of the committee was also changed. The Panchen Rin-po-che became acting chairman, and 'Phags-pa-lha Dge-las Rnam-rgyal (P'a-pa-la Ke-lieh Lang-chieh), vice-chairman; Nga-phod Ngag-dbang 'Jigs-med was also appointed vice-chairman, in addition to his original positions as secretary-general and member of the Standing Committee. Eighteen Tibetan higher officials, who fled with the Dalai Lama to India, were removed as members of the committee and from their other posts.[8]

In June 1958, the Central Government set up a branch of the Supreme People's Court and of the Supreme People's Procuratorate in Lhasa.[9] This Court was a judicial organ for trying cases and rendering judgments. It was responsible to the government of Tibet and was supervised by the Supreme People's Court. The Tibet branch of the People's Procuratorate was independent and not subject to interference from other local organs of state. The procuratorial authority included investigation, prosecution, and general monitoring of all state organs, including the courts.

By December 1964, both the Dalai Lama and the Panchen Lama were officially dismissed from their offices in the Preparatory Committee by the Chinese Communist Central Government. From that date, the combined politico-religious system in Tibetan Government was ended.

The Tibet Autonomous Region

An Election Committee for the Tibet Autonomous Region was formally inaugurated on 25 August 1962; its purpose was to introduce general elections in the Region to prepare the Tibetan people to run their own affairs.

The Tibet Autonomous Region was established through elections carried out in accordance with the "Regulations for Elections for the People's Congresses at all levels in the Tibet Autonomous Region," promulgated by the Chinese Communist Government on 30 March 1963. By August 1965, the basic level election in Tibet had been finished. The delegates to the Tibet Autonomous Region People's Congress convened on 1 September 1965 and proclaimed the formal establishment of the Tibet Autonomous Region.

According to the election law, "all Chinese citizens living in the region, who have reached the age of 18, shall have the right to elect and to be elected irrespective of nationality, race, sex, occupation, social origin, religion, education, property status, or period of residence."[10] General elections are held at the basic administrative level of township. The township people's congresses elect deputies to county people's congresses. The people's congresses established people's councils at each level. The people's congress is a local body of state power, and the people's council is the government.

Lhasa's First Municipal People's Congress met from 15 to 20 August 1965. It was attended by 180 deputies from the district of Lhasa, including the deputies from the eleven counties on its outskirts. Bskal-bzang Rnam-rgyal was elected mayor of the city, and Chang Chen-sheng and four others were vice-mayors. A People's Council of 23 members was also elected.[11]

Heads and deputy heads of all seventy counties in Tibet were elected at Tibet's first county people's congresses, which were held in August 1965. At the same time, county people's councils or governments and deputies to the First People's Congress of the Tibet Autonomous Region were elected. Deputies to the county people's congresses were elected by the people's congress at the township level, held following the completion of the general elections by the end of July 1965.[12] A total of 301 deputies were elected to the First People's Congress of the Tibet Autonomous Region by the county people's congresses. Of the deputies, 226 were Tibetans and 75 were of Han or other nationalities living in the Region.[13]

The First Session of the First People's Congress of Tibet ended with the formal establishment of the Tibet Autonomous Region. During the session, Nga-phod Ngag-dbang 'Jigs-med was elected chairman of the Autonomous Region; Chou Jen-shan, 'Phags-pa-lha Dge-las Rnam-rgyal and five others were elected vice-chairmen. Thirty-seven deputies to the congress were elected members of the Region's People's Council, and again, Nga-phod Ngag-dbang 'Jigs-med was elected chairman.[14]

The People's Council operated on the principle of collective leadership. Each council member was responsible for the work in a particular field of construction or administration. Each department under the People's Council had its own chairman and one or more vice-chairmen, who were responsible to the council. The council met in weekly working sessions at which all major administrative questions were discussed and decided. Together with local functionaries, they kept in close contact with the people. They made regular tours of inspection and on-the-spot investigations of local problems.

The Chinese Communist Party in Tibet

The Central Committee of the Chinese Communist Party directs the entire work of the Party on different levels. The Party organizational levels also match state administrative divisions. The people's councils share with the Party organizations responsibility for government on different levels; they are subordinate politically to Party leadership, and translate its decisions into state action. The Party representative congresses are the highest leading bodies at their respective levels. At the lowest level, primary Party organizations are established in basic level state units, such as townships and communes, and also in many units without formal governmental organs, such as factories, schools, and military divisions.

On 1 September 1965, the Chinese Communist Party Tibet Work Committee was reorganized into the CCP Tibet Autonomous Regional Committee. Chang Kuo-hua, former Second Secretary of the Work Committee was appointed First Secretary of this Regional Committee. T'an Kuan-san, and eight other former deputy secretaries of the Work Committee were reappointed as secretaries in the Secretariat of the Regional Committee.[15] Under the direct control of the Regional Party Committee are Party congresses and committees on the levels of each Special District and county. Congresses or general membership meetings come together infrequently to elect committees which, in turn, elect the standing committees and secretaries that are responsible for actual Party work.

The People's Liberation Army Tibet Military Region

The political role of the People's Liberation Army is less obvious than that of the state or the Party, but it has been an integral part of the communist system. The PLA assumed heavy administrative responsibilities during the early reconstruction years and during the Cultural Revolution. The PLA Tibet Military Region is one of the thirteen military regions in China and is divided into sub-regions, which correspond to the special districts in Tibet. The commander of the military region or a sub-region is also occasionally appointed as chairman of the same area in which he is stationed. For instance, in 1968 Liu Chi-fu was appointed chairman of the Revolutionary Committee of the Shan-nan (Lho-kha) Special District; he was also the commander of the military sub-region of the same district. When the Central Government ordered the PLA to establish military rule in Tibet, the commander of the Tibet Military Region, Tseng Yung-ya, was appointed chairman of the Revolutionary Committee of the Tibet Autonomous Region on 7 September 1968. In August 1971, he was succeeded by General Chen Ming-i.

Each PLA unit has a political department which represents the Party interests and is headed by a political commissar or officer. Thus, a political commissar or officer at each level works alongside the commanding officer of the army headquarters on the same level and is responsible for implementing the Party policies and carrying out educational programs among the troops. Political departments and their commissars or officers are not subordinate to the military commander in their units, but rather to the Party organizational network. The present political commissar of the Tibet Military Region, Jen Jung, also holds the position of vice-chairman of the Revolutionary Committee of the Tibet Autonomous Region.[16]

The Political Framework of the Tibet Autonomous Region
After the Great Proletarian Cultural Revolution

As elsewhere in China, Tibet was seriously affected by the Great Proletarian Cultural Revolution launched by the Chinese communists in May 1966. The Lhasa Revolutionary Rebel General Headquarters was established by the Red Guards in January 1967. It represented the modern and radical thought of the Chinese Communist Party and stood against the conservative Party leaders in the government system headed by Chang Kuo-hua, who supported the Tibet Autonomous Region Proletarian Revolutionaries' Great Alliance Rebel General Command.[17]

When the tide of the Great Cultural Revolution entered the phase of seizure of power, Nga-phod Ngag-dbang 'Jigs-med, chairman of the Tibet Autonomous Region, left Tibet for Peking where he remained a long time. On the other hand, Chang Kuo-hua, former First Secretary of the CCP Tibet Autonomous Regional Committee and commander of the Tibet Military Region, was appointed head of the Preparatory Group of Szechuan Revolutionary Committee and the First Political Commissar of the People's Liberation Army Cheng-tu Military Region on 20 June 1967. About the same time, T'an Kuan-san, former secretary of the Secretariat of the CCP Tibet Autonomous Regional Committee and the political commissar of Tibet Military Region, was appointed vice-president of the Supreme People's Court.[18] Both Chang and T'an had served in the Party and the army in Tibet for more than ten years, and now were transferred to higher posts.

By 28 September 1969, Revolutionary Committees were established in the political system and assumed local governmental authority at every level in the Tibet Autonomous Region. The personnel who occupy government offices are chosen from both the conservative and the radical factions, but their head is always a military commander. Under the Chairman of the Revolutionary Committee of the Tibet Autonomous Region are thirteen vice-chairmen, eight standing committee members, and eighteen regular committee members.[19]

As a result of the Cultural Revolution, the Peking government has reorganized the Party, the military, and political personnel of the Tibet Autonomous Region. In January 1970, the special district of A-li (Mnga'-ris), together with the six counties under its jurisdiction, were transferred into the political system of the Hsin-chiang Uighur Autonomous Region. The A-li area had historically been the western part of Tibet, but the military control of this area has been under the Hsin-chiang Military Region's command for quite a number of years.[20]

At the present time, the Tibet Autonomous Region is divided into 1 municipality, 4 special districts, 64 counties, and 2,100 townships, throughout which 666 communes are being established.[21] These rural people's communes are in many cases in the process of superseding the township administrative structure.

The special district is a subdivision of the regional government that supervises a number of counties. The four special districts in Tibet are the Shan-nan (*Lho-kha*), supervising thirteen counties; the Na-ch'ü (*Nag-chu*), supervising nine counties; the Jih-k'e-tse (*Shigatse*), supervising eighteen counties; and the Ch'ang-tu (*Chamdo*), supervising thirteen counties. The city of Lhasa has its own municipal government, which is now administrated by a Revolutionary Committee chaired by Liang Ch'ao, who is also a member of the Revolutionary Committee of the Tibet Autonomous Region. The municipal government supervises eleven counties[22] in the Lhasa area, which compose the Lhasa Municipality, now directly under the Revolutionary Committee of the Tibet Autonomous Region.

In summary, governmental units at all levels consist of two main organs—people's congresses and people's councils. The congresses are representative bodies designated as the organs of government authority for their levels, while the councils are executive and administrative organs elected by, and responsible to, their respective congresses. Congresses at each level are elected by the congresses immediately beneath them within their administrative unit, except at the basic level where direct election by the citizens occurs. During the Cultural Revolution, new groups known as revolutionary committees assumed local governmental authority.

From the citizen's point of view, the most important units are those beneath the basic level of formal government. These include police stations and small branch offices established by basic level councils, and a variety of residential committees, production teams, agricultural cooperatives, and occupational units. These are really political units as well. They may serve as electoral districts for basic level congresses and as the base for primary Party organization.

Party, state, and army constitute three interlocking hierarchies of organization that dominate the Chinese political system. However, the institutional framework of Chinese politics also includes a variety of additional organizations that provide links with the nonParty masses, and which supplement and support the three dominant institutions. They play a key role in channeling representatives into the state and Party structure and in mobilizing support for the Party policies from different segments of the population. The most important and distinctive of the mass organizations is the Communist Youth League. In Tibet, it has established local committees at each political level, and its headquarters is called Communist Youth League Committee of the Autonomous Region. The others are Lhasa Patriotic Womens' Association, Tibet Patriotic Youth Cultural Association, Chinese Buddhist Association Tibet Branch, and those at the basic level, such as the production and residential groups, the Mutual Aid Teams, etc.

The Constitution and other documents had guaranteed to preserve Tibetan language and culture, and had permitted adjustments of policy to local conditions. However, the long-term trend has been toward fuller political and cultural integration of minority areas into the Chinese system. Since the Cultural Revolution, the problems of minority peoples in China have been seldom discussed, and most of the previous policies toward the minority peoples have been abolished. Obviously, the political system in Tibet has now been gradually changed into the pattern which has been established in the rest of the provinces in China proper.[23]

NOTES

1. About the local political system of the Tibet Autonomous Region, see Union Research Institute, *Tibet: 1950-1967* (Hong Kong, 1968), pp. 357-58, 429, 485, 505, 514. For maps, see Yeh Hsiang-chih, ed., "Hsi tsang tzu chih ch'ü," *Kung fei ch'ieh chü hsia ti chung kuo ta lu fen sheng ti t'u* (Taipei, 1966).

2. The original Chinese text of the "Agreement on Measures for the Peaceful Liberation of Tibet" is found in Kuo Tzu-wen, *Hsi tsang ta shih chi*, [Great events in Tibet], 1949-1959 (Peking, 1959), pp. 35-38. For the English translation, see International Commission of Jurists, *Tibet and the Chinese People's Republic* (Delhi, 1966), pp. 215-18.

3. For the Chinese text of the Program, see Jen min ch'u pan she, *Min tsu cheng ts'e wen chien huei pien*, I (1958), pp. 67-72. For the English translation, see Henry G. Schwarz, *Chinese Policies Towards Minorities: An Essay and Documents*, Occasional Paper no. 2 (Western Washington State College, 1971), pp. 63-68.

.4. Cf. George Ginsburgs and Michael Mathos, *Communist China and Tibet: The first dozen years* (The Hague, 1964), pp. 83-86, 110-11.

5. Ibid., pp. 87-88.

6. A list of the responsible personnel of the commissions and departments is found in *Tibet: 1950-1967*, pp. 739-40.

7. Cf. *Communist China and Tibet*, pp. 114-15, 131-32.

8. The names of the Tibetan officials were listed in the "Order of the State Council of the Chinese People's Republic," issued on 28 March 1959. See *Tibet: 1950-1967*, pp. 357-58, 750-53.

9. *Communist China and Tibet*, p. 115.

10. Cf. *Tibet: 1950-1967*, p. 503.

11. Ibid., p. 507.

12. Ibid., p. 509.

13. Ibid., pp. 520-21.

14. Ibid., p. 758.

15. Ibid., pp. 757-58.

16. With reference to the personnel in Tibet Autonomous Region, from 1959-1969, see Kao Ch'ung-yen, ed., *Chung kung jen shih pien tung* [Changes of personnel in Communist China], 1959-1969 (Hong Kong, 1970), pp. 847-59.

17. For details of the Cultural Revolution in Tibet, see *Tibet: 1950-1967*, pp. 600-700.

18. For the different positions of Chang Kuo-hua, T'an Kuan-san, and Nga-phod Ngag-dbang 'Jigs-med (A-p'ei A-wang chin-mei), see *Chung kung jen shih pien tung*, pp. 5, 404, 812, 820-23, 847-59.

19. Ibid., pp. 847-48. For the establishment of the Revolutionary Committee of the Tibet Autonomous Region, see Chung kung yen chiu tsa chih she [Institute for the study of Chinese Communist problems], *Chung kung nien pao* [Yearbook on Chinese Communism], 1970, 2 vols. (Taipei, 1970), I pp. (IV) 44-45.

20. Ibid., p. (II) 304.

21. Cf. Ch'in T'i, "Hsi tsang ti jen min kung she hua wen t'i" [The establishment of people's communes in Tibet], *Tsu kuo yüeh k'an* [China monthly], no. 85 (1 April 1971), 26-28 pp.

22. For the names of the sixty-four counties in Tibet, see *Chung kung nien pao*, p. (I) 35.

23. For the current situation in Tibet, see Ch'en Chuang-p'eng, "I nien lai chung kung ti 'shao shu min tsu' kung tso" [Chinese Communists' activities in minority races], *Chung kung yen chiu* [Studies on Chinese Communism], vol. 5, no. 2 (February 1971), pp. 89-94. See also the related chapters in *Chung kung nien pao* from 1967 to present. The issues of 1967 and 1968 were entitled *Fei ch'ing nien pao*, published by Fei ch'ing yen chiu tsa chih she, Taipei.

BIBLIOGRAPHY

Ch'en Chuang-p'eng. "I nien lai chung kung ti 'shao shu min tsu' kung tso" [Chinese Communists' activities in minority races]. *Chung kung yen chiu* [Studies on Chinese Communism], vol. 5, no. 2 (Taipei, February 1971): 89-104.

Ch'in T'i. "Hsi tsang ti jen min kung she hua wen t'i" [The establishment of people's communes in Tibet]. *Tsu kuo yüeh k'an* [China monthly], no. 85, (Hong Kong, 1 April 1971).

Chung kung (or Fei ch'ing) yen chiu tsa chih she [Institute for the study of Chinese Communist problems]. *Chung kung (or Fei ch'ing) nien pao* [Yearbook on Chinese Communism], from 1967 to present, Taipei.

Ginsburgs, George, and Mathos, Michael. *Communist China and Tibet: The first dozen years*. The Hague: Martinus Nijhoff, 1964.

Goldstein, Melvyn C. "An Anthropological Study of the Tibetan Political System" Ph.D. dissertation, University of Washington, 1968.

International Commission of Jurists. *Tibet and the Chinese People's Republic*. Delhi, 1966.

Jen min ch'u pan she. *Min tsu cheng ts'e wen chien huei pien*, I. Peking, 1958.

Kao Ch'ung-yen, ed. *Chung kung jen shih pien tung* [Changes of personnel in Communist China], 1959-1969. Hong Kong, 1970.

Kung Szu-hsüeh. *Hsin chung kuo ti hsin hsi tsang*. Peking, 1955.

Kuo Tzu-wen. *His tsang ta shih chi* [Great events in Tibet], 1949-1959. Peking, 1959.

Ram Rahul. *The Government and Politics of Tibet*. Delhi, 1969.

Schwarz, Henry G. *Chinese Policies Towards Minorities: An Essay and Documents*, Occasional Paper no. 2 (Western Washington State College, 1971).

Union Research Institute, *Tibet: 1950-1967*. Hong Kong, 1968.

Yeh Hsiang-chih, ed. *Kung fei ch'ieh chü hsia ti chung kuo ta lu fen sheng ti t'u* Taipei, 1966.

VII.   THE RELIGIONS OF TIBET
AND TIBETAN MISSIONARY ACTIVITIES

The Tibetan Folk Religion

The Tibetans classify their three religions as *lha-chos,* "the divine law" or "religion," i.e., Buddhism; *bon-chos,* or "the Bon religion"; and *mi-chos,* "the law or religion of men," the Tibetan folk religion. Bon was certainly based on an aboriginal Tibetan stratum, but was also introduced in a special form from the western Himalayan countries long before the advent of Buddhism and shows later various connections with Buddhism and the influences of western Asian religions.

The folk religion underwent changes when it came in contact with Buddhism and the Bon religion. It adopted many features from both and therefore should be considered a mixture of ancient nomad, cattle-breeder, and peasant traditions; cosmogonies, theogonies, and the beliefs of Buddhists and Bon-po; and ritualism, magic, and after-life doctrines. This whole melange displays variations in the different regions of Tibet. While folk religion absorbed elements of Buddhism and Bon, these, in their turn, were influenced by indigenous beliefs. This mutual influence could easily come about in view of the obvious analogies between the indigenous inclination for magic of all kinds and a similar stratum of magic and mysticism in the two systematized religions. There had always existed an innate Tibetan interest in magical, occult, and parapsychological phenomena, which had much in common with the Tantric magic that reached Tibet from the countries of Bengal and Uḍḍiyâna (present-day Swât). Belief in the numerous local spirits, demons, and gods who lived in lakes, rivers, creeks, wells, trees, fields, rocks, and mountains in the different parts of Tibet was not suppressed by the new religions. These beings survived as "gods of the phenomenal world," who were tamed by the apostles of the higher religions and bound by oath to function henceforth as "protectors of the religion," employing their negative and terrifying qualities to punish the enemies of Buddhism and the Bon religion. The folk religion during the centuries before the emperor Srong-btsan sgam-po, the unifier of the Tibetans, was not basically different from that which existed until the last days of free Tibet before the Chinese occupation of 1959. The Tibetans' feeling for the numinous nature of the landscape remained almost the same, except that they adopted several deities from Buddhism and the Bon religion. The layman made daily use of the refuge formula (Buddha, the Doctrine, and the Clergy) and the formula of the all-compassionate patron Avalokiteshvara, but he never forgot to sprinkle water and burn incense to the old aboriginal gods and demons. The Buddhist and old

Tibetan gods were, of course, sometimes identified with each other. Thus the *Red rTsiu,* the leader of the red-helmeted and armored *bTsan* demons, seems to have been the old Tibetan god and judge of the dead whose functions were later assigned to the Buddhist-Indian *Yama.*

According to ancient Tibetan belief the world is divided into three parts: sky (or heaven), atmosphere, and earth (including the underworld); or, as the Tibetans say *sTeng-lha* ("the upper gods"), *Bar-bTsan* ("the middle bTsan spirits"), and the *gYog-klu* ("the lower water spirits"). These names, it is true, give no idea of the multitudes of spirit and demon groups included in the respective areas; they are simply prototypes. The lower zone is occupied mainly by the *kLu,* who bear a certain resemblance to the water spirits of the European Middle Ages and who may adopt at will the form of snakes—a characteristic which later made them readily identifiable with the Indian Nâgas. The ancient origin of the *kLu* idea is confirmed by the many theophoric names going back to the Tibetan Imperial period (A.D. 600-842). The bottoms of rivers, lakes, and certain wells comprised the original habitat of the *kLu.* Here they guard secret treasures. Among the trees and the rocks live the *gNyan,* and within the earth proper reside the *Sa-bDag* or "masters of the earth," as well as the dreaded *Sri,* vampire-like creatures who have a preference for small children. The particular spheres of the *kLu,* the *gNyan* and the *Sa-bDag* are occasionally confused. One text, an expiatory poem, reports that the *kLu* lives in strangely formed mounds, in black rocks whose peaks are pointed like the head of a crow, in burial mounds formed in the shape of a black boar's snout, on hills which resemble reclining oxen, in juniper trees which were sacred in the ancient religion, in birch and spruce trees, and in twin mountains, double rocks, and double glaciers. The poem discusses these spirits and their animal entourage as follows:

> The kLu kings are in all streams,
> The gNyan kings are in trees and stones,
> The "Masters of the Earth" are in the five sorts of earth.
> There, it is said, are the "Masters of the Earth," the kLu and gNyan.
> What kind of company is theirs?
> Scorpions with long stings,
> Ants with notched waists,
> Golden frogs,
> Turquoise-colored tadpoles,
> Mussel-white butterflies.
> These are their company.

The *gNyan,* who roam the mountains and valleys and build their lairs in slate rocks, woods, and ditches, are easily upset by human beings, to whom they send sickness and death. The plague, known in Tibet as *gNyan* ("smallpox"), is a scourge attributed especially to them; whereas, if annoyed, the *kLu* send leprosy. As they also make their haunts on mountains, the *gNyan* are closely related to the mountain gods generally found in the central region, the atmosphere. The god *Thang-la* of the powerful Thang-la mountain chain, for instance, is also known as a "Great *gNyan*." Like many of the other mountain gods, he is said to have been "converted" to Buddhism by Padmasambhava, the eighth-century apostle of tantric Buddhism, and thus became incorporated into the Pantheon of Tibetan Buddhism. The "White Goddess of the Sky" (*gNam-lha dKar-mo*) lives in the neighborhood of Mount Everest together with the nearby friendly five "Sisters of Long Life," whose nature is sometimes ambivalent. Each sister has her special pool, with its own distinctive color. Near the frontier of Bhutan lies the domain of *Yar-lha sham-po*, the god of the mountain range of the same name who appears in the shape of a white man or a white yak bull. A saga, which appears in a Tibetan historiographical work, relates that the widow of a murdered Tibetan king conceived a son in a dream in which this mountain god appeared to her in the form of a white man. As the widowed queen awoke she saw a white yak rise from her resting place and go away. Another important mountain god is *Gangs-chen mDzod-lnga*, whose annual feast as the highest god of the Himalayan state of Sikkim (which is half-Tibetan) is celebrated with elaborate mask and sword dances before the temple of Gangtok and in other monasteries throughout the country. To the lower terrestrial sphere belong also the rarely mentioned *gZed, gTod,* and *bSe* spirits whose nature is less clearly defined.

The air is the domain of the *bTsan,* a group of demons feared even today. They are supposed to appear in the form of savage huntsmen, red in color, who wear helmets and armor and ride over the mountains on light red horses, led by their king, *rTsiu dMar-po.* Related to the ancestral spirits (the *Pha-mTshun*), their appearance strikingly resembles the Iranian *Fravashi* of the Zoroastrian religion, who are the surviving souls of heroes. Being also tutelary deities, their name often appears in the sacred onomastic type of names of the Tibetan emperors (e.g., Srong-btsan Sgam-po). Whosoever is unfortunate enough to meet them in the loneliness of the mountains is pierced by their arrows and falls victim to a deadly sickness.

All available information indicates that heaven or sky (both terms are denoted in Tibetan by the same word) was held in high honor by the ancient Tibetans, not only as a natural impersonal reality, but also as the personified god of heaven, who, as a *deus otiosus,* hardly seemed to have played an important role in the men's lives. His role was similar to that of the god of the old Turkish and Mongolian shamanists. The rare sources available suggest that the "King of Heaven" lives surrounded by a host of supernatural spirits, some of whom were gods (*Lha*), others spirits called *dMu, Theu-rang,* and *bDud.* The etymological comparison of the name *dMu* with the respective words in the non-Tibetan but near-to-Tibetan languages of the Zhang-zhung people of western and northern Tibet (*dMu* and *Mu-la*) shows that the original meaning of *dMu* was simply "sky." In the old days the *bDud* also seem to have been heavenly spirits, but in Tibetan Buddhism they were degraded to devils, and their leader, the *bDud* himself, became identified with *Māra,* the tempter of the Buddha. According to the earliest reports, the sky consisted of nine strata or stages, of which the heavenly stage, the cloud stage, and the rain stage are particularly important. Later, as many as thirteen different stages were mentioned, nine and thirteen being holy numbers in the folk religion as well as in the Bon religion.

Evidence that these stages were quite realistically regarded as strata of the universe is found in the belief that to go from one stage to the next a spirit-rope or sky-rope (*dMu-thag*) was necessary for climbing up or down. According to the sagas, the legendary first king, O-lDe-sPu-rGyal, who is also mentioned in Chinese sources relative to ancient Tibet, came down to his people as the son of the gods of heaven by means of this sky-rope. Having fulfilled their earthly tasks, he and his six successors returned to heaven in the same manner. However, the eighth of these kings, Gri-gum, who fell victim to a black magic attack by his minister, cut the rope, and thus made any return impossible. This ruler was therefore the first to leave his body behind when he died, and since then, according to the etiological saga, men began to concern themselves with burial rites.

One particular group of these spirits which includes the "Field God," the "Tent God," the "House God," and the "Hearth God" is more closely connected with man's everyday life. The Hearth God is similar to the Fire God and the "Hearth Mother" of the Mongols, and to the Chinese Hearth God, *Tsao-shen.* The Tibetan Hearth God (*Thab-lha*) is very easily annoyed. Any neglect of his fire he punishes remorselessly with sickness and other misfortunes. If butter is sacrificed to him it gives him pleasure, but woe betide the offender if a hair, an old rag, or dog's dirt finds its way into the fire, or if a pot boils over and defiles the hearth! The offender can expect danger. To ward off the threatening misfortunes when such an accident has happened, the owner of the hearth must call in an experienced sorcerer or priest to perform the appropriate cleansing rites. The soiled hearth is dug out, the priest goes into a trance and takes a lump of the earth, which is then examined. If some living larva is found in it, the ceremony of cleansing and propitiation is regarded as successful. The grub which is now the incorporation of the demon of pollution is immediately destroyed. If no trace of any living thing is found in the lump of earth the demon has obviously made good his escape. The priest is then no longer in a position to help, and the unfortunate owner of the soiled hearth must prepare himself for the advent of misfortune.

The obviously very ancient idea of a "Man-God" (*Pho-lha*), presumably an ancestral spirit, and a "Foe-God" (*dGra-lha*) is of particular interest for the study of the ancient animism of the folk religion. Two such spirits take up their habitation in every human being, and each is to be regarded as a sort of guardian angel who wards off demonic influences. The Foe-God is therefore not regarded as the embodiment of evil in man, but, on the contrary, as an effective helping spirit. Like the *bTsan* spirits, these *dGra-lha* appear as armed warriors. Should they for any reason have to leave the body of the human being in question, whether because of the influence of demons or any kind of ritual pollution, that person is in great danger from the attacks of maliciously inclined fiends. Consequently he may fall victim to sickness and other misfortunes, and unless an experienced priest is called in to conjure the missing two spirits back into their human habitat, the person concerned must surely eventually die.

Very interesting in this connection is the ancient story, referred to in several sources, both Buddhist and Bon-po, which deals with the semimythical king Gri-gum bTsan-po. This king was induced by one of his officials to lay himself open to the black magic arts of his opponent by placing a dead fox on his right shoulder and a dead dog on his left, whereupon the Foe-God left his body through the dead fox, while the Man-God left through the dead dog, with the result that the now unprotected king was easily killed by his enemy. From a number of indications it would appear that these two gods, obviously representing the vital principle, and other spirits are thought to appear as in the myths of other animist peoples, in the form of winged insects. To ward off such evil insects, the Tibetans have from time immemorial devised spirit traps in which the demons are caught as in a spider's web. These devices are known as *mDos-mo* and consist of two or more crossed sticks on which are spun numerous threads, usually of different colored materials. Such *mDos* are found throughout Tibet in all shapes and sizes from small ones, perhaps an inch or two across, to huge nets set up on tall masts. When in the opinion of the priests the evil spirits have been caught in these *mDos*, the latter are burnt.

The general term for the animist vital soul is the *bLa*. It usually resides in the human body, but being mobile, may take up residence in trees, rocks, and animals while still remaining closely connected with the life of the human. If this soul leaves the body for good, the human will fall ill and eventually die. Therefore certain priests specialize in several rites which call back the soul or ransom it from death. Other rites are performed to extend the life of a person, and sometimes a ransom or scapegoat is offered to the evil spirits by sacrificing a dough image of a man or even a live animal. During Imperial times the ancient Tibetan priests provided the sovereign with a highly honored magician whose task it was to protect the emperor's *bLa*, believed to dwell in an ancestral mountain called *bLa-ri*. These powerful priests were allowed to sit to the right of the sovereign while the "Great Minister" had to be content to sit at His Majesty's left.

Among the more important divine beings is the huge bird *Khyung,* a kind of eagle and enemy of the serpent spirits, a bird which Tibetan folk religion shares with the shamanist peoples of Siberia. When Buddhism penetrated into Tibet, this mythical bird was easily identified with the Indian *Garuḍa* since both were of a solar nature. But the *Khyung* is of a more complex and ambivalent character because of the Bon-po idea of an eagle-like bird which was introduced from the country of Zhang-zhung in the Mānasarovar-Kailās area. This *Khyung* can be mischievous and cruel. There is also an attendant of the Bon-po god of death who has a *Khyung*'s head. This conception seems to show Iranian influences, since in the Iranian religion the eagle is known as the bird of death.

Another important characteristic of the ancient folk religion, even during later times, is the offering of animal sacrifices, a practice in total contradiction to all the religious ideas later introduced by the Buddhists. According to information preserved in Chinese records, during imperial times these animal sacrifices played an important part in official state ceremonies. The T'ang dynasty annals record that when the Tibetans swore the oath of fealty they sacrificed sheep, dogs, and monkeys. During an especially solemn ceremony held every three years, horses, oxen, donkeys, and even human beings were sacrificed to propitiate the gods of heaven and earth.

A Bon-po text provides us with the cruelly realistic description of a human sacrifice. To bring about the recovery of a sick prince, one of his subjects had to be sacrificed to propitiate the demon. The text reads: "The soothsayer seized the man by the feet while the Bon priest held his hands. The black hangman then cut open the life orifice and tore out the heart. The two, the soothsayer and the Bon-po, then scattered the blood and flesh of the victim to the four corners of the firmament."

Such sacrifices were also made in connection with the repeatedly concluded state treaties between Tibet and China. These rites were, of course, anathema to the Buddhists. At the end of the monarchy period the Tibetan Buddhist ministers refused to smear their lips with the blood of the sacrificial animals, a practice followed by the other participants of the ceremony. When Buddhism gained the upper hand and obtained state recognition, the defeated adherents of the old religion were forbidden to indulge in such practices; but even down to the present Tibetan Buddhism has not entirely eradicated this form of sacrifice, so deeply rooted is it in the beliefs of the Tibetans. Not only substitutes for living animals such as representations of yaks and sheep or wooden carvings of deer heads were sacrificed, but from the chants of the saint Mi-la ras-pa we learn that when an important Bon-po fell ill, the evil demons were propitiated by hundreds of live yaks, goats, and sheep. In recent times, travellers in eastern Tibet have reported that the followers of the ancient folk religion still use the blood of cocks to conjure peace.

Another characteristic of the old folk religion was a deep concern with death rites. These were later codified by the Bon religion in many treatises and by the Buddhism of the old school (the rNying-ma-pa) in the so-called *Book of the Dead (Bar-do thos-grol)*, a mixture of ancient Tibetan religion, Indian Buddhism, and Iranian influences. Certainly the rites of the "taming of the dead" with a magic knife belong to this oldest stratum of religion. These rites are connected with the idea of preventing the dead from returning to harm the living and are obviously related to similar ceremonies among most primitive peoples. Tibetan Buddhism also seems to have adopted the old indigenous rites for protecting the dead with a ceremony in which the officiating priest places a piece of bone of the deceased or a piece of paper bearing his name on a *maṇḍala*, or "magic circle." For the purifying ceremony grains of sand and white mustard seeds are used. In this connection the piece of bone is certainly remarkable, as in shamanist Inner and Northern Asia bones are the principle of life, and the Siberian shaman is revived by the power of his intact bones after suffering mystic death during his initiation. A strong resemblance to the most ancient Tibetan concepts is also evident in the following instructions for the funeral of a Bon-po priest:

> When a casket of stone slabs has been prepared in a spirit shrine of an appropriate rocky mountain for the corpse of a Shaman Bon-po, the dead man should be clothed in blue silk and placed on a seat in the form of a swastika. Two drums should be put into his hands and before him should be placed the white feathered divine arrow with silk strings of five different kinds and also excellent wine. Amidst the smell of perfumes and the smoke of various kinds of wood, bind the forehead of the dead man with ornaments of white wool and then place his body between grains of corn and wood.

The similarity of this form of burial to that of the Siberian shamans is immediately obvious: the setting out of the body on a mountain, the addition of the typical shaman burial equipment, and a kind of viaticum in the form of corn and wine.

Particularly good information is available concerning the burial customs of the ancient Tibetan emperors of the once powerful and united country. From a number of indications it is evident that the bodies of the dead monarchs were preserved in a mortuary for months, sometimes even for a year, as was done later in Tibet with the bodies of prominent religious personages. They were embalmed by immersion in brine or by boiling in butter, and the actual interment took place only after this preliminary period. The early Tibetan sovereigns were interred beneath a simple, pointed tumulus of stamped earth. Beginning with the death of the great Srong-btsan sgam-po (A.D. 649), extensive underground burial vaults filled with precious things were used. The tomb was guarded by a fraternity of former officials of the emperor known as the "Living Dead," vestige of older times when it was usual to kill the members of the fraternity and bury them together with their lord. One year after the actual interment a memorial service and lamentation was held. This reminds us of the burial customs of the shamanist Turks of Inner Asia from about the same period.

In light of the similarity between ancient Tibetan folk religion and Inner Asian and Northern Asian shamanism, it comes as no surprise that the central concept of shamanism, the so-called "flight of the soul," is also one of the components of Tibetan folk religion. The "flight of the soul" is the shaman's penetration of the upper or nether regions while in a state of trance and is usually undertaken to retrieve a soul which has fled or been carried away by evil spirits. The trance experience, during which the body of the shaman is in a state of cataleptic rigidity, usually occurs spontaneously among the shamans of the Arctic, whereas the southern peoples resort to some sort of narcotics. The desired frenzy is induced by alcohol or an herbal infusion. Occasionally the supernatural experience is simply imitated. Among the Altai tribes it has been observed that a symbolic flight is carried out on a wooden goose or by climbing a tree in which footholds have been notched to represent the stages of heaven. Evidence shows that the ancient Tibetans used this typical shamanist performance of flying through the air riding on the shaman drum or tambourine to bring back a soul which had escaped to heaven or to the lower world. In the eleventh century the Buddhist saint Mi-la ras-pa engaged in a contest of magic with a Bon priest, the agreement being that whoever was first to arrive at the summit of the holy mountain Kailās at dawn should win the prize—command of the holy mountain itself. The Bon-po sought to gain victory by "sitting on a drum, striking a tambourine and flying through the air." Such reports, which could easily be multiplied, are valuable proof of the close typological relationship between ancient Tibetan religion and shamanism.

Ribbach, a missionary to western Tibet, has described a good example of a typical shamanist healing of the sick which took place during the present century. An exorcist of demons was summoned from Lhasa to call back the departed soul of a woman. He used various sorts of Buddhist magic devices, but also, as a narcotic, the fumes of juniper berries and twigs burnt on a charcoal brazier.

> The *Lha-pa* now called on his protective demon to enter his body and went into ecstasy, becoming very agitated, his eyes staring fixedly and his lips foaming, and then leaping on his feet, uttering shrill cries and dancing around wildly. Now the conjured spirit demanded through the mouth of the medium: "Who has called me? " Someone answered: "The *Lha-pa.*" "Who caused the sickness of Parlapang Rolma? " The spirit answered: "The *gNaskorpas* [the wandering pilgrims]." Someone then asked: "What can we do

against the sickness? How can we bring back the departed life of this woman? " The spirit which entered the *Lha-pa* now announced that a sacrificial ceremony must be arranged and sacrificial gifts should be scattered.

This is an authentic shamanist performance characterized by a high degree of trance and by the significant cooperation of a familiar spirit.

An official place was reserved for shamanism even within the framework of the theocratic state of the Dalai Lamas in the institution of the oracle lamas whose opinions were asked in important political matters. The most important of these were the oracles of gNas-chung (in the neighborhood of the great 'Bras-spungs monastery near Lhasa), dGa-gdong, and bSam-yas. The familiar spirit which takes possession of the gNas-chung lama is called *Pe-har*. This lama ejaculates his oracular utterances while in a state of wild ecstasy and writhes on the ground in convulsions. Several oracle lamas who were able to escape from Tibet following the Chinese occupation have recently been examined by the German psychiatrist G. Schüttler, whose findings are described in his book, *The Last Tibetan Oracle Priests* (in German; see Bibliography).

The Bon Religion

The name *Bon* is derived from the verb *bon-pa,* which denotes the conjuring of gods and spirits by the chanting of spells to guarantee their presence. Later, when Bon came into close contact with Tibetan Buddhism, the word *bon* took on all the meanings of the Buddhist word *chos* (Skr. *dharma*), meaning "doctrine" but also "factors of existence." Hence the sphere of the Absolute, *chos-dbyings (dharmadhātu),* "boundless potential existence," is called *bon-dbyings* in the Bon religion.

According to the oldest literary work describing the earliest introduction of the Bon religion into Tibet, the *Genealogy of Kings* by the Sa-skya-pa hierarch Grags-pa rgyal-mtshan (1147-1216), the Bon religion, or rather a form of that religion called "The Bon of Tombs" (*dur-bon*), was introduced following the death of King Dri-gum btsan-po. This religious ritual came from the countries of Zhang-zhung and Gilgit, and though Chos-kyi nyi-ma, a later writer of the Yellow Hat school (1737-1802), also mentions Kashmir, this assumption may be unfounded. (On the Zhang-zhung see pp. 39 f.) The titles of the older canonical Bon-po scriptures are written in the Zhang-zhung language, and thanks to the publications of the Tibetan Bon-po refugees in India we have been able to study them. The language is related to, although not identical with, Tibetan and belongs to the Tibeto-Burmese family. The Bon-po texts appeared in written form only after the creation of the Tibetan script during the reign of the emperor Srong-btsan sgam-po. Prior to that time the Bon tradition was exclusively oral.

The Bon religion of Zhang-zhung was obviously similar to that stratum of the ancient Tibetan folk religion which may also have been called "Bon," since the word *mi-chos* seems to be of later origin.

Dri-gum btsan-po, the king for whose funeral Bon-po priests from Zhang-zhung and Gilgit were invited, is listed among the mythical kings of Tibet. Although he lived at a time when writing in Tibet was nonexistent, and although most of the data known to us portray a rather legendary character, evidence from recently discovered material shows that he was probably an historical personage. His center of power appears to have been in the province of gTsang.

The Bon religion seems to have been a rather primitive animism, but by the time Zhang-zhung was incorporated into the new Tibetan empire the religion must have undergone certain changes connected with the adoption of ideas from Iran and India. This is not surprising since the western Himalayan districts were at all times open to the neighboring Iranian peoples (as shown, for instance, by the Sogdian Nestorian inscription in Ladakh), and Indian commercial and cultural influences could easily make their way into western Tibet by way of the valley of the Sutlej river. Proof of this cultural influence can be found in the great number of Indian loan words in the Zhang-zhung language. When the Bon religion came to Tibet, because of its symbiosis with Tibetan Buddhism, especially with the school of Padmasambhava, the rNying-ma-pa, it adopted an increasing number of religious ideas from Buddhism, which in turn obviously borrowed from the Bon-po.

gShen-rab mi-bo, the founder of this syncretistic and systematized Bon religion, is mentioned in the Bon-po scriptures, although we do not know whether he was an historical personage for his biography is modelled after those of the Buddha Gautama and Padmasambhava. Large portions of the biography are borrowed from texts of the Tibetan Buddhist rNying-ma-pa school, which claims to go back to the teachings of Padmasambhava. gShen-rab is not a personal name, but simply means "the most excellent of gShen priests," while *mi-bo* stands for "man."

Like the Buddha, prior to his birth, gShen-rab looks down at the earth from his heavenly pre-existence in a paradise. The birth itself is miraculous: rays of light from the transcendental world enter the "turquoise bird cuckoo" perched on the top of a sacred willow tree. This bird then alights on the head of the future mother and flaps its wings three times, whereupon a white and a red ray of light from its genitals enter the woman. The white ray symbolizes the active male principle of the polar divine Absolute; the red ray symbolizes the female principle. In their doctrine the Bon-po have the equivalent of the Primordial Buddha of the rNying-ma-pa school, the male aspect called *Kun-tu bzang-po,* "the all-good," and the female, *Kun-tu bzang-mo.* Before beginning his career as savior gShen-rab undergoes baptism in a holy lake, which recalls the baptism of Jesus in the Jordan. Among the Savior's disciples, rMa-lo is the equivalent of the Buddha's disciple Shariputra; gYu-lo may be equated with Maudgalyāyana; and gTo-bu 'bum-sangs, with Ānanda. The great journey of gShen-rab to convert Tibet and adjacent countries is a replica of Padmasambhava's conversion of the demons and spirits of Tibet, which in turn may have been inspired by Manicheism, a rather powerful religion in Inner Asia at that time. The conversion of China by gShen-rab shows similarities with the exploits of Ge-sar, the hero of the great Tibetan Ge-sar epic, although the epic may have borrowed from the Bon-po text. Like the Buddha, gShen-rab attains Nirvāṇa under exactly the same circumstances. A very interesting passage in his long speech of farewell is his promise to send a representative and to return himself in an intermediate world aeon, which reminds us of the words of Jesus who promised the coming of the Paraclete. Christian echoes of this sort suggest familiarity with Western ideas probably originating with the Manicheans. Mani had declared himself to be the Paraclete announced by Jesus. The name of the promised representative is Mu-cho ldem-drug (evidently a Zhang-zhung name). It is believed that he remained three years on earth and "in accordance with the words of the Master constantly preached the gospel, writing it completely and fully." This note is of great importance as it is the first official statement by the Bon-po concerning the creation of their sacred literature.

Mu-cho gathered a large staff of translators (*lo-tsa-ba*) to propagate the Bon teachings in all countries. Three translators went westward as missionaries into the land of Ta-zig, i.e., Iranian countries, from where, according to Bon-po tradition, many revelations of their religion had come. Other translators went to China, India, the country of Phrom where King Ge-sar ruled over the Turks (i.e., eastern Turkestan), to Tibet, the two countries lying between Tibet and China, i.e., Mi-nyag and Sum-pa, and finally to Zhang-zhung, where gShen-rab was born. This interesting information must, of course, be regarded as legendary, but in all probability contains a substratum of truth. We know beyond all doubt that the syncretistic Bon religion and related religions flourished in Zhang-zhung and the neighboring western districts, where we find the "Silver Palace" of Khyung-lung in the upper Sutlej valley described in liturgical texts as a place of pilgrimage and the birthplace and residence of gShen-rab. The Bon religion also probably had earlier adherents in the Indo-Nepalese frontier districts, and we are certain that it had followers in eastern Turkestan where texts proving their existence have been found buried in the sands. The data published by Joseph F. Rock on the religion of the Na-Khi and Mo-so in Yunnan clearly show that the reports of a Bon mission have a factual basis. The sacred writings of the Mo-so reveal an obvious literary dependence on the texts of the Tibetan Bon religion.

A second introduction of the now highly sophisticated and syncretistic Bon religion took place during the reign of the Tibetan emperor Khri-srong lde-brtsan in the second half of the eighth century. Although the sympathy of the emperor was with the Buddhists, he nevertheless, during the period of his minority, had to accept the fact that the majority of his ministers, officials, and noblemen were followers of the Bon religion. A long-lasting struggle ensued between the Bon-po and the nobility on the one hand and the Buddhists and the Imperial dynasty on the other. But when the translating of foreign religious texts began on a large scale, Bon-po priests from Zhang-zhung worked side by side with Buddhist translators in the recently founded Buddhist Avalokiteshvara temple. Outstanding among the Bon-po translators was a certain Shang-rii u-can, who translated into Tibetan the famous work entitled *The Hundred Thousand "kLu" Spirits,* a Bon work which is obviously a combination of the old folk religions and Iranian religious ideas.

An indication that the two religions were more or less coexistent is shown by the Emperor's order in which he called for the building of his funeral monument. He instructed the Buddhists to provide a stūpa and the opposite party to provide a tomb (*bang-so*) built according to ancient Tibetan and Bon custom, at the traditional interment place of the emperors in the valley of 'Phying-yul. When the sovereign felt sure enough of himself, he organized a great debate between the Buddhists and the Bon-po. The representatives of the two religions opposed each other in appropriate pairs: Padmasambhava disputed with the Bon-po scholar Thang-nag bon-po. As a result of this debate the king publicly declared that he had been convinced by the arguments of the Buddhists and that the Bon-po had been defeated. The defeated heretics were exiled. This latter incident, which was to be of great consequence for the future history of Tibet, is graphically described in the biography of Padmasambhava:

> Fox caps were set upon their heads, and half-drums were handed to
>   them,
> Cotton garments were given to them for clothing, and impure food
>   was given them to eat.
> And all the Bon-po customs involving sin were abolished.
> For such Bon rites as were concerned with the warding off of
>   immediately threatening worldly danger
> Wooden stag heads with spreading antlers were made;
> And effigies of yaks and sheep of dough.

As many as gathered from the above quotation, henceforth all animal sacrifices were forbidden and the Bon-po were obliged to use substitutes in place of sacrificial animals. Most important, the Bon-po were banished to the barren lands along the Tibetan frontiers. This was to have great influence on subsequent religious history; for until the last days of independent Tibet, the Bon religion maintained itself in the northern and eastern frontier districts where it had self-sufficient communities with numerous monasteries, whereas few Bon-po remained in central Tibet. Bon-po communities are also to be found in the provinces of Dol-po and Mustang in northwestern Nepal, an area which by mere chance was separated from Tibet proper and incorporated into Nepal.

In addition to the pantheon of the later Bon religion, which was created primarily in Zhang-zhung under Buddhist, Hindu, and Iranian influences, the old gods and spirits of the animist-shamanist folk religion remained alive in the minds of the common people. The highest bipolar principle of the later Bon religion is called Kun-tu bzang-po, the "All-Good," or Kun-tu bzang-mo as in the Buddhist rNying-ma-pa school. He or she represents all-compromising transcendental potentiality, similar to all Buddhist concepts of the Ādibuddha, and is believed to be identical with the "Bon substance" (*Bon-sku*), which may be equated with the *Dharmakāya* of the Buddhists. Existence in this highest state is suggested by the word for the ultimate form of existence which gShen-rab experienced after death in this world and after passing beyond all heavens: "He exists without return, equal to the sky and extended in space."

Occasionally the highest principle in its female form is also denoted as "the Great Mother of Infinite Space," Sa-trig er-sangs. From the primordial principle stems the emanation of a "God of Wisdom" attached to the "Body of Heavenly Pleasure" and a "World God," the real ruler of the phenomenal world. The biography of gShen-rab (gZer-mig) contains a conjuration with a description, both theological and iconographical, of these divinities which provides us with good material for the understanding of that system:

Therefore first veneration for our great Mother!
The Mother of Space, Sa-trig er-sangs,
Who is like in color to essence of gold.
Her finery, her clothing, her Heavenly Palace
Is golden and beautiful with golden light.
In her right hand she holds the heroic letters of the "Five Seeds,"
In her left she holds the Mirror of shining Gold.
She sits on the throne of two strong lions, who shine like jewels.
Through blessings she effects the well-being of creatures.
Veneration to the great Sa-trig er-sangs!

The God of Wisdom gShen-lha od-dkar
Is like in color to essence of crystal.
His finery, his clothing, his Heavenly Palace
Is of crystal, and beautiful with crystal light.
In his hand he holds an iron hook with which he guides through
    compassion.

He sits on the throne of two powerful elephants, which shine like
jewels.
By his compassion he effects the well-being of creatures.
Veneration to the great gShen-lha od-dkar.

The best of effective means, the World God Sangs-po 'bum khri
Is like in color to essence of silver.
His finery, his clothing, his Heavenly Palace
Is of silver, and beautiful with silver light.
In his hand he holds the Precious Banner,
He sits on the throne of two blissful Khyung birds, which shine like
jewels.
Through magical creation he effects the well-being of creatures.
Veneration to the great Sangs-po 'bum-khri!
The teacher gShen-rab mi-bo, perfect in wisdom,
Glows in his colors like a jewel.
His finery, his clothing and his Heavenly Palace
Are like jewels, and beautiful with the lights of jewels.
In his hand he holds the Golden Scepter.
He sits on the throne of Nine Degrees with the Wheel, which shines
like a jewel.
By emitting rays of light he effects the well-being of creatures.
Veneration to the great gShen-rab mi-bo!

The individual figures of the triad (*gShen-lha od-dkar,* the God of Wisdom;
Sangs-po 'bum-khri, the World-ruling God or demiurge; and gShen-rab mi-bo, the
Religious Teacher of our World Period) appear in a pentad form which is
paralleled by the five Buddhas emanating from the Primordial Buddha. Both
doctrines probably originated from Manicheism where the equivalent of the
Primordial Buddha, the "Father of Greatness" or "Father of Light," also has five
spiritual sons which emanate from him. The five forms of gShen-rab are those of
the body, speech, excellences (*yon-tan*), deed (*'phrin-las*), and spirit (*thugs*).

Among the other important deities of the Bon pantheon are the 360
Ge-khod who, according to Bon-po belief, reside on the peak of the sacred
mount Kailās (Tib. Ti-se) and are certainly to be connected with the 360 days of
the lunar year. The texts also mention 360 *Wer-ma,* a Zhang-zhung word.
Possibly these are identical with the *Ge-khod.* In the songs of Mi-la ras-pa, the
famous Buddhist saint and poet (1040-1123) (see below, p. 155), we read that
before he struggled with a Bon-po priest for the possession of the holy
mountain, the Bon-po in his invocation to his gods mentioned the *Ge-khod,*
emanations of the most terrifying deity of the Bon-po, "The Angry King," a
monster with nine heads. The sister of the Angry King is addressed as
Srid-rgyal-ma and seems to be the replica of the Buddhist *dPal-ldan lha-mo.*

The influence of Iranian religion is especially evident in the in the various cosmogonic Bon myths. One of these relates that before the creation of the sun and the moon, time and the seasons, a primordial *Yang-dag rgyal-po* ("The Absolutely Victorious King") existed. From this god first emanated a black man, Myal-ba nag-po ("Black Suffering"). Carrying a spear, he was the being from whom originated all the evil of the world: demons; thunder and lightning; misfortune caused by fire, wind, and water; the 84,000 kinds of diseases; and all discord and hatred among men. From the primordial god also emanated a white man, Od-zer-ldan ("The Bright One"), from whom all virtue and everything good is derived. He created the sun and moon, taught humans how to construct temples, copy holy scriptures, honor teachers, and build bridges and roads. This myth is obviously a replica of primordial events as described in the documents of Zurvanism and Manicheism, both of which played an important role in Iran before being suppressed by orthodox Zoroastrianism during the later Sasanian dynasty. *Yang-dag rgyal-po,* the *deus otiosus,* may be equated with the Iranian god *Zurvan i akanārag* ("Boundless Time"); the black man, with Ahriman; and the white man, with Ohormazd (Ahuramazdah). Concerning the god of time, *Zurvan,* early Indian Mahāyāna Buddhism also adopted this figure as the prototype for one of the most popular Buddhas called "Immeasurable Light" (Amitābha) or "Immeasurable Time" (Amitāyus).

A different version of Bon cosmogony teaches a multiplication of the dualistic principles and adds some interesting details. In the beginning was "Voidness" or "Nothingness" from which "Being" gradually evolved. "Being" then gave birth to two principles; one, bright and paternal; the other, dark and maternal. Then cold developed, followed by dull frost and glittering dew. From frost and dew a mirror-like lake developed, which rolled itself up into an egg. Two birds hatched from this egg: one called "Rich Brilliance" and the other, "Tormented Darkness." From the union of these two birds came three eggs: white, black, and speckled. From the white egg came the hierarchy of the "World Gods" (*Srid-pa*); from the black egg came the "Arrogant Black Man"; and from the speckled egg came an "Intercessional Prayer." The World God, *Sangs-po 'bum-khri,* also called *Ye-smon rgyal-po,* had no control over normal organs of sight, hearing, smell, taste, stretching, or walking, but he had everything he required, thanks to an absolute "Thinking Spirit." The World God then called into being the entire inhabited and uninhabited world. To the right he placed gold and turquoise and spoke an intercessional prayer from which developed a gold mountain and a turquoise valley, and the hierarchy of the *Phya* spirits was born. To the left he placed a mussel and a precious stone and also spoke an intercessional prayer. From this developed a mussel mountain and a valley of precious stones, and the hierarchy of the *dMu* was born. Before him he placed a crystal and a red object and spoke an intercessional prayer. From this developed a crystal mountain and a sea of light, and the hierarchy of the *gTsugs* was born. The *Phya* are human beings, the *dMu* heavenly spirits, and the *gTsugs* animals.

Iranian inspiration seems obvious in this second myth, too. The occurrence of the motif of the world egg and even of three world eggs should be stressed. The world egg mythology may be found in the cosmogonies of different peoples. In addition to China it appears also in Egypt, where it is especially ancient, in India, Phoenicia, and in Greek Orphism. The Bon myth has in common with Orphic cosmogony the "meteriological" phenomena which precede the cosmic egg: the dragon-like Chronos in the latter cosmogony first begets "Wet Ether," "Boundless Space," and "Misty Darkness," and only then does the egg appear, dividing into sky and earth and simultaneously giving birth to the demiurge god. Similar cosmogonic ideas originated in Phoenicia, and the Bon-po cosmogony shows that related traditions also made their way into Inner Asia.

Besides the cosmogonic myth described above another ancient tradition of the origin of the world should be adduced, according to which the world originates from the death or division of a primordial being. This myth was held by several of the peoples of antiquity, for example, the Iranian myth of the Primordial Man, *Gayōmard.* One Bon-po scripture, *The Hundred Thousand Water Spirits,* states that the world originated from a primordial female water spirit, a *kLu-mo,* who is given the indicative name of "The *kLu* Queen who put the World into Order." From the upper part of her head sprang the sky; from her right eye, the moon; from her left, the sun; and from her upper four front teeth, the four planets. When she opened her eyes day appeared; when she closed them, night came on. From her twelve upper and lower teeth emerged the lunar mansions of the zodiac. Her voice became thunder; her tongue, lightning; her breath, clouds; and her tears, rain. Her nostrils produced wind, her blood became the five oceans of Bon-po cosmography, her veins became rivers. Her flesh was converted into earth, her bones into mountains.

This cosmogony has an important parallel in the old Mesopotamian myth of *Tiāmat,* called *Omorka* in the Greek version. This primordial female being had command of the darkness and the waters full of monstrous beings, but was eventually killed by the luminous god *Marduk,* who split her body in two and formed the sky with the upper half and the earth with the lower. Both Mesopotamian and the Bon-po myths agree that the world originated from the body of a water monster. Mesopotamia was for a long time an integral part of the Iranian empire (during the Achaemenid, Arsacid, and Sasanian dynasties), and the Iranians certainly were acquainted with this tradition which may have reached the religious center of Zhang-zhung through Iran.

Another myth found in an old description of the holy area around the Kailās Mountain and the sacred lake of Mānasarovar, also shows Iranian affinities. According to this myth a king of Zhang-zhung, who had no sons, was told by a herdsman that he heard a strange voice from a rock. When the king went there, an eight-year-old boy, supposedly the spiritual son of the king, appeared from the interior of a rock grotto. His body was woven with rainbow-colored rays of light. This story is a replica of the birth myth of the ancient Iranian light god *Mithra,* who js often called, even in the Mithra legends familiar in the Roman Empire, the "rock-born" (*petrogenés*). A later Buddhist text also mentions a ·god of the Parthians, *Vemacitra,* whose name has been translated as the "rock-born." These myths show with sufficient certainty that the Bon-po were correct in claiming that at least several of their religious traditions had come from Persia.

The entire Bon-po doctrinal canon is divided into nine sections, or "vehicles" (*theg-pa*), as is that of the Buddhist school which goes back to Padmasambhava. The first four, known as "Vehicles of Cause," primarily contain the teachings and practices of the old shamanist-animist folk religion. The First Vehicle (*Phyva-gshen*) deals with the 360 *gTo* ceremonies for the healing of the sick; with the "Celestial Drink" (lit.: golden drink, *gSer-skyems*), according to which wine is presented to the kings as a substitute for nectar; with divination by multicolored threads (*ju-thig*); and with the whole oracular aspect of the Bon religion to which the greatest importance has been attributed from earliest times. Whoever is acquainted with this vehicle knows which path leads to good and which to evil and how one may obtain foreknowledge of the events of daily life. This is similar to the shoulder blade oracle, in which the shoulder blade of a sheep is cast into a fire. It is believed that from the shape of the cracks caused by the heat the future can be foreseen.

The teachings of the Second Vehicle (*sNang-gshen*) concern the four kinds of ritual chanting, the eight kinds of lamentation, and the forty-two methods of making thanksgiving offerings. These teachings deal especially with substitute and scapegoat rites known in the old folk religion. The priests of this vehicle owned a drum made from juniper wood on which they could travel through the air like their Siberian shamanist counterparts.

The Third Vehicle (*Phrul-gshen*) is devoted to the practice of magic and taught the adepts how to make rain and call down curses on their enemies. During their exorcisms the priests, donned in tiger skin robes and tiger caps, sacrificed tiger flesh to the gods.

The priests of the Fourth Vehicle (*Srid-gshen*) were able to remove obstacles and dangers for people by protecting the *bla,* the vital soul, and by calling back the souls of the deceased. This vehicle, also called *Dur-gshen*, deals with necromantic rites, too. It teaches 360 ways to die, 4 ways to arrange burial places, and 81 ways to subdue evil spirits. These latter rites are particularly directed against the so-called *Sri* spirits, a species of vampires who are fond of emerging from the ground, particularly in the neighborhood of burial grounds.

The four "Vehicles of Effect" are quite different from the four "Vehicles of Cause," and deal not with shamanist-animist rites, but with higher religious matters. They do not relate to worldly affairs, such as oracular methods, good luck ceremonies, and the burial of the dead; but to the way to salvation, the way of liberation from the sorrowful life cycle of becoming which begins with birth, quite in the Buddhist manner. Vehicles Five (*dGe-bsnyen,* that of the laymen adherents) and Six (*Drang-srong,* that of the ascetics) seem to be similar to Buddhist Mahāyāna and its practice of the virtues by the being destined for Buddhahood, the Bodhisattva. These vehicles consequently deal with moral conduct and asceticism. When, in accordance with these methods, a man has passed through three "Endless World Periods" (*Asaṃkhyeya Kalpa*) he attains salvation.

The adepts of the Seventh and Eighth Vehicles—the "White *A* Vehicle" (*A-dkar*) and the *Ye-gshen* (the "Vehicle of Future Perfect Saints")—need only one incarnation to arrive at the same goal. The sacred *A* is the symbol of the "Pure Sound," the origin of all earthly sounds and of all effects in the phenomenal world. The Bon-po of this vehicle bestow initiation by means of secret incantations. These two vehicles thus contain the tantric teachings and the mysticism of the Bon-po.

The "Vehicle of Supreme Yoga" (*bLa-na-med*) teaches the so-called "Direct Path," the realization of polarity, and is intended to help the seeker merge with the "Bon substance," i.e., the supreme absolute, in this very lifetime. One source notes the existence of a Tenth Vehicle, but until now nothing definite is known about it.

The goal of the Bon mystics and the object of their concentration and meditational practices is union with the original basic essence, the "Bon Essence," or highest Reality, which is described as completely pure, unclouded by passions, void, and shining. Although it is not a "thing," it shines as a "thing." It is unaffected by recognition or non-recognition. Moreover, it contains both good and evil (at this high level both are meaningless); and the cycle of rebirth and salvation are no longer contradictory. Bon mysticism is thus very closely related to the moral and metaphysical relativity of Buddhist Vajrayāna, and a thorough examination would in all likelihood reveal particularly close connections with the school of Padmasambhava. Indicative here, it seems, is the significance of light. The Absolute, which is to be realized through meditation, is practically the same as light. The luminous character of the individual soul and its identity with the realm of the Absolute is described in the following way:

> In the center of the precious palace of the spiritual heart which is located above the eight petals of the mystic arteries, there are five mystic juices. In their center is a ball of the color of the five

wisdoms and spherical in shape. In this center is the "Bon essence," a mass of light. As its essence is void, it is not subject to duration, and as it shines through knowledge neither is it subject to destruction. To look at its essence with fixed eyes in which contemplation and contemplator are one—this is meditation.

This description is basically identical with the experience described in mysticism everywhere in the world:.the perception of the divine spark within the individual and the realization of the substantial identity of the exiled spark with the immeasurable light ocean of the Divine.

In the Bon religion we find a classification of three stages in meditation: the lowest, in which the distraction of the mind is gradually overcome and which allows perseverance in concentration or its abandonment; the middle, which allows the thought of self-salvation to rise in the soul; and the third, which makes the soul of the meditating person one with space when all spiritual impurities become knowledge and the entire visible world is recognized as contained in the completely pure sphere of Bon.

Not all Bon-po mystics, however, devoted themselves to this sort of pure and selfless striving. We know of practices of selfish "Left-hand" tantric rites. Very often such efforts were directed toward the lengthening of one's own life through the practice of magic. Horrible things seem to take place in connection with such practices and some Bon-po priests are supposed to lengthen their own earthly days by appropriating the life force of another who undergoes a painful death by starvation, although to be effective such sacrifices must be voluntary.

The priests of the syncretic Bon religion left an enormous volume of literature, which they had compiled throughout the centuries. Earlier, we discussed the well-established ancient tradition which held that the systematized Bon religion and the first written holy scriptures, subsequently to be translated into Tibetan, originated in Zhang-zhung. Tibetan Buddhist authors, however, never cease to insist that both during the reign of emperor Khri-srong lde-btsan, as well as later, toward the end of the period of the universal monarchy, the Bon-po priests appropriated Buddhist texts and merely made minor alterations in the names of persons and places, sometimes even transforming Buddhist religious tenets into their own. In fact some authors of the Yellow Hat school of Buddhism quote a whole list of Bon texts and compare each of these with the original Buddhist text from which it was appropriated. Such charges will, of course, have to be examined in detail when the Bon texts become more readily available, but the observations made in connection with the analysis of the story of gShen-rab mi-bo do suggest that there is some justification for the Buddhist charges of plagiarism, although this can only refer to the teachings of the "Vehicles of Effect." The old shamanist practices of the first four vehicles and the doctrines influenced by the Iranian religions were certainly not taken from

Buddhism, and it would hardly be possible to produce older Buddhist texts which contain them.

While there cannot be the slightest doubt that the Bon-po texts in the Zhang-zhung language were translated into Tibetan, other mysterious languages mentioned in the Bon-po books, such as the language of the "Svastika Gods" and the language of "Heavenly Iran," are certainly fictitious. The titles of books said to be written in these languages show an uncanny similarity to Zhang-zhung.

Like the Tibetan Buddhists, the Bon-po also codified their sacred literature in two great collections, the *bKa-'gyur,* which contains the authoritative pronouncements of gShen-rab, and the *bsTan-'gyur,* which consists of interpretations and expository literature. In 1931 the late Professor George Roerich stated that during his expedition to northern Tibet he had seen a complete set of each of these two collections in a Bon-po monastery and that the *bKa-'gyur* consisted of 140 volumes, and the *bsTan-'gyur* of 160. It would be a great boon for the history of religion if these texts could be made accessible to scientific research. The Tibetan Bon-po refugee scholars in India may possibly be able to provide more material, in which case research would not have to rely on chance sources.

BIBLIOGRAPHY

GENERAL LITERATURE ON TIBETAN RELIGIONS (Included are books with titles suggesting that Buddhism often contains materials concerning the two other religions of Tibet.)

Emile de Schlagintweit, *Buddhism in Tibet* (first publication of the 2nd ed. which dates back to the previous century), New York 1966; L. A. Waddell, *The Buddhism of Tibet or Lamaism,* 2nd ed., London 1895; Cambridge 1934; reprinted in 1972 as a Dover Paperback under the title *Tibetan Buddhism.* C. F. Koeppen, *Die Religion des Buddha und ihre Entstehung,* vol. 2: *Die lamaische Hierarchie und Kirche,* Berlin 1906; Sir Charles Bell, *The Religion of Tibet,* Oxford 1968; Wilhelm Filchner, *Kumbum Dschamba Ling, das Kloster der hunderttausend Bilder Maitreyas,* Leipzig 1933 (a description of a specific Tibetan monastery but also a compendium of popular Tibetan religion); Robert Bleichsteiner, *Die Gelbe Kirche,* Wien 1937; Giuseppe Tucci, *Tibetan Painted Scrolls,* Roma 1949 (one of the most important books on Tibetan religious history); Marcelle Lalou, *Les religions de Tibet,* Paris 1957; Günther Schulemann, *Geschichte der Dalai-Lamas,* 2nd Leipzig 1958; Helmut Hoffmann, *The Religions of Tibet,* London and New York 1961; Helmut Hoffmann, *Symbolik der tibetischen Religionen und des Schamanismus,* Stuttgart 1967; Giuseppe Tucci, "Die Religionen Tibets," *Die Religionen Tibets und der Mongolei,* Die Religionen der Menschheit 20, Stuttgart 1970.

TIBETAN FOLK RELIGION

Jacques Bacot, *Les Mo-so, leur religions, leur langue et leur écriture,* Leiden 1913; Berthold Laufer, "Bird Divination among the Tibetans," *TP,* ser. 2, vol. 17 (1916): 403-552; A. H. Francke, *Tibetische Hochzeitslieder,* Hagen und Darmstadt 1923; A. H. Francke, Tibetische Lieder aus dem Gebiet des ehemaligen westtibetischen Königreichs," *MSOS* (1929): 93-136; R. A. Stein, "Trente-trois fiches de divination tibétaines," *HJAS* 4 (1939): 297-371; Matthias Hermanns, "Schöpfungs-und Abstammungsmythen der Tibeter," *Anthropos* 41-44 (1946-49); Matthias Hermanns, "Überlieferungen der Tibeter," *MS* 13 (1948): 161-208; René Nebesky-Wojkowitz, "Das tibetische Staats-Orakel," *A V* 3 (1948): 136-55; René Nebesky-Wojkowitz, "A Tibetan Protective Deity," *EA* 5: 87-95; Helmut Hoffmann, "Die Gräber der tibetischen Könige im Distrikt 'Phyongs-rgyas," *NAWG* (1950): 1-14; R. A. Stein, "Mi-ñag et Si-hia, Géographie historique et légendes ancestrales," *BEFEO* 44 (1951): 223-63; Dominik Schröder, "Zur Religion der Tujen des Sininggebietes," *Anthropos* 47 (1952): 620-58, 822-70; René Nebesky-Wojkowitz, "Tibetan Drum Divination 'Nga mo'," *Ethnos* (1952): 149-57; Matthias Hermanns, *Himmelsstier und Gletscherlöwe. Mythen Sagen und Fabeln aus Tibet,* Eisenach u. Kassel 1955; Matthias Hermanns, *Mythen und Mysterien der Tibeter,* Köln 1956; René Nebesky-Wojkowitz, *Oracles and Demons of Tibet,* The Hague 1956; René Nebesky-Wojkowitz, *Where the Gods are Mountains,* London 1956 (on Tibetan shamanism); F. W. Thomas, "Ancient Folk Literature from Northeastern Tibet," *ADAW,* no. 3 (1952); R. A. Stein, *Les K'iang des marches sino-tibétaines, exemple de continuité de la tradition,* Paris 1957; R. A. Stein, "L'habitat, le monde et le corps humain en Extrême-Orient et en Haute Asie," *JA* (1957): 37-74; R. A. Stein, "Le linga des dances masquées lamaiques et les théories des âmes," *Liebenthal-Festschrift, Sino-Tibetan Studies,* nos. 3-4, pp. 1-36; Joseph F. Rock, "Contributions to the Shamanism of the Tibetan-Chinese Borderland," *Anthropos* 54 (1959): 796 ff.; George N. Roerich, "The Ceremony of Breaking the Stone," *Urusvati Journal* 2 (1932): 165-80; Siegbert Hummel, "Der magische Stein in Tibet," *NAE* 49 (1960): 224-40; Siegbert Hummel, "The Tibetan Ceremony of Breaking the Stone," *History of Religions* 8 (1968): 139-42; Siegbert Hummel, "Die Leichenbestattung in Tibet," *MS* 20 (1961): 266-81; R. A. Stein, *Les tribus anciennes des marches sino-tibétaines,* Paris 1961; R. A. Stein, *La civilisation tibétaine,* Collection Sigma, Paris 1962; Giuseppe Tucci, *Tibetan Folk Songs From Gyantse and Western Tibet,* 2nd ed., Artibus Asiae, supplementum 22, Ascona 1966; Friedrich W. Funke, *Religiöses Leben der Sherpa,* Innsbruck/München 1969; Chr. v. Fürer-Haimendorf, *The Sherpas of Nepal,* London 1963; R. A. Stein, "Du récit rituel dans les manuscrits tibétains de Touen-houang," *ETML* (Paris 1971): 479-547; Günter Schüttler, *Die letzten tibetischen Orakelpriester,* Wiesbaden 1971.

For the bibliography of the religious aspects of the Ge-sar epic, see chapter IX.

BON RELIGION

Sarat Chandra Das, *Contributions on the religion, history, etc., of Tibet,* reprint, New Delhi 1970; Anton Schiefner, *Über das Bonpo-Sûtra "Das weisse Nâga-Hunderttausend,"* Mémoires de l'Académie de St. Pétersbourg, VII. série, Tome 28 no. 1, St. Petersburg 1881; Sarat Chandra Das, "A Brief Sketch of the Bon Religion of Tibet," *JBTS* 1 (1893): Part 1, Appendix; Part 2, Appendix; Part 3 Appendix; Berthold Laufer, *Klu Bum Bsdus Pai Sñin Po,* Mémoires de la Société Finno-Ougrienne 11, Helsingfors 1898; Berthold Laufer, *Ein Sühngedicht der Bonpo,* Denkschriften der Wiener Akademie der Wissenschaften, Phil.-Hist. Klasse 1900, no. 7; Berthold Laufer, "Über ein tibetisches Geschichtswerk der Bonpo," *TP* (1901): 24-44; A. H. Francke, "A Ladakh Bonpo Hymnal," *IA* 30 (1901): J. van Manen, "Concerning a Bon Image," *JPASB* (1922): 195 ff.; A. H. Francke, "Die Frage der Bon Religion," *Allgemeine Missionszeitschrift* 49 (1922): 321-31; A. H. Francke, *"gZer-myig.* A Book of the Tibetan Bonpos," edited and translated, *AM* (1924): 243-346; (1926): 321-39; (1927): 161-239, 481-540; (1928): 1-40; N. S. 1 (1949): 163-88; A. H. Francke, "Die Zufluchts-formel der Bon Religion der Tibeter," *NAM* (1927): 150 ff.; A. H. Francke, *Das Christentum und die tibetische Bon Religion,* Deutsche Forschung, Heft 5, Berlin 1928; George N. Roerich, *Trails to Inmost Asia,* Yale University Press, New Haven 1931 (contains important data on Bon-po monasteries in Northern Tibet); Marcelle Lalou, "Les 'cent mille nâga'," *Festschrift Moriz Winternitz,* Leipzig 1933, pp. 79-81; Helmut Hoffmann, "Probleme und Aufgaben der tibetischen Philologie. Mit einem Anhang: Zur Geschichte der Bon-Religion," *ZDMG* 92 (1938): 345-68; Helmut Hoffmann, "Zur Literatur der Bon-po," *ZDMG* 94 (1940): 168-88; René Nebesky-Wojkowitz, "Die tibetische Bon-Religion," *AV* 2 (1947): 26-68; Helmut Hoffmann, *Quellen zur Geschichte der tibetischen Bon Religion,* Abhandlungen der Akademie der Wissenschaften und der Literatur 1950, Nr. 4, Wiesbaden 1950; Marcelle Lalou, "Rituel bon-po des funérailles royales" (fonds Pelliot tibétain 1042), *JA* (1952): 339-61; Marcelle Lalou, "Tibétain ancien Bod/Bon," *JA* (1953): 276-98; Walter Simon, "A Note on Tibetan bon," *AM,* N.S. V (1955): 5-6; Helmut Hoffmann, "Religione Bon (Tibet, Swat, Gilgit)," *Le civiltà dell'oriente,* vol. 3, Roma 1958, 869-81; Marcelle Lalou, "Fiefs, poisons et guérisseurs," *JA* (1958): 157-201; Siegbert Hummel, "Eurasiatische Traditionen in der tibetischen Bon-Religion," *Opuscula Ethnologica, Memoriae Ludovici Bíró Sacra* (1959): 165-212; David Snellgrove, *Himalayan Pilgrimage,* Oxford 1961 (on the Bon-po of northern Nepal); David Snellgrove, *The Nine Ways of Bon,* London 1967; Helmut H. R. Hoffmann, "An Account of the Bon Religion in Gilgit," *CAJ* 13 (1969): 137-45; R. A. Stein, "Un document ancien relatif aux rites funéraires des Bon-po tibétains," *JA* (1970): 155-85.

On the Holy Language of the Bon Religion: Helmut Hoffmann, "Žaṅ-žuṅ, the Holy Language of the Tibetan Bon-po," *ZDMG* (1967): 376-81; Erik Haarh, *The Zhang-zhung Language, A Grammar and Dictionary of the Unexplored Language of the Tibetan Bonpos,* Acta Jutlandica 40, 1, Copenhagen 1968; R.

A. Stein, "La langue Źań-źuń du Bon organisé," *BEFEO* 58 (1971): 233-54; Helmut Hoffmann, "Several Żań-żuń Etymologies," *Oriens Extremus* 12 (1972): (193-201).

On the Bon Religion of the Mo-so and Na-khi: Joseph F. Rock, "The Birth and Origin of Dtom-ba Shi-lo, the founder of the Mo-so Shamanism," *AA* (1937); Joseph F. Rock, *The Na-khi Nâga cult and Related Ceremonies,* 2 vols., Roma 1952; Joseph F. Rock, "The Zhi-mä Funeral Ceremony of the Na-khi of Southwest China," Studia Instituti *Anthropos* 9 (Posieux 1955); Joseph F. Rock, "The D'a No Funeral Ceremony with Special Reference to the Origin of the Na-khi Weapons," *Anthropos* 50 (1955).

Tibetan Buddhism

Outline of the History of Buddhism Before Its Introduction Into Tibet

Before a description of the history of Tibetan Buddhism can be given it is necessary to realize that Buddhism penetrated into Tibet after more than a millenium of development in its homeland, India, and that all forms of Indian Buddhism were still alive when Tibet received the Buddhist heritage. Siddhārtha Gautama, whose followers call him "the Enlightened One," the Buddha (Tib. *Sangs-rgyas*), came from the dynasty of the Shākyas, who ruled a small principality at the foot of the Himalayas. After a youth spent in the pleasures of the world, Siddhārtha left the house of his father to learn from the teachers of Yoga and to satisfy his urge for salvation. But neither Arāda Kalāpa, who led his disciples along the meditative path to the stage of nothingness, nor Rudraka Rāmaputra, who went even further and guided his followers to a sphere beyond both the conscious and the unconscious, nor the harshest asceticism and self-mortifications were able to satisfy him. He separated himself from all other seekers, and under the holy *Bō* tree in the neighborhood of present-day Bodh Gayā in Bihar he at last found enlightenment. After some hesitation he decided to make known his realization which he first revealed to five of his former companions-in-meditation in the famous sermon at Banāras. It is not within the scope of this work to describe the legends which grew up around the Buddha's enlightenment, but we should mention at least one legend which would seem to be a reflection of the inner experiences the Buddha underwent after finding the basic knowledge.

According to the reports of the old texts, the Buddha at first thought it would be difficult and useless to preach his newly-found doctrine because the humans around him would be unable to understand this difficult and deep knowledge. But the highest god, Brahman, appeared before the meditating saint, and in moving words requested him to pronounce the deep doctrine. Then the Buddha perceived the world as a lotus pond in which he saw several lotus buds near the bottom of the pond, others near the surface, and still others in blossom above the water. He realized that there were human beings not greatly given to worldly desires, and that if these humans did not hear his doctrine they would perish; if they did hear it they would understand it. This beautiful simile is the first reference in the Buddhist scriptures to the lotus flower and its unfolding as the symbol of man's spiritual development; and it is still used by the Tibetans. Psychologically it is extremely indicative that at first the Buddha tended to keep his world-redeeming doctrine to himself, a hint that Eastern religious man is not eager to impress his ideas on others, unlike Western man who tends to impose himself on others even to propagate less important ideas.

After a life of eighty years devoted to the spreading of the truth he had discovered, the Buddha died at Kushinagara in present-day Nepal about 480 B.C.

His teachings (*dharma*), originally preserved orally by a growing community of monks (*sangha*), did not represent the traditional popular religion with its rich pantheon of gods and impressive and colorful ritual. It was a strictly philosophical theory of salvation for an elect and was characterized primarily by the *arhat* ideal (Tib. *dGra-bcom-pa*), i.e., the ideal of the religious individual who in a manly struggle accepts the afflictions of life and overcomes them by reaching a state in which the power of the life force (lit. "thirst," *trishnā*) is broken, a state which is known as *Nirvāṇa* (Tib. *Myang-'das*), or the removal of all desires. In this state the accomplished saint is compared to an extinguished lamp. By its very nature *Nirvāṇa* can be described only in negative terms, although this does not imply that it is "nothing." This "bliss unspeakable" denies the following four descriptions of *Nirvāṇa*: that the accomplished one exists as a spiritual personality in heaven, that he is totally annihilated by the disintegration of the four elements which constituted his physical and mental existence, that he only exists as a pure spiritual being, and that he no longer exists as an individual but has found in his redemption the way to the formless Absolute. On the other hand, the old Buddhist texts state that *Nirvāṇa* is permanent, stable, imperishable, immovable, ageless, deathless, and bliss. The old scriptures of the conservative Theravāda school assert in words of great solemnity that there is an Unborn, Unbecome, Uncreated, Unconditioned which offers an escape for the Born, the Become, the Created, the Conditioned. Thus *Nirvāṇa* is something totally different from anything which can be conceived by the intellect; it can only be experienced.

Very soon after the death of its founder, Buddhism began to change and develop, although it is quite clear that the teaching of the four "Noble Truths" was part of the original message, i.e., the truth of suffering, the origin of suffering, the removal of suffering, and the noble eight-fold path which leads to the removal of suffering. It is also very probable that Buddha's original teachings included the doctrine of the "Origin in Dependence" (*pratītyasamutpāda*, Tib. *rTen-'brel*), which describes the development of a living being by a series of twelve factors. These factors represent less a strictly causal series in the sense of Western philosophy than a mutually dependent series whose final basis is described as the ignorance of the holy truths (*avidyā*, Tib. *ma-rig-pa*). Even early Buddhism did not reject the popular Indian gods and their heavens, although they, too, were regarded as subject to the laws of development and decline, the circle of birth and death (*sansāra*, Tib. *'Khor-ba*), whose individual stages were regulated by the law of retribution (*karma*, Tib. *las*). It is important to keep in mind that as Buddha recognized gods but no God, he also recognized no immortal soul. The ego (*ātman*) or individuality is only a conglomeration of life factors, the so-called *dharmas*, and at death their bond is released. However, if *Nirvāṇa* is not realized before death, the nonquiescent *dharma* impulses produce a new life. Thus it is not the ego which is immortal, but only the sorrowful process of development and decline, and the goal of the Buddhist is precisely to avoid this disaster. What Buddha set out to provide was a practical doctrine of salvation; he rejected the preoccupation with metaphysical speculation to which the minds of his age were so devoted.

The Buddha did not claim to be the only Enlightened One. He believed that Buddhas had existed in the world during earlier world periods. Speculation on this idea began very early and provided a basis for a mythology which is peculiar to Indian religious thought. The series of six predecessors of the Buddha, the last of whom was Kāshyapa, probably belonged to a quite early period of development, although the legends connected with them were elaborated only in later times. At least two hundred years after Buddha's passing, rivalry seems to have developed between schools of local traditions (especially concerning the *Vinaya,* the regulations of the order), which quickly led to splits and the formation of sects, as can be clearly gathered from the reports on the early Buddhist rehearsals or synods. The earliest schism was caused by the secession of the conservative Sthaviravāda school, or "Elders," from the Mahāsānghika, the "Great Assemblists." This took place during the reign of the emperor Ashoka in the third century B.C. The latter school, which later became the nucleus for the "Great Vehicle," was less conservative concerning the original *arhat* ideal and did not strictly deny the spiritual possibilities of householders or laymen, women, or less talented monks.

About a century before the beginning of the Christian era a new gospel emerged from the progressive teachings of the Mahāsānghika school which was called by its adherents the "Bodhisattva-career," the "Great Vehicle," or Mahāyāna. The followers of this new doctrine called the old conservative school "The Lesser Vehicle" (Hīnayāna). The *arhat* ideal was replaced by that of the Bodhisattva, the "Buddha-to-be." Unlike the *arhat*, who worked for his own personal perfection alone, the Bodhisattva, out of pity for the suffering world, took an oath not to enter *Nirvāṇa* until the last living being had been saved. The deliberate, cool, and aristocratic simplicity of the older Buddhism now gave way to a more emotional development in which an increasing number of Buddha and Bodhisattva figures developed, offering a more tangible object of devotion to the faithful, similar to the *bhakti* ("devotion") of the Hindus for Vishṇu. Before long the mythical Buddhas in their paradises—far away but effective—such as Vairocana ("Sun"), and Amitābha (the "Buddha of Immeasurable Light"); and Bodhisattvas such as Avalokiteshvara ("the Lord of Mercy," Tib. *sPyan-ras-gzigs*), and Maitreya, the savior of the coming world period, began to surpass in importance and significance the historic Buddha who, however, was never forgotten. Recent research suggests that figures like Amitābha and Avalokiteshvara probably emerged under Iranian influence, since both have the traits of the "light theology" of contemporary Iran. The same is true for the future Buddha, Maitreya, who although of Hīnayāna origin, later became connected with Iranian apocalyptic doctrines, certainly under the influence of an Iranian god whose name is derived from the same Indo-Iranian root: Mithra. It can hardly be regarded as fortuitous that the origin of the Mahāyāna ran more or less parallel to this development in northwest India and eastern Iran, at that time a country with flourishing Buddhist communities. In Iran a hybrid Indo-Greek art emerged, named after the Gandhāra region, but also flourishing in the neighboring regions of Uḍḍiyāna (present-day Swāt) in the adjacent provinces of what is now Afghanistan, and in the area of the old city of Taxila in the Punjab. This art spread not only to India proper but also to eastern Turkestan. Beginning with the first century B.C. Buddhist artists created Buddha images (under the influence of the Hellenistic Apollo images), whereas in previous centuries the Enlightened One had been represented only symbolically, as for instance by the tree of enlightenment with an empty seat before it, or by the wheel of the doctrine.

Beginning with the first century B.C. a multitude of new Mahāyāna texts appeared, including the famous "Lotus of the Good Law" and the whole group of more or less voluminous Sūtras dealing with the "Perfection of Wisdom" (*Prajñāpāramitā*, Tib. *Shes-rab-kyi pha-rol-tu phyin-pa*), a title which may be translated as "Transcendental Wisdom." The emergence of this type of Mahāyāna literature shows that there was more than one original center for the new doctrines. "Transcendental Wisdom" originated in southeastern India in the Deccan, especially between the Godāvarī and Kistnā Rivers in the Telugu-speaking country of present-day Āndhra Pradesh, whose center was at the excavated sites of Amarāvatī and Nāgārjunikonda. Nāgārjunikonda especially is closely connected with the activities of the saint and teacher Nāgārjuna (Tib. KLu-sgrub), who is still famous among the Tibetans and whose teachings provide the basic philosophy for all Tibetan Buddhist studies. According to a legend, the original book of the "Transcendental Wisdom" was given to him by the *Nāga* (water spirits who appear in the form of snakes) in their palace under the sea. This philosophical school, the Mādhyamika or the "Followers of the Doctrine of the Middle Way," flourished in India for about eight hundred years and was adopted by the Tibetans before Buddhism was destroyed by Muslim conquest. To stress the authenticity of this doctrine it is believed that at the same time the Buddha taught the "Small Vehicle" to his earthly disciples, in heaven he taught that deeper doctrine which was first preserved by the snake spirits and then brought to earth by Nāgārjuna. Western influence at the time of the emergence of the early "Transcendental Wisdom" Sūtras is proved by the fact, quite isolated in Indian literature, that Nāgārjuna obtained the book in question which was "sealed by seven seals" from the spirits in exactly the same way that Saint John received the Apocalypse. The doctrine of the "Middle Way" means that Nāgārjuna and his later followers reconciled the *philosophema* of the older view of the dharmas, or "Perishable Factors of Existence," with his newly introduced

"Unlimited," which means that one does not distinguish between oneself and others. The method now recommended is to practice both seemingly contradictory ways simultaneously. Whereas the method of the "Factors of Existence," void by their imminent nature, leads to a boundless contraction of mind, the method of the "Unlimited" leads to boundless expansion of the mind or self. The term "Voidness" (*Shūnyatā*, Tib. *sTong-pa-nyid*) is one of the most important in Mahāyāna philosophy. It means the effacement of the self and is symbolized by an empty circle, a well-known symbol of the ineffable Absolute; hence *Shūnyatā* no longer means an intellectual, but a mystical truth. It stands between affirmation and negation and represents the nonduality of subject and object. Logically, *Nirvāṇa* cannot be distinguished from the phenomenal world. Another term used in this philosophy is "Thusness" (*Tathatā*). The concept of this nondual Absolute was the germ from which centuries later developed in the teachings of the "Diamond Vehicle" the interpretation of the negatively defined Absolute as "Great Bliss."

Moreover, "Transcendental Wisdom" was later represented as a goddess and called the "Mother of all the Buddhas." There is in all probability a connection between Buddhist "Wisdom" and Sophia (which also means "wisdom") in the Gnostic religion of Alexandria, which also emerged during the first century B.C. in the eastern Mediterranean, especially in Alexandria. In this connection Professor Conze has described a Byzantine miniature of the tenth century which is said to go back to an Alexandrian model. The right hand of Sophia shows the gesture of teaching, while the left arm holds a book.

Another development leading to the extension of the doctrine of the Absolute and to a new conception of the individual mind originated in the fourth century with two brothers, Asanga and Vasubandhu, who became the founders of the "Mind-Only" or Yogācārin school, the mere name of which makes it clear that this system is based chiefly on meditational practices. These teachings were based primarily on the *Lankāvatāra* and *Avataṃsaka sūtras* which, like the *Prājñapāramitā*, are ascribed to the historical Buddha. In this system the doctrine of the three bodies of the Buddha, the *Dharma Kāya* (Body of the Absolute), the *Sambhoga Kāya* (the Body of Enjoyment in Heavenly Paradises), and the *Nirmāṇa Kāya* (the Apparitional Body), was fully developed.

The two most important innovations of the Yogācāra school are the "Mind Only" and "Store-Consciousness" doctrines. The adept of this school, through Yogic experience, penetrates to the final subject which is completely beyond intellectual apperception, which is not a thing of this world, and which is transcendental. The Yogin strives for happiness and salvation not in outer things but in the equanimity of the pure inwardness of his thought. The cause of all evil lies in the proclivity of the individual to see things as objects and as separated from the inmost self or mind. The basis of all illusions is derived from the notion that the objectifications of the mind are really its own source and substance.

"Store Consciousness" is defined by Asanga as an overpersonal consciousness which is the foundation of all our acts and thoughts. The experience of past
occurrences is stored in it, which means that it is, so to say, impregnated by all
our deeds and their results. Thus "Store Consciousness" is not a permanent soul
monad, but is rather like a river which changes as a result of constantly receiving
and giving water. This idea goes very well with the teaching of Karma, according
to which the fruits of all deeds, whether good or bad, have to be experienced.
The old "Non-ego" teachings of the Hīnayāna seemed no longer satisfying; and
the new doctrine therefore accounts on the one hand for the sense of the
personal identity of the empirical ego (which, strictly speaking, is wrong), and
on the other hand it lasts until *Nirvāṇa* is realized. The philosophical
developments of the Mahāyāna stipulated beforehand the spiritual conditions for
the origin of the third stage of Buddhism, the Vajrayāna or "Diamond Vehicle."

Along with these highly philosophical innovations an increasingly
emotional attitude was displayed in the popular Buddhism of this time. By daily
services, by promotion of the virtues of the faithful, by removing greed, hate,
and delusion, by generosity, and by love for all sentient beings and especially for
the Buddhas and the Bodhisattvas, the layman hoped for better earthly
conditions as well as for a better rebirth which would enable him to reach the
goal of Buddhism, i.e., redemption from the terrible circle of existence. He also
hoped for reincarnation in "Buddha Fields," heavens like "the Land of Bliss,"
the western paradise of Amitābha, from which he would not return to the
sansāra but enter *Nirvāṇa* directly. An especially strong faith developed in the
Bodhisattva Avalokiteshvara, the All-Compassionate One, the giver of emergency
help in worldly and spiritual difficulties. It was even believed that he could
relieve the unfortunates who fell into hell.

Only after a considerable time, around A.D. 500 or 600, did the Vajrayāna
obtain universal recognition and was no longer practiced exclusively by secret
circles. The *vajra* (Tib. *rDo-rje*) is a universal symbol whose most important
significance is "diamond," a symbol of the Indestructable. The "Indestructable,"
of course, is another symbol for the "Absolute," "Voidness," "Thusness," and
the "Ineffable Light," terms which were taken over from the preceding teachings
of the "Great Vehicle." Vajrayāna is also called Buddhist tantrism and emerged
approximately at the same time as Hindu tantrism. Tantra (Tib. *rGyud*)
originally meant "thread, cord," and signified the uninterrupted chain of
spiritual teachers or gurus. More specifically, it meant a secret esoteric system
given to the disciple only from mouth to ear. The Vajrayāna is a typical mystery
religion in which, accordingly, initiations (*Abhisheka*, Tib. *dbAng-bsKur*) play a
most important role. This form of Buddhism uses three methods to achieve
spiritual perfection and salvation: first, the recitation of secret spells (*mantra*,
Tib. *gSang-sngags*), using thus the innate power of the "Word" in its highest
sense, and reminding us of the great importance of the Logos in the

Mediterranean world; second, the performance of ritual gestures (*mudrā*) by which the human body itself becomes a symbolic thing; and third, the experience of identification with superhuman powers by means of a special kind of concentration and meditation. Thus the Vajrayāna is a combination of mysticism and magic. It is distinguished from mere mysticism by the active character of its realization of the Divine, and it may be called neither subordination nor supraordination, but inordination in the laws of the spiritual world whose experience is sought.

Mythologically and philosophically the pentad speculation, most probably of Manichean origin, was codified by the teaching of the "Five Buddhas," wrongly called Dhyāni Buddhas, but denoted in the original texts as "The five Victors" or the "Five Tathāgatas," namely, Vairocana, Akshobhya ("the Imperturbable"), Ratnasambhava ("The Jewel Born"), Amitābha ("The Immeasurable Light"), and Amoghasiddhi ("Unfailing Perfection"). Whereas some of the Buddhas as single holy individuals go back to the early Mahāyāna, their arrangement in the four cardinal directions and in the center of the world as well as in a sacred *maṇḍala*, which is a representation of the world, was probably not introduced before A.D. 750. The five Buddhas are believed to be emanations of the Primordial Buddha, the Ādibuddha, who does not act in the phenomenal world and is the first manifestation of the "Voidness" or the "Ineffable Light." The Ādibuddha has different names in the different schools of Buddhism: Samantabhadra, Vajradhara, Vajrasattva, and, in East Asian Buddhism, the Great Vairocana. The holder of the central position also shows no consistency in the different tantric schools: often Vairocana is the central figure, but in other cases it is Akshobhya.

A doctrine which developed an exceptional importance in later Vajrayāna concerns the teaching of the polarity of the world and of the Divine, which meant an increase in the importance of the female element in rites and mythology. In early Buddhism there was no place for a doctrine of polarity, and the feminine received anything but high esteem. In fact, the Buddha is believed to have at first established only an order of monks, later, he reluctantly gave permission for the founding of an order of nuns at the request of his foster mother, Mahāprajāpatī, but not without adding the prophecy that the pure doctrine would then come to an end within five hundred years. By the time of the "Great Vehicle" and the "Diamond Vehicle," this attitude had greatly altered and now found expression in the concept of numberless female divinities, the most important of whom, besides "Transcendental Wisdom," was Tārā (Tib. sGrol-ma), the Great Savioress.

In many respects Vajrayāna runs parallel to Hindu tantrism with, however, many basic differences. Whereas in Hinduism the divine masculine aspect of the macrocosm-microcosm is portrayed as passive, meditative repose symbolically represented by the god Shiva as an ascetic, and whereas the Shakti or "Divine

Energy" personified as Kālī-Durgā, the mother goddess in her manifold manifestations, represents the active, productive force, the very opposite is the case in the Tantrism of the Vajrayāna: the masculine aspect of the macrocosm-microcosm, usually called *upāya* (Tib. *thabs*), "means, method," or *karuṇā*, "compassion" (Tib. *sNying-rje*) is active-productive, while the feminine aspect, as is well known, is passive-receiving. The central concept is *prajñā*, "wisdom," a term certainly connected with the "Transcendental Wisdom" of earlier Mahāyāna.

In the tantric Buddhist texts, active-passive polarity is symbolized by numerous other pairs of concepts in a secret and highly symbolical language which the adepts of that system call the "Language of Suggestion" (*sandhābhāshā*). Polarity can be expressed by heaven and earth, consonants and vowels, and sun and moon. The latter two are frequently used as the crown of the late Buddhist *stūpas*, their union in the "Great Bliss" (*mahāsukha*) symbolized by the flame of the *bindu* or "drop" which appears above them. Another polarity-pair in the Vajrayāna which corresponds *mutatis mutandis* to the mystical concepts of the Kuṇḍalinī Yoga of Hinduism are the mystical right- and left-hand arteries, called in Buddhism *Rasanā* and *Lalanā* respectively. From these the mysterious material of Bodhicitta, generally known as "Thought of Enlightenment" but denoting here the vital force or sperm, is pressed into the central artery called *Avadhūti*, by which process the holy *unio mystica* is realized.

Other important polarity pairs are knowledge and ignorance, sperm and menstrual blood, and, especially, subject and object in meditation, to be united by mystical realization and from which finally the union of the polarities of *nirvāṇa* and *sansāra* (the circle of rebirth) proceeds, a teaching already created by the Mahāyāna. This entire religion thus centers on the removal of the contradictory antithesis in early Buddhism and its transformation into a polar one.

In the rituals of the Vajrayāna cult the *vajra* (Tib. *rDo-rje*), meaning thunderbolt, diamond, and phallus, is the symbol for the active aspect and has its counterpart in the bell or the lotus, *Padma*, as the passive aspect.

Since Vajrayāna is a mystery religion, its secret revelations can be acquired only by initiation, called *abhisheka* (lit. "sprinkling") in Sanskrit, but *dbAng-bsKur* (conveying of a power) in Tibetan. For an effective initiation, the personal guru of the initiate, the latter frequently having completed the very hard training of a neophyte, must be present as a guide in the room of initiation where the rite is commonly celebrated before a cosmic diagram or *maṇḍala*. Also indispensable is a consecrated woman called *prajñā* or *vidyā* (both of which mean "wisdom") and *mudrā* ("seal"), whom the guru or the neophyte has selected in accordance with certain physical or spiritual priorities and with whom the initiate must perform symbolical erotic rites in order to close the polarity. Actual physical union of the initiate and the woman was successfully suppressed by the famous teacher Atīsha in Tibet during the eleventh century and is today practiced only by debased and coarse Buddhism.

The hypostasis of the female aspect of the Divine is called Vajrayoginī (Tib. rDo-rje rnal-'byor-ma) and is represented as a naked goddess with a garland of skulls draped between her legs. As "Divine Wisdom" she has the function of a typical goddess of initiation who appears to the yogin at various stages of his spiritual path, especially during the treading of the path and at consummation. A special form of Vajrayoginī is called by the strange name of Vajravarāhī which means "Diamond Sow," and is represented in the same attitude and the same iconographic details except that she wears a suggestive pig's head at the left side of her head. Vajrayoginī is the prototype of an entire group of initiation goddesses, (each yogin has his own goddess) called the ḍākinīs or "sky travellers," who originated in the primitive religion of the country of Uḍḍiyāna (Swat) in northwestern India (present-day Pakistan) and were taken over in spiritualized form by the Vajrayāna.

If we summarize the polar relationship between Vajrayoginī and her counterpart Heruka, from the mythological as well as from the philosophical standpoint, it is clearly evident that no logical reason within Indian ideas can be adduced for an explanation as to why in the Vajrayāna the female aspect of the macrocosm-microcosm should be conceived as passive, which is certainly contrary to genuine Hindu development. This discrepancy can only be ascribed to foreign influences which came from the West by way of Iran, namely, the acceptance of ideas and mythologemes from the Gnosis of late antiquity. The Buddhist prajñā ("wisdom") is nothing but a replica of the Gnostic Sophia who originated in the early example of Helena (who functioned terrestrially as the consort of the adept Simon Magus) and continued throughout the latest manifestations of this system. Helena was also called Selene, "moon," and in the Vajrayāna the moon is an important symbol of the feminine aspect of polarity.

Very little chronological information is available about the masters of the Vajrayāna—the Indians, as is well known, paid little attention to correct dates in religious history—but we can hope that the investigation of the tantric commentaries and the additional data of the Tibetan historiographers will be helpful in this respect and eventually allow us to compile at least some sort of relative chronology. The figure of Saraha would seem to begin the history of eroticized Vajrayāna. Some sources make him the teacher of a "perfect saint" (siddha, Tib. grub-thob) Nāgārjuna, who, however, should not be confused with the great philosopher Nāgārjuna, the founder of the Mādhyamika and "Void-ness" doctrine, who lived in the second century A.D. The later Nāgārjuna was also an important alchemist. Tradition states that Saraha came from a Brahmin family of Orissa, but lost caste because of his fondness for intoxicating liquor (a "weakness" not uncommon among the other Vajrayāna masters or *siddhas*) and also because he lived with a low caste woman who served as his *vidyā* in the polarity rites. This yoginī was the daughter of an arrow-maker. By using arrows, it is said, she guided him to an understanding of the nature of things (*dharma*). He conferred the *mudrā* ("seal") initiation on her and henceforth, wandering with her through many parts of India, pursued the trade of arrow-making. As his wisdom steadily grew he received the name of Saraha, or "he who hits with the arrow."

We may regard this report as typical for it characterizes the spiritual climate of the times and the paradoxical and highly symbolical behavior of these *siddha,* eighty-four of whom later became canonized and are still worshipped among the Tibetans. Saraha, like other Vajrayāna saints, compiled paradoxical mystical verses, the so-called *dohā*, composed in the *Sandhā-bhāshā* or "secret symbolical language" in which, for instance, "flower of the sky" means the Absolute, and "sun" the male. Some of the other great mystics, such as Lūi-pā, Jālandhari and his disciple Krishnacārin, Kambala, Indrabhūti, and Padmasambhava (the last three of whom come significantly from northwest India, the land of the *dākinīs*) probably belong to a somewhat later period. The group of the "eighty-four Perfect Ones" also includes females called *yoginī*. They all devoted themselves primarily to the cult of mystic Buddhas and newly-arisen grotesque tantric tutelary gods, such as Yamāntaka ("the Killer of the God of Death"), Saṃvara, Hevajra, and Heruka who were conjured in meticulously executed magic circles or *maṇḍalas*. The last-named three *yi-dam* are deified hypostases of the active polar element, i.e., the conjuring *yogin* himself. Each of the chief divinities has its own definite and exclusive *maṇḍala* in which a display of the physical and spiritual universe with all its divine hierarchies is symbolically represented. Also characteristic of this epoch is the importance attached to the "sky-goers," both male (*dāka*) and female (*dākinī*), in whom we see the reflection of the perfected mystics who either still live in the phenomenal world or are deceased and who transmit mystic doctrines to their disciples directly or indirectly, occasionally making it possible for them by means of special instructions to "discover" hidden religious documents of esoterism, the so-called "treasures."

The "First Propagation of the Doctrine"

When primitive, illiterate Tibet—adhering to animist-shamanist belief—came into contact with Buddhism in the seventh and eighth centuries, the innovations of the Vajrayāna were found to be particularly appealing. But one would create a false picture of the spiritual climate of the time if one failed to note that the older Buddhist teachings, such as the philosophic Mahāyāna of Nāgārjuna and Asanga, were still fully effective. In fact there was even a school of the old Hīnayāna, that of the Sarvāstivādins, which seems to have been of importance at the time, at least if we judge from the quite considerable number of the doctrinal texts of this school which were translated when Buddhism began to be accepted in Tibet.

Tibet made its appearance in world history during the reign of the great emperor Srong-btsan sgam-po. In the Tibetan historical accounts, a legend has been preserved which describes how at an earlier time the Tibetans mysteriously came into possession of Buddhist sacred objects—they are alleged to have fallen from heaven—among which were Buddhist writings and a miniature representation of a Stūpa. This event, ascribed to the reign of the fifth predecessor of Srong-btsan sgam-po, Lha-tho-tho-ri, who was still a petty chief in the neighborhood of the Yar-klungs valley, might point to early but superficial contacts with Buddhism. We are informed by the chronicles that the Tibetans did not know what to do with these objects.

While in all secular matters such as the institutionalizing of a state chancellèry, the introduction of paper and ink, and civilized social behavior, the Tibetans turned to the Chinese as their teachers, in spiritual and religious matters they turned, though not exclusively, to India, the abode of Buddhist beliefs. Buddhism had by the seventh century A.D. spread to almost the whole of Asia Major: eastern Iran, Turkestan, China, Japan, Indochina, and Indonesia. The emperor realized that without a written language any higher culture was impossible. As mentioned before (see p. 15 f) he sent one of his ministers, Thon-mi Sambhoṭa, to India and entrusted him with the task of creating a Tibetan script. The new literary language was now used for government documents as well as for the translation of a few Buddhist texts. Supervised by Thon-mi Sambhoṭa, the work of translating was done by foreign monks together with Tibetans. Among the monks invited to take part in this work was a Chinese Buddhist.

The relationship of Tibet with both India and China at this time is also reflected in the emperor's marriages. Apart from a number of Tibetan wives chosen from the ranks of the Tibetan aristocracy, he also wed a Chinese and possibly a Nepalese princess (see above p. 42). Although these two marriages were primarily of a political nature, it seems that both of the princesses were zealous followers of Buddhism and no doubt contributed to the spread of the Buddhist doctrine in the higher Tibetan society. Both the Nepalese princess,

Bhrikutī, and the Chinese princess, Wen-ch'eng, brought Buddhist images and other religious objects with them from their homes, which were in later times believed to have been incarnations of the green and the white goddess Tārā. The emperor himself, while making use of the new religion predominantly as an instrument for the desired advance of Tibetan civilization, is called in the monastic chronicles "the first religious king" (Skr. *Dharmarāja*), one of a series of three religious kings. He, too, is believed to have been an incarnation of the Bodhisattva of Mercy, Avalokiteshvara. It seems certain that he erected two sanctuaries at Lhasa, his new capital: the famous "Cathedral of Lhasa," the Jo-khang, and the smaller but likewise renowned sanctuary called Ra-mo-che ("The Great Enclosure"). He is also credited with having built four temples in central Tibet, as well as four temples for the "Conversion of the Frontiers" and four temples for the "Conversion of Countries beyond the Frontiers." Sober historical consideration shows that we can hardly speak of any actual "imposition" of the new religion by the emperor Srong-btsan sgam-po. A century after his reign the Tibetan people were still attached to the religion of their forebears, and the Bon-po priests maintained their official position in state affairs. The first Buddhist monastery was not built until the following century, and therefore the Chinese Buddhist pilgrim Huei-ch'ao, who went to India and returned to China in 727 through eastern Turkestan, has nothing to say about Buddhism in Tibet. "As far as the country of Tibet in the East is concerned," he writes in his report of his travels, "there are no monasteries there, and the teachings of Buddha are unknown," the last statement being only conditionally true. Nevertheless, these old Tibetan contacts with Buddhism were of great importance for later developments.

During the reigns of the first two successors of Srong-btsan sgam-po, Indian Buddhist beliefs do not seem to have made much progress in Tibet, though one may assume that the dynasty itself and a minority among the influential aristocratic families showed a certain interest in the cultural aspects of Buddhism. It was the time of major-domo leadership of the mGar clan as well as an era of military expansion into western China, eastern Turkestan, Ferghāna, Gilgit, and other more western countries. Not until the reign of Mes-ag-tshoms (704-55) was there anything of importance to note in the history of religion. This emperor is reported to have founded a number of new temples, and under his reign several other Buddhist texts, including the legends of the "Karma-shataka" and the famous "Gold Luster Sūtra" of the Mahāyāna (*Suvarna-prabhāsa*), were added to the translated store of early Tibetan religious literature. On the other hand, the messengers sent by the emperor to the Kailās region to invite two Indian masters engaged in meditation returned without success. All they brought back with them was five Mahāyāna *sūtras* which they had learned by heart so that, as it is reported, they could be put into writing on their return to Tibet.

The cause of Buddhism was greatly advanced by Chin-ch'eng, wife of the emperor Mes-ag-tshoms. It was certainly because of her influence that representatives of Chinese Buddhism, the so-called Ho-shang, again began to play a role at the Tibetan court. Moreover, she pleaded successfully for providing refuge to a group of Buddhist monks from the kingdom of Khotan (Tib. Li), supplying them with food and clothing during their sojourn in Tibet. Assumably the arrival of a group of foreign monks greatly furthered the cause of Buddhism, although it also created political resentment on the part of the jealous nobility. The exponents of the nobility looked for an opportunity to get rid of the unwelcome guests. During a smallpox epidemic, which occurred three years after the monks arrived (740-41) and took the life of Chin-ch'eng, the Tibetan ministers publicly pronounced the pestilence to be a sign of the anger of the ancient gods, caused by the incursion of the monks. On this pretext the expulsion of the hated strangers, who once again had to take to the road, was secured. This event was an important landmark in the two-hundred-year struggle between, on the one hand, Buddhism and the imperial house, and, on the other, the powerful noble families and the Bon religion, encouraged and developed as a counterweight to Buddhism. During the last years of Mes-ag-tshoms, probably at the insistence of the imperial house, four Tibetans were sent to China under the leadership of Sang-shi to collect and bring back Buddhist writings. They actually obtained permission to examine Chinese translations of the "Gold Lustre Sūtra" and parts of the *vinaya* (the collection of Regulations of the Order), and certain medical texts. When they returned, accompanied by a Chinese monk, they found that the emperor had died and that the general situation in Lhasa was much less favorable to Buddhism than before they had left.

The Tibetan feudal nobility took advantage of the minority of the new emperor Khri-srong lde-brtsan (755-97) to prepare the final overthrow of Buddhism, detested by them for political rather than for religious reasons. Chinese and Nepalese monks residing in the temple of Ra-mo-che were sent back to their respective countries, and an edict was issued which suppressed Buddhism throughout the country. It is recorded that an attempt was made to remove the famous Buddha image of the Jo-khang and send it back to China, but eventually it was transported to the southern part of Tibet.

The principal leaders of the anti-Buddhist reaction were sTag-sgra klu-gong and Ma-zhang Khrom-pa-sKyabs, who seems to have been all-powerful during the minority of the young emperor. Ma-zhang's motives for opposing Buddhism were political rather than religious; this was generally true of the anti-Buddhism of the old Tibetan nobility from whom the ministers and other high officials were selected. Considering the origin of the Tibetan imperial dynasty, it seems quite natural that the emperor was only a *primus inter pares* and that the feudal aristocracy were highly jealous of their privileges. When Khri-srong lde-brtsan reached maturity he thoroughly justified the fears of the nobility and used

Buddhism and the Buddhist party at his court as a tool with which to establish his own absolutist regime. Obviously, a weak emperor would have fallen under the political pressure of the aristocracy as it took place during the reign of the later emperor Ral-pa-can. The aristocracy's politics allowed Bon to develop into a more sophisticated religion with its own written literature, translated into Tibetan with the help of priests invited from Zhang-zhung.

Khri-srong lde-brtsan had to be very cautious, and the Buddhist texts which Sang-shi had brought back from China were kept secret. An influential young Tibetan, gSal-snang, who also favored Buddhism, was appointed governor of the southern Tibetan province bordering Nepal. Here he established closer contacts with the Indian Buddhists, notably the famous Indian teacher Shāntirakshita, a representative of Mahāyāna philosophy and an important writer, whose basic works are still extant. Meanwhile, the Buddhist party at the capital had succeeded in getting rid of their prominent adversary, Ma-zhang Khrom-pa-sKyabs, by an evil stratagem which could hardly be called Buddhist. Consequently Shāntirakshita was invited to Tibet, and the banished Buddha image from the Jo-khang was triumphantly brought back to Lhasa. Because opposition to Buddhism was still strong, Shāntirakshita was able to spend only four months in Tibet. Before his departure he advised the emperor to send for a powerful magician, strong enough to overcome what he called the "evil spirits" of Tibet. This powerful tantric sage and exorcizer of demons was Padmasambhava of Uḍḍiyāna, a man well-suited to overcome all impediments. He is reported to have subjugated all the evil spirits and to have converted them to act henceforth as "protectors of the Buddhist law." While the foundation of bSam-yas seems to have been carried out under the supervision of Shāntirakshita, it was Padmasambhava who prevented the "demons" from destroying the rising walls and who by means of astrological calculations chose the right hours for special phases of the building activities. Judging from the different historical sources, his importance seems to have been exaggerated by the Buddhist tantric school which reveres him as its founder and glorified him later with the title of "the Second Buddha." bSam-yas was modeled after the Buddhist temple of Otantapurī, and was constructed according to the cosmographic ideas of Buddhism. The three-storied main temple with the Avalokiteshvara sanctuary was erected in the center to represent the world mountain Meru. In keeping with Buddhist cosmography, four different world continents surround the world mountain, one at each of the four directions, and four *stūpas* in white, red, black, and blue completed the cosmic symbolism as do the two temples of the sun and moon. The whole layout was enclosed by a great wall decorated with a multitude of miniature *stūpas*. Inside the sacred complex was also a chapel for the oracle god *Pehar* who in later times transferred his headquarters to a place near 'Bras-spungs in the neighborhood of Lhasa.

Following the foundation of bSam-yas, twelve Indian monks of the *Hīnayāna* sect of the Sarvāstivādins were invited, perhaps in order to counterbalance the magical tendencies of Padmasambhava. This important personage seems not to have stayed very long in Tibet. Certain chronicles express doubt about the capability of the Tibetans of that time to embrace the spiritual life. The first seven volunteer Tibetan monks were therefore known as "the Trial Candidates" (*sad-mi mi-bdun*), although all seven stood the test. Prominent among them was Vairocanarakshita, who devoted himself successfully to the translation of Buddhist texts. All these candidates were ordained by Shāntirakshita. According to Buddhist custom, this was reflected in the spiritual names they were given, all of which had the second component of -*rakshita* to record their relationship with the revered Indian Buddhist philosopher and guru. The foundation of bSam-yas was a landmark in the religious history of Tibet and was followed as early as 779 by the recognition of Buddhism as the state religion. This meant the complete victory of Khri-srong lde-brtsan over his feudal opponents (even if the struggle against Buddhism was not totally extinct), and the attitude of the emperor was later honored by incorporating him in the triad of the "Three Religious Kings," or Dharmarāja, as an incarnation of Mañjushrī, the Bodhisattva of wisdom and literature. The expulsion of the Bon-po priests was the logical consequence of these developments.

But the Buddhist-Bon-po struggle was not the only religious problem of this time requiring a solution. An internal struggle had developed among the Buddhists themselves, where disagreement in doctrinal points was connected with the struggle for power of two alien Buddhist schools: the Indian and the Chinese. Old records have revealed that considerable numbers of Chinese monks who followed the Ch'an tradition of Buddhist teachings gained great influence during the time of Khri-srong lde-brtsan. Quite a few names of these monks (Ho-shang, in Tibetan orthography Hva-shang) are listed in the *bKa-thang sde-lnga*. Their leader seems to have been the Ho-shang Mahāyāna or Mahāyāna-deva. The most controversial points which led to serious discussions concerned the path leading to *Nirvāṇa* and enlightenment. The adherents of Shāntirakshita, guided after his death by the Tibetan *Jnānendra,*   stressed the old *Mahāyāna* career of the Bodhisattva which led to the goal by way of the ten perfections (*pāramitā*) ascending from one degree of Bodhisattvahood (*bhūmi*) gradually (*rim-gyis*) to the next, eventually reaching the highest, the tenth. The method of the Chinese, *ch'an* (Japanese *zen*), is called in the Tibetan texts *cig-car.*

Much time has been spent by scholars in an effort to establish the exact meaning of this word which according to recent research means "simultaneous," although the meaning "instantaneous, sudden" cannot be excluded. Whether or not this semasiological problem has been solved correctly, the description of the way of reaching enlightenment is "sudden" as well as "simultaneous." "Sudden enlightenment" needs no explanation. It was totally and unreconcilably rejected by the adherents of the *bhūmi* doctrines because the traditional Buddhist virtues such as generosity, moral conduct, patience, effort, meditation, wisdom, etc., besides the study of the holy scriptures, would be totally superfluous. This attitude need not be explained by Tibetan sources on the Ch'an Buddhists, but very clear examples may be gathered from their own books. Thus it has been reported that the *ch'an* master Tê-shan reached sudden enlightenment when an old woman extinguished a candle and left him in complete darkness. The next day Tê-shan burnt the Buddhist *sūtras* which were now useless to him. This story reveals another typical feature of *ch'an*: a predilection for paradox and even the burlesque. But what "simultaneous enlightenment" means and what may be simultaneous in enlightenment needs further elucidation. According to some Tibetan scriptures the defilements in the "three spheres," i.e., the "sphere of desire" (*kāmadhātu*), "the sphere of forms" (*rūpadhātu*), and the "sphere of the formless" (*arūpadhātu*), are removed simultaneously. But we also find evidence of this in the biography of an Indian perfect saint (*siddha*) called Bhusuku, who reached enlightenment by the perception of the unity of body, speech, and thought and attained the goal "instantly" (here instead of the controversial expression *cig-car* the clear-cut term *sKad cig* "instantly" is used). The followers of Hva-shang Mahāyāna also frowned on theological learning and discursive thinking and stressed direct experience. This trend is very near to the doctrines of many Indian *mahāsiddha*, and although Indian chronology does not provide us with exact dates, the origin of Chinese *ch'an* seems also to go back to an Indian development. It is also quite possible that the symbiosis of this form of Buddhism with Chinese Taoism may have enforced the special trend of this school. Even if the legend of the introduction of the doctrine by the patriarch Bodhidharma, later called *ch'an* in China, is a later seventh-century fabrication, this by no means excludes the basically Indian origin of Chinese *ch'an*.

During the Sino-Tibetan Buddhist struggle a representative of this doctrine of "simultaneousness" visited Tibet. He was Vimalamitra, an Indian by birth and a close collaborator of Padmasambhava. To back the defenders of "gradualism," another high authority, the famous Kamalashīla, a disciple of Shāntirakshita, was invited from India by the Tibetan government. The whole controversy was decided in a lengthy public debate (792-94) in the presence of the Tibetan emperor as had been done once with the Bon-pos and Buddhists. According to Chinese sources the *Ch'an* monks were victorious, but according to the testimony of the Tibetan historiographers the Chinese were defeated. It may very well be possible that the Chinese adduced excellent arguments to prove their case, but the decision rested with the emperor and in his opinion the Chinese had been defeated. Consequently they had to leave the country; and it was proclaimed that in Tibet the Mādhyamika school of Nāgārjuna should be practiced as true, orthodox Buddhism, a statement which with respect to the preceding controversy was quite insignificant. The emperor and his entourage certainly were not in a position to judge the quality of theological arguments, and Khri-srong lde-brtsan's decision was merely a political one. This becomes obvious if one bears in mind that during the period in question Tibet was involved in a permanent war with the Chinese. At any rate this decision proved to be an event of great historical importance since it assured for the further development of Tibetan Buddhism the orthodox Pāramitā way and the close adherence to this special form of Indian Buddhism. This does not mean that the way of simultaneous and instantaneous enlightenment disappeared totally. It was the later bKa-brgyud-pa, and even more the rNying-ma-pa school of Tibetan Buddhism, which succeeded in maintaining that tradition. Most important in this field is the school of the "Great Perfection," the rDzogs-chen-pa.

In external politics and religious affairs the last years of Khri-srong lde-brtsan were less fortunate than the preceding ones as has been described earlier (pp. 44). After his death and that of his son Mune-btsan-po, his other son Sad-na-legs took the throne (see p. 55 ff). Though personally inclined to propagate Buddhism, he had to obey the wishes of the nobility during the early years of his reign, although officially the attitude toward Buddhism, which had remained the state religion, was not changed. But many Tibetans who had nominally converted to Buddhism actually adhered to the old religion in their heart, "while their bodies and their tongues practiced Buddhism." During the later reign of the emperor two Buddhist religious men, Myang Ting-nge-'dzin and especially Bran-ka dPal-yon, were very influential among the highest officials. This state of affairs continued under the emperor's son Ral-pa-can (815-838), who was certainly the most fervent Buddhist to sit on the emperor's throne and, like Khri-srong lde-brtsan and Srong-btsan sgam-po, was called a "Religious King." The Buddhists called him an incarnation of the Bodhisattva Vajrapāṇi (Tib. Phyag-na rdo-rje). His most important service to Buddhism was undoubtedly the interest he showed, like his father, in the encouragement of Buddhist literature. During the course of generations a tremendous number of texts had been translated, but it was now seen that the lack of uniformity of terminology had resulted in near chaos. It was not merely that the original texts had been translated from many languages (in addition to Sanskrit and the different Indian dialects, also from Chinese and from Khotanese) but that, more important, the primitive Tibetan language did not lend itself readily to the expression of complex philosophical ideas. Foreign translators of very disparate backgrounds and religious traditions had been involved and had translated the technical terms of Buddhism in various ways.

The creation of a uniform and universally valid literary language became an urgent necessity. A commission of scholars, set up by Ral-pa-can's father, had already worked on this difficult task with admirable skill, and apparently the work was completed during the reign of Ral-pa-can himself. Indian Pandits such as Jinamitra, Surendrabodhi, Shilendrabodhi, Dānashīla, and Bodhimitra were members of this commission and were assisted by Tibetan translators among whom Jnānasena (Ye-shes-sde), Ratnarakshita, Dharmatāshīla, etc., were outstanding. The names of these men are part and parcel of the history of Tibetan canonical literature. Even before beginning their work they compiled the Buddhist compendium *Mahāvyutpatti*, which established the authorized translation of every Buddhist name and technical term. During this period new translations of *Hīnayāna* and *Mahāyāna* writings were made (the texts of the "Lesser Vehicle" were those of the Mūla-Sarvāstivāda school). The translations made in earlier times by other scholars were subjected to a general revision and amended to bring them into line with what had now been laid down as standard terminology. The totality of the sacred writings was not yet brought together in a recognized canon such as the later Kanjur, but a list of titles was drawn up of those books which had obtained the imprimatur of the commission.

Undoubtedly Ral-pa-can rendered an outstanding service to Buddhist literature and Buddhism in general, but his personal relation to that religion was almost thraldom, and he left nothing undone to further the interest of the clergy or to afford them personal advantage. It is reported that his veneration for the priesthood was so excessive that he would humbly bow down at the feet of the priests and fasten silk ribbons to his hair, attaching the other ends to the seats on which the priests sat. This behavior offended Tibetan national sentiment, but much more important than such outward signs of subordination was the steadily growing power of the Buddhists, especially the chief minister, Bran-ka dPal-yon. A law was issued that seven Tibetan families must make themselves responsible for the maintenance of one Buddhist monk. Not only the common people but also the nobles were compelled to conform, outwardly at least, to Buddhist standards of morality. In the end popular resentment and anger burst out in violent anticlerical demonstrations, but the purblind emperor supported the Buddhist clergy recklessly and severely punished anyone who had been guilty of any offense against the monks. Some of the offenders had fingers hacked off; others even had their eyes put out. The effect of this brutal repression (so alien to the spirit of Buddhism) brought about a conspiracy among the Tibetan nobles led by the minister rGyal-to-re. Cleverly and systematically, the conspirators isolated the emperor before they delivered their decisive blow. Under various pretexts they succeeded in obtaining the banishment of the emperor's brother gTsad-ma, who had himself become a Buddhist monk. Charges were also made against Bran-ka dPal-yon, the chief minister, alleging that he was guilty of improper relations with one of the emperor's wives. Unfortunately, Ral-pa-can fell into the trap: the accused minister was put to death, and the lady in question committed suicide. When the nobles had succeeded in isolating the emperor and dispersing the Buddhist camarilla on which he had relied, they launched their coup: when the emperor was asleep, assassins broke into his apartment and murdered him in his bed.

The victorious conspirators enthroned Ral-pa-can's elder brother as the new emperor but his personality was no stronger than that of his predecessor. He leaned toward the nobles and the Bon-po just as Ral-pa-can had been partial to Buddhism. All the influential posts were now, of course, occupied by the conspirators and their friends. rGyal-to-re became chief minister, and immediately began a fierce campaign of oppression against Buddhism, at the same time doing everything possible to restore the Bon religion. Buddhist teachings were prohibited throughout the country, and the persecution extended even to the remotest parts of the empire. The work of translation which had been so promising was now, of course, stopped altogether; even the premises where it had taken place were destroyed. The solemn dedication of Ral-pa-can's newly built temple at On-cang-rdo did not take place as arranged, and even those sanctuaries which could look back on some tradition, those built under Srong-btsan sgam-po and Khri-srong lde-brtsan, were now deliberately exposed to public contempt. Their doors were bricked up, and the frescoes were painted over with pictures of beer-swilling monks in order to deprecate Buddhism in the eyes of the people. The numerous Buddha images, including those from the temple of Jo-khang, were removed. The original intention was to throw them into the water, but because of their weight the vandals contented themselves with burying them in the sand. The Chinese consort of Srong-btsan sgam-po was declared to be an evil spirit for it was she who had brought the most venerable of these images from China. The Jo-khang itself was turned into a cattle shed, and a rope was placed around the effigy of the Bodhisattva Vajrapāṇi, the "Master of Secrets." The wave of repression, of course, did not spare Buddhist literature, and many of the carefully translated texts were burned or thrown into the water. Nevertheless some part of the literary treasure was saved by hiding it away in caves in the neighborhood of Lhasa.

The fiercest fury was directed, of course, against the Buddhist monks. The Indian pandits who but recently enjoyed respect and even veneration were now compelled to seek safety in flight, and many Tibetan religious men fled with them. Among them one outstanding personage, Ting-nge-'dzin bzang-po, was killed by hired murderers. Those who remained behind had to give up their religion and priesthood. The new authorities took malicious pleasure in forcing the ex-monks to perform humiliating tasks, for example making them butchers, and sending them out to hunt with bows, arrows, and dogs.

But neither the persecution nor the reign of gLang-dar-ma were destined to last. A tantric hermit, dPal-gyi rdo-rje, killed the emperor with an arrow while he was reading an inscription on the big obelisk in front of the Jo-khang. As a true tantric, the murderer claimed that he had acted out of compassion: he wished to prevent the emperor from committing further sins, and thus help him to a better rebirth. The murderer made his escape without any impediment, and the capital was left in a state of utmost bewilderment. The prestige of the monarchy suffered severely from this series of murders. The overall results of the political and religious turmoil were that Buddhism was not immediately restored after the death of the apostate emperor, nor did the dynasty recover from the deadly blow. The once powerful and culturally developing country disintegrated and before long broke up into numerous small principalities, while the power of the central government could not make itself felt outside the capital.

Both Buddhism and the systematized Bon religion had received serious blows, and for almost a century and a half it looked as though Tibet would fall back into the original primitive condition from which Srong-btsan sgam-po had raised it.

BIBLIOGRAPHY

For some general books on Tibetan religion (dealing also with Buddhism), see the section of the bibliography entitled *The Diamond Vehicle*, below.

BUDDHISM IN GENERAL (only a selection of important books is quoted here)

Hermann Oldenberg, *Buddha. His Life, His Doctrine, His Order*, London 1882 (several reprints); T. Stcherbatsky, *The Central Conception of Buddhism and the Meaning of the Word Dharma*, London 1923; T. Stcherbatsky, *The Conception of Buddhist Nirvāna*, Leningrad 1927; Edward Conze, *Buddhism. Its Essence and Development*, Oxford 1951, also Harper Torchbook 1959; Edward Conze, *Buddhist Texts through the Ages*, Oxford 1954; Edward Conze, *Thirty Years of Buddhist Studies*, University of South Carolina Press, Columbia, S.C. 1968; André Bareau, *Les sectes bouddhiques du petit véhicule*, Saigon 1955; Nalinaksha Dutt, *Buddhist Sects in India*, Calcutta 1970; Sukumar Dutt, *Buddhist Monks and Monasteries of India*, London 1962; Louis de la Vallée Poussin, *Bouddhisme: études et matériaux*, Bruxelles 1896-98; Nalinaksha Dutt, *Aspects of Mahāyāna Buddhism and Its Relations to Hīnayāna*, London 1930; Marie-Thérèse de Mallmann, *Introduction à l'étude d'Avalokiteçvara*, Annales du Musée Guimet 57, Paris 1948; Étienne Lamotte, *Histoire du bouddhisme indien des origines à l'ère śaka*, Bibliothèque du Muséon, Louvain 1967.

THE DIAMOND VEHICLE

Anton Schiefner, *Târanâtha's Geschichte des Buddhismus in Indien*, Aus dem Tibetischen übersetzt, St. Petersburg 1869; Albert Grünwedel, *Tāranātha's Edelsteinmine. Das Buch von den Vermittlern der Sieben Inspirationen*, Bibliotheca Buddhica 18, Petrograd 1914; Albert Grünwedel, "Die Geschichten der vierundachtzig Zauberer (Mahāsiddhas), aus dem Tibetischen übersetzt," *BA*

V (1916): 137-228; Giuseppe Tucci, "Some Glosses upon the Guhyasamāja," *MCB* 3 (1935): 339-53; Ferdinand D. Lessing, *Yung-Ho-Kung. An Iconography of the Lamaist Cathedral in Peking*, vol. 1 (all published), *The Sino-Swedish Expedition* 8, 1. Stockholm 1942; S. B. Dasgupta, *An Introduction to Tantric Buddhism*, Calcutta 1950; Anagarika Govinda, "Solar and Lunar Symbolism in the Development of Stupa Architecture," *Marg* 4: 1 (Bombay 1950): 185ff.; Toni Schmidt, *The Eighty-five Siddhas*, Stockholm 1958; Anagarika Govinda, *Foundations of Tibetan Mysticism*, New York 1960; Giuseppe Tucci, "Oriental Notes," *EW* 14 (1963): 133-45; Agehananda Bharati, *The Tantric Tradition*, London 1965; P. H. Pott, *Yoga and Yantra. Their Interrelation and Their Significance for Indian Archaeology*, The Hague 1966; Edward Conze, "Buddhism and Gnosis," *Studies in the History of Religions (Supplements to Numen)* (1967): 651-67; Herbert V. Guenther, *The Royal Song of Saraha*, Seattle and London 1969.

EARLIEST TIBETAN BUDDHISM

W. W. Rockhill, *The Land of the Lamas*, London 1891; Albert Grünwedel, *Mythology of Buddhism in Tibet and Mongolia*, Leipzig 1900; Albert Grünwedel, *Die Tempel von Lhasa, SBHAW* no. 14, Heidelberg, 1919 (description of the old sanctuaries of Lhasa); Marcelle Lalou, "Les textes bouddhiques au temps du roi Khri-srong lde-bcan," *JA* (1953): 313-53; Giuseppe Tucci, "The Symbolism of the Temples of bSam-yas, *EW* 6 (1956): 279ff.; R. A. Stein, *Une chronique ancienne de bSam-yas: sBa-bžed*, Paris 1961; Paul Demiéville, *Le concile de Lhasa*, Paris 1952 (deals with the debate of bSam-yas according to Chinese sources); Giuseppe Tucci, *Minor Buddhist Texts II*, Roma 1958 (study of the bSam-yas debate according to Tibetan sources); R. A. Stein, "Illumination subite ou saisi simultanée. Note sur la terminologie chinoise et tibétaine," *RHR* 179: 1 (1971): 1-30 (concerning the bSam-yas debate).

LITERATURE ON PADMASAMBHAVA

Emil Schlagintweit, "Die Lebensbeschreibung von Padmasambhava," Teil 1/2, *AKBAW* 21 (1899): 417-44; 22 (1905): 517-76; Albert Grünwedel, "Ein Kapitel des Ta-she-sung," *Festschrift für Adolf Bastian*, Berlin 1896, pp. 461-82; Albert Grünwedel, "Drei Leptschatexte, mit Auszügen aus dem Pad ma thang yig," *TP* 7 (1896): 526-61; Albert Grünwedel, "Padmasambhava und Mandārava," *ZDMG* 52 (1898): 447-61; Berthold Laufer, "Die Bru-ža Sprache und die historische Stellung des Padmasambhava," *TP* (1908): 1-46; Berthold Laufer, *Der Roman einer tibetischen Königin*, Leipzig 1911; Albert Grünwedel, "Padmasambhava und Verwandtes," *BA* 3 (1912): 1-37; S. H. Ribbach, *Vier Bilder des Padmasambhava*, Mitteilungen aus dem Museum für Völkerkunde in Hamburg, 5. Beiheft, Hamburg 1917; G. C. Toussaint, *Le dict de Padma*, Paris

1933 (translation of Padmasambhava's biography); W. Y. Evans-Wentz, *The Tibetan Book of the Great Liberation*, London 1954 (contains an abstract of contents of a Bhutanese edition of Padmasambhava's biography); F. A. Bischoff and Charles Hartman, "Padmasambhava's Invention of the Phur-bu," Ms. Pelliot tibétain 44, *ETML*, pp. 11-28, Paris 1971; Anne-Marie Blondeau, "Le Lha-'dre bka'-thañ," *ETML*, pp. 29-126 (describes the suppression of Tibetan demons by Padmasambhava).

The "Second Propagation of the Doctrine"

The collapse of the Tibetan empire after the murder of gLang-dar-ma in 842 was accompanied by an almost universal disintegration of Tibetan Buddhist culture. The failure of the central authority to make its influence felt in eastern and western Tibet however, created possibilities for some kind of survival of Buddhism. In many regions Buddhism deteriorated very quickly, contaminated by its inherent magical tantric components. This Buddhism became a kind of left-handed tantra worship which indulged in coarse sexual rituals and sometimes even in human sacrifices, a development which might have been furthered by contact with non-Buddhist Shivaist doctrines. The paradoxical rituals of the old tantras translated during Imperial times were understood literally, and sacrifices of human sperm, blood, and feces were offered to the tantric gods. The few remaining genuine Buddhists abhorred these practices of the tantric celebrations which included the "Five Makāra," i.e., the five objects which in the Indian language begin with the syllable *ma: māmṣa* ("meat"), *matsya* ("fish"), *madya* ("intoxicating beverages"), *mudrā*, and *maithuna* ("sexual intercourse"). The original meaning of *mudrā* was "seeds of an aphrodisiac plant," but later the same word was used to denote a "consecrated woman." A few Buddhist devotees made their escape from central Tibet to Amdo in eastern Tibet, where they happened to meet with several like-minded Buddhists, both Tibetan and Chinese, and were able to be ordained according to the original rules of the *vinaya.* When the persecution of Buddhism in central Tibet came to an end, a group of genuine Buddhists returned to the Lhasa region and embarked on what was called later "the second propagation of the doctrine" (*phyi-dar*). The most eminent personages devoted to this work were dGongs-pa Rab-gsal and his disciple kLu-mes (circa 950-1025), who, after a century and a half of spiritual darkness, fostered a process which is called by the chronicles "the rising of Buddhism from the embers" (*me ro langs*).

The work of these enthusiasts was eventually strengthened by succour from western Tibet, where a scion of the old imperial dynasty, sKyid-lde ñi-ma-mgon, had established a new independent kingdom in Gu-ge (the center of the old Zhang-zhung state). The dynasty of this kingdom had been known for its zeal in the cause of Buddhism since the times of 'Khor-re, the grandson of the founder of the dynasty. The king himself became a Buddhist priest and took the name of "the Royal Monk," Ye-shes-'od ("Light of Knowledge"). As his two sons also became monks, the actual government was handed over to the king's brother, Srong-nge, although it is clear from the sources that Ye-shes-'od did not surrender power completely but remained head of state as priest-king, while Srong-nge took care of the current business of government under the title of viceroy.

Ye-shes-'od was very concerned about the debased form of contemporary Tibetan Buddhism. He regarded the philosophical teachings of the "Great

Vehicle" as the authentic word of Buddha and felt that many tantric practices of his time were of doubtful authenticity. Therefore he sought direct contact with India, the sacred country of the Buddhist religion, and had some of his subjects study under the guidance of the great Indian masters of the Buddhist law. He chose twenty-one young men, among whom was Rin-chen bzang-po (958-1055), who later achieved fame as a translator of Buddhist texts and for his activity in the erection of Buddhist temples in western Tibet. The party of youths set out for Kashmir, at that time a center of Buddhist tradition as important as Magadha in the east. As in many similar cases, most of the young Tibetans were unable to stand the climate of India, and after seven years Rin-chen bzang-po returned home with only one companion. The rest had died in India. The success of this first of Rin-chen bzang-po's great journeys, however, was complete. This talented man, later called the "Great Translator," had studied Buddhist Mahāyāna philosophy under various masters, but also many tantras of the so-called "New Tantra" type. (The other group, translated by the adherents of the Padmasambhava school, the "Old Tantras," were looked upon as not in accordance with genuine Buddhist doctrine.) Among the "New Tantras" the *Guhyasamāja* was of special importance, and the translator was able to obtain the cooperation of famous Indian masters like Shraddhākaravarman, Kamalagupta, etc., to translate a tremendous number of the Buddhist scriptures into Tibetan. It is clear from the above data that, far from being neglected, the study of the tantras was vigorously encouraged, although these mystical-magical practices were no longer performed in the coarse fashion which king Ye-shes-'od condemned. Rin-chen bzang-po is said to have studied under no less than seventy-five Indian pandits and to have made three journeys to India, the second of which took him to the holy places of Magadha, the country where the Buddha had done most of his preaching.

The importance of Rin-chen bzang-po is by no means confined to his translations, which also included the revision of old translations made during the reign of the great emperors. He was also the guiding spirit in the construction of numerous temples and monasteries begun by king Ye-shes-'od and his successors. Among the new religious buildings with which his name is connected are said to be the temples of Kha-char and the "Golden House" (*gSer-Khang*) in mTho-gling, the capital of the western Tibetan kingdom at that time. It received its name because on its eastern side there stood a golden stūpa which caught the rays of the rising sun and reflected them onto the sanctuary.

In the course of strengthening Tibetan Buddhism, Rin-chen bzang-po had to fight and subdue the cult of a water spirit (*kLu*), called sKar-rgyal, a survival of the Bon religion, the center of which had been for centuries in western Tibet.

The royal monk Ye-shes-'od was still unsatisfied with the results of his efforts to purify and consolidate Buddhism in his own country. Upon learning that the most famous Buddhist teacher of those times, whom the Tibetans called

Atīsha (Jo-bo-rje), "The Noble Lord," was residing at Vikramashīlā in Magadha, he sent messengers to invite him to Tibet. His first effort failed, for Atīsha's abbot refused him permission to leave. The untiring royal enthusiast then organized expeditions into the neighboring countries for the purpose of collecting a large amount of gold to offer to Atīsha and other famous Indian teachers. During one of these expeditions he was captured and taken prisoner by the Muslim Qarluq who at that time were very powerful in eastern Turkestan and adjacent regions. The Qarluq ruler declared that he would release his prisoner only if he would embrace Islam or could ransom himself with his weight in gold. The king's grand nephew, Byang-chub-'od, tried his best to liberate the prisoner, but he only had enough gold to ransom the body of the captured king, not his head. The chronicles record the moving conversation of the uncle and the grand nephew. Imprisoned in a terrible jail, the heroic Ye-shes-'od said he was now an old man broken by illness, and the young king should not waste gold on a man whose life was no longer of value in the cause of Buddhism. He advised Byang-chub-'od to use the gold he had collected to invite famous religious teachers to Tibet. Byang-chub-'od went away in tears, but willing to carry out the order of Ye-shes-'od, who subsequently was murdered in jail.

The intention of Ye-shes-'od to invite a Buddhist teacher of high standards to the kingdom of western Tibet was based to a large degree on his concern for the purification of the degenerated tantric Buddhism of his time, and it was because of this that he could not rest content with the enormous number of books which had been collected by Rin-chen bzang-po or with the doctrines that master had acquired through many initiations. Eventually Atīsha accepted an invitation to visit Tibet presented to him by another Tibetan mission to India, headed by the "Translator of Nag-tsho" (Nag-tsho Lo-tstsha-ba). The famous monk-scholar acquired the name Atīsha (Tib. Jo-bo-rje "the Noble Lord") because he was the son of a noble family.

Because Atīsha had a great impact on the further development of Buddhism in Tibet, it is necessary to deal with his religious education and life prior to his arrival in Tibet. According to his biography, based on data provided by Nag-tsho, his first religious experiences were within the field of Vajrayāna. It has been reported that even in his childhood he had a vision of the goddess Tārā who remained his tutelary deity throughout his lifetime. While still in his teens he was initiated by a tantric sage called Rāhulagupta at a place known as "the Black Mountain," possibly situated near Rājagriha. After this he listened to the tantric teachings of teachers like Avadhūtipā, also known as Maitripā, who was a forerunner of the later bKa-brgyud-pa school as well. The famous Virūpāksha was also among his Vajrayāna teachers, and we are informed that in a dream the young Atīsha swallowed the sun and moon, an indication that his religious activities during that time were certainly of a tantric nature. Later he felt the necessity of a normal Buddhist monk's career and became a novice at Nālandā and later a full monk (*dGe-slong*) and even "Master of the three Piṭaka" of the four classical Buddhist schools (Sarvāstivādin, Sthaviravādin, Mahāsānghika, and Sammitīya). Not satisfied with all the learning available in India, at age thirty-one he proceeded to Suvarṇadvīpa (present-day Sumatra), where at that time Buddhism flourished. He became the disciple of a famous teacher called Dharmakīrti, usually mentioned in the existent sources as Suvarṇadvīpin "the Man of Suvarṇadvīpa," with whom he studied for twelve years the practice of *bodhicitta*, i.e., the impetus needed for following the path of Bodhisattva. After his return to India he was summoned to the monastery or monastic university of Vikramashīlā where together with the abbot Ratnākara he soon occupied a most respected position.

Nag-tsho, and another Tibetan sent to Vikramashīlā to invite the venerable Atīsha, offered him a generous amount of gold. At first they met with refusal from the great Ratnākara, who was opposed to Atīsha's going abroad, but as Atīsha himself was much impressed by the persistence of the Tibetans he consulted his tutelary goddess, Tārā. She told him that his journey to Tibet would be for the benefit of numerous beings, and he finally accepted the invitation. Eventually the opposition of Ratnākara was overcome, although Nag-tsho had to promise that Atīsha would be allowed to return to India after a stay of three years. Atīsha and his party left Vikramashīlā in 1040. They spent about a year in Nepal where the master, honored by the king, worshipped the famous *stūpa* os Svayambhū Nāth. When they reached western Tibet in 1042, a grand reception was organized for him by the rulers of western Tibet, Byang-chub-od and the acting king, 'Od-lde, the elder brother of the monk-king. Atīsha's activities in western Tibet had, as we shall see, lasting effects.

Rin-chen bzang-po, who was twenty-four years older than the Indian master, was not at first ready to acknowledge the newcomer, but when Atīsha, viewing the wall paintings of the tantric deities in the temple of mTho-gling, extemporized laudatory verses in their honor, he humbly submitted to the Indian teacher and later was initiated by Atīsha into special methods of propitiation. These various events make it evident that Atīsha did not totally reject the tantric teachings of the Vajrayāna, but that his primary aim was to purify the debased forms of tantric worship. It was also to stress the basic teachings of the Mahāyāna, moral conduct, and the Bodhisattva way by means of the stages of perfection (*pāramitā*) and meditation. For the special use of the Tibetans he composed, among other works, his "Lamp for the Way of Enlightenment" (*Bodhipatha Pradīpa*) to which he added a large commentary stressing the practical method of acquiring enlightenment. In this text he distinguished between three personality types: the inferior, mediocre, and superior. The inferior man acts in every way with a view to worldly pleasures; the mediocre man is indifferent to pleasures and opposed to sinful acts; but the superior man not only follows the ideal of his individual salvation, but strives to help all sentient beings, which means that his efforts tend toward Bodhisattva-hood. The teachings of the *Bodhipatha Pradīpa* later became the basis for bTsong-kha-pa's *lam-rim* teachings.

An important event occurred when Atīsha met a religious man called rGyal-bai 'byung-gnas, more generally known as 'Brom-ston (1004-64). This man, who out of modesty simply called himself a Buddhist layman, also strove for improvement of the moral conduct of the Tibetan Buddhists of central Tibet, where the religion had begun to flourish again as a result of the previous activities of dGongs-pa rab-gsal and kLu-mes. When Atīsha was invited to come to the Lhasa province, Nag-tsho felt very concerned and pointed out that he had promised Ratnākara of Vikramashīlā that Atīsha would return to India after three years. But Atīsha pointed out that in special cases it is more important to help human beings than to fulfill a promise. Accordingly, the Indian master went to central Tibet and taught at important centers like bSam-yas, Yer-pa, Lhasa, and sNye-thang south of Lhasa, a small village where he died in 1054 after having instructed 'Brom-ston to complete his work. It was this great Tibetan Buddhist who finally succeeded in establishing Buddhism firmly in Tibet. In 1057 he founded the monastery of Rva-sgreng (pronounced Reting), which became a center of a new Buddhist school based on the teachings of Atīsha: the bKa-gdams-pa, "the School Based on the Direct Advice of the Teacher."

Atīsha's activity in Tibet was highly important for another reason: his work on chronology (1051). In this booklet the reckoning of dates according to the well-known animal cycle of twelve (hare, dragon, snake, horse, sheep, monkey, hen, dog, pig, mouse, ox, and tiger) in use throughout Inner Asia was complemented by a method which combined the twelve animals with the group of the five elements (fire, earth, iron, water, and wood), thus constituting a cycle of sixty years which allowed a much more accurate time computation. The first year of the first cycle of sixty years is the year A.D. 1027. Also about this time another great Vajrayāna Buddhist, Abhayākaragupta, wrote his "Comprehension of the Wheel of Time" (*Kālacakrāvatāra*). It seems that Atīsha did not actually introduce the new chronology but merely systematized and adapted it for use by the Tibetans. The system was introduced several years earlier by the "Translator of Gyi-jo" together with the Kālacakra (*Dus-kyi 'khor-lo*) on which the whole new chronology was based.

The Kālacakra "Wheel of the Time" tantric system represents the ultimate phase of the Vajrayāna in India and was introduced to that country from the northwest, i.e., from Buddhist countries inhabited by a non-Indian population. This is evident from its highly syncretistic nature. It obviously came from a country where the Buddhists were in contact with the adherents of other religions, such as Islam and Manicheism, for its basic sources mention Western prophets, e.g., Adam, Enoch, Abraham, Moses, Jesus, Mani, and Mohammed. The name "Wheel of Time" very probably indicates a chronological cycle.

Astronomy and astrology are the basis of the whole system, but the astrological elements are deified and raised to the status of a means to salvation. At the back of the Kālacakra also lies the ancient universal belief in the identity of microcosm and macrocosm, whose most condensed expression is contained in the famous magic symbol of "the Powerful One in Ten Forms" (*dashākāro vashī*). This symbol may be seen everywhere in Tibetan temples and comprises the elements of air, fire, water, earth, the central world mountain Meru, the "Sphere of Desire" (*kāmadhātu*), the "Sphere of Forms" (*rūpadhātu*), the "Sphere of the Formless" (*arūpadhātu*), the signs of the crescent and sun disk (the symbols of polarity), and, above all, the so-called planet Rāhu, which in the microcosmic field signifies the flame of the *unio mystica*.

The Kālacakra Tantra belongs to the class of so-called "Mother Tantras" which transmit the teachings concerning "Transcendental Wisdom" (*shes-rab*), while the "Father Tantras" are devoted to the active realization of the ideal of compassion (*karuṇā*). There is also a personification of Kālacakra as a deity of the Yi-dam type like that of Cakrasamvara and Guhyasamāja. Most important, however, is the Primordial Buddha (Ādibuddha), the concept of which now reaches the apogee of importance in the whole Vajrayāna.

According to the Kālacakra texts, Buddha preached this system in the "Sphere of the Absolute" (*Dharmadhātu*) at the *stūpa* of Dhānyakaṭaka near the delta of the river Kistnā either one year after his enlightenment or in his eightieth year (the sources are not consistent on this point). By some mysterious means, King Sucandra of the faraway country of Shambhala joined the audience of numerous Bodhisattvas and deities. One year later the basic text (*Mūlatantra*) of twelve thousand verses was recorded in Shambhala. Sucandra himself is regarded as the incarnation of the "Master of Secrets," the Bodhisattva Vajrapāṇi, the inspirer of several mystic Vajrayāna teachings. Originally the name Shambhala no doubt referred to a real country located somewhere outside India. As time went on it faded in the mind of the Tibetans into a purely mythical kingdom where, even during the worst world period, the true doctrine will be preserved and from where at the end of the present Kalpa the apocalyptic army will come and overthrow all enemies of Buddhism. These apocalyptic ideas are not in accordance with the cyclic thinking of Indian Hindu and Buddhist religions, but were borrowed from Iranian doctrines which were fully developed by the end of the Sasanian period. According to the sources, Shambhala was situated somewhere to the north of the river Sītā which in later books certainly represents the river Tarim, but may have been identified during the earlier periods with either Amu Darya or Syr Darya in western Turkestan. Shambhala is described as being surrounded by eight snow-capped mountain ranges resembling an eight-petalled lotus. In the center of this lotus lies the capital with the king's palace called *Kalāpa*, and to the south of this is a great park in which is situated a *maṇḍala* of the Kālacakra built by King Sucandra.

According to tradition, Sucandra was the first in a lineage of seven "Priest-Kings" of Shambhala, who were succeeded by a line of twenty-five rulers known as Kalki, each of whom reigned for one hundred years. The conception of Kalki seems to have been borrowed from Hinduism in which there is only one Kalki, the tenth and last incarnation of the god Vishnu. This Hindu Kalki is also an apocalyptic hero whose origins go back to the time when India suffered greatly from incursions of foreign, mostly Iranian, peoples such as, the Saka, Kushāṇa, and White Huns. The twenty-fifth and last Kalki, Rudra Cakrin ("Rudra with the Wheel"), will ascend the throne of Shambhala in the year 2327 of our era, and his task will be to destroy all enemies of Buddhism, especially the hated Muslims, in a tremendous battle which is described in glowing apocalyptic colors. These future hopes are alive in the minds of many Tibetans and Mongols even today.

Tibetan historians agree that the Kālacakra was introduced into India sixty years before its arrival in Tibet. Since the year 1026 is accepted as the time of its official introduction into Tibet, this would mean that it penetrated into India in the year 966. However, there is a great deal of inconsistency in the sources regarding the master who first brought the new teachings to India, and a careful study of the respective sources as preserved by the different Tibetan religious schools (the rNying-ma-pa, bKa-brgyud-pa, Jo-nang-pa, and dGe-lugs-pa) should be devoted to this subject. This first guru of the Kālacakra teachings is variously called Tsi-lu-pa, Pi-ṭo-pa, or the "Great (i.e., older) Kālacakrapāda." The last name is probably the right one, while the other two are open to controversy. A historical Buddhist teacher, Nāropā, was initiated by him; and in the Tibetan Canon commentaries written by Nāropā on Kālacakra doctrines actually do exist. From our sources we learn that the first Kālacakra teacher in India travelled miraculously to Shambhala where he was initiated by the Kalki king. After returning to India he proceeded to the monastery of Nālandā, where he wrote the macrocosm-microcosm symbol of Kālacakra over the gate of that monastery, and below the symbol he inscribed several statements concerning the Ādibuddha teachings of the new system. Nāropā and five hundred pandits were defeated in a disputation by the Kālacakra teacher and accepted his doctrines.

The first introduction of the Kālacakra by the "Translator of Gyi-jo" who had studied the subject under Bhadrabodhi, a disciple of Tsi-lu-pa, had little impact. He had only four pupils, and even they did not maintain the tradition. A second and more important chain of teachers, however, began with the Kashmirian guru Somanātha, who was invited by the translator 'Bro Shes-rab-grags. Because of the activities of these two men the greatest representative commentary of the tantra, the "Immaculate Lustre" (*Vimalaprabhā*), was translated into Tibetan. 'Bro Shes-rab-grags established the 'Bro school of the Kālacakra tradition. The second important chain of gurus was founded by Rva Chos-rab and was called "the School of Rva." This scholar studied in Kashmir with the pandit Samantashrī, a former pupil of Nāropā. The Rva school was to become particularly significant because of the later Buddhist sects of the Sa-skya-pa and the Jo-nang-pa. The latter in particular was given to the mystical experiences of the Kālacakra. To this line of tradition belongs also the famous "omniscient" Bu-ston, whose extensive writings on the subject are still much appreciated by the Tibetans.

BIBLIOGRAPHY

THE LATER INTRODUCTION OF BUDDHISM

Giuseppe Tucci, *Indo-Tibetica II, Rin c'en bzang po e la rinascità del Buddhismo intorno al mille*, Roma 1933; Giuseppe Tucci, *Indo-Tibetica III, part 2: I templi del Tibet occidentale e il loro simbolismo artistico, Tsaparang*, Roma 1936 (description of west Tibetan temples connected with the activities of Rin-chen bzang-po); Helmut Hoffmann, "Die Qarluq in der tibetischen Literatur," *Oriens* 3 (1950): 190-203 (contains materials concerning the pious king Ye-shes-od); Alaka Chattopadhyaya, *Atīśa and Tibet*, Calcutta 1967; Sarat Chandra Das, *Indian Pandits in the Land of Snow*, 2nd ed., Calcutta 1965.

MATERIALS ON THE KĀLACAKRA

Alexander Csoma de Körös, "*Note on the origin of the Kāla Chakra and Ādi-Buddha Systems*," *JASB* 2 (1833): 57-59; Albert Grünwedel, *Der Weg nach Shambhala*, AKBAW 1915, no. 3, München 1915; George N. Roerich, "Studies in the Kālacakra," *Urusvati Journal* 2 (1932): 153-64; Biswanath Bandyopadhyaya, "A Note on the Kālacakratantra and its Commentary," *JASB*, N.S. 18 (1952): 71-76; G. N. Roerich, *The Blue Annals of gZhon-nu-dpal*, vol. 2, Calcutta 1953 (pp. 753-838 contain important data on Kālacakra); Mario E. Carelli, *Sekoddeśaṭīkā. Being a commentary of the Sekoddeśa Section of the Kālacakra Tantra*, Sanskrit text edited with an introduction, Gaekwad Oriental Series XC, Baroda 1941; Helmut Hoffmann, "Literarhistorische Bemerkungen zur Sekoddeśaṭīkā des Nāḍapāda," *Beiträge zur indischen Philologie und Altertumskunde. Festschrift Walther Schubring*, Hamburg 1951, pp. 140-47; Helmut Hoffmann, "Das Kâlacakra, die letzte Phase des Buddhismus in Indien," *Saeculum* 15 (1964): 125-31; Klaus Hahlweg, "Der Dhânyakaṭaka-Stûpa," *ZDMG* 115 (1965): 320-26 (translation of a treatise by Klong-rdol bLa-ma on the famous stûpa, but with a wrong identification of the site); Raghu Vira and Lokesh Chandra, *Kalacakra Tantra and Other Texts*, 2 vols., Satapitaka series vol. 69, New Delhi 1966 (texts in Sanskrit, Tibetan, and Mongolian); André Bareau, "Le stūpa de Dhānya Kaṭaka," *AAS* 16 (1967): 81-88; Helmut H. R. Hoffmann, "Kālacakra Studies I, Manichaeism, Christianity, and Islam in the Kālacakra Tantra," *CAJ* 13 (1969): 52-73; 15 (1972), pp. 298-301.

ON KĀLACAKRA RECKONING OF TIME AND ASTRONOMY

Paul Pelliot, "Le cycle sexagénaire dans la chronologie tibétaine," *JA* (1913): 633-67; Berthold Laufer, "The Application of the Tibetan Sexagenary Cycle," *TP* (1913): 569-96; A. von Staël-Holstein, "On the Sexagenary Cycle of the Tibetans," *MS* 1 (1935/36): 277-314; Winfried Petri, "Uigur and Tibetan Lists of the Lunar Mansions," *Indian Journal of History of Science* 1 (1966): pp. 83-90; Winfried Petri, "Colours of Lunar Eclipses According to Indian Tradition," *Indian Journal of History of Science* 3 (1968): 91-98 (also uses Tibetan material); Winfried Petri, "Tibetan Astronomy," *Vistas in Astronomy*, vol. 9, 1968, pp. 159-64.

The Development of the Tibetan Buddhist Schools

The bKa-gdams-pa

    As Atīsha himself founded no special school of Buddhism, this task was left to 'Brom-ston (1005-1064), who not only erected the monastery of Rva-sgreng, but was regarded as the first teacher of the bKa-gdams-pa school.

    This school received its name because it held fast to the authoritative word of the master Atīsha and of Poto-ba (died 1082), the important third abbot of the monastery. These traditions were concerned primarily with the cleansing of the mind and the implementation of moral conduct and esoteric principles as given in Atīsha's *Lamp for the Way of Enlightenment*. They were less engaged in complicated theories as developed by the school of Nāgārjuna and Asanga than in trying to guide the individual to the perception of the nature of mind and the Void. This knowledge of the Void was regarded as the "reaching of the utmost limit" (*mt'ar t'ug*), but the theory and practice of the esoteric doctrines were by no means neglected. 'Brom-ston studied under four other spiritual leaders besides Atīsha. He himself was venerated as the incarnation of Avalokiteshvara, and the cult of this Bodhisattva continued to be most important among the later *dGe-lugs-pa* who inherited the traditions of the *bKa-gdams-pa,* calling themselves "the New *bKa-gdams-pa* School." Po-to-ba founded a monastery in the 'Phan-yul province to the north of Lhasa which was named after him. A considerable number of the *bKa-gdams-pa* centers arose in the neighborhood of this monastery, and 'Phan-yul was regarded as the classic stronghold of the school.

    In general, the religious institutions of the bKa-gdams-pa were noted for their moral strictness and in this respect certainly followed the tradition of Atīsha. This did not prevent the followers of the sect from enjoying a high reputation as experts on ritual which had penetrated deep into the philosophically based tantric teachings. It is reported that most of these lamas had looked on the faces of numerous Bodhisattvas and gods in their meditation. The followers of 'Brom-ston regarded as the seven basic elements of their doctrine the three sections of the traditional Buddhist collections of the doctrine (*Tripiṭaka*); the person of the historic Buddha Shākyamuni; Avalokiteshvara, the great Boddhisattva of mercy; his female counterpart, the goddess Tārā; and as their special tutelary deity, Acala (Tib. Mi-gyo-ba), the "King of Religion."

The Zhi-byed-pa

    The *bKa-gdams-pa* played no role in the secular historical developments which later transformed Tibet into a theocratic state, nor did the Zhi-byed-pa school, founded at about the same time. Its name was derived from one of its basic esoteric traditions, *zhi-byed,* ("bringing to peace and disappearance all misery and suffering by the incantations of their mantras"). This school goes back to a South Indian teacher, Pha-dam-pa Sangs-rgyas ("Illustrious Father

Buddha") and his Tibetan disciple, rMa Chos-gshes, who met the master in 1073. Pha-dam-pa had been a monk in the monastery of Vikramashīlā and, like Atīsha, he was introduced to mysticism by Suvarṇadvīpin of Indonesia, but also by other gurus. He devoted himself to meditation and the conjuration of tantric gods in many parts of India, including Bōdh Gayā where the Buddha had received enlightenment, and in one of the famous eight cemeteries of India, the Shītavana or "Cool Grove," which in earlier times was also visited, according to tradition, by Padmasambhava. He mastered not only the eight lower "perfections" (*siddhi*), i.e., walking beneath the earth, the power of the magical sword, the destroying of impediments, the ability to make a person pliable, the production of pills which cause invisibility, the eye ointment by which it is possible to find hidden things, the detection of treasures, and the "swift feet" or "seven league boots," but also the highest *siddhi* pertaining to a perfect saint. He was believed to have looked on the face of twelve deities, including Mañjushrī, Avalokiteshvara, and Tārā.

According to one tradition, Pha-dam-pa paid seven visits to Tibet though other sources speak of only three. When he visited Tibet for the first time he was not thought to be a Buddhist but one of the Shivaist ascetics who frequented the Kailās area, a detail which shows how different from the bKa-gdams-pa path was his own approach to Buddhism. He taught that the mind should not love the body nor should the body love the mind. Mind and body should be free to rest in themselves. In 1117 Pha-dam-pa founded a monastery near the little town of Ding-ri close to the Nepalese border.

Another important teaching of Pha-dam-pa was the so-called *gCod* (the abscission of all the roots of defilements), which developed two branches: the male *gCod* and the female *gCod*. The outstanding representative of the second one was Ma-gcig lab-sgron ("Unique Mother, Lamp of Eloquence"), who met Pha-dam-pa during his third stay in Tibet (1055). The goal of *gCod* is the destruction of the dichotomy of the mind and the phenomenal world which is identical with that of subject and object. This also implies liberation from the dichotomy of good and evil, and therefore from all illusions (*sgyu-ma*). This typical Vajrayānist goal is attained by special Yogic practices carried out at lonely and terrifying places, such as cemeteries, where the adept intends to experience the fact that all gods and demons are simply emanations of thought created by the power of imagination. The human body which itself is unreal must be sacrificed to the likewise unreal demons by a psychologically awe-inspiring process. *gCod* has been appropriately called a mystic drama with one actor, the conjuring mystic himself, and only during the course of the proceedings is he joined by unearthly beings and demons created by his imagination. Certain magic equipment is necessary for the ritual: a small double drum (*ḍamaru*) made of two calottes, a flute made from a human thigh bone (*rKang-gling*), a bell, and a symbolic tent which has to be erected in a certain prescribed fashion. First, in the morning the adept celebrates the so-called "white sacrificial repast" during which his body is converted into nectar and offered to the "Three Precious Ones" (*Triratna*); during the day it is followed by the "speckled sacrificial repast," which implies that the body is imagined to have become a garden, food, and garments for the "protector deities" (*mgon-po*) like Mahākāla. At dusk the "red" ritual takes place, and flesh and blood are sacrificed to the evil demons. The "black repast" during the night, the most terrifying of all, means sacrificing one's own body as a compensation for a selfish life and selfish actions through the aeons. Similar to the process of the "awakening" of a *maṇḍala,* a goddess created by the imagination rises from and severs the adept's head. The body is then cut into pieces and offered to the accompaniment of the following words: "The day has come on which my debt must be paid. Therefore, I offer up as sacrifice this so-beloved body of mine. I give my body to the hungry, my blood to the thirsty, my skin to the naked, and my bones as fuel to those who suffer from cold. . . . Shame on me if I draw back from this sacrifice! Shame on all who hesitate to accept it." Understandably this ritual has been compared to a similar one in shamanism, where the shaman in the course of his initiation is cut into pieces during his trance experiences.

The Zhi-byed-pa did not long exist as an independent sect; its teachings were taken over by other schools, especially by the rNying-ma-pa.

The Sa-skya-pa and the First Missionary Activity Among the Mongols

The Sa-skya-pa school received its name from the monastery of Sa-skya in gTsang, founded in 1073 by 'Khon dKon-mchog rgyal-po. It played a much greater role in church organization than the two aforementioned sects. The teaching of this school, the "cause" (*rgyu*) and "fruit or effect" (*'bras*) doctrine, goes back to the "translator of 'Brog-mi," who studied in India under Virūpāksha and was the most important teacher of the founder of the Sa-skya monastery. The tutelary deity of the Sa-skya-pa is either Hevajra or Vajrakīla (rDo-rje phur-pa). The Bodhisattva Manjushrī is also of great significance in this school, as is seen from its traditional beliefs that seven reincarnations of Mañjushrī have appeared in the lineage of dKon-mchog rgyal-po, whose family is traced back to the country of Bru-sha (Gilgit).

The central concepts of the Sa-skya-pa teachings are obviously derived from the "Thought Only" (*cittamātra*) teachings of the Yogacāra, as is the case with several other sects of Tibetan Buddhism such as the bKa-brgyud-pa, differences being but minor. According to Sa-skya-pa teachings, "Thought Energy" or "Mind" is of a luminous nature, while the Absolute, the "Void," is the essence of thought. Luminosity cannot be derived from the Void or vice versa. The coincidence of these two principles in a doctrine of "photism" denotes the means for reaching the extreme limit by thought (*sems*). According to the Sa-skya hierarch bSod-nams rtse-mo (1142-82), who gave a comprehensive description of the sect's esoteric doctrine, thought is beyond all duality, beyond beginning, permanence, or end, and beyond discursive thinking (*rnam-rtog*). It is thus described in negative terms only, as is usual in most of the Buddhist sects. *Sems* is marked by three immanences. For "cause" (*rgyu*), it is innate luminosity; for the "way" (*lam*), the adept, using the highest class of tantras (Anuttarayoga) through the "process of unfoldment" (*utpannakrama*) and the "process of integration" or "state of perfection" (*sampanna-krama*), realizes first luminosity and then "voidness." Having by meditation obtained the "effect" (*'bras-bu*), the process culminates in the identity of the apparitional body (*sprul-sku*) and luminosity, and of voidness and the Dharmakāya. Therefore all phenomena appear only in the mind, and because in the mind duality is impossible, all appearances are only deceptions or a kind of magical play.

Especially significant for the development of a spiritual and secular hierarchy was Kun-dga rgyal-mtshan, usually known as Sa-skya Paṇḍita (1182-1253). It was this hierarch who established relations with the rising world power of the Mongols. The Mongol armies seem not to have penetrated to the center of Tibet at that time, and the correspondence which is supposed to have passed between the great conqueror Chingis khan and Sa-skya Paṇḍita is probably only a pious invention. On the other hand, the Sa-skya abbot was actually invited to the court of the Mongol prince Godan, and it is reported that the High Lama cured the prince of a serious sickness by reciting a powerful spell (1244). Sa-skya Paṇḍita succeeded in arousing the friendly interest of this descendant of the Great Khan in the cause of Buddhism, and later Buddhism was to become as culturally important for the Mongol nomads as it had been for the Tibetans in the days of Srong-btsan sgam-po.

The nephew of Sa-skya Paṇḍita, the lama 'Phags-pa (1235-80), completed the work of his uncle, and about A.D. 1260 succeeded in obtaining the unconditional recognition of the secular dominance of the Sa-skya lamas over all three Tibetan districts (*chol-kha*) of the great Mongol emperor Khubilai. This event took place when 'Phags-pa, like his uncle an eminent Buddhist scholar, was invited by the Great Khan, the first of the Mongol emperors to rule over the whole of China. 'Phags-pa visited the emperor at his court and, according to the records, conducted himself proudly, insisting on his equality in rank with the emperor. Thanks to the mediation of one of Khubilai's wives, the two finally came to an understanding whereby in all spiritual and Tibetan affairs the Grand Lama should take precedence, while in all secular affairs of concern to the great Mongol empire the emperor should be supreme.

An interesting discussion between the emperor and the lama on historical matters is recorded. In order to stress his high position 'Phags-pa reminded the emperor that the kings of Tibet once ruled over two thirds of Jambudvīpa, that they had defeated China, and that on the re-establishment of peaceful relations a Chinese princess had come to Tibet with the famous Buddha image, the Jo-bo.

'Phags-pa thus showed himself an expert in the earlier history of his country. It is known that 'Phags-pa pursued historical studies, and a treatise of his called "Genealogy of the Tibetan Kings" has come down to our times. The emperor doubted what 'Phags-pa had told him and had his Chinese scholars consult the pertinent historical documents, i.e., the annals of the T'ang dynasty, where they found the statements of the hierarch brilliantly confirmed. Thereafter the emperor had full confidence in his distinguished guest and allowed himself, with a number of his notables, to be initiated in the Hevajra cycle. 'Phags-pa was also appointed "Imperial Teacher" (*ti-shih*). This report is also quite probably true, because, although for political reasons the Mongol rulers tolerated and even encouraged many religions, including Islam and Nestorian Christianity, they did show a special leaning toward Buddhism, with which they were already acquainted through their Uighur subjects.

As a consequence, as we have seen (p. 54), Khubilai not only gave jurisdiction over the whole of Tibet to the Sa-skya lamas, but also proposed to enact a law compelling all Buddhists to embrace the Sa-skya form of the doctrine. It is very characteristic that 'Phags-pa dissuaded him, beseeching him to allow everyone to follow his own conscience according to ancient Buddhist custom; for Buddhism has never shown a tendency to establish a compulsory dogma for all its adherents. The privileges 'Phags-pa obtained were of very real significance: exemption of the monasteries from all taxation, and an order to the famous Mongol couriers to cease using the houses of the clergy as posting stations. These privileges were continued under the successors of Khubilai; but when Mongol power waned the influence of the Sa-skya-pa in Tibet also decreased, and the Phag-mo gru-pa, originally a branch of the bKa-brgyud-pa, deprived their former overlords of power (1354).

'Phags-pa had also pleased the emperor by providing the Mongols with an alphabet modeled on the Tibetan script but written vertically so that it could be used in government documents along with Chinese. Since this "square script" was used only in official inscriptions and documents, it was discarded after A.D. 1300 in favor of that of another Sa-skya lama, Chos-sku od-zer, who based his alphabet on the Uighur script.

In later times a split occurred among the Sa-skya-pa, and the members of the Ngor monastery (founded in 1429 by Kun-dga bzang-po) established their independence as a separate sect.

The moral status of the Sa-skya-pa does not seem to have been particularly high in the later period. The exhortations of Atīsha for sterner monastic discipline and strict celibacy were largely ignored. In general the monks of the big monasteries conducted themselves in a very worldly fashion. The great religious communities were less centers of religious endeavors than strongholds in the struggles between the rival sects.

The bKa-brgyud-pa

The school of the bKa-brgyud-pa is based, as shown by its name, on the oral tradition of its gurus, i.e., on secret, esoteric teachings passed on from teacher to disciple by word of mouth. Although mystic and magical doctrines are the very heart of these traditions, the "steps of Bodhi" have not been neglected as is shown by the *Jewel Ornament of Liberation* by sGam-po-pa, the third guru of the Tibetan spiritual lineage. The sect was founded by Mar-pa of Lho-brag (1012-98), often called "Mar-pa the Translator," who received his initiation from one of the most famous Vajrayāna teachers of the time, Nā-ro-pā (Skr. *Nāḍapāda*). He had already learned Sanskrit at the age of fifteen from 'Brog-mi lo-tstsha-ba, who was also the spiritual master of the founder of the Sa-skya monastery. While still a young man he sold all his possessions for gold with the help of which he made his way to India. There he found his guru, Nā-ro-pā, at Phullahari, not far from the famous monastery of Nālandā. He was given a joyful reception by the great Vajrayāna teacher and initiated into profound doctrines, especially the tantric cycle of Cakrasamvara, the tutelary deity of the bKa-brgyud-pa school. He was also sent by his guru to other *siddhas* and introduced to the *Guhyasamāja* tantra, the *Tantra of the Great Illusion* (*Mahāmāya* tantra), bestowed upon him by the strange "dog ascetic" Kukuri-pa, who lived alone on an uninhabited island in a poisonous lake. By Maitri-pa (also called Advayavajra) he was taught the Doctrine of *Mahāmudrā*, the "Great Symbol," which means the convergence of the universe in the highest consciousness. One of the most important doctrines Mar-pa received from his main teacher was called—in the bKa-brgyud-pa tradition—"The Six Principles of Nā-ro-pā" (*Nā-ro chos-drug*). It comprised the doctrine of the "Inner Yoga Fire" (*gTum-mo*), the "Illusory Body" (*sGyu-lus*), the "Dream State" (*rMi-lam*), the "Clear Light" (*Od-gsal*), the "Intermediate State" between two incarnations (*Bar-do*), and the "Transference of Consciousness" (*'Pho-ba*).

Because the "Six Principles of Na-ro-pā" have been adopted not only by the bKa-brgyud-pa but by all other schools of Tibetan Buddhism, including even the reformed school of the Yellow Church, a short elucidation of the "Principles" should be given here. The "Mystical Heat" or the "Inner Yogic Fire" means an intentional increase of the body temperature by forcing the vital energy, the carrier of the "Thought of enlightenment" (*bodhicitta*), from the two mystical arteries *rasanā* (Tib. *ro-ma*) and *lalanā* (*brKyang-ma*) into the central artery (*avadhūti,* Tib. *dbU-ma*), which the *bodhicitta* ascends through all the body lotus centers (*cakra*). The doctrine of the "Illusory Body" (*sGyu-lus*) implies the assumption of a subtle body basically different from the ordinary "coarse" body which consists of the "five heaps" (*skandhāḥ*) or constituents of the perishable outer body: *kāya* (the body), *vedanā* (feelings), *samjñā* (perception), *samskārāḥ* (impulses which are the cause of rebirth if not mastered by meditation and cleansed from all the engrams of defilements), which develops its innate luminous character and becomes a "pure magical body" ascending to the highest status of the Perfections (*pāramitā*) and producing eventually the *vajrakāya* (*rdo rjei sku*) and thereby salvation. In the "Dream State" the illusory manifestations of the dream are used as vehicles of salvation. If the adept has already visualized in his wakeful state the identification of *vajradhara* (the male cosmic component) and *prajñā* (wisdom, female cosmic component), a hexagram (*chos-'byung*) consisting of a white and red triangle appears below his navel. By this process, even in a dream the yogin plunges into the state of the *unio mystica* and experiences the fourth principle, the "Clear or Radiant Light," which is identical with the now-purified mind (*sems,* Skr. *citta*). Beyond all duality is at the same time the experience of immeasurable light and the primordial "sound" which contains potentially all possible sounds. The "Intermediate State" (*bar-do,* Skr. *antarābhava*) means the condition the adept (like all humans) experiences after his earthly death. Even in this state man may reach the "radiant light" if he has purified his mind (*sems*) by yogic training. If this is not possible he may be helped by a lama to obtain at least a favorable rebirth by whispering the teachings of the so-called "Book of the Dead" into his ear. Different forms of this teaching are found among the literatures of the different Tibetan Buddhist schools. The Transference of Consciousness takes place at the very moment of death, but this will be possible only if the adept has already trained himself during his lifetime in the "art of dying" (*ars moriendi*). The transference of the mind takes place by the repeated pronunciation of the mantra *hik,* by which the mind through the fontanel leaves the space which is covered with a membrane at angles between the bones of the skull. If the yogin does this only for provisional exercise, the sems returns by the pronunciation of the mantra *Ka.* An example of transference of the mind into a corpse will be given below in connection with the activities of the guru Mar-pa.

The untiring Mar-pa did not rest content with his first stay in India but returned twice to the mother country of Buddhism to obtain more spiritual instruction and to bring to Tibet more sacred books of the Vajrayāna tradition which he later translated. In Tibet he also met Atīsha but did not accept his teachings. In one mystic teaching Mar-pa was disobedient. He refused Nā-ro-pā's order to initiate his main disciple, the hermit and poet Mi-la ras-pa, into the practice of the "Transference of Consciousness," or more specifically, the *Grong-'jug,* the ability to transfer consciousness of a dying person to another body. Out of paternal love he bestowed this initiation upon his own son, Dar-ma mdo-sde, and was punished therefore by the premature death of his son. According to a legend, there was no other human corpse in the neighborhood, and consequently the consciousness had to pass into the body of a dove.

To trace the bKa-rgyud-pa school back to its origin, some data must be given concerning the two inspiring Indian gurus of the sect. Ti-lo-pā (also written

Tilli-pā) received his initiation directly from the Adibuddha Vajradhara (Tib. rDo-rje 'chang), and the circumstances of his initiation, though legendary, prove to be very informative for the Buddhist school in question. When Ti-lo-pā grew tired of the "cycle of life," or *sansāra*, he was ordained as a monk and devoted his life to Buddhist studies. One day a horrible, bearded old woman appeared before him and asked him whether he would like to receive the necessary spiritual instructions (*upadesha*) for his studies. Ti-lo-pâ immediately recognized this old crone as an initiation goddess, a *ḍākinī*, and begged for her instructions. The old woman now observed that the normal Mahāyāna way of the "Six Perfections" (*pāramitā*) was extremely onerous and progress on this way very slow. On the other hand, the direct path of the "Vehicle of Mantras and the *vajra*" involved fewer hindrances and would quickly lead him to his goal—liberation. She then initiated him into the *maṇḍala* of the God of Wisdom, *Cakrasamvara* (Tib. *'Khor-lo sdom-pa*), who mysteriously appeared in the air before him.

In another story found also in the biography of Padmasambhava, which was certainly borrowed from the bKa-rgyud-pa school, it is stated that the *ḍākinī* instructed Ti-lo-pā to proceed to the land of the queen of the *ḍākinīs*. To aid him on his journey, the *ḍakīnī* taught him a magic formula which enabled him to overcome all the dangers he met on his "Direct Path" terrible deserts, tumultuous waterfalls, fearful chasms, murderous demons, and deceptive wills-o'-the-wisp. After many trials and tribulations he finally made his way to the palace of the *ḍākinī* queen, whose walls of metal gave forth a tremendous heat and brilliance. But neither this nor other terrors discouraged him, and he forced his way into the enchanted palace, walking through endless, splendid apartments until finally he reached the queen. She sat on her throne in superb beauty, bedecked with jewels, and smiled gently at the brave adept. But he kept repeating his magic formula, ripped off the queen's jewels and clothing, and raped her. This fantastic and highly symbolical story, a reflection of meditative experiences, may be regarded as typical, and recalls parallel stories in the legends of other peoples. Due to his success Ti-lo-pā mastered the "Inner Magic Heat" (*gTum-mo*), which results from forcing the vital energy from the two mystic side arteries (*rasanā* and *lalanā*) into the central artery, the *avadhūti*.

Ti-lo-pā's main disciple and the second guru of the bKa-brgyud-pa school, the above-mentioned Nā-ro-pā, was also summoned by an old ugly witch-like *ḍākinī*, who told him to seek his predestined guru in the eastern part of India. Because Nā-ro-pā had committed sins by using black magic, his spiritual path was even more horrible than that of his teacher. He had to pass through many major and minor trials. The teacher ordered him to jump down from the roof of a huge temple (but when he lay on the earth with a crushed body Ti-lo-pā restored his health). He was forced to rob and steal for the guru and was almost beaten to death. He had to stay in a pool full of blood-sucking leeches. Another time, the guru pressed burning torches into his body. All these cruel experiences had to be undergone for the purification of the neophyte's mind and as a test of confidence and devotion to the guru. Only after endless suffering was Nā-ro-pā eventually initiated into all the secret doctrines. It seems most probable that the tantric teachings which Nā-ro-pā obtained from his teacher included the Kālacakra, since one literary source of the bKa-brgyud-pa states that Ti-lo-pā is identical with the saint Tsi-lu-pa or Mahākālacakrapāda who was the first to introduce that system into India. Several commentaries by Nā-ro-pā demonstrate his relations with the Kālacakra and are found in the Tibetan Canon, and several later authors of the bKa-brgyud-pa have maintained the tradition of the "Wheel of Time" and written important commentaries and compendia on this subject.

The main disciple of Mar-pa was the great ascetic and poet Mi-la ras-pa (1040-1123), whose famous songs are still very popular among the Tibetans. He was born in the district of Gung-thang not far from the Nepalese border. When a youth, his life was saddened by the death of his father who left his family destitute. Because Mi-la's mother refused to marry her late husband's brother, this man seized the family property, leaving the widow and her children in great despair. The widow, temperamental and revengeful, lived on solely in hope of eventual retaliation for her suffering and brought up her son in this spirit. It was she, therefore, who was responsible for the sinful actions later carried out by young Mi-la. The youthful Mi-la actually found two much-feared magi who fully instructed him in black magic. In particular, he learned from these sorcerers the art of killing people by means of tantric magic circles, an art taught in a tantra as old as the "Basic Tantra of Mañjushrī" (*Mañjushrī Mūla Tantra*), where this conjuration is called *māraṇa*. He also learned how to conjure hailstorms to destroy the crops of his enemies. It is recorded that after the completion of some deadly ceremonies, the terrifying spirits Mi-la had conjured appeared before him carrying the bloody heads of his enemies in their hands while at the same time the victims perished because their houses collapsed above their heads. Mi-la then conjured a terrible shower of hail which destroyed the crops of those enemies who were not in their houses. While the mother expressed her satisfaction in a furious song of triumph, young Mi-la was seized with deep remorse for his terrible, sinful deeds.

He realized that his next incarnation would, beyond any doubt, be in hell, and that only the dangerous Vajrayāna "direct path" could save him. He consequently looked desperately for a holy guru who would be willing to initiate him into the highest spiritual mysteries and lead him to salvation and inner peace. Thus in his thirty-eighth year he became the disciple of the famous Mar-pa in whom he had the greatest confidence from the very beginning. Mar-pa made him serve a probation period of not less than six years during which time he tormented him cruelly, just as Ti-lo-pā had once tormented Nā-ro-pā. Mi-la was ordered to erect a house, but when it was nearly completed the relentless teacher had it pulled down again on one pretext or another and ordered the pupil to start again elsewhere. When Mi-la begged for the promised initiation he was abused and beaten. In his desperation Mi-la made several attempts to escape, but always his confidence in Mar-pa caused him to return. When Mar-pa was convinced that his best and most heroic disciple was really purified he eventually rewarded him with the longed-for initiations into the profoundest secrets. The highest "Secret Initiation" (Guhyābhisheka) bestowed upon the neophyte implied also drinking a beverage containing among other ingredients the so-called "five impurities," including the sperm of the guru; and it seems that in the case of Mi-la's initiation the beverage (nang-mchod) was a real one, whereas in other initiation rituals the beverage is only created in the imagination of the disciple. After this decisive ritual Mi-la devoted his whole life to lonely meditation in the Tibetan mountains, mostly in the area adjacent to Nepal. His spiritual experiences and his outward style of life are described in clear detail in the famous mGur-'bum ("Hundred Thousand Songs"). Here the unique personality of this noble and truly holy man is depicted through vivid legends, which include the poetical and mystical songs of the saint. The literary genre of these songs goes back to the paradoxical so-called dohā verses of the Indian "Perfect Saints" (siddha), but Mi-la's poetry is pervaded by a typical Tibetan atmosphere which made it very popular among Tibetans of all social classes.

During the first years after his initiation by Mar-pa, Mi-la avoided all contacts with human beings. Even during the icy Tibetan winter he remained in the caves of high glacier mountains, cut off from all human aid and clad only in a light cotton garment, which brought him the honorific title of a Ras-pa, a "Cotton-Clad Saint." Heir of all the teachings of the bKa-brgyud-pa, he also possessed the ability to produce the "Mystic Heat," one of the "Six Principles of Na-ro-pa." In later times he had eight "spiritual sons" and thirteen "lesser sons." Of the former group, Ras-chung (1084-1161) and sGam-po-pa (1079-1153) are the most important. While Mi-la himself had never travelled in India, Ras-chung visited the holy Buddhist country where he was initiated into the "Nine Circles of the ḍākinī teachings." He appears to have been rather self-willed, mainly interested in his own practical experience of the Vajrayāna secrets. As a consequence the main stream of the bKa-brgyud-pa tradition does not flow through him, but through sGam-po-pa, also called the "Doctor of Dvags-po" (Dvags-po lha-rje). sGam-po-pa had first studied the teachings of Atīsha's school, and it was only in his thirty-second year that he met Mi-la ras-pa and became his outstanding disciple. Mi-la transmitted all teachings to him, including the "Six Principles of Nā-ro-pā" and the Mahāmudrā.

In later life, residing in his home province of Dvags-po, sGam-po-pa carried on important literary activity and attracted many disciples who became the heads of different branches of the bKa-brgyud-pa school. Among them was Phag-mo gru-pa (1110-70), who founded the monastery of 'Bri-gung, although the center of the sub-sect named after him was later transferred to the Yar-klungs valley where it acquired high political importance and eventually replaced the Sa-skya-pa as overlord of Tibet. Another disciple of sGam-po-pa, 'Jig-rten mgon-po (1143-77), became the head of the 'Bri-gung-pa sect with headquarters at the 'Bri-gung monastery. From the 'Bri-gung-pa a sub-sect was formed, founded by sTag-lung bKra-shis-dpal (1142-1210), another pupil of Phag-mo-gru-pa. This sect was named the sTag-lung-pa. Still another important sub-sect was the 'Brug-pa, founded by gLing-ras-pa Padma rdo-rje (1128-88). The name *'Brug* actually means thunder and derives from an experience by the head of this order who, while building the first monastery in the province of gTsang, is said to have been surprised by extremely violent thunder and lightning. In the seventeenth century followers of this sect did missionary work in the country of Bhutan, and even today this country is the stronghold of the sect. Another disciple of sGam-po-pa, Dus-gsum mkhyen-pa (1110-93), erected the famous monastery of mTshur-phug (1189) and became the founder of the sub-sect of the Karma-pa which later split into two branches, the "Red Hat Karma-pa" and the "Black Hat Karma-pa." The last sub-sect of the bKa-brgyud-pa was the Shangs-pa bKa-brgyud-pa, founded by 'Ba-ra-ba (1310-91).

Genealogical Table of the bKa-brgyud-pa

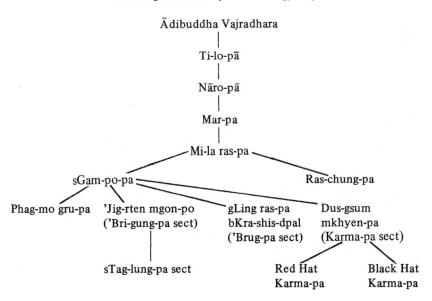

The Zha-lu-pa

In 1040 the monastery of Zha-lu in the province of gTsang was founded by lCe-ston-pa who had studied the Kālacakra according to the tradition of Somanātha and his translator 'Bro Lo-tstsha-ba. Even though this monastery was not especially influential, it became highly important because one of the most eminent polymaths and tantric adepts of Tibet, the great Bu-ston rin-po-che (1290-1364), whose numerous writings were to influence most of the schools and sects of Tibet, belonged to it. His fame and outstanding learning brought him the name "the Omniscient Bu-ston," and his tradition was called Bu-pa or Bu-lugs-pa, "adherents of the teachings of Bu(-ston)," rather than Zha-lu-pa. Although he stressed the importance of the Kālacakra and other tantric systems, he undertook the enormous task of commenting on all the important teachings of Tibetan Buddhism. Nor did he neglect to comment on monastic discipline (vinaya) or the revelations of the sūtra texts and the tantras. The basis of his doctrinal approach does not differ greatly from that of the Sa-skya-pa, but is more extensive.

The Jo-nang-pa School

Another school, primarily based on the Kālacakra but also on the tantric cycle of the Tathāgatagarbha, was the Jo-nang-pa, founded by Shes-rab rgyal-mtshan (1292-1361) and named after the Jo-mo-nang monastery, situated in gTang west of bKra-shis lhun-po. The monks of this school were looked upon by the other schools with considerable suspicion because their teachings in general, especially their exegesis of the "Thought Only Doctrine" of Asanga, seemed heretical. Among the best known teachers of this sect were Dol-po-pa (1292-1361), famous also for his knowledge of the Kālacakra, and Tāranātha (born 1575), the author of the well-known *History of Buddhism in India* and of several important writings of the Kālacakra. Although the reformer and founder of the Yellow Church, bTsong-kha-pa, studied the Kālacakra at Jo-mo-nang in the seventeenth century, the Fifth Dalai Lama was hostile to the sect and suppressed it. He also confiscated and sealed the wood blocks containing the Jo-nang-pa texts so that with the exception of two historical works by Tāranātha, the writings of this sect became very difficult to obtain.

The teachings of the Jo-nang-pa, so violently attacked by the Yellow Church, might be called "substantialism." According to the Jo-nang-pa doctrine, everything perceptible or phenomenal is non-existent; only the essence of the Tathāgata exists, i.e., Buddhahood, which is also called the "Highest Truth" (*don dam* Skr. *paramārtha*) and is identical with the "Void" or "Thusness," as in the doctrines of the other schools. This highest entity, called *rgyud*, is innate not only in the "Enlightened One" but also in the continuum of all sentient beings. Compared with the viewpoints of the other schools, this doctrine is certainly heretical. There is an identity of all the Buddhas, whether past, present, or future, in the so-called Tathāgatagarbha or "matrix of Buddhahood," and this primordial matrix is believed to be beyond time and space and identical with the Dharmakāya (the Body of boundless potentiality). The path to enlightenment may be called "cause" (*rgyu*) only verbally, and the "effect" (*'bras-bu*) is primordially immanent within the cause. Therefore there is no real purifying of the defilements (*klesha*) because these are in reality non-existent. Nothing is to be eliminated because an entity is absolute purity from the very beginning. This "absolute" may also be called "the Eternal Svastika," a term which may have been borrowed from Bon-po mysticism. In contrast to this, empirical and conditional truth is not real and the Jo-nang-pa therefore deduce that the unreal cannot be the cause of the defilements.

Thus in these teachings we find two "Voids," exemplified by these similes: first, the phenomenal world is compared to a coiled-up rope which may be considered a snake though, of course, it is not; second, the innate highest truth is comparable to a garment which occasionally is stained, yet when the garment is cleaned all dirt disappears and it regains its original state of purity. If the defilements of the mind were innate, the mind itself would have to be eliminated. Thus the phenomena of the world are simply "names," *nomina*, as in medieval European nominalism. Hence in the Jo-nang-pa there is a convergence of relative (*kun-rdzob*) and highest (*don-dam*) truth, so that the "Void" is not simply characterized by negation but by a negation of negation. It is not always easy to render Buddhist existential teachings in Western terms, and it must be remembered that these doctrines are not formal philosophy and are accessible only to meditative experience.

The rNying-ma-pa

The only school of Tibetan Buddhism which may lay claim to an origin earlier than the "Second Propagation of the Doctrine" is the rNying-ma-pa, the "adherents of the older tantras" called so in contrast to the adherents of the "later tantras" introduced into Tibet during the time of Atīsha by Mar-pa and other famous teachers of the eleventh century. Although many of their scriptures may be later than the "First Propagation of the Doctrine" and certain of their tantras of doubtful origin, it must be recalled that Atīsha, on his visit to bSam-yas, discovered tantras "which did not exist in India." Although certain ones do indeed go back to Indian sources, these scriptures are connected with Padmasambhava, the central figure of this school. Although his historical existence is certainly not subject to doubt, later times have deprived him of practically all human characteristics and converted him into a kind of supernatural personage, a "Second Buddha," a title strongly objected to by the other schools. There is little doubt that he and his later adherents attempted to create a kind of religion of their own which—as it is highly syncretistic—shows influences of non-Buddhist beliefs. Padmasambhava came from the western country of Uḍḍiyāna or Swat, a well-known center of religious syncretism. It is possible that the religion of "Padmaism" borrowed certain tenets from Manicheism and that these borrowings were not restricted to the universally accepted teachings of the five emanations of the Primordial Buddha (the Pañca Tathāgathāḥ), but were related to other pentad teachings (see below). Also indicative is the manner in which "Padmaism" adopted materials from the traditions of other "Perfect Saints" or Siddha, such as Sa-ra-ha, Virūpāksha, and Krishnācārin, who were real individuals although later parts of their biographies became identified with that of the rNying-ma-pa master. Since even the Kālacakra, which originated considerably later than the time of Padmasambhava, is ascribed to his teachings, it seems highly probable that the process of syncretism continued even during the later development of this school. Manichean is both the unusually strong stress on a light theology and the adoption of indigenous religious terminology.

The entire problem of the transmission of Padmasambhava's teachings is highly mysterious. It has been stated that he obtained his different tantric teachings not only from Indian sources but from certain books in the language of Swat, and that others were revealed to him by different ḍākinīs. He is reported to have hidden these secret, esoteric doctrines at different places—in temples, caves, and under rocks—to be discovered at a later period when humans would be able to understand them. It is stated in his biography that over the whole area between the Kailās region and China he hid 108 "treasures" of scriptures (gTer-ma), 125 important tantric images, and "five very rare essences," i.e., the most secret doctrines. These "treasures" were later unearthed by the so-called discoverers of treasures such as O-rgyan gling-pa, who lived during the time of declining Sa-skya power. O-rgyan gling-pa (died A.D. 1379) discovered Padmasambhava's biography and the *Five Scrolls Containing his Words to the Demons, Kings, Queens, Ministers, and the Clergy*. These books contain, along with later apocryphal material, a considerable amount of genuine information dating back to the time of Khri-srong lde-brtsan and Padmasambhava himself. It will be left to later investigation to separate the original material from later accretions.

Besides these materials other evidence of an uninterrupted tradition from the times of the ancient emperors to the later codified teachings of the rNying-ma-pa exists. It is especially worthwhile to consider the tradition transmitted by Vimalamitra, Padmasambhava's Indian collaborator and the only representative of the doctrine of "simultaneous" and "instantaneous" enlightenment (*cig-car-pa*), besides the Chinese monks expelled by the emperor. It is stated that Vimalamitra transmitted a basic text of the later rDzogs-chen or "Great Perfection" section of the rNying-ma doctrine through the Tibetan Myang Ting-nge-'dzin. This fundamental text, the *sNying-thig* (in four volumes: *ya-bzhi*), a basic work of later times, was hidden by his Tibetan disciple in a temple. Another, originally oral, transmission of the same doctrine, the *sNying-thig*, was discovered by Zhang-ston in the twelfth century. Later this work was elucidated by the rNying-ma-pa lama Klong-chen-pa (1308-63) in a commentary which enjoys the universal recognition of the entire sect. Thus the school obtained its definitive theological *summa*, which codified the doctrine of the unsubstantiality of the phenomenal world and the way of sudden enlightenment.

It seems that the great collection of *rNying-ma* tantras (not accepted as canonical by the other Tibetan schools) was "discovered" or rather compiled during the twelfth century. The collection of all the "treasure" books was later compiled in sixty-one volumes which, in addition to a special version of Padmasambhava's biography and the short biographies of the "discoverers of treasures," contain a huge amount of liturgical manuals, prayers, and conjurations of deities.

The teachings of the rNying-ma-pa, like those of the Bon-po, are subdivided into "nine vehicles," one of the many indications of interdependence between the two religions. The first three are connected with the "Body of Change" (*Nirmāṇakāya*) and were taught by the historical Buddha: the Vehicle of the Disciples (*shrāvaka*); the Vehicle of the Pratyekabuddhas, who obtain enlightenment by themselves but do not preach the doctrine to the world; and the Vehicle of the Bodhisattvas (i.e., the Mahāyāna teachings of the stages of the "perfections" or *pāramitā*). The next three vehicles are ascribed to the "Body of Enjoyment in Heavenly Paradises" (*Sambhogakāya*): the *Kriyā, Upāya,* and *Yoga* Vehicles, which comprise the doctrines of the lower tantras with their ritualism and *mantra* speculations. The three highest and most esoteric vehicles are attached to the "Body of the Absolute" (*Dharmakāya*), the Ādibuddha Samantabhadra: the *Mahāyoga, Anuyoga,* and *Atiyoga* Vehicles, which comprise the teachings of the highest tantras that lead to the *unio mystica*.

The most direct path is represented by the *Atiyoga* Vehicle which leads to perfection in one lifetime and is based on rituals of polarity. During the initiations the *vidyā* of the master must be present. The "thought of enlightenment" (*bodhicitta*), identical with the sperm, also means the light imprisoned in the body. The "essential body," symbolized by the form of Samantabhadra, transcends *sansāra* as well as *Nirvāṇa*, thus being beyond all dichotomies. This essence unfolds into *rig-pa*, "luminous knowledge," which is identical with the innermost essence of the individual. The realization of the pure *rig-pa* is the cause of enlightenment, which is obtainable gradually or by a direct and sudden unveiling of the truth. Luminous innate knowledge reveals itself through five rays of light which appear in their stainless form as the five families (*pañcakula*) of the five Buddhas, but in the defiled world of *sansāra* as the five *skandhas* or "constituents of the personality." For the practice of the way to salvation the human body is looked upon as the essential instrument.

With the physical eye the adept stares at the morning or evening sun, although he sometimes uses another light: the moon, three lamps, or a mirror. Eventually this light divides and transforms itself into five concentric circles, the central one of these being the symbol of the Void. If this central point is widened by constant meditation it eventually pervades immeasurable space and the difference between subject and object disappears.

The teachings concerning the "Intermediate State" or *Bar-do*, which were discussed earlier in the section describing the "Six Principles of Nā-ro-pā," are common to all Tibetan Buddhist schools. An entire literature on this subject has developed, of which only the *rNying-ma-pa* version has been translated and studied, and even this insufficiently. These books are called *Bar-do thos-grol*, which means "salvation by the mere hearing (of the holy text) when in the Intermediate State." This holy text is to be whispered into the ear of a dying or dead man, but also studied during one's lifetime so that the individual may find his way through the deceptions and terrors of this state. The *rNying-ma-pa* version is a *gTer-ma,* a "treasure," which according to tradition was found by a *gTer-ston* in the form of an old manuscript.

In this work the psychical experiences during the maximum forty-nine days in the Bar-do are described. While in this state experiences depend upon the spiritual progress which the deceased had been able to acquire during his lifetime. If he had meditated successfully before death it may happen that even during the first stage, the *'Ch'i-k'ai Bardo,* i.e., "the Bar-do of the very moment of dying," he will attain the "Radiant Light" (*Od-gsal*), the manifestation of the Absolute. For the unprepared the Radiant Light will be darkened again, and he will have to enter the *Chos-nyid Bar-do,* the "*Bar-do* of the experience of reality," in which he sees the symbolical visions of several cycles of mild and terrifying deities. These are simply manifestations of his own mind and indicate to the somewhat experienced person the level of spiritual maturity he has attained. The text teaches him to overcome awe and terror. In the *Srid-pai Bar-do*, the "*Bar-do* of seeking a new rebirth," it is still possible for an individual to obtain a rather good rebirth if while passing through this state he is not totally given over to worldly desires and sins. During this period the "Judgment of the Dead" takes place, presided over by the god gShin-rje.

gShin-rje has been identified with the Indian god of the underground world *Yama*, usually represented in Tibet as a terrifying figure with a bull's head. It would seem, however, that the Tibetan god of the dead is not of Indian origin for no descriptions or art representations of the Indian *Yama* in a similar form exist. The entire concept of the judgment most probably is a borrowing from western Asia. In fact the systematized Bon religion, which is strongly influenced by Western doctrines, presents a very similar description of *gShin-rje* and the hell with all its torments. The judgment requisites and the whole process show an astonishing similarity to the religious concepts of the West. The apprentices of *gShin-rje* are animal-headed: dog-headed, ape-headed, and bird-headed (especially the *Garuḍa*). The god of death looks into a mirror which reflects the sins and virtues of the deceased. The dead one is accompanied by his "good and bad innate gods" (*Lhan-cig skyes-pai 'dre*), which recalls the Zoroastrian idea of the good and evil *Daēnā* who meet the deceased, a teaching found even in the Avesta, as well as in later Middle-Persian books. Scales are also mentioned, on either side of which white and black pebbles are placed, the destiny of the dead man depending upon the amounts of these pebbles. The good and the evil genii and the white and black pebbles suggest Iranian dualism. Other features suggest Egypt, where the after-death experiences are described in the so-called *Book of the Dead*. The Egyptian judgment scene, presided over by Osiris (who does not have a bull's head, a special idea which may go back to representations of the Mesopotamian god Nergal), offers parallels of animal-headed apprentices: Thot, the Ibis-headed scribe of the gods, who records the meritorious and evil deeds; Thot's companion, a dog-headed ape; and the jackal-headed Anubis, who makes certain that the beam of the scales is exactly horizontal. According to Egyptian beliefs, the heart of the dead is weighed on the scales against a feather, the symbol of right and truth, and the wicked may be devoured by a terrible monster from the underground world. In the Tibetan texts, which are closer to the Iranian pattern, the "bridge of *gShin-rje*" (equivalent to the famous Cinvat Bridge in Iranian religion) plays an important role. The wicked fall from this bridge into the black river of the underground, infernal world. This highly interesting subject requires more detailed investigation.

The dGe-lugs-pa (the Yellow Church)

Although from the eleventh to the fifteenth century A.D. Tibetan Buddhism included the development of several spiritual teachings, its image darkened because the equal validity of the basic branches of the Buddhist doctrine (*vinaya*, the philosophy of the *pāramitās*, and the mysticism of the tantras), which had been the goal of Atīsha's endeavors, did not last very long. Besides high idealism in search for salvation, some schools displayed a regrettable, quite un-Buddhistic craving for political power which was manifested in a very real militant attitude. This was especially true of the Sa-skya-pa, the 'Bri-gung-pa, and the sTag-lung-pa. The work of Atīsha, a reform of all Buddhist monastic life, thus had to be redone.

The man destined to carry out this task was bTsong-kha-pa, who, as his name indicates, came from the bTsong-kha district of the Amdo country. His monastic name was bLo-bzang grags-pa, but the venerating Tibetans called him "The Precious Lord" (rJe rin-po-che). This great man, born in 1357, was the fourth son of poor parents. At his birthplace a sacred tree now stands and writings are said to appear miraculously on its leaves. Today the huge compound

of the Kumbum (sKu-'bum) monastery encompasses this tree. The lad is said to
have been initiated into the Buddhist religion at an astonishingly tender age by a
Karma-pa hierarch, Rol-pai rdo-rje; but from his third year his most important
teacher was a monk from Amdo, Don-'grub rin-chen. He was early honored with
tantric initiations of the *Hevajra, Cakrasamvara,* and *Vajrapāṇi* cycles, whereupon he was given the mystic name of Amoghavajra. At seven he took the vows
of a novice. When he was sixteen his teacher considered it essential for this
industrious young pupil to have the opportunity of widening his range of studies
at the most famous religious centers of central Tibet and to undergo an
all-embracing and systematic program of studies. The youth was urged to devote
himself especially to the teachings of the outstanding Indian founders of
schools: Nāgārjuna and Maitreyanātha (both representatives of the Mādhyamika
and Yogācāra schools), and the great logician Dharmakīrti. These suggestions suited the promising young scholar's own inclinations perfectly, although he did not
neglect the other aspects of Buddhism. He began his studies at 'Bri-gung with an
introduction to Tibetan medicine. Then, devoting himself to the fundamentals
of Mahāyāna philosophy, he sat at the feet of the famous teachers of the various
sects at Sa-skya, sNar-thang, Lhasa, Yar-klungs, and even Jo-mo-nang. Of
outstanding importance to him in Buddhist logic and philosophy was the master
Red-mda-pa, who introduced his pupil to logic according to the Sa-skya
traditions. Displaying keen interest in Buddhist logic, he followed the example
of the famous early Indian teachers of this branch of the Buddhist doctrine.
Soon his knowledge surpassed that of his schoolmates. He was able to recite
several philosophic works by heart, and was successful in monastic debates
through his complete mastery of the five basic branches of Buddhist learning:
logic, the "Perfection of Wisdom," the "Middle Way" doctrine of Nāgārjuna, the
Hīnayāna scholastic compendium of the *Abhidharma Kosha,* and, most
important, the *vinaya.* His teacher of the *vinaya* represented the older school of
Atīsha and 'Brom-ston, the bKa-gdams-pa, for which bTsong-kha-pa showed a
predilection even in his later days, thus guaranteeing a continuation of these
traditions. It would be a serious mistake, however, to assume that he neglected
or even rejected the tantric teachings. He was initiated into the mysteries of the
tantric forms of Mañjushrī, the Guhyasamāja, the Cakrasamvara, and especially
the Kālacakra in which he became an authority. Later he was to transmit these
initiations to his own disciples. He favored a balance of all branches of the
Buddhist teachings and condemned the attitude of many of his contemporaries,
some of whom only recognized the *pāramitā* path and neglected the tantras,
while others sought tantric knowledge and neglected the "Perfection of
Wisdom."

bTsong-kha-pa should thus be regarded as a Buddhist who attempted to
avoid all one-sidedness and who was a true representative of the "Middle Way"
in all respects. Evaluating this remarkable personality, we see him primarily as a

great scholar and polymath rather than a charismatic yogin like Mi-la ras-pa. He left to posterity a very large literary work in sixteen volumes, the *gsung-'bum*, which contains information on practically every aspect of Buddhism. He worked for what was most important for the Buddhism of his day, not by manifesting warm sympathy and impulsive love but by subjecting his followers to a strict and severe monastic discipline.

The *Summa* of his teachings is found in his "Gradual Path to Enlightenment," (*Byang-chub lam-rim*) completed at the old bKa-gdams-pa monastery of Rva-sgreng in 1403. This work was based on the "Entrance to the Bodhi Way" (*Bodhicaryāvatāra*) by the Indian teacher Shāntideva and, more especially, on Atīsha's *Lamp for the Bodhi Way* with its commentary. In this book, which has still not lost its importance, he gives advice about how man should purify himself by the *pāramitās*, beginning with resort to a spiritual teacher and ending in the highest spheres of profound spiritual peace. He points out that this gradual way to moral purification is also binding on the followers of the tantric path. For those unable to achieve the highest spheres of religious life, in 1415 he prepared a special abbreviated version of his main work. That bTsong-kha-pa did not reject the tantric way is shown by his composition of another basic work "The Great Gradual Way of the *Mantras*" (*sNgags-rim chen-mo*), in which, in an authoritative manner and for the sake of his own followers he set out the four basic tantric systems which he recognized. Following Atīsha, he showed a special tendency to purify Tantrism and to prevent evil men from exploiting the study and practice of the tantras to satisfy their lower instincts.

It was inevitable that the great scholarship and the blameless life of this distinguished teacher should attract an ever-growing number of pupils who subsequently formed the nucleus of a new school or church of Tibetan Buddhism, the "School of the Virtuous" (*dGe-lugs-pa*), or the Yellow Church, destined to assume a leading position in Tibet. In 1393 only eight pupils listened to the teachings of the master, but by 1409 his following had grown enormously, and there was not the slightest doubt about the immense importance of the new school which professedly aimed at no more than a continuation of the old tradition of the bKa-gdams-pa. The Jo-khang of Lhasa was cleansed of all misuses and became the center of solemn processions at which votive offerings were made to the sacred Buddha image, the Jo-bo. In 1409 the Tibetan New Year celebration was combined with the great *sMon-lam* festival or "Wishing Prayer," institutionalized by bTsong-kha-pa for the well-being of all living beings. This *sMon-lam* festival usually began on the fourth day of the first Tibetan month (according to the Western calendar in February-March). A great prayer assembly was held in the Jo-khang, in front of the Jo-bo, to increase the people's collective merits and to disseminate the Buddha's teachings in all directions for the sake of peace, prosperity, and light. The ceremonies were also performed to hasten the advent of the future Buddha,

Maitreya. The Prayer Festival brought multitudes of layman and monk-pilgrims to Lhasa, doubling the population of the capital. For the duration of the celebrations the administration of Lhasa was entrusted to two monks of the 'Bras-spungs monastery who, after the death of bTsong-kha-pa, were appointed by the Dalai Lama. In addition to religious services during the *sMon-lam* celebrations, public debates took place among highly reputed Tibetan monk-scholars, covering the entire field of Buddhist philosophy, logics, and ethics. The most successful competitors were given the high title of a *Lha-ram-pa*. During the night of the fifteenth, or the full moon, the "butter festival" took place in which huge triangular offerings made entirely of butter were displayed by different monastic communities along the inner circumambulation road of the Jo-khang. The winner in this competition received a generous prize. On the outskirts of the city folk sports and a military parade were organized. In 1409, the year of the institutionalizing of the *sMon-lam*, bTsong-kha-pa and one of his disciples founded the dGe-lugs-pa monastery of dGa-ldan of which the reformer became the first abbot. He was followed by others who were given the honorary title of Khri-rin-po-ché. Other outstanding religious centers of the school were Se-ra, founded in 1419, and 'Bras-spungs, founded in 1416. The latter received its name from the Dhānyakaṭaka Stūpa in India, where according to tradition the Buddha had preached the Kālacakra. bTsong-kha-pa, because of a revelation from the Bodhisattva Mañjushrī, never traveled into India, where by the end of the twelfth century Buddhism had been destroyed by the Muslims. Nor did he accept an invitation from the Yung-lo emperor of the Ming dynasty to visit China, although his disciple, Byams-chen chos-rje, later spent some years at the Chinese capital.

By the time of his death at dGa-ldan in 1419, bTsong-kha-pa had truly reformed Tibetan Buddhism among his disciples; and his followers differed strikingly from the adherents of the older schools, much to the displeasure of the latter. In his school he had reintroduced the strict observance of celibacy and abstention from intoxicating liquors. Certain tantric practices were forbidden, and even the "purified" tantras were allowed to be practiced only outside the monastic institutions. Of bTsong-kha-pa's disciples it was rGyal-tshab-rje (1364-1432) who was destined to succeed the master as abbot of dGa-ldan. The most learned disciple, mKhas-grub-rje (1385-1438), a great scholar and adept of the Kālacakra, succeeded rGyal-tshab-rje in 1432 and held the position until his death in 1438, when dGe-'dun grub-pa, the nephew of bTsong-kha-pa, became the leader of the Yellow Church. The latter worked for the consolidation of the hierarchical system of the dGe-lugs-pa Church and founded the first monastery of this order outside the Lhasa area: bKra-shis Lhun-po in gTsang near the city of Shigatse. A prophecy going back to the time of the reformer himself had foretold that incarnations of mKhas-grub-rje and dGe-'dun grub-pa would appear again and again in an endless series of incarnations. Based on this prophecy, dGe-'dun grub-pa seems to have laid the foundation for the reincarnation system of the Yellow Church.

According to this teaching the protector of Tibet, Avalokiteshvara, is permanently reincarnated in a series of monks beginning with dGe-'dun grub-pa, who bears the title of rGyal-ba rin-po-che "Precious Victor" (the title "Dalai Lama" is of later origin). On the other hand the hierarchs of bKra-shis lhun-po, the first of whom had been installed by dGe-'dun grub-pa, are the incarnations of Amitābha, the Buddha of Infinite Light. Owing to a later development of this incarnation dogma, dGe-'dun grub-pa was to become the first Dalai Lama; and the first abbot of bKra-shis lhun-po was considered to have been the first Paṇ-chen Rin-po-che. The reincarnation of the two hierarchs, who soon enjoyed great and increasing prestige, was carried out in the following manner. It was believed that forty-nine days after his passing away, the "soul" of the deceased hierarch occupied the body of a newborn baby. It very often happened that the previous incarnation had given some general indication concerning the neighborhood in which he was due to appear, but the State Oracle was also consulted in quite a few cases. The baby should possess certain physical characteristics, and certain signs and wonders should be connected with his birth. A committee of high lamas was sent to trace the new incarnation. In cases of doubt, i.e., if there were several candidates, the decision might be made by casting lots. The boy finally chosen was then brought in triumph to Lhasa where for the time being he continued to live with his parents. Beginning with his seventh or eighth year he received a systematic and increasingly austere education and was initiated, according to his progress, first as a novice and later as a full monk.

At the time of dGe-'dun grub-pa and his successor dGe-'dun rgya-mtsho (1475-1542) the dGe-lugs-pa school had begun to spread throughout the whole of central Tibet and to squeeze out the older "Red-Capped Sects," although the political importance of the school remained modest. In this chapter political developments will be dealt with only briefly as they have been described in the chapter on history. It seems quite likely that even during this early period the Red Lamas began to move away from the centers of dGe-lugs-pa influence, a process which was later enormously accelerated by the action of the Fifth Dalai Lama and ultimately led to the conversion of the southern Himalayan countries—Sikkim by the Karma-pa and Bhutan by the 'Brug-pa. The Yellow Church also spread steadily in eastern Tibet where a milestone in its development was the foundation of the sKu-'bum (Kumbum) monastery at the birthplace of bTsong-kha-pa in 1578. Because of the tremendous increase in the number of the Yellow Church establishments under dGe-'dun rgya-mtsho, it became necessary to create the office of sDe-pa, or major domo, to look after administrative and economic matters. During the time of the second rGyal-ba the "Palace of Joy" (dGa-ldan pho-brang) was erected. Later it became the seat of the Tibetan government.

The third rGyal-ba rin-po-che, bSod-nams rgya-mtsho (1543-88) played a role of considerable importance in the history of Tibetan Buddhism, for he succeeded in converting the Mongols for the second time. Invited by Altan khan of the Tumet, the Grand Lama arrived in Mongolia in 1578. This is an important date in the history of Inner Asia, since from this time the Mongols became the most devout followers of Tibetan Buddhism, which later greatly influenced the inter-relations of Tibet, Mongolia, and China. With the aid of missionaries, dGe-lugs-pa monasteries were erected, and the old indigenous animist-shamanist religion of the Mongols was persecuted. Altan khan conferred on bSod-nams rgya-mtsho the title of "Dalai Lama," by which the rGyal-ba rin-po-che lineage subsequently became known to world history. The fourth hierarch, Yon-tan rGya-mtsho (1589-1617), was born in the family of Altan khan, but was eventually brought to Lhasa, and the Mongols were compensated for their loss by an important incarnation of their own regarded as an incarnation of the Buddha-to-come, Maitreya. Called Maidari Khutukhtu or rJe-btsun dam-pa Khutukhtu by his own people, he was installed at Urga.

The next and perhaps most important dGe-lugs-pa hierarch, Ngag-dbang blo-bzang rgya-mtsho (1617-82), usually called "the Great Fifth," was destined to complete the development of Tibet as a priest state. He did this with the help of the war-like Mongol prince Gu-shri khan (1582-1654) of the Khoshot, who, for the benefit of the Dalai Lama, subdued all temporal and religious competitors in the gTsang province and in eastern Tibet and put down the Bon-po-sponsored rebellion of the prince of Be-ri (1641). The office of the *sDe-pa*, or temporal administrator of church property, was now transformed into that of sDe-srid, or regent. In 1669 this office was entrusted to the shrewd and learned Sangs-rgyas rgya-mtsho, who was to play an important role in the politics of the new theocratic state, and who played off the powerful Dzungar Mongols against the expansionist Chinese-Manchu empire. As a symbol of religious and temporal power the Dalai Lama began the erection of the Red Palace on the Potala hill, which was closely connected with Tibet's patron, Avalokiteshvara, and which during Tibetan Imperial times had been the governmental center of Srong-btsan sgam-po.

Tremendously successful as a politician, the "Great Fifth" was also a great religious leader and Buddhist scholar. As an outstanding polyhistor he left a huge collection of writings on almost every subject of Buddhist erudition such as history, Indian poetry, and even biographies of some red-capped rNying-ma-pa lamas. This latter group of literary works owes its origin to the fact that several rNying-ma-pas had been among the Dalai Lama's teachers. Although he suppressed the Red Sects he showed a keen interest in their religious teachings, an interest which was also shared by the regent, Sangs-rgyas rgya-mtsho.

When the "Great Fifth" died in 1682, the regent for political reasons

concealed his death and kept secret the discovery of the sixth incarnation especially because he did not want the Chinese to know about these developments.
This incarnation was the son of a rNying-ma-pa family, and he later showed
inclinations toward these teachings so greatly frowned upon by the dGe-lugs-pa.
The young hierarch (1683-1706) was enthroned in 1696, still before the regent
Sangs-rgyas rgya-mtsho was murdered by Lha-bzang khan of the Khoshot in
1705, following long political and military troubles. Lha-bzang was a Mongol
ruler of Gu-shri khan's family from whom the Fifth Dalai Lama had acquired
temporal rule over Tibet. The new hierarch, although causing much disappointment to the leaders of the Yellow Church because of his dissolute life, was
nevertheless very popular and respected by the Tibetans because they believed
him to be the true incarnation. The legend of the libertine Dalai Lama would
seem to have a serious and important background. It probably grew out of the
Dalai Lama's participation in erotic tantric rituals disapproved of by the
orthodox monks. A small collection of his writings confirms his tantric
predilections and studies. A corroboration of this interpretation is offered by a
letter of the Dzungar prince Tshe-dbang rab-brtan (preserved only in a Manchu
translation), addressed to the K'ang-hsi emperor of the Ch'ing dynasty of China,
in which the young hierarch is charged with following the doctrines of the
rNying-ma-pa "Treasure discoverer" (gTer-ston) Padma gling-pa, which are
believed to be influenced by "the dissident White-Hat" teachings. It is quite true
that the rNying-ma-pa wore white garments although they donned red hats.
Therefore this secret, almost anti-Buddhist, religion most probably represents an
echo of a later and degenerated form of Inner Asian Manicheism, for the Manicheans concealed themselves behind Buddhist terminology and are, in fact, portrayed
in Central Asian murals wearing white hats. This surprising statement seems also to
be supported by a note on the history of Tibetan Buddhism found in the index
volume of the Lhasa edition of the bKa-'gyur. The note says in effect that
Tshangs-dbyangs rgya-mtsho followed a "heretical doctrine of the North," which
suggests the Manichean centers of eastern Turkestan. The great sinologist Pelliot
also traced a late crypto-Manichean community as far as the remote Chinese
province of Fukien.

    In 1702 the young Dalai Lama formally renounced his dGe-slong vows to
the Paṇ-chen Rin-po-che from whom he had taken them. However, he still retained
his secular powers. A congregation of orthodox monks then decided that the
spirit of Avalokiteshvara had abandoned the body of Tshangs-dbyangs rgya-
mtsho and entered that of another lama, Pad-dkar 'dzin-pa. This candidate
enjoyed the support of the Chinese, but not of the majority of the Tibetans. The
Khoshot khan Lha-bzang deposed the Dalai Lama and took him prisoner. The
successful attempt of the clergy of the 'Bras-spungs monastery to free the
hierarch only postponed his tragic end. Tshangs-dbyangs was again captured and
escorted to the Koko Nor region in the east where he died, perhaps violently, in
1706.

The Chinese failed to obtain recognition of their candidate; but because of the political intrigues and military interference of the Dzungars and the Chinese, the peace and satisfaction of the Tibetans were established only after bsKal-bzang rgya-mtsho, the incarnation of the unfortunate Sixth Dalai Lama born in the east near Li-thang (1708-57), was universally recognized. He proved to be a deeply religious and learned hierarch and was greatly revered by all Tibetans.

For the study of Tibetan religion the period from the eighth to the twelfth incarnations offers little of interest. This entire period is replete with mundane affairs, and the emergence of Chinese colonialism and interference in Tibet. Most of the Tibetan hierarchs did not even reach the age of majority for they were murdered by representatives of various, mostly pro-Chinese, groups. The eminent thirteenth incarnation, Thub-bstan rgya-mtsho (1876-1933) managed to avoid a premature death, but during his lifetime the Tibetan theocracy slid into the whirlpool of world politics and became a pawn between the British, the Russians, and the Chinese. Twice this Dalai Lama had to flee: first to Mongolia in 1904; and later, to India after the Chinese invasion of 1910. After the Chinese revolution of 1911, Tibet and the Tibetan religion enjoyed comparative peace, but when the fourteenth incarnation (born in 1935) was enthroned in 1940, the deadly danger of the invasion of the Chinese communists was already a reality, and in 1959 Tibetan freedom and religion succumbed to Chinese violence and were totally destroyed. This would seem to spell the sad and tragic end of a highly spiritual religion. All the Fourteenth Dalai Lama, bsTan-'dzin rgya-mtsho, can do at present is to maintain the ancient spiritual traditions and protect his refugee subjects for whom he is the only symbol of hope.

BIBLIOGRAPHY

The most important book for the study of all Tibetan Buddhist schools is Giuseppe Tucci, *Die Religionen Tibets,* cited in full on page 112.

OTHER GENERAL INFORMATION
P. J. van Durme, "Notes sur le lamaisme," *MCB* 1 (1932): 263-321; Matthias Hermanns, "Tibetan Lamaism up to the time of the Reform by Tzoṅ Khapa," *Journal of the Anthropological Society* (1951): 7-56; G. N. Roerich, *The Blue Annals of gZhon-nu-dpal,* 2 vols., Calcutta 1949 and 1953 (information on all Tibetan Buddhist Schools); His Holiness the Fourteenth Dalai Lama, *The Opening of the Wisdom Eye and the Advancement of Buddhadharma in Tibet,* Bangkok 1968 and Wheaton, Ill. 1972.

GENERAL INFORMATION ON BUDDHIST TANTRISM

Albert Grünwedel: *Tārānātha's Edelsteinmine*, Bibliotheca Buddhica 18, Petrograd 1914; Albert Grünwedel, "Die Geschichten der vierundachtzig Zauberer (Mahāsiddhas)," aus dem Tibetischen übersetzt, *BA* (1916): 137-228; Berthold Laufer, *Use of Human Skulls and Bones in Tibet*, Chicago 1923; R.F.G. Müller, "Die Krankheits-und Heilgottheiten des Lamaismus," *Anthropos* 22 (1927): 956 ff.; M. Shahidullah, *Les Chants mystiques de Kāṇha et de Saraha, en apabhraṃśa avec les versions tibétaines*, Paris 1928; Alexandra David-Neel, *Magie d'amour et magie noire. Scènes du Tibet inconnu*, Paris 1928; Alexandra David-Neel, *With Mystics and Magicians in Tibet*, London 1931; Giuseppe Tucci, "Teorie ed esperienze dei mistici tibetani," *Il progresso religioso* 4 (1931): 1-14; W. Y. Evans-Wentz, *Tibetan Yoga and Secret Doctrines*, Oxford 1935; Giuseppe Tucci, *Tibetan Painted Scrolls*, 3 vols., Roma 1949 (contains important information on Tantrism); David Snellgrove, *Buddhist Himalaya*, Oxford 1957; Toni Schmid, *The Eighty-five Siddhas*, Stockholm 1958; Anagarika Govinda, *Foundations of Tibetan Mysticism*, New York 1960; David Snellgrove, *Himalayan Pilgrimage*, Oxford 1961; Giuseppe Tucci, *Theory and Practice of the Mandala*, London 1961; Alex Wayman, "Buddhist Genesis and the Tantric Tradition," *OE* 9 (1962): 127-31; Alex Wayman, "Female Energy and Symbolism in the Buddhist Tantras," *History of Religions* 1962, pp. 73-111; Giuseppe Tucci, "Oriental Notes I: The Tibetan 'White-Sun-Moon' and Cognate Deities," *EW* 14 (1963): 133-45; Agehananda Bharati, *The Tantric Tradition*, London 1965; F. Sierksma, *Tibet's Terrifying Deities*, The Hague and Paris 1966; David Snellgrove, *Four Lamas of Dolpo*, 2 vols., Oxford 1967/68; Helmut Hoffmann, *Symbolik der tibetischen Religionen und des Schamanismus*, Stuttgart 1967; John Blofeld, *The Way of Power. A Practical guide to the Tantric Mysticism of Tibet*, London 1970; Alex Wayman, "Contributions on the Symbolism of the Mandala Palace," *ETML* (Paris 1971): 557-66; Helmut Hoffmann, "The Doctrine of Polarity in Late Buddhism," *TSB* 4, 2 (1971): 18-35; Helmut Hoffmann, "Zen und später indischer Buddhismus," *Asien, Tradition und Fortschritt, Festschrift H. Hammitzsch*, Wiesbaden 1971, pp. 207-16.

ON THE SCHOOL OF THE SA-SKYA-PA

An-che Li, "The Sakya Sect of Lamaism," *JWCRS* 16 (1945): 72-86; George N. Roerich, "Kun-mkhyen chos-kyi ḥod-zer and the Origin of the Mongol Alphabet," *JASB* 11 (1945): 52-58; Shoju Inaba, "The Lineage of the Sa skya pa. A chapter of the Red Annals," *Memoires of the Research Department of the Toyo Bunko* no. 22 (Tokyo 1963): 107-23; Turrell V. Wylie, "Mortuary Customs at Sa-skya," *HJAS* 25 (1965): 229-35; Helmut Eimer, "Ein

Sa-skya-Gebet," *ZS* 2 (1968): 151-78; Sherab Gyaltsen Amipa, *Historical Facts on the Religion of the Sa-skya-pa Sect,* Rikon/Zürich 1970.

THE BKA-BRGYUD-PA AND THEIR SUB-SECTS

Sarat Chandra Das, "A Short History of the House of Phagdu," *JASB* (1905): 202-07; Satis Chandra Vidyabhusana, *Mgur-hbum or Songs of Mi-la-ras-pa* (edition of chapters 25 and 26), Darjeeling 1912; Berthold Laufer, *Milaraspa. Tibetische Texte in Auswahl,* Hagen und Darmstadt 1922; Jacques Bacot, *Le poète tibétain Milarépa. Ses crimes–ses épreuves–son nirvána,* Paris 1925; Giuseppe Tucci, "Apropos the legend of Nāropā," *JRAS* (1935): 677-88; Albert Grünwedel, Die Legenden des Nāropa (translation of his biography; full of misunderstandings), Leipzig 1933; Jacques Bacot, *La vie de Marpa le "traducteur",* Buddhica 1, 7, Paris 1937; Mary Shi-yü Yü, "The Tibetan Story of Transferring of One's Soul into another Body," *JAF* 62 (1949): 34-41; An-che Li, "bKa-brgyud Sect of Lamaism," *JAOS* 69: 2 (1949): 51-59; Helmut Hoffmann, *Mila Raspa. Sieben Legenden,* München-Planegg 1950; Toni Schmid, *The Cotton-clad Mila: the Poet-Saint's Life in Picture,* Stockholm 1952; Humphrey Clarke, *The Message of Milarepa. A Selection of poems,* London 1958; Hugh Richardson, "The Karmapa Sect," *JRAS* (1958): 139-64; (1959): 1-17; J. W. de Jong, *Mi la ras pa'i rnam thar,* Texte tibétain de la vie de Milarépa, édité, s'Gravenhage 1959; H. V. Guenther, *The Jewel Ornament of Liberation by sGam-po-pa,* London 1959; Antoinette K. Gordon, *The Hundred Thousand Songs. Selections from Milarepa, poet-saint of Tibet,* Rutland-Vermont 1961; Garma C. C. Chang, *The Hundred Thousand Songs of Milarepa,* translated, 2 vols., New York 1962; H. V. Guenther, *The Life and Teaching of Nāropa,* London 1963; Turrell V. Wylie, "Mar-pa's Tower: Notes on Local Hegemons in Tibet," *History of Religions* 3 (1964): 278-91; F. Wilhelm, *Prüfung und Initiation im Buche Pauṣya und in der Biographie des Nāropa,* Wiesbaden 1964; Claus Vogel, "On the Nā-ro-pai rnam-thar," *CAJ* (1968): 8-30; Bireshwar Prasad Singh, "Nāropā. His Life and Activities," *JBRS* 53 (1967): 117-29; W. Y. Evans-Wentz, *Tibet's Great Yogi Milarepa. A biography from the Tibetan,* 2nd ed., London and New York 1969; F. R. Hamm, "Studien zur Überlieferungs-geschichte des Mi la'i Mgur 'Bum," *ZS* 4 (1970): 29-79.

ZHA-LU-PA SCHOOL: D. Seyfort Ruegg, *The Life of Buston Rin po che,* Roma 1967.

JO-NANG-PA SCHOOL: D. Seyfort Ruegg, "The Jo-naṅ-pas, a School of Buddhist Ontologists," *JAOS* (1963): 73-91.

RNYING-MA-PA SCHOOL: G. Ch. Toussaint, *Le dict de Padma* (translation of Padmasambhava's Biography), Paris 1933; P. Poucha, "Das Tibetische Toten-buch," *Ar.Or.* 20 (1952): 136-62; An-che Li, "rNying-ma-pa, the Early Form of Lamaism," *JRAS* (1948): 142-63; Giuseppe Tucci, *Il libro Tibetano dei morti,* Milano 1949 (the best translation); W. Y. Evans-Wentz, *The Tibetan Book of the Dead,* 3rd ed., London 1957; W. Y. Evans-Wentz, *The Tibetan Book of the Great*

Liberation, London 1954 (contains a summary of Padmasambhava's biography); Ch. von Fürer-Haimendorf, *The Sherpas of Nepal*, Berkeley and Los Angeles 1964; Friedrich W. Funke, *Religiöses Leben der Sherpa*, Innsbruck/München 1969. For additional literature on Padmasambhava cp. page 136-137.

The DGE-LUGS-PA SCHOOL: Johannes Schubert, "Eine Liste der Abte von Kumbum," *AA* 4 (1930/32): 220-35; Wilhelm Filchner, *Kumbum Dschamba Ling, das Kloster der hunderttausend Bilder Maitreyas*, Leipzig 1933; Eugene Obermiller, "Tsoṅ-kha-pa le Pandit," *MCB* 3 (1935): 319-38; Robert Bleichsteiner, *Die Gelbe Kirche*, Wien 1937; Giuseppe Tucci, "Tibetan Notes 2: The Diffusion of the Yellow Church in Western Tibet and the Kings of Gu-ge," *HJAS* 12 (1949): 481-96; Günther Schulemann, *Geschichte der Dalai-Lamas*, 2nd ed., Leipzig 1958; Ferdinand D. Lessing and Alex Wayman, *Mkhas-grub-rje's Fundamentals of the Buddhist Tantras*, The Hague and Paris 1968; Rudolf Kaschewsky, "Briefe Tshongkhapas an Geistliche und Laien," *ZS* 2 (1968): 15-20.

VIII. THE SOCIAL AND ECONOMIC STRUCTURE IN TRADITIONAL TIBET

The Peasants

In general the Tibetan peasant's standard of living compared most favorably with that of the other peoples of Asia. While his heavy homespun apparel might not have given the impression of material prosperity and creature comforts, he never experienced a severe lack of the basic necessities of food, clothing, and housing. Actual dire poverty was extremely rare.

Along the rivers such as the Brahmaputra were fertile valleys and fruitful plains which provided the peasant with productive farmland. Although the elevation at Gyantse is more than 13,000 feet above sea level, some excellent crops grew here. Tibet was not the arid land many believed it to be. Some of her products were enviable; for instance, her fruits, native to temperate climates, grew in abundance. The fertile areas produced apricots, peaches, pears, small apples, strawberries, raspberries, and walnuts.

It was customary for a peasant to occupy a piece of land belonging to a monastery or a wealthy landlord. In return for the use of the land, the peasant cultivated the remainder of the estate and provided other services, such as working on the roads, sending one of his family for military service, or providing transportation for official travellers. Though this may have been the general rule, some peasants were able to rise to the status of landowners.

No evidence of discontent appears on the faces of these kind, gentle, honest, cheerful people. They were self-reliant and naturally courteous, with a keen sense of humor, giving not the slightest sign of being driven or overburdened. The Tibetan peasant's way of life seemed enviable, for he possessed what all men desire—ample time to enjoy his leisure independently.

To take advantage of the sunshine, the peasants usually built their houses facing south. They were constructed of brick and stone and consisted of eight or nine rooms. Some were beautifully decorated, for many peasants were gifted with a keen artistic sense of beauty. As a safeguard against thieves, the firewood was kept on the roof. Here again was evidence of the Tibetan's fine appreciation of pleasing form and symmetry, for the wood was not stacked haphazardly, but arranged in attractive designs. In deference to strong religious convictions, the Tibetan kept a prayer flag above his roof.

The house was built around a central courtyard. It was not customary for the family to live on the first floor, which was reserved in part for animal shelter and forage. Generally they occupied the upper floor where the kitchen formed the center of the home. The chapel, the bedrooms, and the storerooms surrounded the kitchen. If a monk were a guest, he was assigned to the chapel, where only the privileged were invited to sleep.

The domesticated animals were the *dzo* and *dzomo*, common cattle, sheep, pigs, donkeys, horses, mules, cats, and chickens. The entire farm was protected most efficiently by ferocious black-haired dogs. The most useful animals were the *dzo* and *dzomo*, cross-breeds of the yak. A *dzo* is the male cross-breed between a bull and a cow yak or *dri*, while the female cross-breed is called a *dzomo*. The *dzomo* is unsurpassed as a good milker. The *dzo* is more tractable than other animals.

The irrigation systems were worked jointly with the landlords. The peasant-tenant supplied the labor for the construction of the irrigation channels and for necessary repairs. The amount of work each tenant was required to do depended on the quantity of seeds he sowed in the fields he cultivated, rather than on the amount of land he possessed. Ploughing was done by the men with the *dzo*. The sowing, as well as the weeding, was done by the women.

Except for mutton, yak meat was eaten more often than any other. Fish and chicken were eaten infrequently. The chief crop was barley, both white and black. Peas, wheat, oats, mustard, radishes, and turnips also were important agricultural products. Mustard provided a valuable oil used not only for cooking, but also for lamps and for the care of babies and young children.

In Tibet, childbirth, marriage, and death were accompanied by special rites differing somewhat from one place to another and carried out in accordance with the family's circumstances.

Childbirth was considered a natural function, taking place at home without the benefit of doctors or midwives. However, the mother-to-be was assisted by her mother-in-law or grandmother. Should they be unavailable, an aunt or elder sister helped in delivering the infant. At times the village lama offered protective prayers for a safe, easy birth. Notwithstanding the age-old tradition of prayers and talismans, the rate of infant mortality was high. Regardless of the fact that male children were preferred, all babies, male or female, were received with great joy. The child was tenderly washed and rubbed with mustard oil and kept comfortably warm. A mother often breast-fed the child until it was two or three years old.

A few days after a baby was born some families called in the *tsipa* ("astrologer") to note the most auspicious moments or misfortune in the child's life. Generally the child's name was chosen by a lama. As a rule two names were given. Frequently, the first was the day of the week on which the child was born, e.g., a boy born on Wednesday could be called Lhagpa Tshering, or Wednesday Long Life. If the boy or girl entered the monastery or the nunnery the name was changed at that time by the chief priest.

Though the Tibetan woman always enjoyed great freedom, she had little or nothing to say in the choice of her husband. But in Tibet, too, times changed and rules became less stringent. In all probability the girl was acquainted with the groom-to-be. An astrologer was consulted about the marriage. If the girl was born in one of the fire years, it was not propitious for her to marry a boy born in a water year, for fire and water were believed to be incompatible. However, one born in an earth year would find one born in a wood year suitable for marriage, for wood needed soil to grow. Once the horoscopes were cast, the boy's parents visited the girl's parents to offer them the traditional *khatag* ("ceremonial scarf") and gifts. Once the parents of the girl gave their consent, a favorable day was set for the bridegroom's party to visit the bride's home, where they were lavishly entertained. On that day the bridegroom's parents presented from five hundred to a thousand *srang* (a one-ounce silver coin) together with an apron for the bride's mother. It was not until the final ceremony, when the bride was ready to leave her home, that her parents presented her dowry consisting of ornaments and some clothing and money.

While in Tibet monogamous marriages were the rule, polyandry was practiced—a woman might marry one man and his brothers as well. In such cases the offspring were recognized as the children of the eldest brother. The younger brothers were addressed as "uncle."

When death came to the Tibetan, he was not faced with a feeling of finality, for he had completed another segment in his chain of lives. If possible, a lama or monk came to help him relinquish the earthly things to which he had clung while in his temporary body. His mind was directed to his guardian deity and most of all to the "Root Lama" who was his connection between his imperfect self and the Buddha, the All-Merciful One. The service for the deceased, conducted in his house, lasted about half an hour. For another half hour the lama sat in meditation to assist the *namshe* ("consciousness") to escape from the body. The *tsipa* ("astrologer") decided how long the corpse should remain in the house.

The corpse was disposed of in several ways. Since the body was composed of four elements—earth, fire, air, and water—it was thought fitting to consign it to one of these. Fire or cremation was reserved for religious teachers. Burial in the earth was confined to babies and victims of infectious diseases such as smallpox. The very poor were sometimes placed in the rivers. Some babies, too, had water burials. The commonest form of corpse disposal was to dismember the body in some wide, open space and leave it for the vultures to consume. In this manner the body returned to the air. If some of the remains were left at the disposal grounds, wild animals consumed them. The family did not accompany the deceased to the disposal grounds, for this was not considered fitting.

The Nomads

Nomads constituted the mobile population of Tibet, occupying the highlands at altitudes of from 9,000 to 15,000 feet. In general, they inhabited the northeastern and the south-central plateaus, extending over a considerably wide area.

Many tribes are found among the nomads. Living within the tribal boundaries were various groups, some small, some numbering over a thousand families. The average family had approximately five or six members. According to their circumstances, some families occupied a single tent while others had two or three additional tents. Some tribes counted more than six thousand tents under their jurisdiction. The tribe was autonomous, having its individual, highly respected name, and strongly aware of its rights. Tribal decisions were rigidly enforced. Fundamentally, the tribe was similar to a well-administered political system.

Nomads were completely dependent upon their animals. *Nor*, ("yak"), and *dri* ("cattle"), *chug* ("sheep"), and *lalo* ("horses") were the source of their wealth and security. It was inconceivable to envisage the nomad without the *nor*, for it was doubtful if he could have existed without it. The *nor* was the source of food—both meat and dairy—, clothing, shelter, and transportation. Sheep ranked equally with cattle in importance and were also used for transportation, being able to carry thirty pounds for long distances. Nomads who lived at lower elevations often added goats and common cattle to their herds.

In early summer the nomads looked for pasturage at higher elevations. Many halts were anticipated. However, the first halt was shortened to nine or ten days owing to the tenderness of the new growth of grass, which was quickly consumed. However, by the time the second move was made, the animals were stronger and had greater endurance for the higher climbs. As summer progressed the grass grew more vigorously and became more nourishing. The nomads were able to lengthen their sojourn at each location. By autumn the grass had reached its maximum growth, and it was possible to graze the animals for almost a month in one area. The pasturage was gauged according to the animals themselves. During grazing the animals were separated, each to its own kind.

At the end of summer the nomads prepared to return to their permanent winter quarters in the protected valleys suitably situated to escape the sweep of the icy winter winds and inclement weather. Immediately upon arriving at their new quarters, the nomads erected tents. Only natural barriers, such as rivers and mountains, served as boundaries to separate the tribes. For protection against marauding bandits and animals, the communities of nomads sought to remain within calling distance of each other.

Their black tents were made of *nor* hair, which had been spun into thread and woven into cloth. Though the tents might vary in size, the average tent was about thirty square feet and about six to seven feet high. A pole at either end supported the center of the tent. Strong *nor*-hair rope was stretched between the poles and secured to outside posts, which held the roof taut. The more prosperous nomads erected second and possibly third tents for chapels, guests, and storage. Generally, they were located either at the side of or behind the principal tent. In winter an open passage extended between the tents and about the five foot *nor* dung fence, which served as a windbreak.

Inside the tent, wooden boxes, measuring a foot and a half in height by three feet in length and two feet in width and covered with *nor* skins, were piled against the back wall together with *nor* skin bags. Food and grains were stored in these containers on top of which the father of the group reverently set up the altar. Here were placed the religious treasures—a Buddha or holy image, incense burners, a butter lamp, holy books, and seven bowls containing holy water. In front of the containers a mattress was placed to accommodate the elderly member of the household, a guest, or a monk who had come to render religious service.

Along the side walls clothing was stored in *nor* skin bags, three feet in height and two feet in diameter. Resting on top of the bags were the saddles. In one corner near the entrance was the grinder which turned parched barley into meal for tsampa. In the opposite corner was the tall wooden churn with its long-handled dasher. Also, the skin of a *nor* or sheep was often used for a churn. After drawing the entire skin from the animal, it was tanned to render it pliable. The flexible skin was then securely tied at all extremities, leaving the neck open to receive the milk to be churned. The bulky bag was placed across a log. Two nomads, either men or women, then pushed it from one to the other across the log, until the butter came.

Near the center of the tent was a stove which was continually lit. Generally a pit about five inches deep was dug into the ground and was built up of mud and stones to a height of one foot above the ground, with the fireplace at one end. A fire burned along the entire length of the stove under two cooking vessels. The rim of the stove, made of earth and sand firmly tamped, formed a ledge on which small kitchen utensils were placed. The meal was served from the stove after the family had gathered around it to eat.

At night members of the group settled anywhere in the tent to sleep. However, the younger members of the family slept outside under felt coveralls or in small shelters. There were always those who acted as scouts and remained vigilant throughout the night.

Firearms and swords were usually tied to the front pillar of the tent. The sword was kept in a sheath made of wood covered with tanned sheep leather. The hilt of the sword sometimes was decorated with turquoise. The most effective protection, however, was provided by the highly trained, fierce mastiffs. Since the dogs were constantly alert, their savage barking warned the encampment of the approach of an intruder, no matter how stealthy he might be. Even the most intrepid person feared and was wary of the Tibetan mastiff.

The nomads' diet was simple and seldom varied. Vegetables and grains were eaten only occasionally. Mutton and *dri* meat were staples and were eaten raw, dried, boiled, or frozen. For religious reasons, frying and roasting were looked upon with disfavor. A great variety of dairy products were consumed in abundance. Rich *dri* milk was churned into butter and placed in skin bags to be packed away, leaving some for immediate use. This was followed by cheese-making. By heating the buttermilk, curds were formed. After draining the whey from the curds through a cloth bag, a soft product very similar to cottage cheese resulted. Some of this was served to the family, but the greater part was spread out in the sun to dry. It was then finely crumbled and could be stored for several months. Yoghurt was also an important dairy product.

During the winter months the nomads visited nearby towns and villages, taking advantage of the various festivals of the season to buy and sell goods. On these occasions they purchased supplies they were unable to produce them-selves—tea, sugar, rice, grain, dried vegetables and fruit, wheat flour, and dried noodles. In addition, the nomads sold or bartered skins; the furs of wolves, fox, lynx, wildcats, leopards, and brown bears; leather; *nor*-hair rope; and some live animals. Both men and women wore long sheepskin *chupa* ("garments") with the fleece worn inside, which were snugly wrapped about the body with a sash. The women's *chupa* were decorated differently from the men's and touched the ground. The men, using a tight girdle of either hair rope or leather thongs about the hips, wore their *chupa* at calf-length. A coarse silk girdle was preferred by most of the men. Women did not wear undergarments, and men seldom wore trousers. The summer garments differed only in the length of the fleece. In summer this measured about an inch, while in winter it was about six inches. Seven or eight skins made an ample sized *chupa*. The children wore shorter garments very much like those of the adults. Tanning the skins and sewing the garments required great skill.

Footwear, too, was an important item. Though the design might differ, the boots were basically the same. The upper part of the boots was made of leather and lined with felt, but the sole, cut larger than the foot itself, was left unlined. Felt filled the sole of the boot, providing a comfortable padding which allowed free circulation. The felt was changed often to avoid the discomfort of packing.

It is virtually impossible to overestimate the value of animal hides to the nomads. They served a myriad of uses. In addition to clothing, they provided containers for food. They were indispensible for saddles, bridles, and other items needed for the horses. Hides were converted into leather ropes. Because of the constant use of hides there was always a need for more of them.

The nomads had an innate love of beauty which they satisfied through the use of decorations. In the left ear, men wore a round gold or silver hoop about one or one and a half inches in diameter set with a coral or turquoise. It was not uncommon to find a man wearing rings in both ears. Five or six large coral beads strung on woolen threads or leather cords along with six or seven turquoise and amber beads were worn around the neck. An ivory ring about one half inch deep and one half inch thick was worn on the thumb. This ring was often made of gold, silver, or copper and decorated with various stones. On the middle finger a gold or silver ring twisted around five or six times was worn by wealthy men. At times prayer beads of one hundred and eleven beads were combined with turquoise or coral and worn about the neck. Thick ivory bangles, imported from India, were worn on men's wrists.

Women, too, indulged in their love of beauty. Their headbands, two or three inches in width and four to five feet long, were decorated with silver plates, amber, coral, and turquoise. Unmarried girls rarely had headdresses, but sometimes they wore a long, narrow band decorated with a few silver coins. Women favored earrings three to four inches in diameter made of gold or silver. Different colored stones adorned the front of the ear plate. Unmarried girls threaded coral or turquoise beads through the ear lobes. Huge beads of coral, amber, and turquoise were strung on woolen threads or leather cords to be worn around the neck. The woman's wealth determined the number of necklaces she wore. Both married and unmarried women wore silver or gold rings with a rectangular top about an inch long and half an inch wide, a turquoise or coral set in the center. Two or three rings of this type were often worn on the middle or small finger. A round gold or silver ring was decorated with different colored small stones and pearls. They also used gold and silver bangles adorned with stones. Often they wore two or three on both hands, again depending upon their wealth.

Both men and women wore charm boxes around their necks to keep away evil spirits and prevent accidents. These boxes, of various sizes and styles, contained written prayers, relics, and figures of the Buddha. The boxes were fashioned of gold, silver, copper, wood, or leather. Those made of metal and decorated with turquoise and coral were especially prized by women.

The nomads led an uncomplicated life with the work amicably divided between the men and women. The children played happily with puppies and other young animals, as well as with stones and other natural objects found in their immediate environment. The fierce dogs which guarded each group prevented the children from playing with their neighbors.

The Nobility

In Tibet, as in other countries, the nobility was a class set apart. Between it and the ordinary people a wide chasm existed. Common people showed great deference to the nobility, even using a different manner of speech in addressing them, and were especially careful in their use of vocabulary.

There were three sources by which a Tibetan noble traced his ancestral lines:

1. An ancestor may have performed an exceptional service for Tibet. Recognition of this by the government was cause for his ennoblement.

2. When a Dalai Lama took birth in a family, it was ennobled and presented with a large estate by the government. Some of the principal nobles of Lhasa were descendants of the families of previous Dalai Lamas. During the lifetime of a Dalai Lama, his family was recognized as *Yabshi Sarpa* (The New Patrimony). A few years later the family took a new name, which would identify them with the ranks of the nobility.

3. The smallest section of the nobility was the oldest. Its ancestry was traced to Tibet's ancient rulers, dating back to the seventh century.

Some members of the nobility received special titles, such as *kung* and *dzasa*. With a sizeable grant of land, the father of the Dalai Lama received the title of *kung*. The *kung* had little or no power, as a rule, but his honorary degree of nobility was the highest granted to a layman. *Dzasas* were selected from either laymen or members of a monastic order. Certain persons received the title for outstanding services performed. Though it carried with it very little power, it entitled the recipient to attend the meetings of the National Assembly.

Monks and Nuns

To the Tibetan nothing is more important than his religion. Throughout the villages, towns, and cities of Tibet literally thousands of Buddhist monasteries and nunneries existed. No hamlet was too mean to possess one or the other, or perhaps both. Indeed, the monasteries had a significant role in the development and formation of Tibet's history.

Life in the monasteries differed only slightly, depending upon the size and sect of the monastery. The general term for all monasteries was *gompa*. Some monasteries, including the small ones, were referred to as hermitages (*ridro*). The large monasteries were spoken of in two ways, i.e., *dansa* (Residence of the Monks) or *chode* (Religious Institution). The *dGe-lugs-pa* sect administered the famous monasteries of Drepung, Sera, Ganden, and Tashilhunpo.

Members of all classes of the population were free to ask admission to a monastery. It was customary for a boy to be received into the monastery at the age of seven or eight. He was dressed in monastic robes, and his head was shaved, except for the small tuft of hair at the crown. This was left to be offered to the

Abbot or Teacher, who removed it with a blade during the prescribed ceremony. The boy became known by a new name, and his formal education began. He was taught the rudiments of reading and writing. Also, he memorized the scriptures. Following a two-year period of elementary training, the young boy took the vow of *getsul.*

Getsul was the first stage of the monastic life. The novice attended classes devoted to higher studies and was required to apply himself industriously to an intensive course of study for a long period of time. Eventually, he completed the following subjects: canon of monastic discipline, dialectics, logic, metaphysics, the doctrine of the middle path, and *Pharchin* ("perfection of wisdom").

When he reached maturity at eighteen or twenty, the young monk might take the vow of a *gelong*, a fully ordained monk. The monastic discipline of a *gelong* was rigidly enforced. The *gelong* vow was often taken before the monk had completed his higher studies. If he was a member of a large monastery, the monk might aspire to higher degrees by pursuing further studies of theological and philosophical texts. The successful completion of these additional subjects enabled the *gelong* to become *Lharim Geshe, Dorim Geshe,* and *Tshogrim Geshe* ("Doctor of Philosophy").

It must not be assumed that a member of one of the smaller monasteries was excluded from seeking higher degrees. Upon presenting himself at the monastery of his choice and satisfactorily passing the required examination, he was admitted to further study.

One holding an advanced degree had the choice of remaining in the monastery for life, or of retiring to a *ridro* ("hermitage") for meditation to prepare himself to enter society and teach. Some monks undertook even more advanced esoteric studies in a separate monastic college, *Gyu* ("tantrism"). Upon being graduated from this advanced branch of learning, the monk was worthy to become a *khenpo* ("abbot"). It was also possible for him to aspire to be recognized as the most erudite religious figure in Tibet—the *Ganden Tripa* ("Enthroned one of Ganden Monastery"). By the time a dGe-lugs-pa monk became a candidate for such an exalted title, he might be well into his sixties.

In all monasteries the monks were required to lead a life of simplicity and chastity. Like a Western university, a Tibetan monastery was divided into colleges and dormitories, which were supported by contributions from wealthy patrons. Monks received monetary gifts from donors in the same manner as Western students receive assistance through scholarships.

The Traders

In Tibet the traders stood between the landed nobility and the peasants and nomads. Tibetans by instinct are experts at bargaining. Hence, it was to be expected that Tibet should have developed trade routes. In the south and west the routes led into India; in the east, into China; and toward the north, into Mongolia.

Exports were limited to the principal products of the country, such as wool, the largest item. Most of it found its way into India. Nepal was a ready outlet for rock salt. Kashmir proved to be an excellent market for borax and carpets. Tibet also exported woolen cloth, and some rather unusual goods such as otter skins, musk, bears' bile, herbs, fresh deer horns, which were highly prized in China's pharmacopoeia, and white yak tails used in the United States for Santa Claus beards. Since no embargo was levied on either imports or exports, the rate of exchange was irregular. Supply and demand were the controlling factors in trading, which depended also on weather conditions.

Tibet was self-sufficient except for tea, rice, and some fruit and sweets which were imported. However, to satisfy the wealthy, many items were brought into Tibet. India provided a variety of products: hardware, some machinery, iron, copper, glass, kerosene, woolen and cotton materials, rice, dried fruits, sugar, molasses, tea, matches, needles, soap, tobacco, medicines, and coral and precious stones. From China came the all-important tea, pressed into bricks. Exquisite porcelains and enamel, together with matchless silks, satins, brocades, cotton goods, buttons, ceremonial scarves, and ponies from Kansu were also among the Chinese imports. Mongolia sent silver, especially in the shape of horses' hoofs (also some made of gold but smaller), silk, and a moderate number of ponies. Hats were imported from Japan and Europe.

The great monasteries monopolized some branches of the trade, especially those dealing with silks and damasks, indispensable for the ceremonial robes of the dignitaries and monks. A few wealthy families which had interests in foreign countries relied on their own agents to import expensive articles for their use.

Currency

In Tibet's early days, trading was carried on by exchange of commodities. To the present day in remote sections of Tibet bartering continues. Since barley, butter, mustard oil, salt, wool, and animals' hides were necessities in Tibet, they were generally used to make purchases and could be exchanged for everything from clothing to horses.

Later silver came to be used as a standard of value. In the beginning before it was minted, its value as a medium of exchange depended on its weight. After a lapse of time the officials saw the importance of standardization. Therefore, the Tibetans developed their own form of currency. The silver pieces were known as *ngul* ("coins"), taking the following forms: ten *karma* to one *sho*; ten *sho* to one *srang*; fifty *srang* to one *dotse*.

After 1750, for a period of forty years, Nepalese coins were used in Tibet. The Nepalese *tamka* was added to the coinage, being the equivalent of about one and one half *sho*.

In 1792 the Tibetans established their own system of currency with the coins bearing a Tibetan inscription. Later, copper coins, sized according to value, appeared. All coins bore the seal of the lion. No longer were the coins considered mere units of weight. They were recognized in other countries and had an exchange value with the Indian rupee.

After a visit by Tibetan officials to British India to study the administration of the mint in Calcutta, paper currency, backed by gold reserves held by the government, was introduced in 1890. All the coins and notes in circulation were embossed with the date of issue and the government seals. The paper notes were called *srang* and appeared in denominations of five, ten, twenty-five, and one hundred *tamkas*. Silver coins were issued in units of five, ten, thirty, and one hundred *sho*. Only one gold coin was issued, having a value of twenty *srang*. Paper money bore the red seal of the Dalai Lama and the black seal of the cabinet minister. Until the Chinese occupation this currency was in continuous use.

The Traditional Political System of Tibet

The Tibetan government was a theocracy with its leadership—both spiritual and secular—invested in His Holiness, the Dalai Lama. (The government in exile continues to be theocratic with the Dalai Lama recognized by both the Tibetans and the Western world as Tibet's titular leader.) The Dalai Lama held absolute power, although in actual practice, with exemplary discretion, he exercised authority only in consultation with his cabinet and the prime ministers.

No political parties existed in Tibet, but the government did recognize two groups: the *tse-kor* ("the monastic group") and the *sho-kor* ("the lay group").

When a monk had successfully passed his examination, he was qualified to become a member of the monastic group, and was admitted to membership in the *Drung-kyu*; although a monk belonging to the nobility, after passing his examination, was entitled to take his place as a *Drung-drag*. Following qualification, special monastic titles were issued to monks, who became known as *Drung-dring*. All monks desiring to join the monastic offices had to be approved by the *Yig-tsang* ("the secretariat"). The *Yig-tsang* was composed of four *drung-yig che-mo* ("monastic secretaries").

The duty of the *Yig-tsang* was the direct supervision of the monasteries with the exception of those at Sera, Drepung, and Ganden. It was responsible also for the selection, control, and instruction of the monks of the civil service. The *Yig-tsang* also presided over the National Assembly (*Tsong-du*). Although the monastic officials and the lay officials served together in the administration, the National Assembly had no power to interfere with monastic appointments and discipline. In actual practice the monastic officials were considered a personal retinue of the Dalai Lama and were accustomed to attend his daily levee, from which the lay officials were excluded.

Ambitious laymen, desiring to become government officials, had to pass an examination and seek the approval of the *Tsi-kang* ("finance ministry"). The *Tsi-kang* was composed of four *tsi-pon* ("finance ministers"). The finance ministry presented the laymen's credentials to the cabinet ministers who in turn presented them to the One in Charge of Appointments. The lay officers who served in a lesser capacity than the monastic officials were divided into three groups: 1) *De-pon*—the smallest group, comprised of members of the Ancient Families; 2) *Mi-drag*—a group made up of laymen in the service of cabinet ministers; and 3) *Ger-pa*—a group composed of members who ranked below the first and second groups.

Immediately below the cabinet ministers in rank was an entire series of officers, each following the other in traditional administrative importance. As stated above, the highest were the four *tsi-pon*. Their duties were to maintain the records of the income of the government, to estimate property values for taxation, and to transfer claims on revenue. They were also responsible for the training of lay officers to help them gain more proficiency.

The first among the high officials of the Tibetan government was the *Gyal-tshab* ("regent"), elected by and responsible to the *Tsong-du*. In recent times, the regent was usually chosen from among the incarnate lamas of the *Ling-shi* ("four monasteries") in and near Lhasa. While those incarnate monks of the four monasteries ranked very high in the ecclesiastical hierarchy, they possessed little or no political power. If none of them were considered qualified to act as regent, the customary practice was to appoint the *Tri Rinpoche* ("Enthroned One") of Ganden as regent.

During the absence or during the minority (before age eighteen) of a Dalai Lama, the regent administered the government. He acted, too, in the event of the retirement of a Dalai Lama. After the death of a Dalai Lama, a regent was appointed to administer the government until the accession to power of the Dalai Lama's reincarnation. In the administration of the secular government the regent was invested with great authority, although he invariably consulted the *Tsong-du* in matters of importance.

The *Tsong-du*, a peculiar, ancient political organization of Tibet, was comprised of two bodies: *Tsong-du du-pa* ("Lesser Assembly") and *Tsong-du gye-dzom* ("Greater Assembly"), which served as intermediaries between the administrative branches. The assembly was unique in the sense that it was not a permanent body meeting regularly. It met only when called by the *Kashag* ("Cabinet") to render an opinion on some particular matter.

The *Tsong-du du-pa* was an official group made up of the *drung-yig che-mo*, the *tsi-pons*, the *da-pons* and other lay and monastic officials of the fourth rank. The *Tsong-du du-pa* convened when the *Ka-shag* issued a summons naming those called to attend, giving the date and hour of the meeting. This summons came only when the *Kashag* was considering government matters which required consultation. If, after consideration, the *Tsong-du du-pa* felt the matter was beyond their scope, the *Kashag* called a meeting of the *Tsong-du gye-dzom*.

Lay and monastic officials attended meetings of the Greater Assembly. The abbots of Sera, Drepung, and Ganden, together with nine representatives of the above-mentioned monasteries and representatives of every class and occupation, e.g., craftsmen, soldiers, traders, and householders, came to discuss the subject in question. The presiding officers were the *drung-yig che-mo* and the *tsi-pon*. After thorough discussion and lengthy deliberation, the assembly came to a decision. The conclusion was presented to the *Kashag* which in turn presented it to the Dalai Lama, who then passed down his decision giving more attention to the *Tsong-du's* views than to the *Kashag's* opinions.

Even though the *Tsong-du* had no legislative role or power to direct the executive branch, it played an important part in the governmental system and often a very vital part. No discussion of any issue concerning Tibet was completed without hearing the opinion of the *Tsong-du*. The recommendations of the *Tsong-du gye-dzom* were always accepted by the Dalai Lama and the *Kashag*.

Next in command after the regent (*Gyal-tshab*) were the prime ministers (*se-lon*). Since the essential character of the government was dualistic, the administration was divided into a civil and a religious branch. Therefore, one *se-lon* was a monk while the other was a senior lay official, selected by the Dalai Lama from candidates submitted by the National Assembly. The prime ministers served as liaison between the Dalai Lama and the *Ka-shag*, although the prime ministers did not sit with the cabinet. Their duties were to pass on the recommendations of the cabinet to the Dalai Lama. However, the *se-lon* were allowed to include a note outlining their own views. The prime minister presented to the Dalai Lama the views of the *drung-yig che-mo* and the Lord Chamberlain on matters of religious issues.

The principal executive body of the Tibetan government was the *Kashag*. Four *Ka-lon* ("ministers"), three lay officers, and one high-ranking monk, who was recognized as the senior member, were appointed by the Dalai Lama. Inasmuch as the cabinet represented the chief executive branch of Tibet, it administered the affairs of the country. All government business, including relatively inconsequential issues of every kind, came to the cabinet for consideration. Its authority extended over a wide area including administrative, judicial, and political decisions. Petitions were also received by it. Any Tibetan was privileged to petition the *Kashag* regarding decisions made by the provincial governors. Often, disputes which originated between great families came before the cabinet for review. Even decisions made by the cabinet itself, which did not satisfy the parties involved, could be appealed to the Dalai Lama, who was the supreme judge. All the recommendations of the cabinet were forwarded to the Dalai Lama for decision through the prime ministers. In one department the *Kashag* had full power. The cabinet could and did issue decrees on land-holding without referring to the Dalai Lama. In cases which involved monks, the *Kashag* had no power to act. The *Yig-tsang* dealt with them.

The *Chi-kyab Ken-po* ("lord chamberlain") was the highest ranking monastic official below the Dalai Lama. In status he was equal to a member of the *Kashag,* and had access to the Dalai Lama at almost any time. He was responsible for the personal household of the Dalai Lama, composed of a number of highly placed monastic officials. The lord chamberlain was also the treasurer of the Dalai Lama's personal treasury as well as the official treasury of the Potala. In addition, he was in charge of the care of Norbulingka (the summer palace) and the public parks around Lhasa. An important part of the lord chamberlain's duties was the supervision of the two *Chib-pon Chen-mo* ("superintendents of government stables"), who controlled the work of the mounted couriers engaged in delivering the government mail. Acting with the lord chamberlain upon religious affairs was the *drung-yig che-mo*, which presented their views and recommendations to the Dalai Lama through the prime minister's office. When issues of secular importance arose, a joint session of the *drung-yig che-mo* and the *tsi-pon* was called to discuss the matter. Likewise, when the National Assembly was convened to discuss important national issues, the two councils—*drung-yig che-mo* and *tsi-pon*—presided jointly over the meeting. The *Kashag* and the office of the prime minister presented the decisions to the Dalai Lama. The lord chamberlain also attended the meeting.

The department of Justice (*Sher-khang*) consisted of two lay and one monastic official who took care of disputes and quarrels. The laws of the city were under the *Nang-dzi-shag.* Justice was guided by custom, for which the Tibetans had great regard. Only a repetition of a crime by an offender brought forth severe punishment. Otherwise, severe penalties were never lightly inflicted. Treason was considered the most heinous crime. After 1898, the most severe punishment was flogging, the Thirteenth Dalai Lama having abolished capital punishment.

In 1922 a police force was planned for Lhasa but it never became fully operative. If an offender disappeared, he was traced by a body of couriers, a unique organization of long standing, supervised by the lord chamberlain.

Judgments in criminal cases were delivered in accordance with the various proclamations of previous Dalai Lamas. In civil suits judgments were made in accordance with the aspects of the case. The judgments could be appealed right up to the Dalai Lama.

Civil or criminal cases referred by the *Kashag* were decided by the two *Sher-pang* ("judicial investigators"), whose jurisdiction extended over all Tibet. Should the case be an exceptionally serious one, two civil and two military officials were consulted. The results of the completed investigation were sent to the *Kashag* and the Dalai Lama for the final decision.

Two *da-pon* commanded the military administration—a monk and a layman. They held the titles of *dza-sa* and *the-ji* respectively. The regimental commanders were known as *mak-pon*.

The Tibetan army numbered about eight thousand in peacetime. The greater concentration of soldiers was on the eastern border of Tibet with about fifteen hundred men billeted in Lhasa, including the Dalai Lama's bodyguard. Smaller detachments were distributed at strategic places in the north and west.

Men were drafted for military service from landlords in lieu of taxes. The Tibetan peasant generally made an excellent fighting man, for he was brave, dutiful, and accustomed to working many hours each day. In critical times men between the ages of eighteen and forty were drafted into the army. Even the monasteries sent volunteers from the ranks of the uneducated monks, who formed their own military unit. Military service was not strenuous, since the men were called only for a few days at a time on two or three occasions annually. Training varied according to the weapons supplied. After 1921 a number of officers were sent to India to receive their training.

In more recent times the function of Tibet's military organization was twofold: to preserve the country's internal peace and to protect it from external invasion. Military organization was a matter of great concern to the Thirteenth Dalai Lama. Before his death in 1933, he gave this wise note of warning to his people: "Unless we now learn how to protect our land, the Dalai Lama and the Panchen Lama, the Father and the Son, the upholders of the Buddhist Faith, the glorious Incarnations, all will go under, disappear and leave not a trace behind. The political system inherited from the Three Great Kings will become a matter of history. All beings will suffer great hardship and pass their days and nights slowly in a reign of terror." To strengthen the army, the Dalai Lama improved military equipment. The Dib Arsenal at Lhasa produced small arms, which represented a great advance over the swords, spears, flintlock muskets, and matchlocks used previously.

Tibet was comprised of approximately one hundred *dzongs* ("districts"), each of which was administered by two *dzong-pon* ("district officials"), a monk and a layman. This might be considered a control system, for while the monastic branch of the government was able to keep the layman under surveillance, the layman acted as a check on the religious branch.

A *dzong-pon* served a term of three years and dealt with affairs of the land, the people, and the law, according to the administrative regulations. Military matters were beyond his jurisdiction.

While the provincial or regional governor functioned as the supervisor of the district officials, it was conceded that the *dzong pon* were guided only by the traditional rules and enjoyed a virtually free jurisdiction.

The amount of revenue due from each *dzong* was on record in Lhasa. These amounts were collected by the *dzong-pon,* whose own income was in the form of dues collected from the people within his jurisdiction, proceeds from fines he imposed, and private trading in which he compelled traders to sell to him at his own price. Often he received luxurious gifts from traders and enjoyed *u-la* ("free transportation").

Large estates in Tibet supported many farms and vast acres of pasturage where from fifteen to twenty families resided. The government exacted revenue from these estates, but very little of the revenue collected was in actual currency. A large portion of the government's income was taken in grain, mainly barley. The tenant farmer paid his revenue to the landlord both in grain and in service. The shepherd did not meet his revenue with service. The peasant, who owned his own farm, paid his revenue in three ways—in cash, in grain, and in actual labor—directly to the government.

Occasionally, the need arose to levy extra taxes. This occurred especially when some great event took place, or a war was declared. Generally such contingencies were met with a tax on grain.

After the seventeenth century the principal administrative regions in Tibet were *U Tsang* ("central Tibet"), *Do-kham* ("eastern Tibet"), and *Ngari* ("western Tibet"). *Chi-kyabs* ("governors") administered these regions. It is clearly impossible to give detailed accounts of them in this study.

Below the council were the various departments of the administrative body. All had their significant functions in the operation of the Tibetan government; and all were administered in much the same way as the government, having at the head a monastic official and a lay official. Each department had the power to make decisions within definite limits. If issues arose beyond these limits they were sent to the Council for its decision. Significant among these departments were: *Drag-tar Le-khung* (Office of Communications), post office and telegraph office; *Shib-khang* (Department of Accounting); *So-nam Le-khung* (Agriculture Office), information on the availability of seeds and the allotment of land; and *Cha-tsha Le-khung* (Office of Taxation), regulating taxes on musk, tea, salt, wood and wood products, yak tails, and fresh deer horns.

Discovery and Installation of the Dalai Lama

Choice or selection has no part to play in the designation of a new Dalai Lama. He is not elected nor is his position hereditary in the material sense of this word. He is the reincarnation of the protective deity *Chen-ri-zig* (Avalokitesh-vara) and, as such, must be discovered by those in charge of state and church.

The mechanism of this search can be described as follows. After the death of a Dalai Lama, when his true self has left his body, a regent takes charge of the country's administration until the reincarnation is discovered. The most arresting feature of the search for the child in which the Dalai Lama is reborn is the consultations of the oracles, visions in the sacred waters of Lake Lha-mo la-tsho, and the continuous prayers of the whole Tibetan people. The search begins at a time thought propitious for the purpose and is conducted with the greatest possible thoroughness. All safeguards to avoid a possible mistake are taken. The search committee, composed of seven or eight men chosen among lamas, officials, and servants, does its work in secret. They travel in disguise and no region is omitted from the itinerary. Bhutan, Sikkim, Nepal, Mongolia, and even China are visited in search of the child. Great care is taken not to arouse suspicions or to create false hopes in the families visited. The great oracles of Ne-chung, Sam-ye, Ka-dong are consulted as are astrologers. Finally the regent in the company of high officials, civil and religious, visits the sacred lake where the silent waves reveal not only the whereabouts of the dwelling place, but even the name and the dress of the holy child's family.

Discrete investigations are conducted to correlate the fund of information collected. The results are sent to the National Assembly, where they are studied in depth. From the scores of names presented, a few special ones are selected for further scrutiny. Finally, when the child is believed to have been found, he, young as he may be, has to pass rigid examinations, so that no error is made.

As a rule the investigation group, well-disguised, comes to the house asking for a night's lodging. During the visit, the child is judiciously exposed to various personal belongings of the departed Dalai Lama. Among the relics are rosaries, bells, drinking cups, and drums presented together with imitation duplicate objects. If the child is the true incarnation, he seizes his former possessions with joy, completely disregarding the other objects even though they are newer and brighter. Also, the servant who had served the deceased Dalai Lama accompanies the party. Again, with no hesitancy, the child recognizes him. All through what would have been an unendurable trial to an impostor, the holy child conducts himself in a mature manner, showing excellent judgment, rare intelligence, and faultless deportment.

While the above is the usual procedure, cases have been known where the child announced his own rebirth, and insisted upon recognition. Also, at times, the incumbent Dalai Lama, before relinquishing his body, would indicate some details of his rebirth, which would help locate the child.

When the child successfully passes the many tests and his identity is confirmed, there is great rejoicing in Tibet. When the Dalai Lama reaches the appropriate age of between five and seven, he and his family are brought to

Lhasa for the installation by the government and by the Tibetan people as the spiritual ruler of the country. The family takes up residence in Lhasa, while the child is taken to the Potala and put in the care of selected monks and an incarnate lama, who becomes his teacher. From the beginning the routine is rigid. The studies progress until the Dalai Lama's age permits him to assume full direction of his land as its spiritual and temporal leader. However, circumstances demanded that the present Dalai Lama assume control of the secular government before he reached his majority. In the winter of 1950 when he was only 16, the Fourteenth Dalai Lama assumed full control of his government. He was the youngest Dalai Lama to do so.

BIBLIOGRAPHY

Sir Charles Bell, *The People of Tibet*, 2nd ed., Oxford 1968; Sir Charles Bell, *Tibet Past and Present*, 2nd ed., Oxford 1968; P. Carraso, *Land and Polity in Tibet*, Seattle 1959; C. W. Cassinelli and Robert B. Ekvall, *A Tibetan Principality, The Political System of Saskya*, Cornell University, Ithaca, New York 1969; Matthias Hermanns, *Die Nomaden von Tibet*, Wien 1949; Matthias Hermanns, *Die Familie der Amdo-Tibeter*, Freiburg/München 1959; T. J. Norbu, *Tibet. An Account of the History and the People of Tibet*, New York 1968; M. Oppitz, *Geschichte und Sozialordnung der Sherpa* Innsbruck/München 1968; Günther Schulemann, *Geschichte der Dalai Lamas*, Leipzig 1958; E. H. C. Walsh, "The Coinage of Tibet," *MASB* 2: 2 (1907): 11-23; Prince Peter of Greece and Denmark, "The Tibetan Family," *Comparative Family Systems*, edited by M. F. Nimkoff, Boston 1965, pp. 192-208; Robert Ekvall, *Fields on the Hoof: Nexus of Tibetan Nomadic Pastoralism*, New York 1968; Melvyn C. Goldstein, "Stratification, Polyandry, and Family Structure in Central Tibet," *Southwestern Journal of Anthropology* 27 (1971): 64-74; Melvyn C. Goldstein, "Serfdom and Mobility: An Examination of the Institution of 'Human Lease' in Traditional Tibetan Society," *JAS* 30 (1971): 521-34.

IX. TIBETAN LITERATURE

Folk Literature

Tibetan literature is extremely extensive, and its full extent may never be known. A considerable part of it may have been destroyed by the Chinese occupants and lost forever. Its oldest branch is certainly folklore, which existed throughout the whole period of Tibetan history from the time when Tibet had no script until the present period. Originally literature was transmitted orally—a tradition that has continued down to the present, although after the adoption of writing, i.e., from the time of the ancient emperors, folklore texts were also written.

The most ancient specimens of Tibetan folk literature that we have were found in the sand-buried ruins of eastern Turkestan—at one time part of the Tibetan empire—especially in the library of Tun-huang. A collection of these texts, written in the ancient preclassical language of Imperial Tibet, has been published by F. W. Thomas, but there are also specimens in the French collection (fonds Pelliot). These texts deal with various divinations (*mo*) and are quite similar to a Turkic text of about the same period. Prognostications are sought for business enterprises, trading, petitions to superiors, arrival of travellers, sick persons, meeting an enemy, making a family connection, and recovery of lost property. Fragments of a similar divination book have been found at the Turfan oasis. Proverbs with which later Tibet also abounds are found in the *Sum-pa Mother's Sayings,* which are believed to have been translated from the language of the Sum-pa people who lived at the time of Tibetan domination in present-day rGyal-mo-rong.

Besides the ancient folklore documents, several works exist (one of them connected with Skyi, the Lhasa Valley) which indicate a transition from a Golden Age to an Age of Decline. These texts are of a pessimistic nature. Instead of one king who came down to the earth to be the ruler of men, there are several, and the Golden Age is replaced by the "Age of Debts and Taxes" following the disappearance of the heaven-born kings. Humans are now disturbed by fiends and demons, whose placation is most important. The religious background of these documents shows no acquaintance with Buddhism but describes an increasingly sophisticated Bon religion, although the latter displays characteristics of the ancient folk religion which also might be called Bon and is later frequently called "The Religion of Men" (*mi-chos*). The Skyi documents end with a scapegoat ritual. The texts include several proverbs and mythological riddles which stylistically are very close to the songs of the *Tun-huang Annals* (cf. section on the sources of Tibetan history) and to later oral folklore. Also found among these texts are the great traditional myth of the battle between the wild horse and the wild yak, and the story of the separation of the domesticated horse from the wild one.

Later folklore, both oral and written, is very conservative. An examination of materials collected in western Tibet by A. H. Francke and G. Tucci, in eastern Tibet by M. Hermanns, and in central Tibet by G. Tucci makes this apparent. The meter shows a striking similarity to the T'ang period texts; its rhythm is dactylic rather than trochaic like the verses of Buddhist literature. As does ancient folklore, later folklore makes much use of parallelisms.

Much of the folklore is in the form of song: weddings songs, (*nyo-pai glu*), songs for the different seasons and beer songs (*chang-glu*). The religious background occasionally shows the impact of Buddhism and Bon, but the general tone is that of the old *mi-chos*, as is the case with the *Ge-sar* epic (see below). The themes of these sometimes very elaborate songs are cosmogony (sometimes influenced by Bon: mention is made of the "world-egg" or rather "world eggs," concepts borrowed from the Bon religion which drew this idea from western Asia); theogony, genealogies of gods and kings; and the so-called "origin themes," which describe the origin of the wedding, clothing, the cap, etc. One of the cosmogonic texts published by Hermanns shows literal borrowings from a Bon text. Very often the songs are in the form of question and answer, as in the case of, for instance, the wedding songs exchanged between relatives of the bride and seven friends of the bridegroom who attempt to get access to the bride's house by answering at successive stages difficult and detailed questions. If their answer is wrong or if they do not know an answer they will be whipped with willow rods by the family of the bride. After having satisfied the people of the house, the Nyo-pa gain access to the drinking hall where the "beer song" will be sung. This song is in the form of a catechism and consists of two parts: one dealing with barley, the source of *chang* ("beer"); and one with reed, denoting the arrow and the spindle. The songs often combine quite modern material with ancient reminiscences: in one folklore text from eastern Tibet, for instance, the city of Khotan is called "the dark red grove of willows," an expression used in eighth- or ninth-century literary texts.

Until the present, lot books (*mo-dpe*) for mantic purposes have been popular with the Tibetans. There are also books dealing with divination from dreams, which include a *Treatise of the Goddess of the Dream* (*rmi lam lha moi bstan bcos*). No less popular is a short text, the *Treatise of the Goddess of Tea and Beer*. For worldly wisdom there is a small booklet giving the advice of a Kashmirian father to his son (*Kha-che pha-lugs*), which seems to have been translated from a Muslim Kashmiri original for it contains several foreign words. Other favorite tales such as those of *A-khu sTon-pa* (*Uncle Teacher*), sometimes scabrous, do not seem to have ever been printed.

As regards tales and fables it seems obvious that original Tibetan materials such as the *A-khu sTon-pa* tales exist as well as fairy tales and fables which were adopted from other peoples, especially the Indians, the latter presenting interesting parallels to the Pañcatantra and Aesop's fables. As in the animal fables of other peoples, animals such as the fox (the symbol of slyness), the raven (the symbol of disaster), birds, monkeys, parrots, lions, tigers, cats, turtles, and even lice and ants play an important role. Some ant stories from western Tibet seem to be especially old for they are related to the legend of the gold-digging ants. Extremely popular even at present are the *Stories of the Corpse Demon* (*ro-langs,* Skr. *Vetāla*), which adopted the famous fairy tales from the Indian *Vetāla-pañca-viṃshatikā* in a version which no longer exists in Indian languages but became the model for the respective Mongolian tales (*Siddhi Küür*). In several instances, such as the *Vetāla* stories, the milieu was adjusted to the Tibetan scene and way of life. From an Indian source stems also the tale of the wicked king Ha-shang De-ba, translated from a Hindi original. Certainly of Indian Buddhist origin is the narrative of the nun dPal-mo and the Kashmirian king Dharmapāla. Of Buddhist or Bon-po inspiration but intermixed with popular ideas are those tales which describe the experiences of people who were able to travel to the beyond and who returned, the so-called *'Das-log* books (literally "return of the deceased").

Proof exists that Indian Hindu motifs found their way into Tibet even during the Imperial period. The Tun-huang collections contain no less than six manuscripts dealing with the Indian hero Rāma. This explains the presence of Rāmāyaṇa tales and names in later Bon-po literature (*rGyal-rabs bon-gyi 'byung-gnas*).

The most important non-Buddhist contribution to folklore in Tibetan literature is the cycle of the Ge-sar epic, which spread over vast parts of Inner Asia and is found in the Mongolian, Soyon Turkic, Lepcha (Sikkimese), and Burushaski (Hunza Valley) literatures. This primitive cycle seems to have developed in northern Khams and Amdo around the end of the fourteenth or the fifteenth century, but it must be conceded that older elements are also found in the different versions of this epic, both oral and written. A kingdom of gLing certainly existed in this area (the word originally meant "world continent" or the "known countries of the world") from which the hero's name, gLing Ge-sar, is derived. But undoubtedly the name *Ge-sar,* derived from the Byzantine *Kaisar,* was connected in earlier texts with the country of *Phrom* (Rome—Byzantium, in its Sogdian form, *Frōm*). We do not know how this name came to be adopted by eastern Tibetan literature, but because the title *Phrom Ge-sar* is connected with the Turks (*Dru-gu*) in the old texts and because we know from other occurrences that the Byzantine emperors bestowed the then outmoded title on barbarian chieftains, it may have made its way into Tibet through the intermediary of the western Turks. The names of all the peoples with whom Ge-sar makes war in the respective cycles were also known even during Tibetan Imperial times. However, the spirit which pervades the epic is definitely neither Byzantine nor Turkish, but goes back to the genuine old Tibetan *Mi-chos* and Bon-po genealogies.

Practically every region of Tibet has its own version of the epic, either oral or written. The most voluminous written version comprises not less than nineteen sections in twenty-four volumes. The first part deals with the antecedents in the heavens, the land of gods (*Lha-gling*), and shows a striking similarity to the heavenly events before the birth of the Bon-po teacher gShen-rab. Part two sings of the hero's birth and his early exploits as an infant; part three tells of the famous horse race in which Ge-sar emerges as the victor and consequently becomes king of the gLing country. The following parts deal with Ge-sar's campaigns in different countries: China (four); the land of the devil (*bdud*) of the north (five), both showing Bon-po affinities; the Hor country under its ruler "White Tent" (six and seven), which includes the abduction and the recovery of Ge-sar's wife 'Brug-mo; lJang, the country of Yunnan, during Imperial times an independent kingdom (eight); Mon, the countries south of the Himalayan crest (nine); sTag-gzig, Iranian or Muslim territory in the west (ten); Sog, Mongols or Central Asian Iranians (eleven and twelve); Bye-ri in the north (thirteen); Kashmir in the southwest (fourteen); the Turks (Dru-gu, fifteen); and sBe-ra (Nepal?) and the Women's Kingdom (sixteen, seventeen). The eighteenth part deals with the winning of the nine-eyed pearl; the nineteenth and last, with Ge-sar's descent to hell (*dMyal-gling*). Ge-sar is regarded as the savior and messiah who at the end of this age will conquer the evil ones in an apocalyptic battle, an idea which seems to be influenced by the Buddhist Kālacakra doctrines and goes back ultimately to Iranian religious inspiration. The epic is chanted by special non-Buddhist bards, and paintings representing Ge-sar are not to be found in Buddhist monasteries.

The Tibetan drama developed from the mask dances (*'cham*), which go back to pre-Buddhist times and are devoted to fertility rituals and the expelling of demons. Such dances, performed especially during the New Year celebrations, employ no words although they are accompanied by music. Their ritual is described by the "dance books" (*'cham-dpe*), which also give the score for the musical accompaniment. Buddhism later adopted these *'cham* dances and introduced Buddhist innovations, additions, and reinterpretations. The so-called "black hat dancers" became representatives of the tantric saint Lha-lung dPal-gyi rdo-rje, who killed the anti-Buddhist king gLang-dar-ma, the Chinese monks (*Hva-shang*) playing the role of clowns and symbolizing the expulsion of Chinese Buddhism in the eighth century. All these performances, including the later spoken dramas, took place in the open air—in monastery courtyards if religious, at an enclosure in the countryside or in the courtyard of a layman's house if secular—and were presented by travelling actor groups.

Most of the later dramatic works contain pious Buddhist legends, adapted to Tibetan conditions and thus combining elements of Indian and Tibetan folklore. Some of the best known dramas borrowed their subjects from Buddhist *Jātaka* tales (rebirth stories of the Buddha), such as the famous play *Dri-med kun-ldan* (*The Totally Pure One*) which describes the moving story of the heroic self-sacrifice of the Indian prince Vishvantara; and the *Life of the Religious King Nor-bu bzang-po*, which goes back to the *Sudhana Jātaka* and is the only drama whose author, sDings-chen smyon-pa, is known. Another drama, *The Life of the Youth Padma 'Od-'bar*, has a rNying-ma-pa sect setting but certainly goes back to Indian sources, for it tells the story of a pious Buddhist youth, son of a guild master, and a wicked Hindu king. The subject of another popular play, *The Life of the Seer's Daughter "Sun-of-Beauty"* (*gZugs-kyi ñi-ma*), is also derived from Indian sources. The girl becomes the wife of a Bengal king but because of false accusations is expelled from the palace and handed over to the executioner. She realizes that these events can only be the result of previous *karma,* and being a pious Buddhist, she renounces all selfishness and follows the Bodhisattva model of self-sacrifice. Exposed to beasts of prey, she realizes that these animals which encircled her in veneration are more sensitive to saints than humans. After many physical and psychical trials she directs a prayer to the compassionate Bodhisattva Avalokiteshvara and even renounces her own redemption and religious merits for the benefit of all living beings.

The drama *'Gro-ba bzang-mo* displays the characteristics of an adopted Indian fairy tale. The heroine, an incarnation of the Goddess *Tārā*, is miraculously born to a brahmin couple which had long been childless. The girl proves to be beautiful and virtuous, but it is predicted that she will later forget her parents and even give up her children. When she comes of age, she is discovered by an impious Hindu king who, struck by her beauty, marries her without telling this to his principal queen who in reality is a man-eating ogress (*rākshasī*). For some time the young queen remains in hiding and brings forth a son and a daughter, but eventually the ogress-queen discovers both her and the children. Furiously she attempts to devour the three humans, but the prediction of yore becomes fulfilled: wrapped in her scarf, the fairy queen flies up into the sky, abandoning her children. In order to devour the boy and the girl, the wicked queen, with the aid of her ministers and by means of a magic potion, causes the king to lose his senses. The ministers are ordered to bring to the queen the hearts of the children (a motif very common in Indian fairy tales), but they substitute the hearts of two dogs. Later, the ogress-queen learns that the children are still alive, and orders them thrown over a precipice. The executioner saves the girl; and the young prince, who is thrown into the sea, is saved by a vulture and brought to shore by a fish. The prince then makes his way to the Lotus

Country where he becomes king. His sister, guided by shepherds, eventually meets him, and the two siblings reign together. When the wicked queen learns of these events, she makes war with the Lotus Country and is killed by the prince's unfailing arrow. The siblings free their father who had been thrown into prison, and all three rule together in both kingdoms.

The *Younger Brother Don-yod* (*gcung-po don-yod*) shows some slight similarities to the *'Gro-ba bzang-mo* play. The plot seems to be of Indian origin and deals with the love of two brothers, although the drama is intermingled with genuine Tibetan problems: the rivalry between the provinces of dbUs and gTsang and between the factions of the Dalai Lama and the Paṇ-chen Rin-poche, preference being shown for the latter. The villain of this play is the heretical and unbelieving prime minister of the Dalai Lama, whereas in the fairy-tale section the stepmother of the older boy is displayed as the embodiment of all evil. Like the ogress-queen of the drama just described, she would like to have his heart served to her on a platter. But both boys go into exile because of their mutual love, and it is the elder one who unselfishly cares for the younger, depriving himself of food. In the end the younger one dies but is revived; and both brothers marry a princess, a theme which hints at Tibetan polyandry.

Quite different is the setting of another drama entitled *sNang-gsal* (*Clear Light*), which is also the name of the heroine. This work describes the character of a woman striving for Buddhist sainthood who is unhappy in the house of her parents and in the palace of the governor of gTsang whom she marries. Eventually she flees, and after a search she is found meditating in a grotto. The work contains very little dramatization; the greater part is filled with the religious monologues of sNang-gsal. Other characters are represented rather hazily and the work impresses one more as a collection of Buddhist homilies than as a drama. However the style of this drama is beautiful.

A favorite dramatical representation *rGya-bza Bod-bza* is the description of the Chinese and Nepalese marriages of the great emperor Srong-btsan sgam-po. This work would seem to have been borrowed from the respective chapter of the book entitled *Maṇi bka-'bum*. An episode taken from the *Hundred Thousand Songs* of the Saint Mi-la ras-pa, namely, the story of the great hunter mGon-po rdo-rje who is converted by the holy man and henceforth abstains from killing animals, is also popular among the Tibetans.

BIBLIOGRAPHY

GENERAL SURVEY

A. H. Francke, *Geistesleben in Tibet,* Gütersloh 1925; Matthias Hermanns, *Die Familie der Amdo-Tibeter,* Freiburg/München 1959; Sir Charles Bell, *The*

People of Tibet, 2nd ed., Oxford 1968; R. A. Stein, *La civilisation tibétaine,* collection "Sigma," Paris 1962. In English: *Tibetan Civilization,* Stanford University Press 1972.

ANCIENT TIBETAN FOLK LITERATURE

J. Bacot, F. W. Thomas, Ch. Toussaint, *Documents de Touen-houang relatifs à l'histoire du Tibet,* Paris 1940/46 (contains several ancient Tibetan songs); F. W. Thomas, *Ancient Folk Literature from Northeastern Tibet,* Deutsche Akademie der Wissenschaften, Klasse für Sprachen, Literatur und Kunst 1952, no. 3, Berlin 1957 (also contains folk literature from Skyi-central Tibet); Ariane MacDonald, "Une lecture des Pelliot tibétain 1286, 1287, 1038, 1047, et 1290," *ETML* (Paris 1971): 190-391 (this is more a book than an article and contains, in addition to historical interpretations, much information on ancient Tibetan poetry. It is regrettable that this amount of information has not been made more accessible by an index); F. W. Thomas, "A Rāmāyaṇa Story in Tibetan from Chinese Turkestan," *Indian Studies in Honor of Charles Rockwell Lanman,* Cambridge, Mass. 1929, pp. 193-208; Marcelle Lalou, "L'histoire de Rāma en tibétain," *JA* (1936): 560-62; J. K. Balbir, *L'histoire de Rāma en tibétain,* Paris 1963; J. W. deJong, "Un fragment de l'histoire de Rāma en tibétain," *ETML* (Paris 1971): 127-44 (the most important study of the ancient Tibetan Rāma tale); A. H. Francke, "Tibetische Handschriftenfunde aus Turfan," *SBAW* (1924): 5-20 (deals with fragments of an ancient Tibetan divination book among other material).

FOLK SONGS AND PROVERBS

H. Hanlon, "The Folk Songs of Ladakh and Baltistan," *Transactions of the 9th International Congress of Orientalists,* London 1892; H. Hanlon, "The Wedding Customs and Songs of Ladakh," *Actes du 10eme Congrès des Orientalistes,* Genève 1894; A. H. Francke, "The Ladakhi Pre-Buddhist Marriage Ritual," *IA* 30 (1901); A. H. Francke, "On Ladakhi Poetry," *Globus* 75, no. 15; A. H. Francke, S. Ribbach and Dr. F. Shawe, "Ladakhi Songs," *IA* 31 (1902); A. H. Francke, "Ten Ancient Historical Songs from Western Tibet," *IA* 38 (1909); A. H. Francke, "The Ancient Historical Songs of Western Tibet," *IA* (1909); Dawasamdup Kazi, "A Tibetan Funeral Prayer," *JASB,* N. S. 12 (1916); Johan van Manen, "Three Tibetan Repartee Songs," *JASB,* N. S. 17 (1921), no. 4; A. H. Francke, *Tibetische Hochzeitslieder,* Hagen und Darmstadt 1923; A. H. Francke, "Tibetische Lieder aus dem Gebiet des ehemaligen westtibetischen Königreichs," *MSOS* (1929): 93-136; Yu Dawchyuan, *Love Songs of the Sixth Dalai Lama,* Academia Sinica, Peiping 1939; A. F. C. Read, "Balti Proverbs," *BSOAS* 7 (1933-35): 499-502; J. H. Edgar, Verse of the Tibetan Border (from eastern Tibet), *JWCBRS* 8 (1936); René Nebesky-Wojkowitz, "Hochzeitslieder der Lepchas," *AS* 6: 30-40; Marion H. Duncan, *Love Songs and Proverbs of*

Tibet, London 1961; Giuseppe Tucci, *Tibetan Folk Songs from Gyantse and Western Tibet*, Artibus Asiae, supplementum 22, Ascona 1966; Pavel Poucha, "Le vers tibétain," *Ar Or* 18, pt. 4 (1950): 188-235; pt. 22 (1954): 563-85; J. Vekerdo, "Some Remarks on Tibetan Prosody," *AOH* 5 (1955): 101-22; Chang Kun, "On Tibetan Poetry, *CAJ* 2 (1956).

THE TIBETAN EPIC

A. H. Francke, *Der Frühlings-und Wintermythus der Kesarsage*, Mémoires de la Société Finno-Ougrienne 15, Helsingfors 1902; A. H. Francke, *A Lower Ladakhi Version of the Kesar Saga* (Tibetan text, English Abstract of Contents), Calcutta 1905-1941; George N. Roerich, "The Epic of King Kesar of Ling," *JASB* 8 (1942): 277-311; Alexandra David-Neel, *The Superhuman Life of Gesar of Ling*, 2nd ed., London 1959; R. A. Stein, *L'épopée tibétaine de Gésar dans sa version lamaïque de Ling*, Paris 1959; R. A. Stein, *Recherches sur l'épopée et le barde au Tibet*, Paris 1959; R. A. Stein, "Une source ancienne pour l'histoire de l'épopée tibétaine, le Poti bse-ru," *JA* (1962): 77-106.

THE TIBETAN DRAMA

Jacques Bacot, "Drimed Kundan. Une version tibétaine dialoguée du Vessantara Jātaka," *JA* (1914): 221-305; E. Denison Ross, *The Story of Ti-Med-Kun-Den* (edition of the text), Calcutta 1912; M. H. Morrison, *Ti Med Kun Dan* (translated), London 1925; Jacques Bacot, *Trois Mystères tibétains*, Paris 1921; H. I. Woolf, *Three Tibetan Mysteries*, London 1924; M. H. Duncan, *Harvest Festival Dramas of Tibet*, Hong Kong 1955; Jacques Bacot, *Zugiñima*, 2 vols., texte et traduction, Paris 1957; Thubten Jigme Norbu and Robert B. Ekvall, *The Younger Brother Don Yod. A Tibetan Play Translated* (the original text has been added), Bloomington and London 1969; J. Bacot, "Le mariage chinois du roi tibétain Sron bcan sganpo" (extrait du Mani bKa' 'bum), *MCB* 3 (1935): 1-60; J. Bacot, "La conversion du chasseur" [the text underlying the story of the hunter mGon-po rdo-rje], *EORL* (Paris 1932): 131-43.

FOLK TALES

W. F. O'Connor, *Folk Tales from Tibet*, London 1906; A. H. Francke, "Die Geschichte des toten No-rub-can. Eine tibetische Form der Vetālapañca-vimśatikā aus Purig," *ZDMG* 75 (1921): 72-96; A. H. Francke, "Zur tibetischen Vetālapañcavimśatikā (Siddhi Kür)," *ZDMG* 77 (1923): 239-54; A. H. Francke, "Two Ant Stories from the Territory of the Ancient Kingdom of Western Tibet. A contribution to the question of the gold-digging ants," *AM* 1 (1924): 67-75; A. L. Shelton, *Tibetan Folk Tales*, Saint Louis 1925; A. H. Francke,

"Wa-tsei-sgruṅs. Fuchsgeschichten, erzählt von dKon-mchog-bKra-shis aus Kha-la-tse," *AM* 2 (1925): 408-31; A. H. Francke, "Zwei Erzählungen aus der tibetischen Vetālapañcaviṃśatikā," *ZII*, 6 (1928): 244-54; Matthias Hermanns, *Himmelsstier und Gletscherlöwe. Mythen, Sagen und Fabeln aus Tibet*, Eisenach und Kassel 1955; Helmut Hoffmann, *Märchen aus Tibet* (Märchen der Weltliteratur), Düsseldorf und Köln 1965; A. W. MacDonald, *Matériaux pour l'étude de la littérature populaire tibétaine I. Édition et traduction de deux manuscrits tibétains des "Histoires du cadavre"*, Paris 1967; L Lörincz, "Les recueils Ro-sgruṅ tibétains contenant 21 contes," *AOH* 21 (1968): 317-37; Geoffrey Taylor Bull, *Tibetan Tales*, London 1969.

The Buddhist Canonical Scriptures

The earliest Tibetan texts put into writing, if we omit folklore texts, government documents, and chronicles (for the latter see chapter on the sources of Tibetan history), are the canonical Buddhist scriptures. According to the monastic chronicles this work of adoption began shortly after the invention of the Tibetan alphabet by Thon-mi Sambhoṭa. Among the texts translated during this early period the sources mention the book of legends, *Karmashataka,* and the famous *Gold Splendor Sūtra* (*Suvarṇaprabhāsa*) of which fragments have been found in eastern Turkestan. These do not fully agree with the later Tibetan versions. The translation of the enormous corpus of the Buddhist scriptures, however, went on very slowly during the seventh and the first half of the eighth century A.D. According to the chronicles, during the time of Mes-ag-tshoms five Mahāyāna *sūtras* were brought to Tibet from the Indian Buddhist sages who were meditating in the Kailās area.

Large-scale translation of the Buddhist scriptures, first initiated together with the translation of Bon-po scriptures by teachers from Zhang-zhung, was not begun before the time of Khri-srong lde-brtsan. This work was especially furthered after the foundation of the first Tibetan monastery of bSam-yas (about 775) and the acceptance of Buddhism as the state religion in 779. Many Chinese and Indian monks at bSam-yas worked as *paṇḍitas* together with Tibetan translators (*lo-tstsha-ba*), the most famous of whom were perhaps the Tibetan Vairocanarakshita and the Indians Vimalamitra, Jinamitra, and Dānashila.

The work of translating the holy scriptures and the scholastic compendia and commentaries was continued under Khri-srong lde-brtsan's successors and reached its apogee during the reign of the devout emperor Ral-pa-can (817-36) and his father, Sad-na-legs, after which time the nobility and Bon-po reaction brought all translation work to a halt. During the time of Ral-pa-can and Sad-na-legs, the work of translation was done more systematically than it had been done previously and older translations were revised. Under Imperial auspices a committee of Indian and Tibetan scholars was set up to establish uniformity in the translation of Buddhist technical terms. The committee compiled the *Mahāvyutpatti,* a compendium in Sanskrit and Tibetan of Buddhist terms arranged according to subject. The texts were translated primarily from Indian languages, but also from Chinese, the languages of Uḍḍiyāna (Swat), 'Bru-sha (Gilgit), and Uighur.

About A.D. 1000 after the revival of Buddhism in Central Tibet, in centers in eastern Tibet and in Gu-ge in the west new translations were produced with the help of contemporary Indian tradition. Because the old tantras of the Imperial period were recognized only by the old school, which goes back to the period of "the earlier propagation of the doctrine" (*snga-dar*), other "orthodox" tantras were adopted for Tibetan religious literature. Among them was the extremely important Kālacakra (*dus-kyi 'khor-lo*), "Wheel of Time," first introduced into Tibet by Gyi-jo Lo-tstsha-ba in 1026, sixty years after its arrival in India. The work of translating Indian Buddhist books continued as long as the Tibetans were able to obtain Indian teachers, notwithstanding the Muslim conquest of Bihar and the disappearance of Buddhism in the country of its origin. Even then the famous Jo-nang-pa author Tāranātha (born 1575) added new translations such as *The Itinerary to Kalāpa* (Kalāpa was the capital of the country of Shambhala) to the treasury of Tibetan religious works of Indian origin.

The Tibetans, like other Buddhists, call the collection of their holy scriptures *The Three Baskets* (*Tripiṭaka*, Tib. *sDe-snod gsum*). From earliest times it consisted of the three sections of *Vinaya* ("monastic discipline"), *Sūtra* ("epitome or aphorisms of the Buddha"), and *Abhidharma* ("systematical philosophy, compiled by later authorities"). The division actually used by the Tibetans is that of the two great collections: *bKa'-'gyur, Translation of the Word* [of the Buddha], and *bsTan-'gyur, Translation of Compendia and Commentaries* [on the *bKa'-'gyur* texts], written by Buddhist masters of the law. According to tradition, the *bKa'-'gyur* collection goes back to the thirteenth century; that of the *bsTan-'gyur* is closely connected with the polymath Bu-ston (1290-1364) and is called the *bsTan-'gyur of Zha-lu*, Zha-lu being Bu-ston's monastery. Originally, these collections circulated only in handwritten copies.

The first printed edition was made in 1410 in China, not Tibet, during the reign of the Yung-lo emperor of the Ming. According to recent research, it seems to have been printed on copper plates. A second edition, the so-called *Wan-li bKa'-'gyur* comprised of 105 volumes, was made in 1605 and was followed by the third edition in 1684 during the K'ang-hsi period. Both collections were printed for the fourth time in 1737. The blocks of the third edition were destroyed during the Boxer uprising in 1900, although copies survived in libraries.

The oldest edition printed in Tibet was carved during the time of the Seventh Dalai Lama at sNar-thang where the blocks were also kept. The *bKa'-'gyur* was completed in 1731 and the *bsTan-'gyur* in 1742, the first comprising 100, the latter 225 volumes. The sDe-dge edition, which goes back to an older Li-thang edition now lost, was printed in red ink in 1733 and was based on the Ming edition.

The Lhasa edition of the *bKa'-'gyur*, printed by order of the Thirteenth Dalai Lama, comprises 100 volumes. The script is large and very legible. A corresponding *bsTan-'gyur* edition was planned, but stormy times prevented the realization of the plan. Another printing of the canon which belongs to the "sDe-dge family", is kept in Co-ne, the *bKa'-'gyur* having been printed earlier than the *bsTan-'gyur*, the latter being completed in 1773. Other Tibetan *bKa'-'gyur* editions are reported to have been printed at Ch'ab-mdo and Punakha in Bhutan. The printing blocks of the Tibetan *bKa'-'gyur* of Ulan Bator were manufactured in Tibet in 1804 by the fourth rJe-btsun Dam-pa Khutukhtu. They consist of gold letters soldered to copper sheets.

Traditionally the three subdivisions of the *bKa'-'gyur* are the following: *Vinaya, Sūtra* and *Tantra* ("magical and mystic texts"). The *Sūtra* section contains not only the old Hīnayāna but also the Mahāyāna texts. In the later printed editions, however, the arrangement of the sections varies. The *bKa'-'gyur* generally consists of the following subdivisions: 1) *'Dul-ba* (*Vinaya*); 2) *Sher-phyin* (*Prajñāpāramitā*, "attainment of perfect transcendental wisdom"); 3) *Sangs-rgyas phal-po-che* (*Buddhāvataṃsaka*, "a large number of Buddhas"), a huge *sūtra* with several subsections; 4) *dKon-mchog brtsegs-pa* (*Ratna Kūṭa*, "jewel summit"), another large collection of Mahāyāna sūtras describing the names and attributes of the Buddha. Some editions also contain the *Kāshyapaparivarta*, the Tibetan translation being less complete than the Chinese. Then follow 5) the *mDo* (*Sūtra*) and 6) *rGyud* (*Tantra*). Certain editions have also extracted from the *sūtra* division the texts dealing with the passing away of the Buddha and have formed a *Nirvāṇa* section (*Myang-'das*).

The *bsTan-'gyur* is subdivided into the two large sections: *rGyud-'grel* ("*Commentaries on the tantras*") and *mDo'grel* ("*Commentaries on the sūtras*"). Certain *bsTan-gyur* editions have in addition a section of hymns (*bStod-tshogs*) to the historical Buddha as well as to other Buddhas, Bodhisattvas, and gods of the vast Mahāyāna and Vajrayāna pantheon, and another section, *sNa-tshogs*, "*Various Texts*," which contains translations of the secular Indian sciences such as grammar, theory of poetry (*Kāvya*), painting, construction of images, mathematics, astronomy, astrology, alchemy, medicine, etc.

The collection of old tantras (*rNying-ma'i rgyud 'bum*) is accepted as authoritative by the rNying-ma school; not, however, by the dGe-lugs-pa.

BIBLIOGRAPHY

CATALOGUES OF THE ENTIRE CANON

A Complete Catalogue of the Tibetan Buddhist Canons (BKaḥ-ḥgyur and Bstan-ḥgyur), 2 vols., ed. by Hakuju Ui, Munetada Suzuki, Yenshô Kanakura, Tôkan Tada, Tôhoku Imperial University, Sendai 1934 (generally quoted as the "Tôhoku Catalogue").

CATALOGUES OF THE BKA'-'GYUR

I. J. Schmidt, *Index des Kandjur*, Kaiserliche Akademie der Wissenschaften, St. Petersburg 1845 (an index of a handwritten *bKa'-'gyur* in St.

Petersburg); Alexander Csoma de Körös, *Analyse du Kandjour*. Traduite de l'anglais et augmentée de diverses additions et remarques par M. Léon Feer, Annales du Musée Guimet 2, Paris 1881; Hermann Beckh, *Verzeichnis der tibetischen Handschriften der Königlichen Bibliothek zu Berlin I: Kanjur*, Berlin 1914; *A Comparative Analytical Catalogue of the Kanjur Division of the Tibetan Tripiṭaka edited in Peking during the K'ang-hsi Era*, Otani Daigako Library, Kyoto 1930/32 (generally quoted by the name "Otani Catalogue"); Taishun Mibu, *A Comparative List of the BKaḥ-ḥgyur Division in the Co-ne, Peking, Sde-dge and Snar-thaṅ Editions*, Taisho Daigaku Kenkyokiyo no. 44, Tokyo 1959; F. A. Bischoff, *Der Kanjur und seine Kolophone*, 2 vols., The Selbstverlag Press, Bloomington 1968.

CATALOGUES OF THE BSTAN-'GYUR

Alexander Csoma de Körös, *Abstract of the Contents of the Bstangyur*, Asiatic Researches 20, Calcutta 1836; Palmyr Cordier, *Catalogue du Fonds Tibétain de la Bibliothèque Nationale, Partie II et III*, 2 vols.: Index du Bstan-ḥgyur, Paris 1909-15; Marcelle Lalou, *Répertoire du Tanjur d'après le catalogue de P. Cordier*, Paris 1933.

STUDIES IN THE BUDDHIST CANON

Georg Huth, "Verzeichnis der im tibetischen Tanjur, Abteilung mDo (Sûtra), Band 117-24, enthaltenen Werke," *SBAW*, phil.-hist. Classe, pp. 267-86, Berlin 1895; Georg Huth, "Nachträgliche Ergebnisse bezüglich der chronologischen Ansetzung der Werke im tibetischen Tanjur mDo, 117-24," *ZDMG* 49 (1895): 279-84; Berthold Laufer, *Bulletin de l'Académie Impériale de St. Pétersbourg*, "Die Kanjur-Ausgabe des Kaisers K'ang-hsi" (1909): pp. 567-74; Paul Pelliot, "Notes à propos d'un catalogue du Kanjur," *JA* series 4, XI (1914): 111-50; Marcelle Lalou, *Catalogue du Fonds Tibétain de la Bibliothèque National, Partie IV, Les mdo-maṅ*, Buddhica, 2ème série: documents, Paris 1931; L. D. Barnett, "Index der Abteilung mDo des handschriftlichen Kanjurs im Britischen Museum," *AM* 7 (1931/32): 157-78; Friedrich Weller, "Zum Kanjur und Tanjur von Derge," *OLZ* (1936): 201-18; Kenneth K. S. Ch'en, "The Tibetan Tripiṭaka," *HJAS* 9 (1946): 53-62; Arnold Kunst, "Another Catalogue of the Kanjur," *BSOAS* 12 (1945/48): 106-21 (dealing with a manuscript Kanjur at Cambridge); G. Tucci, "Tibetan Notes: 1. The Tibetan Tripiṭaka," *HJAS* 12 (1949): 477-81; R. O. Meisezahl, "Über zwei mDo-maṅ Redaktionen und ihre Editionen in Tibet und China," *ZS* 2 (1968): 67-149; A. Fonahn, *Notes on the Tanjur in Oslo*, Oslo Etnografiske Museums, Skrifter Bind 3, no. 4, Oslo; R. D. Badaraev, "Notes on a list of the Various Editions of the Kanjur," *AOH* 21 (1968): 339-51.

IMPORTANT EDITIONS AND TRANSLATION OF CANONICAL SCRIPTURES

I. J. Schmidt, *Der Weise und der Tor*, Tibetischer Text und deutsche Übersetzung, 2 vols., St. Petersburg 1843; Philippe Édouard Foucaux, *Rgya tch'er rol pa, ou dévelloppement des jeux, contenant l'histoire du Bouddha Çakya Mouni*, traduit sur une version tibétaine du Bkah hgyour, 2 vols., Paris 1847-1848 (the Tibetan version of the Lalita-vistara); Anton Schiefner, *Ergänzungen und Berichtigungen zu Schmidt's Ausgabe des Dsanglun*, St. Petersburg 1852; W. Woodville Rockhill, *The Life of the Buddha and the Early History of His Order*, (derived from Tibetan works in the bKah-hgyur and Bstan-hgyur), London 1884; Léon Feer, *Fragments et textes tirés du Kandjour*, Annales du Musée Guimet 5, Paris 1884; H. Wenzel, *Suhṛllekha. Brief des Nāgārjuna an König Udayana*, Übersetzung aus dem Tibetischen, Leipzig 1886; P. Ghosha, *Sher-Phyin*, 3 vols., Bibliotheca Indica, Calcutta 1888/89 (Tibetan text of the Śatasāhasrikā Prajñāpāramitā); Sarat Chandra Das, *Avadāna Kalpalatā*, 2 vols., Bibliotheca Indica, Calcutta 1889-1917 (a collection of legends with their Tibetan translations); Julius Weber, "Das buddhistische Sūtra der 'Acht Erscheinungen', Herausgegeben von Georg Huth," *ZDMG* 45 (1891): 577-91; W. Woodville Rockhill, *Udânavarga. A collection of verses from the Buddhist canon* compiled by Dharmatrâta, translated from the Tibetan of the Bkah-hgyur, London 1892; Anton Schiefner, *Tibetan Tales, derived from Indian Sources*, translated from the Tibetan of the Kah-gyur, translated from the German by W. R. S. Ralston, London 1906; Hermann Beckh, "Die tibetische Übersetzung von Kālidāsas Meghadūta (edited from the *bsTan-'gyur*)," *ABAW* (1906); Anhang, Berlin 1907; Hermann Beckh, *Udānavarga, Eine Sammlung buddhistischer Sprüche in tibetischer Sprache*, Berlin 1911; Berthold Laufer, *Das Citralakṣana*. Nach dem tibetischen Tanjur herausgegeben und übersetzt, Dokumente der indischen Kunst I., Heft "Malerei," Leipzig 1913; Satis Chandra Vidyabhusana, *So-sor-thar-pa*, edited and translated, Calcutta 1915 (the Tibetan Version of the Vinaya Prātimoksha text); W. L. Campbell, *She-rab Dong-bu or Prajnya Danda by Lu-trub (Nagarjuna)*, edited and translated, Calcutta 1919; M. Shahidullah, *Les chants mystiques de Kaṇha et de Saraha*, en Apabhraṃśa avec les versions tibétaines, Paris 1928; Friedrich Weller, *Das Leben des Buddha nach Aśvaghoṣa's Buddhacarita*, tibetisch und deutsch, 2 vols., Leipzig 1928; Marcelle Lalou, *Iconographie des étoffes peintes (paṭa) dans le Mañjuśrīmūlakalpa*, Buddhica, 1ème série, tome VI, Paris 1930 (with the Tibetan text of three chapters of the Mañjuśrīmūlakalpa); Friedrich Weller, *Das tibetische Brahmajālasūtra*, Leipzig 1934; Friedrich Weller, "Das tibetische Brahmajālasūtra" (German translation), *ZII* 10 (1935): 1-61; F. W. Thomas, *Tibetan Literary Texts and Documents Concerning Chinese Turkestan, vol. 1: Literary texts* (from the Tibetan canon), London 1935; N. N. Chaudhuri, *Studies in the Apabhraṃśa Texts of the Ḍākārṇava*, Calcutta Sanskrit Series 10, Calcutta 1935 (with Tibetan version); P. C. Bagchi, *Dohākośa*, Calcutta Sanskrit Series no. 25c, Calcutta 1938 (with the Tibetan translation); Helmut Hoffmann,

Bruchstücke des Āṭānāṭikasūtra aus dem zentralasiatischen Sanskrit-Kanon der Buddhisten (with a Tibetan version), Königlich Preussische Turfan-Expeditionen, Kleinere Sanskrit-Texte 5, Leipzig 1939; Johannes Nobel, Suvarṇaprabhāsottama-Sūtra. Die tibetischen Übersetzungen mit einem Wörterbuch herausgegeben, 2 vols., Leiden/Stuttgart 1944/50; Ernst Waldschmidt, Das Mahāparinirvāṇasūtra, Teil 2 und 3, Textbearbeitung, ADAW 1950, no. 2, Berlin 1951 (with a Tibetan version); D. R. Shackleton Bailey, The Śatapañcāśatka of Mātṛceṭa, Cambridge 1951 (a Buddha hymn with Tibetan translation); Jacob Ensink, The Question of Rāṣṭrapāla, Zwolle 1952 (Tibetan text with English translation); Friedrich Weller, Tibetisch-Sanskritischer Index zum Bodhicaryāvatāra, ALAW 46, no. 3, 47 no. 3, 2 vols., Leipzig 1953/55; Edward Conze, Abhisamayālankāra, Serie Orientale Roma, Roma 1954 (translation with Sanskrit-Tibetan index); Johannes Nobel, Udrāyaṇa, König von Roruka, die tibetische Übersetzung des Sanskrittextes, 2 vols. (vol. 1: Tibetan text and German translation, vol. 2: glossary), Wiesbaden 1955; Giuseppe Tucci, Minor Buddhist Texts, 2 vols., Serie Orientale Roma, Roma 1956/58; Ernst Waldschmidt, Das Catuṣpariṣatsūtra, Teil 2 und 3 (Textbearbeitung), ADAW 1956, no. 1, Berlin 1956 (with Tibetan version); F. A. Bischoff, Ārya Mahābala-nāma-mahāyānasūtra, tibétain (Mss. de Touen-houang) et chinois, Buddhica, série 1, tome X, Paris 1956; Johannes Nobel, Suvarṇaprabhāsottamasūtra. I-tsing's chinesische Version und ihre tibetische Übersetzung, 2 vols., Leiden 1958; David Snellgrove, The Hevajra Tantra, 2 vols., London 1959 (Sanskrit and Tibetan texts with translation and notes); E. Obermiller, Prajñāpāramitā-ratnaguṇasaṃcaya-gāthāḥ, Bibliotheca Buddhica 29, Leningrad 1937, reprint, The Hague 1960 (Sanskrit and Tibetan texts); R. O. Meisezahl, "The Amoghapāśahṛdayadhāraṇī," critically edited and translated, MN 17 (1962): 265-328; Friedrich Weller, "Betrachtungen über einen Ratnakūṭa-Text," FF (1963): 369-74; Friedrich Weller, Zum Kāśyapaparivarta, Heft 2: Verdeutschung des Sanskrittibetischen Textes, ASAW 57, no. 3, Berlin 1965; Tilman Vetter, Dharmakīrti's Pramāṇaviniścaya, 1. Kapitel: Pratyakṣam, SÖAW 250, Abh. no. 3, Wien 1966; Ernst Steinkellner, Dharmakīrti's Hetubinduḥ, 1. Abhandlung, Wien 1967 (with Tibetan text); R. E. Emmerick, Tibetan Texts Concerning Khotan, London Oriental Series, vol. 19, London 1967; Dieter Schlingloff, Die Buddhastotras des Mātṛceṭa, ADAW 1968, no. 2, Berlin 1968 (with Tibetan translation); Herbert V. Guenther, The Royal Song of Saraha, Seattle and London 1969 (Dohās of Saraha); J. Terjék, "Fragments of the Tibetan Sūtra of 'The Wise and the Fool' from Tun-huang," AOH 22 (1969): 289-334; Helmut H. R. Hoffmann, "Kālacakra Studies I: Manichaeism, Christianity and Islam in the Kālacakra Tantra," CAJ 13 (1969): 52-73 (verses from the Kālacakra Tantra, book 1 with Tibetan version); Claus Vogel, The Teachings of the Six Heretics, according to the Pravrajyāvastu of the Tibetan Mūlasarvāstivāda Vinaya, AKM 39, 4, Wiesbaden 1970; Walter Fuchs, Die Mandjurischen Druchausgaben des Hsin-ching (Hṛdayasūtra), AKM 39, 3, Wiesbaden 1970 (also contains the photomechanical reproduction of the Tibetan version). There are additional texts published by Tibetan publishing houses, appeared after the final proof reading.

Tibetan Buddhist Literature
Compiled by Tibetan Authors*

Tibetan Buddhist literature is primarily an exegesis of the canonical scriptures, including the sciences, contained in the *sūtra* or "textbooks" of the *bsTan-'gyur* on quasisecular matters such as medicine and law. To give a full survey of this literature or even a "history of literature" would be premature. Only the main characteristics of this enormous mass of literary activity can be described at present. More time is needed to review even the many books recently published by Tibetan scholars, many of whom only began publishing the literature available to them after they fled communist occupied Tibet for other countries, such as India, and these are only a part of the total of Tibetan Buddhist literature. Therefore, each day may provide the scholar with more Tibetan scholastic works.

The most ancient examples of original Tibetan literature which have come down to us are represented by two seventh century treatises on Tibetan grammar by Thon-mi Sambhoṭa, the minister of Srong-btsan sgam-po: the *Sum-cu-pa, The Thirty Letters* (i.e., the alphabet), and the *rTags-kyi 'jug-pa The Description of the Genders of Tibetan Sounds,* where the functions of the prefixes according to the imminent character of the Tibetan language are explained. These treatises, written in memorial verse, have been used by all later authors, who commented on them according to the different grammatical schools which later developed. This may be seen from a study of the available grammars of Si-tu paṇ-chen, Zha-lu lo-tsa-ba (1441-1528), and lCang-skya Rol-pai rDo-rje (born A.D. 1714), to mention only the most well-known instances.

The next available examples of Tibetan literary composition date back to the eleventh century. These are letters and verses of praise of famous religious teachers, such as the thirty verses of 'Brom-ston in honor of Atīsha. Some of these letters were composed by the monk-kings of Gu-ge, Ye-shes-'od and Zhi-ba-'od, and by the "Great Translator" Rin-chen bzang-po. All are of a doctrinal nature and are devoted primarily to the refutation of some misleading interpretation of the tantras. There are also handbooks of ascetics of the *bLo-sbyong* ("Cleansing of the Mind") type patterned after Atīsha's *Bodhipatha-pradīpa (Lamp for the Way to Enlightenment),* extant also in a Sanskrit version. Certainly many of the songs of the poet-saint Mi-la Ras-pa (1040-1123), which follow the pattern of the *Dohā* or Vajragīti songs ("Diamond Songs") of the Indian Siddhas, have a personal, genuinely Tibetan touch. The books containing these verses, the *Hundred Thousand Songs* and the *Biography of the Saint (rNam-thar),* were not compiled by the master's disciple Ras-chung-pa (1084-1161), as previously assumed, but by a later bKa-brgyud-pa lama, "the

---

* Chronicles dealing with Tibetan history will be excluded from this chapter as they have already been discussed in the chapter on sources for Tibetan history.

Madman of gTsang" (gTsang-smyon he-ru-ka). A careful study of the *Hundred Thousand Songs* shows that portions of other traditions were incorporated into the book of the "Madman," such as the chapters of the mountain goddesses, *Tshe-ring-ma,* in the Mount Everest area which contain a separate colophon by Mi-la's personal disciples, Bodhi-rāja and bZhi-ba-'od. A survey of Mahāyāna teachings, the *Jewel Ornament of Liberation* by sGam-po-pa, has been preserved and is available in English translation.

On the writings of the great hierarchs of Sa-skya, we are fortunate enough to possess their *Collected Works (gSung-'bum)* in the large collection of the *Sa-skya bka-'bum,* which includes the writings of Kun-dga snying-po (1092-1158), bSod-nams rtse-mo (1142-82), Grags-pa rgyal-mtshan (1147-1216), the great Sa-skya Paṇḍita (1182-1251), and 'Phags-pa (1235-80). These authors discussed the tantric doctrines of their school, especially the *Hevajra,* although they did not neglect the other cycles such as the *Cakrasamvara,* the *Sampuṭa,* and the *Gur-mgon.* There also exist general descriptions of the entire tantric field, such as the *General Analysis of the Tantra* (rGyud sde spyii rnam par bzhag) by the first hierarch. This work contains the later generally accepted classification of the tantras, such as *kriyā, caryâ, yoga,* and *anuttara yoga,* as well as the two groups of father and mother tantras (cp. chapter VII on religion). Although the Sa-skya-pa stressed Tantrism they did not restrict themselves to this field but composed works giving a general introduction to the essentials of Buddhism, such as bSod-nams rtse-mo's *Door for Entering the Religious Law (Chos-la'jug-pai sgo)* or 'Phags-pa's *General Instructions* for the use of the emperor Khubilai and certain mongol princes. Historical and chronological works are also to be found among the Sa-skya lamas' writings and include the *Royal Lineage of the Shākya Family* by Grags-pa rgyal-mtshan. There are also letters (by Sa-skya Paṇḍita and 'Phags-pa), medical works (by Grags-pa rgyal-mtshan) and books on philosophy and logic (by Sa-skya Paṇḍita), and poetics (Indian *Kāvya* style) by 'Phags-pa. Sa-skya Paṇḍita is especially famous for his *Legs-bshad (Subhāshita),* a collection of maxims written in an extremely florid style, which is a guide to worldly as well as religious life.

Similar *gSung-'bum* by many other polymaths of the different Tibetan Buddhist schools also exist. These relate to the different branches of the bKa-brgyud-pa, rNying-ma-pa, dGe-lugs-pa, and Jo-nang-pa. An outstanding example is the *gSung-'bum* of Bu-ston Rin-po-che (1290-1364) who wrote on practically all subjects of Tibetan Buddhism: tantra (stressing the Kālacakra of which he is perhaps the supreme authority), religious art and iconography, general history, the *History of the Kālacakra (Dus-'khor chos-'byung), Perfection of Wisdom,* logic, and grammar.

The "old school" of Buddhism, the rNying-ma-pa, which claims to go back to the times of Padmasambhava and Vimalamitra (eighth century), is characterized by its having most of its important books, the so-called *gTer-ma,* "treasures," allegedly hidden by Padmasambhava or his disciples for later times when the teachings could be understood. This is true of the basic work on the "Great Perfection" doctrine, the *sNying-thig*, whose authoritative commentator was Klong-chen rab-'byams-pa (1308-63) and through whom the school obtained the definitive codification of its doctrine. The rNying-ma-pa also have its own collection of tantras, the *rGyud-'bum*, which is not acknowledged by the other schools because it is believed to be of doubtful origin. The other schools of Tibetan Buddhism were also offended by the interconnection of rNying-ma-pa and Bon-po doctrines. Among the *gTer-ma* are two basic and well-known books of this sect: the *Biography of Padmasambhava (Padma thang-yig)*, of which many versions exist, and the five separately discovered "Scrolls of the Commands of Padmasambhava," which speak of gods, demons, the kings, the queens, the *paṇḍits* and translators, and the ministers. The discoverer of all these works was O-rgyan gling-pa, who probably found and edited them with apocryphal additions in 1347 and 1352 respectively. The *Rin-chen gter-mdzod*, a huge collection of many other *gTer-ma*, not only includes the history of the "Treasure Discoverers" and another version of Padmasambhava's biography, but also masses of liturgical, ritualistic, and magical treatises. It was printed as late as the beginning of the last century. The other Tibetan religious schools, i.e., the bKa-brgyud-pa, dGe-lugs-pa, and Bon-po have their own *Bar-do* literature which has not yet been studied. The famous *Bar-do thos-grol*, the so-called *Tibetan Book of the Dead*, is also believed to be a *gTer-ma*. The text, at least in the form in which it became known in the West, shows striking resemblances to Bon-po materials. Another famous *gTer-ston* who "found" several important mystical rDzogs-chen works was Nyang-ral Nyi-ma od-zer (1136-1203).

One of the most representative *gSung-bum* is, of course, that of the great reformer and founder of the dGe-lugs-pa school, bTsong-kha-pa, (1357-1419), whose works became the prototype for the *Collected Works* of all later important dGe-lugs-pa scholars and incarnations, especially those of the Dalai Lamas and the Paṇ-chen Rin-po-che. The most important of his works is his *Byang-chub lam-rim chen-mo, Gradual Path to Enlightenment*, which in its literary style is influenced by the Indian master Shāntideva's *Bodhicaryāvatāra* and Atīsha's *Bodhipathapradīpa*. bTsong-kha-pa's work covers the entire field of Mahāyāna Buddhism and is also extant in an abbreviated form (*Lam-rim chung-ngu*) for those who are unable to study the longer version. Although the master struggled against the abuse of the tantras he nevertheless appreciated them and devoted several treatises to this field. In addition to the representative *sNgags-rim chen-mo*, The *Gradual Way of the Mantras* he wrote different specialized works on the cycles of *Guhyasamāja, Saṃvara*, and *Kālacakra*, on which the respective writings of his disciples rGyal-tshab-rje (1364-1432) and mKhas-grub-rje (1385-1438) are based. Other works of his are devoted to the *Perfection of Wisdom*, logic, and the Mādyamika doctrine of *Nāgārjuna*.

While rGyal-tshab-rje stressed systematic philosophy, mKhas-grub-rje excelled in the tantric field. His main contributions are *The Explicit Description of the Tantras in General* (*rGyud-sde spyi rnam-par bzhag-pa*) and his vast subcommentary to the Kālacakra according to the two main chains of tradition ('*Bro and Rva*). He also wrote on the *Perfection of Wisdom*, logic, and *vinaya*.

The *gSung-'bum* of bTsong-kha-pa and his disciples are representative samples of the writings of the great dGe-lugs-pa hierarchs who had nothing new to add to the framework established by these three authors. However, the *gSung-'bum* of the Great Fifth Dalai Lama, Ngag-dbang blo-bzang rgya-mtsho (1617-82), contains in addition to treatises on the subjects already described, an interesting book on the incarnations of Avalokiteshvara as far as his predecessor, the Fourth Dalai Lama; a collection of valuable documents dealing with the erection of religious buildings and objects; descriptions of the *sMon-lam* ceremonies; and donations by Mongol princes. They are written in an elegant style characteristic of this hierarch. It seems remarkable that he was vividly interested in Indian poetics as described in the *Kāvyādarsha* of Daṇḍin, upon which he wrote a large commentary. He is also the author of a stylistically remarkable description of the sanctuaries of Lhasa (*Lha-ldan sprul-pai gtsug-lag khang-gi dkar-chag*), now well known in the West, and of a book on Indian and Chinese astrology. But most astonishing and differing greatly from the works of other dGe-lugs-pa hierarchs is an entire section, sealed and available only to those dGe-lugs-pa monks who have special permission to peruse it, which contains four volumes of the secret doctrines of the rival sect, the rNying-ma-pa (and even of a 'Brug-pa master). The Fifth Dalai Lama was educated by several rNying-ma-pa teachers and had mastered their doctrines.

Of significance in connection with the works of the Fifth Dalai Lama is an unusual collection of writings by a layman, the regent (*sde-srid*), installed by the ruler. Sangs-rgyas rgya-mtsho, who became regent in 1679 and died in 1705, mastered the knowledge of nearly all religious schools including the Bon religion, and compiled several important and voluminous works: the *Vaiḍūrya dkar-po* (*White Lapis Lazuli*), which deals with astrology and chronology as well as burial rites and demons of the folk religion: the *Vaiḍūrya gya-sel* (*Remover of Rust from the Vaiḍūrya*), which refutes the author's critics in this field; the *Vaiḍūrya ser-po* (*Yellow Lapis Lazuli*), which describes the history and diffusion of the Yellow Church; the *Dvangs-shel me-long* (*The Pure Crystal Mirror*), which deals with law; and the *Vaiḍūrya sngon-po* (*Blue Lapis Lazuli*), a medical treatise which is a commentary to the *rGyud-bzhi* or *Four Roots,* the anonymous old authoritative work on medicine, with its supplement the *Lhan-thabs* (*The Addenda or The Appendix*).

Among the Paṇ-chen Rin-po-che, the first, Blo-bzang Chos-kyi rGyal-mtshan (1569-1662), wrote an important subcommentary to the Kālacakra work *Vimalaprabhā* (*Immaculate Lustre*) from which information was taken by the third incarnation, bLo-bzang dpal-ldan ye-shes, in his *Shambha-la'i lam-yig* (*Description of the Way to Shambhala*), containing different kinds of curious geographical information. Among his sources the Paṇ-chen mentions the *Shambhala-pai lam-yig*, i.e., the *Itinerary of Shambhala-pa*. This author, also called Man-lung gu-ru, was a Tibetan pilgrim born in 1239, who described the areas he visited according to the cardinal points: east (China), south (India, Bōdh Gayā and Dhānyakaṭaka), west (Udyāna), north (Shambhala), and center (Tibet).

Among the many other dGe-lugs-pa polymaths, kLong-rdol bla-ma (born in 1719) and the third Thu-kvan blo-bzang chos-kyi nyi-ma (1737-1802) are important. The latter has done interesting work on the religions known to him, including Confucianism and Taoism. kLong-rdol bla-ma is important for his bibliographical "book lists" (*thob-yig*) and for his encyclopedic writing.

Just as bTsong-kha-pa and his chief disciples created a *summa* of the Buddhist doctrine for the dGe-lugs-pa school, about two centuries later the same was done for the bKa-brgyud-pa by Padma dkar-po (1526-92) of the 'Brug-pa sub-sect. Padma dkar-po left an extremely important and voluminous *gSung-'bum* printed in Bhutan (Tib. *'Brug-yul*). As a great polymath he wrote on all subjects on Buddhism: logic, the *Perfection of Wisdom*, medicine, etc., but because of the typical character of his school, esoterism is the outstanding feature of his *gSung-'bum*. Cakrasamvara, the *yi-dam* of the bKa-brgyud-pa, plays an important role, but other tantric cycles including the Tārā tantra and Kālacakra were not neglected. Of these he wrote a summary according to his tradition in *The Treasure Which Explains All Secrets of Categories Concerning the Highest Ādibuddha* (*mChog-gi dang-poi sangs-rgyas rnam-par bye-ba gsang-ba thams-cad bshad-pai mdzod*). In his *History of Buddhism* (*Chos-'byung*), Padma dKar-po treated the Kālacakra as a most important subject. In another treatise the Yoga techniques of the Mahāsiddha schools are profoundly studied. Especially important are those works which give detailed information on his own school: a commentary on the "Six Principles of Nāro-pā" (*Nāro chos drug*), a list of the bKa-brgyud-pa masters and books whose teachings were followed up to the time of the founder of the 'Brug-pa sub-sect, as well as certain *rNam-thar* (biographies) of outstanding lamas of his spiritual lineage. One among them devoted to gTsang-pa rgya-ras-pa contains mystical songs (*mgur*) in the style characteristic of Mi-la ras-pa. A special collection of his own mystical songs, *Garland of Vajra Songs,* is also included in his works.

The greatest author of the Jo-nang-pa, a sect considered heretical by the dGe-lugs-pa and other schools of Tibetan Buddhism, was Tāranātha Kun-dga snying-po (born 1575), who wrote a seventeen-volume *gSung-'bum*. This collection begins with his very important autobiography, a work which deserves detailed investigation for it reveals the sources of his knowledge and proves that during his lifetime there was direct contact with Indian masters with whom he studied. In this work as in his historical books such as the famous *rGya-gar chos-'byung* (*History of Buddhism in India*), the tantras are prominent. His overwhelming interest lay in the forms of Buddhist Tantrism or Vajrayāna, to which his other historical work, the *Mine of Jewels*, which describes seven esoteric Vajrayāna lineages of Gurus, is exclusively devoted. His works also contain a long biography of the Buddha Shākyamuni compiled from various sources. The historical style is also characteristic of the *Religious History of the Cycle of the King of Tantras, the Yamāntaka*, which describes the chain of gurus who had devoted themselves to the visualization of the red and black forms of that *yi-dam* (*rGyud-rgyal gshin-rje-gshed skor-gyi chos-'byung*). The traditions of the Indian Siddha Krishnācārin are studied in a commentary to his *Dohā* mystical verses. A most important work is his *Ocean of Tutelary Gods, a Jewel Mine of Sādhana* (*Yi-dam rgya-mtsho sgrub-thabs rin-chen 'byung- gnas*), which describes the manner of realizing all the *Yi-dams* with their symbols, colors, and postures.

Traditionally the foremost place among the tantric teachings is considered to be held, as in the studies of the earlier Jo-nang-pa authors such as Dol-po-pa (1292-1361), by the Kālacakra to which system Tāranātha devoted several treatises. These include the important *History of the Kālacakra*, a commentary to the Kālacakra initiation ritual according to Nā-ro-pā's *Sekoddesha Ṭīkā*, and a large work of 278 pages on the mystical experiences and evocations of this system. Tāranātha also wrote numerous smaller works dealing with prayers, *sādhana*, yoga, and the astrology of the Kālacakra.

Among the works of the later unreformed schools the *gSung-'bum* of Mi-pham 'Jam-dpal dgyes-pai rdo-rje (1846-1912), a rNying-ma-pa polygraph, is outstanding. His nineteen volumes of writings comprise all the rNying-ma teachings. They also contain authoritative interpretations of the Kālacakra as practiced by the rNying-ma-pa, e.g., "The Lapis Lazuli Mirror Which Makes Clear the Essence of the Vajra-Yoga in the Utpannakrama of the Glorious Kālacakra" (*dPal dus kyi 'khor lo'i rdzogs rim rdo rje'i rnal 'byor gyi dgongs gnad gsal byed baiḍūryai me long*).

Important literature continues being produced even today. Contemporary refugee lamas in India, for instance, are publishing valuable works. One of these is the voluminous History of the *rNying-ma Doctrine* (*rNying-mai chos-'byung*) by the rNying-ma-pa incarnation bDud-'joms rin-po-che, a mine of valuable information.

BIBLIOGRAPHY

The most important books dealing with aspects of Tibetan literature are the following: Giuseppe Tucci, *Tibetan Painted Scrolls*, Roma 1949, vol. 1, pp.

94-170; Lokesh Chandra, *Materials for a History of Tibetan Literature*, Śatapitaka Series 28, 3 vols., New Delhi 1963; Lokesh Chandra, *Eminent Tibetan Polymaths of Mongolia*, Śatapitaka Series 16, New Delhi 1961. Catalogues of Tibetan block-prints and manuscripts: I. J. Schmidt and O. Boehtlingk, *Verzeichnis der Handschriften und Holzdrucke im Asiatischen Museum der Kaiserlichen Akademie der Wissenschaften*, Bulletin historico-philologique de l'Académie Impériale des Sciences de St. Pétersbourg, 4, 1847, no. 6-8; W. P. Wassilieff, "Die auf den Buddhismus bezüglichen Werke der Universitäts-Bibliothek zu Kasan," *Mélanges Asiatiques* 2, pp. 347-86; L. D. Barnett and A. H. Francke, "Tibetan Manuscripts and Sgrafitti discovered by Dr. M. A. Stein at Endere." In M. A. Stein, *Ancient Khotan* 1, pp. 548-69, Oxford 1907; Alexander Csoma de Körös, "Enumeration of Historical and Grammatical Works to be met with in Tibet," *JPASB* 7 (1911, extra no.): 81-87; L. A. Waddell, "Tibetan Manuscripts and Books etc., collected during the Young-husband Mission to Lhasa," *Asiatic Quarterly Review* 34 (1912): 80-113; J. van Manen, "A Contribution to the Bibliography of Tibet," *JPASB* 18 (1922): 445-525; Andrew Vostrikov, "Some Corrections and Critical Remarks on Dr. Johan van Manen's Contribution to the Bibliography of Tibet," *BSOS* 8 (1934): 51-75; J. Bacot, "La collection tibétaine Schilling von Canstadt à la Bibliothèque de l'Institut," *JA* (1924): 321-48; G. Tsybikov: *Musei Asiatici Petropolitani Notitiae IV* pp. 1-7, St. Petersburg; B. Baradijn: *Musei Asiatici Petropolitani Notitiae VII*, pp. 49-84, St. Petersburg; Marcelle Lalou, *Catalogue du Fonds Tibétain de la Bibliothèque Nationale IV: Les mdo-maṅ*, Buddhica, 2me série, Documents, Paris 1931; Louis Ligeti, "Ouvrages tibétains rédigés à l'usage de Csoma," *TP* 30 (1933): 26-36; J. Filliozat, "Liste des manuscrits de la collection Palmyr Cordier à la Bibliothèque Nationale," *JA* (1934): 168-70; M. Lalou, *Inventaire des manuscrits tibétains de Touen-houang conservés à la Bibliothèque Nationale* (Fonds Pelliot Tibétain), 3 vols., Paris 1939-61; L. J. Nagy, "Tibetan Books and Manuscripts of Alexander Csoma de Körös in the Library of the Hungarian Academy of Sciences," *Analecta Orientalia memoriae Alexander Csoma de Körös dicata*, Budapest 1942-47, pp. 29-56; René Nebesky-Wojkowitz, "Einige tibetische Werke über Grammatik und Poetik," *AV* 4 (1949): 154-59; Pentti Aalto, *Le Mdo-maṅ conservé a la Bibliotèque Universitaire de Helsinki*, Eripainos, Miscellanea Bibliographica 6, Helsinki 1952; *A Catalogue of the Tôhoku University Works on Buddhism*, edited by Yensho Kanakura, Ryujo Yamade, Tokan Tada, and Hakuyu Hadano, Tôhoku University, Sendai 1953; J. Bacot, "Titres et colophons d'ouvrages non-canoniques tibétains," *BEFEO* 44 (1954): 275-334; Gombojab, "Mongolčud-un töbed kele-ber jokiyagsan jokiyal-un jüyil," *Studia Mongolica* 1 fasc. 28, pp. 1-40, Ulan Bator; R. O. Meisezahl, "Die tibetischen Handschriften und Drucke des Linden-Museums in Stuttgart," *Tribus*, Neue Folge 7 (1957): 1-166; R. O. Meisezahl, *Alttibetische Hand-schriften der Völkerkundlichen Sammlungen der Stadt Mannheim im Reiss-Museum*, Libri 11: 1 (48 pp.), Copenhagen; Manfred Taube, "Verzeichnis der Tibetica des Leipziger Völkerkunde-museums," *Jahrbuch des Museums für Völkerkunde zu Leipzig* 17 (1958): 94-139; René Nebesky-Wojkowitz, "Tibetan

Blockprints and Manuscripts in Possession of the Museum of Ethnology in Vienna," *AV* 13 (1958): 174-209; Lokesh Chandra, "The Authors of the Sumbums," *IIJ* 2 (1958): 110-27; Lokesh Chandra, "Tibetan Works Printed by the Shöparkhang of the Potala," *Jñāna muktāvalī* (Sarasvatî Vihâra Series), New Delhi 1959, pp. 120-32; Wesley E. Needham, "The Tibetan Collection of Yale," *The Yale University Gazette* 34 (1960): 127-33; Wesley E. Needham, *Tibetica. Exhibitions in the Yale University Library on the Occasion of the 170th Meeting of the American Oriental Society*, Yale University 1960; B. D. Dandaron, *Opisanie tibetskikh rukopisej i ksilografov Buryatskogo Kompleksnogo naučno-issledovatelskogo instituta*, vyp. 1, Moskva 1960; Lokesh Chandra, "Les imprimeries tibétaines de Drepung, Derge et Peping," *JA* (1961): 503-17; Manfred Taube, *Tibetische Handschriften und Blockdrucke*, 4 vols. (Verzeichnis der Orientalischen Handschriften in Deutschland 11, 1-4), Wiesbaden 1966; David S. Snellgrove, *A Catalogue of the Tibetan Collection. Chester Beatty Library* (together with C. R. Bawden, *Catalogue of the Mongolian Collection*), Dublin 1969; Josef Kolmaš, *Tibetan Manuscripts and Blockprints in the Library of the Oriental Institute of Prague*, Academia, Prague 1969; Josef Kolmaš, *Prague Collection of Tibetan Prints from Derge*, edited, 2 vols., Asiatische Forschungen 36, Wiesbaden 1971.

Editions and translations of Tibetan original literature (with the exception of historical works on Tibetan history): Anton Schiefner, *Târanâthae de doctrinae Buddhicae in India propagatione narratio*, contextum Tibeticum, Petropoli 1868; Anton Schiefner, *Târanâtha's Geschichte des Buddhismus in Indien*, Aus dem Tibetischen übersetzt, St. Petersburg 1869; Georg Huth, *Geschichte des Buddhismus in der Mongolei*, Aus dem Tibetischen des 'Jigs-med nam-mk'a (should be: 'Jigs-med rig-pai rdo-rje), 2 vols., Strassburg 1892/96; Sarat Chandra Das, *Kah Bab Dun Dan*, compiled by Tāra Nātha (edition of the Tibetan text), Calcutta 1901; Albert Grünwedel, *Târanâtha's Edelsteinmine, das Buch von den Vermittlern der Sieben Inspirationen*, aus dem Tibetischen übersetzt, Bibliotheca Buddhica XVIII, Petrograd 1914; Berthold Laufer, *Der Roman einer tibetischen Königin*, Leipzig 1911 (Tibetan text and translation of the *bTsun mo bkai thang yig*); Albert Grünwedel, "Der Weg nach Śambhala," *AKBAW* 1915, no. 3, München 1915 (text and translation of *Pan-chen bLo-bzang dPal-ldan Ye-shes' Shambha-lai lam-yig*); Albert Grünwedel, *Die Tempel von Lhasa, Gedicht des ersten Dalai Lama, für Pilger bestimmt, SBHAW*, 1919, no. 14 (Tibetan text and German translation); Berthold Laufer, *Milaraspa, Tibetische Texte in Auswahl übertragen*, Hagen und Darmstadt 1922; Helmut Hoffmann, *Mila Raspa, Sieben Legenden*, München-Planegg 1950; Antoinette K. Gordon, *The Hundred Thousand Songs*, Selections from Milarepa, poet-saint of Tibet, Rutland/Vermont 1961; Garma C. C. Chang, *The Hundred Thousand Songs of Milarepa*, 2 vols., New York 1962 (complete translation); F. R. Hamm, "Studien zur Überlieferungsgeschichte des Mi-la'i Mgur 'Bum," *ZS* 4 (1970): 29-79; G. N. Roerich, "The Author of the Hor-chos-ḥbyuṅ," *JRAS* (1946): 192-96; Emil Schlagintweit, "Die Berechnung der Lehre von Sureçamatibhadra," (aus dem Tibetischen übersetzt), *AKBAW* (1896): 589-670; Berthold Laufer,

"Studien zur Sprachwissenschaft der Tibeter. Zamatog," *SMAW* (1898): 519-94
(about the lexicographical work *Za-ma-tog*); Emil Schlagintweit, "Die
Lebensbeschreibung von Padma Sambhava," I/II, *AKBAW* 21 (1899): 417-44;
22 (1905): 517-76 (texts and translations of parts of the *Padma thang-yig*); Sarat
Chandra Das, *An Introduction to the Grammar of the Tibetan Language, with
the Texts of Situi-sum-rtags, Dag-byed gsal-bai me-long and Situi zhal-lung*,
Darjeeling 1915; Jacques Bacot, *Une grammaire tibétaine du tibétain classique,
les slokas grammaticaux de Thonmi Sambhota, avec leur commentaires*, 2 vols.,
Annales du Musée Guimet, Bibliothèque d'Etudes 37, Paris 1928; Johannes
Schubert, "Tibetische Nationalgrammatik. Das Sum cu pa und Rtags-kyi 'ajug-pa
des Lama Dbyaṅs can grub pai rdo rje," *MSOS* 31 (1928): 1-59; 32 (1929):
1-54; Yu Dawchyuan, *Lovesongs of the Sixth Dalai Lama*, Academia Sinica,
Peiping 1930; G. C. Toussaint, *Le dict de Padma*, Paris 1933 (translation of the
Padma thang-yig); Albert Grünwedel, *Die Legenden des Naropa*, übersetzt, in
Umschrift herausgegeben und mit einem Glossar versehen, Leipzig 1933;
Giuseppe Tucci, "À propos the Legend of Naropā," *JRAS* (1935): 677-88; H. V.
Guenther, *The Life and Teachings of Nāropa*, Oxford 1963; Claus Vogel, "On
the Nā-ro-pai rnam-thar," *CAJ* 1 (1968): 8-30; Johannes Schubert, "Das
tibetische Mahātmya des Wallfahrtplatzes Triloknāth," *AA* 5 (1935): 76-78,
127-36 (a dKar-ch'ag); W. Y. Evans-Wentz, *Tibetan Yoga and Secret Doctrines*,
Oxford 1935 (translation of several esoteric texts); Johannes Schubert, "Das
tibetische Mahātmya von Lamayuru," *AA* 7 (1937): 205-9; Jacques Bacot, *La
vie de Marpa le 'traducteur', suivie d'un chapitre de l'avadāna de l'oiseau
Nīlakaṇṭha*, Buddhica 1, 7, Paris 1937; Johannes Schubert, *Tibetische National-
grammatik. Das Sum cu pa und Rtags Kyi 'ajug pa des Grosslamas von Peking
Rol pai rdo rje, mit Übersetzung und Anmerkungen versehen*, Artibus Asiae,
Supplementum Primum, Leipzig 1937; Giuseppe Tucci, *Travels of Tibetan
Pilgrims in the Swat Valley*, Calcutta 1940 (extracts from biographies); M.
Lalou, "Texte médical tibétain," *JA* (1945): 209-11; Giuseppe Tucci, *Il libro
tibetano dei morti*, Milano 1949 (the best translation of the *Bar-do thos-grol*); W.
Y. Evans-Wentz, *The Tibetan Book of the Dead*, London³ 1957; P. Poucha,
"Das tibetische Totenbuch," *Ar.Or.* 20 (1951): 136-62; Jacques A. Durr. *Deux
traités grammaticaux tibétains*, Heidelberg 1950; W. Y. Evans-Wentz, *The
Tibetan Book of the Great Liberation*, London 1954 (contains in addition to a
summary of *Padma thang-yig*, translations of different mystical treatises);
Alfonsa Ferrari, *Mkhyen-brtse's Guide to the Holy Places of Central Tibet*,
edited by L. Petech and H. Richardson, Roma 1958; Johannes Schubert,
Publikationen des modernen Chinesisch-Tibetischen Schrifttums, Institut für
Orientforschung, Deutsche Akademie der Wissenschaften zu Berlin, no. 39,
Berlin 1958; J. W. de Jong, *Mi la ras pai rnam thar*, texte tibétain de la vie de
Milarépa édité, 's-Gravenhage 1959; W. Y. Evans-Wentz, *Tibet's Great Yogi
Milarepa*, A biography from the Tibetan translated with introduction and
annotations, London and New York² 1969; Humphrey Clarke, *The Message of
Milarepa*, A selection of poems, London 1958 (songs from the *rNam-thar*);
George Roerich, *Biography of Dharmasvāmin*, Patna 1959 (text and translation

of the biography of Chag-lo-tsā-ba Chos-rje-dpal); Lokesh Chandra, *Vaiḍūrya ser-po*, 2 vols., Satapitaka Series 12, New Delhi 1960 (Tibetan text); Raghu Vira, ed., *The Samye Monastery*, Śatapitaka Series 14, New Delhi 1961 (text of a *dKar-chag*); Turrell V. Wylie, *The Geography of Tibet According to the 'Dzam-ling rgyas-bshad* Roma 1963; Turrell V. Wylie, "Dating the Geography 'Dzam Gling Rgyas Bshad through its Description of the Western Hemisphere," *CAJ* 4 (1959): 300-11; bDud-'joms rin-po-che, *Bod snga rabs gsang chen rnying mai chos 'byung*, Kalimpong 1964 (text of a history of the rNying-ma-pa); bDud-'joms rin-po-che, *snga 'gyur rnyin-ma pa'i bstan pai rnam bzhag legs bshad snang bai dga ston*, Kalimpong, n.d. (text of a systematical description of the rNying-ma-pa doctrine); D. Seyfort Ruegg, *The Life of Buston Rin po che*, Rome 1967 (text and translation); D. Snellgrove, *Four Lamas of Dolpo*, 2 vols., Oxford 1967/68 (four rNam-thar); *Sa skya pai bKa-'bum*, 15 vols., edited by the Toyo Bunko, Tokyo 1968 (the text of the complete works of the Sa-skya hierarchs until 'Phags-pa); Lokesh Chandra, ed., *Yu thok's Treatise on Tibetan Medicine*, Śatapitaka Series 72, New Delhi 1968 (Tibetan text); W. A. Unkrig, *Die Tollwut in der Heilkunde des Lamaismus*, The Sino-Swedish Expedition, Stockholm 1942; P.C. von Krasinski, *Tibetische Medizinphilosophie*, Zürich 1953 (with an introduction on Tibetan medical literature by W. A. Unkrig); Theodor Burang, *Tibetische Heilkunde*, Zürich 1957; Fr. Hübotter, *Chinesisch-Tibetische Pharmakologie und Rezeptur*, Ulm 1957; Yeshey Donden, "Tibetan Medicine—a Brief History," *TSB* 5 (1972): 7-24; Manfred Taube, "Zur Textgeschichte einiger gZuńs-bsdus Ausgaben," *ZS* 2 (1968): 55-66; Lokesh Chandra, ed., *Tibetan Chronicle of Padma dKar-po*, with a foreward by E. Gene Smith, Śatapitaka Series 75, New Delhi 1968; Ferdinand D. Lessing and Alex Wayman, *Mkhas-grub-rje's Fundamentals of the Buddhist Tantras*, The Hague and Paris 1968 (text and translation); James E. Bosson, *A Treasury of Aphoristic Jewels: The Subhāṣita ratna nidhi of Sa skya Paṇḍita in Tibetan and Mongolian*, Indiana University Publications, Uralic and Altaic Series, vol. 92, Bloomington 1969 (texts with English translation); Namgyal Dorje Dalama, ed., *The Penetration and Spread of Buddhism in China by Gung mGonpo skyab*, Berkeley 1969 (Tibetan text only); Lokesh Chandra, ed., *A 15th Century Tibetan Compendium of Knowledge by Don-dam smra-bai senge*, with an introduction by E. Gene Smith, Śatapitaka Series 78, New Delhi 1969; Ngawang Gelek Demo, ed., *The Autobiography of the first Panchen Lama Blo Bzang Chos Kyi Rgyal Mtshan*, with an English introduction by E. Gene Smith, New Delhi 1969; Nga-wang Gelek Demo, ed., *Collected Works of Thu'u bkwan Blo bzang Chos kyi nyima*, 10 vols., New Delhi 1969; Nga-wang Gelek Demo, ed., *Three Karchacks*, with an English introduction by E. Gene Smith, New Delhi 1970 (contains also the Lhasa dKar-chag of the Fifth Dalai Lama); Lokesh Chandra, ed., *Kongtrul's Encyclopaedia of Indo-Tibetan Culture*, with an introduction by E. Gene Smith, Śatapitaka Series 80, New Delhi 1970; *Bka brgyud gser 'phreng chen mo*, biographies and autobiographies of eminent gurus in the lineage of transmission of the teachings of the Barawa branch of the Drookpa Kargyudpa sect, 4 vols., Dehra Dun 1970; Nga-wang Gelek Demo, ed., *The Secret Biography of the Sixth*

Dalai Lama, together with Rong-po grub-chen's collection of biographies of eminent Gelugpa masters, New Delhi 1970; Anne-Marie Blondeau, "Le Lha-'dre bka'-thaṅ," *ETML* (Paris 1971): 29-126; Car pai Blama Saṅs-rgyas bstan-'jin ed. Alexander W. Macdonald, *Documents pour l'étude de la religion et de l'organisation sociale des Sherpa,* avec un avant-propos de A. W. Macdonald, Junbesi and Paris-Nanterre 1971; Nga-wang Gelek Demo, *Tāranātha's Life of the Buddha and His History of the Kālacakra and Tārā Tantra,* with a foreword by Prof. D. Seyfort Ruegg, New Delhi 1971; Lokesh Chandra, ed., *Bu-ston's Collected Works,* 28 vols., Śatapitaka Series 41-68, New Delhi 1965-70.

The Literature of the Bon-po

The difficulty in giving a satisfactory survey of Tibetan literary history becomes even more evident when we turn to the field of Bon-po literature, which until now has been undeservedly neglected by Western scholars. Consequently, the data given here cannot be but incomplete. Before the arrival of the Tibetan Bon-po refugees in India after the catastrophe of 1959, very few prints or manuscripts existed in Western libraries. Thus the first book which undertook a general investigation of Bon—Hoffmann's *Quellen zur Geschichte der tibetischen Bon-Religion*—was of necessity based on scattered materials excerpted from Buddhist sources. The results of this extensive study were criticized as giving partial and incorrect information because of Buddhist influence, but when genuine Bon texts became known, much of the material furnished by the Buddhists proved to be correct; and a comparative study of both materials must now be made.

There cannot be the slightest doubt that Bon in its primitive stage of a Tibetan folk religion was far older in Tibet than Buddhism, and it certainly possessed an oral literature which dealt with the propitiation and suppression of gods and spirits. The Bon-po in their own later literary sources claim to have possessed a kind of script earlier than that introduced by Thon-mi Sambhoṭa, but this certainly is untrue. No specimen of such a script is extant, and the special Bon-po alphabet found in later sources is certainly derived from the well-known alphabet in use since the first half of the seventh century.

The systematized Bon religion was introduced—to quote the oldest text available, the *Bod-kyi rgyal-rabs* of the Sa-skya hierarch Grags-pa rgyal-mtshan—from Zhang-zhung and Bru-sha (Gilgit) during Tibet's period of illiteracy. This event is connected with the period following the murder of King Gri-gum btsan-po (Dri-gum in the Tun-huang annals) who, according to good evidence, seems to have been a historical not a mythological person although the dates of his life are unknown. The first introduction of Zhang-zhung Bon with its funeral rites used at the obsequies of this king goes back to a period considerably prior to the introduction of writing into Tibet. Therefore even at that time the Zhang-zhung priests and their Tibetan pupils could only have been in possession of an oral literature.

The earliest period during which literary Bon-po texts were translated into Tibetan was the period of the minority of Khri-srong lde-brtsan (755-97), and in all probability the texts represent a more sophisticated Zhang-zhung Bon religion, by then subjected to Hindu, Buddhist, and Western (primarily Iranian) influences. The rNying-ma-pa scriptures furnish us with the names of several Zhang-zhung pandits such as Sha-ri u-chen (written also: dbu-chen), Dran-pa Khod-spungs, sTag-lha me-'bar (Zhang-zhung; La-sad ne-bar), and Li-shi stag-rings, all now confirmed by original Bon-po sources. These men worked together with Tibetan translators in the Avalokiteshvara temple of bSam-yas, where Buddhist texts were translated from the Indian languages. The *Padma Thang-yig* states that even Vairocanarakshita, disciple of Shāntirakshita, translated Bon texts. The only Bon-po work mentioned by name in this source is *The Klu-Hundred-Thousand in Four Pothis* (*klu 'bum pod bzhi*). In all probability the large, tripartite Klu-'bum ("white," "black," and "speckled") or perhaps an earlier version of it is meant. It is now available as a Tibetan blockprint. In the "speckled" section not only the title of the whole work is given first in Zhang-zhung, but also that of several chapters. The chapter titles appear also in the Sum-pa language. The text of the *klu-'bum* is an interesting and typical mixture of primitive animist-shamanist beliefs and other materials such as cosmogonies which are undoubtedly of Iranian origin and show distinct traces of Iranian dualism. The Zhang-zhung Bon religion itself actually claims to be of Iranian (*Ta-zig*) origin, and Bon-po literary texts of later times give titles not only in Zhang-zhung but also in two imaginary languages, "The Heavenly Iranian language" (*mu-sangs ta-zig*) and "The Language of the Svastika Gods of Ka-pi-ta" (*ka pi ta gyung drung lhai skad*). These titles would seem to be fictitious, but their phonology is in many respects very similar to that of Zhang-zhung. An abbreviated form of the *klu-'bum* also exists, but the booklet published by Laufer under this title is not a Bon text.

To the older stratum of Bon literature belongs also the "Expiatory Poem" published and translated by Laufer. Its purpose is to reconcile and pacify the *kLu, gNyan,* and *Sa-bdag* spirits.

Since the travels of George N. Roerich in northern Tibet (the Hor-pa country, gNam-ru and Nag-tshang) and the Great Lake Area, it is known that the Bon-po have the equivalent of the Buddhist *bKa'-'gyur* and *bsTan-'gyur*. Evidently in later times much literary material was added to the older stratum translated from Zhang-zhung. The major part of it though seems to have been borrowed from the rNying-ma-pa. The Bon-po now have their own *tantras, sādhanas,* and initiation texts, which greatly resemble their rNying-ma-pa counterparts.

To the older materials introduced from Zhang-zhung probably belongs the Treasure (*mDzod-phugs*) with its commentary by Dran-pa nam-mk'a, perhaps dating back to the times of Khri-srong lde-brtsan. The basic text is reproduced in Tibetan as well as in Zhang-zhung and is somewhat similar to the encyclopaedic *Abhidharma Kosha* of the Buddhists.

The basic material of the biography of gShen-rab, the founder, or more correctly, systematizer of the Bon religion, also points to Zhang-zhung origins. One version, the *gZer-mig* (*Key for the Memory* in the Zhang-zhung language), has been partially translated by A. H. Francke, and an abstract of the contents has been given elsewhere. But here also rNying-ma-pa borrowings are obvious:

practically the entire first and third section of the *bKa'-thang sde-lnga* have been adopted and adjusted to the requirements of the Bon-po.

A detailed version of gShen-rabs's biography, obviously much later than the *gZer-mig,* is the *Precious Compendium, the Blazing Sūtra Immculate and Glorious.* Recently published by the Bon-po Foundation, it comprises no less than sixty-one chapters. Nine chapters, edited and translated by D. Snellgrove, describe the "Nine Vehicles" of the Bon religion. From these chapters and from the copious additional materials included in this enormous work, it is obvious that the 'Dus-pa rin-po-che dri-ma-med-pa gzi-brjid rab-tu 'bar-bai mdo (abbreviation: *gZi-brjid*) is not a simple biography but an entire compendium of the later Bon doctrine. Extensive studies of its literary history are necessary. A biography of gShen-rab compiled by the Bon-po scholar Tenzin Namdak and excerpted not only from the *gZer-mig* and the *gZi-brjid* but including eleven other sources must also be studied before the genesis of gShen-rab's biography becomes clear.

The Bon-po holy scriptures are not only systematized according to the "Nine Vehicles," but are also divided into "Four Bon Portals and the Treasure as Fifth" (*bon sgo bzhi mdzod lnga*). This term cannot refer to five treasures as implied by G. Tucci (*Die Religionen Tibets,* p. 252). The term has already been adequately translated (*ZDMG* [1938]: 363ff.). The "Treasure" is the aforementioned *mDzod-phugs.* To the first "portal" belong the Zhang-zhung *snyan-rgyud* ("Oral Tradition from Zhang-zhung") and other texts of the "Great Perfection" (*rDzogs-chen*) literature which the Bon-po share with the rNying-ma-pa (published by Tenzin Namdak). The "Portals and Treasure" problem is described in full in an unedited manuscript, "The True Essence of the Four Bon Portals and the Treasure as Fifth" (*Bon sgo bzhi mdzod lngai yang snying*).

The Bon-po also wrote interesting books on the history of their religion, a literary genre which may be compared to the Buddhist *Chos-'byung* (*History of Buddhism*) literature. The only published work of this type is the *rGyal-rabs bon-gyi 'byung-gnas* (*The Royal Lineage and the History of Bon*) written by Khyung-po Blo-gros rgyal-mtshan in 1439. A fragment of another book of this kind, the *bsTan-'byung* (*Origin of the Doctrine*), describes the development of Bon in Bru-sha (Gilgit).

A specimen of religious geography comparable to mKhyen-brtse's *Guide to the Holy Places of Central Tibet* in Buddhist writings, but covering the whole area of Tibet is *The Book of the* [Bon-po] *Monasteries* (*dGon-deb*), which contains much interesting historico-geographical material.

BIBLIOGRAPHY

Anton Schiefner, *Über das Bonpo-Sùtra "Das weisse Nâga-Hunderttausend,"* Mémoires de l'Académie de St. Pétersbourg, 7, série, tome 28 no. 1, St. Pétersbourg 1881; Berthold Laufer, *Über ein Sühngedicht der Bonpo*, Denkschriften der Wiener Akademie d. Wissenschaften, Phil.-hist. Klasse 1900, no. 7; Berthold Laufer, "Über ein tibetisches Geschichtswerk der Bonpo," *TP*, pp. 24-44 (a study of the following text); Sarat Chandra Das, ed., *rGyal-rabs bon gyi 'byung gnas*, Calcutta 1915 (many misprints); A. H. Francke, "A Ladakhi Bon po Hymnal," *IA* 30 (1901); A. H. Francke, "gZer myig. A Book of the Tibetan Bonpos," *AM* (1924): 243-49, (1926): 321-39, (1927): 161-239, 481-540, (1928): 1-40, new series 1, (1949): 163-88; Marcelle Lalou, "Rituel Bon-po des funérailles royales (fonds Pelliot tibétain 1042)," *JA* (1952): 339-61; Helmut Hoffmann, "Probleme und Aufgaben der tibetischen Philologie. Mit einem Anhang: Zur Geschichte der Bon-Religion," *ZDMG* 92 (1938): 345-68; Helmut Hoffmann, "Zur Literatur der Bon-po," *ZDMG* 94 (1940): 169-88; Helmut Hoffmann, Gšen. Eine lexikographisch-religionswissenschaftliche Untersuchung," *ZDMG* 98 (1944): 340-58; "Tibetan Žang Žung Dictionary" and "Sangs rgyas kyi bstan rtsis ngo mtshar nor bui phreng ba," Tibetan Bonpo Foundation, Delhi 1961; *'Dus pa rin po chei rgyud dri ma med pa gzi brjid rab tu 'bar bai mdo*, 12 vols., Delhi, n.d.; Tenzin Namdak, ed., *Mdzod phug*, basic verses and commentary by Dran-pa nam-mkha, Delhi 1966; Dgongs-mdzad Ri-khrod chen-po, *A-tri Thun-Tsham cho na dan*, Tibetan Bonpo Foundation, Delhi 1967 (the "great perfection" teachings of the Bonpo); David Snellgrove, *The Nine Ways of Bon*, London 1967; Helmut Hoffmann, "Žaṅ-žuṅ: the Holy Language of the Tibetan Bon-po," *ZDMG* (1967): 376-81; Helmut Hoffmann, "An Account of the Bon Religion in Gilgit," *CAJ* 13 (1969): 137-45 (publication and translation of a fragment of the Bonpo Church History *bsTan-'byung*): Tenzin Namdak, *The Life of Lord Gshen rab excerpted from original texts*, 2 vols., Delhi 1971 (Tibetan text from thirteen different sources); *Ma rgyud sangs rgyas rgyud gsum*. The three basic mother tantras with commentaries by Rgyal-gshen-Mi-lus-bsam-legs, Delhi 1971 (Tibetan text); Tenzin Namdak, *Sources for a History of Bon*, New Delhi 1972 [in Tibetan]; Lokesh Chandra and Tenzin Namdak, *History and Doctrine of the Bon-po. Niṣpanna Yoga*, Satapitaka Series 73, New Delhi 1968 (contains the Zhang-zhung snyan-rgyud doctrines); Samten G. Karmay, *The Treasury of Good Sayings: A Tibetan History of Bon*, London Oriental Series, vol. 26. London 1972.

X. TIBETAN RELIGIOUS ART

Tibetan art is pervaded by the all-comprising spirit of the Tibetan religion. This holds true for Buddhist as well as Bon-po artifacts. The only exception is the construction of houses, palaces, and castles, although even here we find features which obviously combine secular and religious architecture.

Even today the scholar who attempts to present a general outline of Tibetan art is seriously handicapped. Although there is certainly no lack of publications on Tibetan objects of art, it is still almost impossible to give a general description of this art. With few exceptions, the relevant literature (enumerated in the bibliography) has been written either by dilettantes, enthusiasts who have collected material during their travels in Tibet or in adjacent Himalayan districts, or by scholars who merely describe the iconographic or symbolical aspects of Tibetan art. The *rara avis* group of scholars, which has gone deeper into the subject, is represented by Giuseppe Tucci, George N. Roerich, and Pieter H. Pott. Their valuable works show that the time has not yet come to write a history of Tibetan art and that careful stylistic studies are needed to extricate the various foreign influences and explain the Tibetan synthesis of these ingredients. Another difficulty which makes the discussion of Tibetan art in this handbook unsatisfactory is the impossibility of adding illustrations of the works described.

It is uncertain whether the earliest specimens of Tibetan artifacts discovered on Tibetan soil were really created by the Tibetans or, in a wider sense, by the Ch'iang peoples. These artifacts are represented by the megalithic monuments (menhirs, cromlechs, and alignements) found in the Amdo area, the country of the great salt lakes, and even in the west (Mānasarovar area and Kulu). These simply form a branch of the Eurasian belt of barrows, which extends from the plains of Hungary to western China. In Tibet the earliest of these monuments, which certainly are of a religious nature, can be dated to before the seventh century A.D., but objects older than the bronze age may well exist.

The Tibetan megalithic monuments are identical with specimens of the "Animal Style" which closely resemble the Scythian art and metal work of the presumably Indo-European nomads of Central Asia who penetrated as far as China. In motif the monuments are also similar to the so-called "Luristan Bronzes." The objects found by G. Roerich in the Amdo, Hor, gNam-ru, and eastern Nag-tshang provinces, and those collected by G. Tucci in western and central Tibet may well go back to models of the Hsiao Yüeh-chih who, in Former Han time, rather than follow the major part of this (probably Iranian) people to the west, wandered into the mountain country south of present-day Kansu province, and gradually became amalgamated with the autochthonous Tibeto-Ch'iang population of the Nan-shan mountains and the high plains (*Byang-thang*). This would seem to be confirmed by anthropological studies. This animal style survived as a "New Animal Style" among the Tibetan nomads (*'brog-pa*). It is represented by metal ornaments on tinder and flint pouches, and on brass buckles which, for instance, display the two-headed eagle motif within a circle. Later the animal style was also adopted for Buddhist ornamentation as shown by charm boxes where the Buddhist "eight auspicious signs" (*bKra-shis rtags brgyad*) have been combined with figures of a running deer, a survival of the ancient "hunting magic." Stylized figures of a sitting deer, well-known from Scythian and Siberian antiquities, are also found on silvered-iron pen cases and silver sword and dagger sheaths. Some objects from western Tibet also use an animal motif, such as a plaque portraying two dogs facing each other in the same manner as do animals in theEurasian animal style. Of considerable importance are several bronze horned *Khyung* plaques which stylistically cannot be connected with the Indian *Garuḍa* bird, but which later became identified with the indigenous sacred eagle. Most probably some of these eagles are not of later Bon-po origin, but belong to the prehistoric period.

Some information on Tibetan architecture dates back to the period prior to the unification of the tribes by Srong-btsan sgam-po. The annals of the short-lived Chinese Sui dynasty (589-617) contain ethnographic information on a "Kingdom of Women," called *Su-p'i* by the Chinese and *Sum-pa* by the Tibetans. While it was a part of the Tibetan empire it had its center at present-day rGyal-mo-rong, but during Sui times covered a larger zone of influence to the north. These Sum-pa were known to erect nine-story-high, tower-like houses and palaces with sloping walls. These were certainly fortresses, for upon being warned of an enemy attack, the villagers and nomads would hasten to the towers whose doorways were often at some distance from the base. Similar ruins, found in the west at Uḍḍiyāna (Swat) by Sir Aurel Stein, may well have been once inhabited by semi-Tibetan peoples, probably the Zhang-zhung. In Manchu times in rGyal-mo-rong these high tower-houses were still used for protection against Chinese invasions. Towers like these have also been discovered in the southern provinces of Lho-brag and rKong-po. In contrast to its usual function, a tower was erected at the command of the guru Mar-pa by the saint Mi-la ras-pa to atone for his sins.

The castles of the competing princelings in the Yar-klungs valley had the same sloping walls and were constructed of heavy stones mortared with sun-dried mud. The internal structure was supported by wooden columns and beams, and the windows were high and narrow in the form of embrasures through which stones might be hurled at attacking enemies. Remnants of these old castles still exist, and the ruins of one of them has been identified as the castle of the dynasty of the Tibetan emperors-to-be, Phying-ba sTag-rtse, built, according to tradition, by one of Srong-btsan sgam-po's semimythical predecessors, sTong-ri stong-btsan. Another Yar-klungs chieftain, Lha-tho-tho-ri snyan-shal, who lived before the Imperial period, inhabited a castle still standing today. It was known by the name *Yum-bu bla-mkhar* or *Om-bu bla-sgang,* and the Tibetans referred to it as "the oldest house of Tibet." Its basic structure certainly goes back to pre-Imperial times, while the Chinese-style roof on the tower is a later addition.

The austere and warlike appearance of the old Tibetan castles was adopted for the construction of several ancient temples: the Khra-'brug chapel in Yar-klungs and the dbU-ru ka-tshal, erected by Srong-btsan sgam-po, and Kva-chu and Has-po-rgyab in the bSam-yas area erected by Khri-srong lde-brtsan. All of them retain their ancient style characterized by the massive inward-sloping walls, making them resemble castles rather than temples. This style of fortress was used even later, as shown by the ruined castle of Yar-klungs Pho-brang erected during the Phag-mo-gru-pa dynasty (fourteenth and fifteenth centuries). It also seems likely that the most important early Buddhist temples built by Srong-btsan sgam-po, the Jo-khang (which marked the navel [*lte-ba*] or center of the empire), and the *Ra-mo-che,* originally displayed the same features. Later, however, these sanctuaries were extended by new structures and courtyards and altered by a reconstruction of the facades so that only their lower floors can be regarded as dating from the seventh century. These have now been destroyed by the Chinese.

While the outward appearance of the monasteries and temples became more sophisticated and highly decorated—walls were whitewashed and Chinese gilt roofs were introduced—the basic architecture of Tibetan buildings changed very little throughout the later centuries. Thus the wall structures of the Potala Palace at Lhasa still show the well-known sloping walls. According to the old chronicles, Srong-btsan sgam-po hired workers and craftsmen from abroad. Thus a part of the Imperial palace erected on the hill where the Potala now stands was called the "Saka style Palace" (*Sog-po lugs-kyi mkhar*), *Sog-po* at that time meaning of course not "Mongol" but *Saka* of Khotan (Tib. *Li-yul*). It is well-known that Nepalese craftsmen were also hired by the emperors; hence in these early times appeared both Khotanese (*Li-lugs*) and Nepalese (*Bal-poi lugs*) influences in styles.

Very few examples of early sculpture have survived, the outstanding example being the stone lion on the funeral compound of the emperor Ral-pa-can. The sculpture is surprising because of its unquestionably Iranian stylistic features, which did not reach Tibet directly from Iran but through the peoples of the Tarim basin. Ral-pa-can's lion has a striking counterpart in a lion found at Tumshuk on the northern silk road.

Among the oldest monuments are the obelisks (rDo-ring) set up by the emperors in different parts of the country. Because of the contemporary inscriptions which most of them bear, they are of special importance. The most ancient obelisk is at Zhol. Since no Buddhist features appear in the text of the inscription, one may assume that the rDo-ring symbolism in Tibet (as a kind of "omphalos" of the pre-Buddhist religion) in its simple setting is a typical Tibetan creation. Later obelisks, such as that of bSam-yas, show Buddhist symbolism: sun, moon, and bindu (the symbol of Vajrayāna polarity), and a lotus throne. The sKar-chung pillar of the ninth century has a fluted stone canopy and conch-shell finial, and the two Zhva'i Lha-khang obelisks have rectangular bases adorned by the symbol of two crossed vajras (vishvavajra, Tib. sNa-tshogs rdo-rje).

The entire plan of Tibet's first monastery-compound at bSam-yas, encircled by a wall adorned by many miniature stūpas, is expressly stated to have been conceived according to an Indian Buddhist mode copied from the Vihāra of Otantapurī in Bihar. It displays a representation of the Buddhist universe in which the central temple represents the world mountain Meru and the temples at the four cardinal points, flanked by two minor temples each, represent the world continents and minor continents (dvīpa). Although the temples were greatly damaged by a conflagration during the previous century, the original plan is still quite evident and the restored buildings follow the original pattern. Solidly built, the stūpas of the four directions escaped disaster. These are painted in the traditional style: white, red, black, and blue as symbols of the disciples of the Buddha, the religious world emperor, the Pratyeka Buddha, and the world-saving Buddhas who descend from a heavenly region. The various foreign influences in early Tibet are reflected in the religious images in the lower story cast in the "Tibetan style" (which seems to mean a reconciliation of different foreign styles in a Tibetan synthesis); the images in the middle story are in the Chinese style, while those of the upper story are Indian. Knowledge of Chinese Buddhist images certainly existed at that early period, for the Chinese consort of Srong-btsan sgam-po had brought to Tibet the famous Jo-bo image as well as what are probably other specimens of Chinese Buddhist art. These images may not all have been of cast bronze since it was quite usual to make a core of clay covered with metal leaf.

Originally the Tibetan stūpas, like their Indian predecessors, portrayed the macrocosm-microcosm symbolism, but by degrees their form changed and became typically Tibetan. The large dome, for instance, globular in India, assumed a form which grew larger at the top and was therefore no longer called "egg" (aṇḍa) as in India, but kalasha (Tib. bum-pa), "flask." The cubic represents the element earth; the kalasha water (whose geometrical form is the circle which is more obvious in the Indian specimens); and the conical spire fire (symbolized by a triangle pointing upward). In Tibet this spire generally consists

of thirteen discs which symbolize the "stages (*bhūmi*) of enlightenment."
Originally, they represented umbrellas. Above the thirteen discs which rest on
"the little house" (*harmikā*, Tib. *pu-shu*), the entire structure is crowned by the
symbols of polarity (crescent and sun) and at the apex by the "flaming drop"
(*bindu,* Tib. *thig-le*), representing the *unio mystica* and the element ether. The
harmikā may portray the eyes of the Primordial Buddha on its four sides.

Two other forms of Tibetan art used exclusively for religious purposes are
of a highly hieratic character—painting and sculpture. In the study of these art
forms the individualistic enthusiasm of dilletantes and art collectors and even of
some art historians is entirely out of place. Such works of art are anonymous
since, in contrast to Chinese and Japanese Buddhist practice, the names of the
artists are generally unknown and considered of no importance.

Paintings (murals and painted scrolls or *thang-kas*) and images are
instruments of religious invocation. The artist first must prepare himself by Yoga
to attain a state of ecstasy in which he actually sees with his spiritual eye the
Buddhas and gods whom he will represent in his work of art. The artist becomes
an apotheosized instrument of the "Absolute" (*tathatā) or "Radiant Light" (od
gsal*), and preparations must be made by liturgical ritual before he may begin his
work. He must be neither old nor ill and must await an astrologically auspicious
day and hour before he may undertake his work, which is not the creation of an
individual but a reproduction of a preexisting reality. His merit is therefore
restricted to his ability to reproduce his visions. The painter is generally a
layman but he must work under the leadership of an instructing priest.

The methods of painting and casting images were adopted from Buddhist
India, and authoritative treatises dealing with them were translated into Tibetan
and incorporated in the *bsTan-'gyur.* Examples of these are the *Citralakshaṇa*
(characteristics of painting) and the *Pratimānalakshaṇa* (characteristics of
images). Only the latter has been preserved in the original Sanskrit. For painting,
even older instructions have been found in a canonical text, the *Mañjushrī
Mūlatantra,* which have been excellently translated and published by M. Lalou.
The Sanskrit equivalent of the Tibetan word *thang-ka* is *paṭa* (lit.: "a piece of
cloth"). The original Tibetan literature on this subject, which may be called
iconometry, follows the Indian pattern. Among the authors who have dealt with
this subject are sMan-thang-pa, Padma-dKar-po of the 'Brug-pa school (1526-92)
and, among the more recent dGe-lugs-pa authors, kLong-rdol bla-ma (born 1729)
and Sum-pa mKhan-po (1704-77).

Painted scrolls are generally painted on linen cloth or, more rarely, on silk.
The cloth is stretched over a frame by passing twine through its edges. The fabric
itself is spread with lime mixed with animal glue. To eliminate any porosity, the
cloth is rubbed with a piece of shell. When the whole surface is even, the figures
are outlined in charcoal. This procedure always starts with the central figure
which is then surrounded by lesser images or scenes. The respective symbolic

colors which contain several traditional mineral and vegetable substances are then applied. Unfortunately Western chemical paints are now used. As a rule, the *thang-kas* are rectangular; only the *maṇḍala* representations are executed in a square form.

The material for most cast images is *li* or "bell metal," and different qualities are used: an inferior rind called *khro*, and a better rind called *mkhar*, an alloy with brass. Other images are made of pure natural copper or silver. Another appreciated variety, *ji-khyim,* is composed of eight metals: gold, silver, copper, white iron, rock crystals, white and black lead, and mercury. Of course, stone sculptures cut from the living rock also exist. Wooden images are comparatively rare.

When the images have been cast or the *thang-ka* painting finished a consecration cermony is required, for only by this means can the sacred object be animated and contain divine and effective power. The priest in charge performs the usual *sādhana*-style tantric ritual. First he must become through meditation the representation of the deity in question. The image is placed in the center of a *maṇḍala* in the form of an eight-petalled lotus. Each of the petals is provided with a ritual *bum-pa* ("vase") filled with water and other pure substances such as perfume, butter, fruit, seeds, and other ritual ingredients. The priest now visualizes the deity by evocation and recites 108 times the holy *ye dharmā hetuprabhavāḥ* formula, an epitome of the entire Buddhist teaching. Praises of the Buddha follow while the sacred object is honored with flowers, incense, and music. After this the religious merit of the consecration is offered for the benefit of all sentient beings. This is followed by the most essential moment, the *rTen-bskyed* ("creation of the object in which the divine spirit is to be installed"). After sprinkling the object from the *Las-bum* ("vase of action"), the priest invokes the deity to descend into the object. The protection of the sacred object from evil spirits or impediments (*bgegs*) is done with the syllable *hūm*, which causes a terrifying "protector of the law" to emanate from the heart of the officiating priest. A last sprinkling of holy water with the middle finger of the priest's right hand on the mouth, nose, eyes, ears, hands, navel, and head of the image concludes the complex ritual.

Further study is needed on different styles on Tibetan religious art, although it is obvious that it has been influenced by three major styles, which later became to a certain extent amalgamated in a typical Tibetan synthesis. Tibetan authors differentiate between Indian, Chinese, and Khotanese styles (*rGya gar-gyi-lugs, rGya-nag-gi lugs,* and *Li-lugs*). Understandably, the Indian influences entered Tibet through different channels, one of which, as described by Tāranātha in the final chapter of his *History of Buddhism in India,* was the style of the Pāla art of Bengal which made its way into Tibet through Nepal. Tāranātha points out that this tradition goes back to the school of Dhīmān and Bitpalo, who lived in the era of the fervent Buddhist Pāla kings Devapāla and

Dharmapāla (eighth and ninth centuries). Western Tibet shows the influence of another Indian tradition, the Kashmiri school of Hasarāja. G. Tucci, in his outstanding studies on the religious objects of the Gu-ge kingdom of the tenth and eleventh centuries, points out the importance of this school. The Mang-nang and Alchi murals undoubtedly display influences of the art of Kashmir. The Pāla-Nepalese influence penetrated to the west as far as Kojarnāth, while the Chinese style made itself felt only when favored by political and military contact. The latter occurred during the Imperial period which was contemporary with the Chinese T'ang dynasty, and later, very strongly, during the rule of the Manchu dynasty. It is the Indo-Nepalese style, however, which runs through the entire history of Tibetan art. The influence of eastern Turkestan, more precisely that of Khotan, was important from the time of the great Tibetan emperors when Khotanese artisans and craftsmen were hired along with the Nepalese. The Central Asian style, recently unconvincingly denounced as a banal mixture of different influences, certainly has proved its importance in the art of Ivang and Samada in central Tibet and in the Bon-po murals in western Tibet (Sutlej Valley and the area of the Sutlej tributaries). It was through Khotan that an echo of Indo-Hellenistic art (commonly called Gandhāra art) made itself felt, for instance, in the drapery of the garments of certain Buddha images. But Iranian motives, such as friezes of birds and the characteristic pearl design, are also found in the Bon-po murals of the west. The Chinese style did not change the basic arrangement of the old thang-ka patterns, but its influence can be seen (especially in Khams) in the Tibetans' use of space as expressed in landscapes with mountains, rivers, trees, plants, birds, gazelles, clouds, and dragons.

BIBLIOGRAPHY

Materials on the Indian foundation of Tibetan art: Berthold Laufer, *Das Citralakṣaṇa* (nach dem tibetischen Kanjur herausgegeben und übersetzt), Dokumente der indischen Kunst, vol. 1, Malerei, Leipzig 1913; Marcelle Lalou, *Iconographie des étoffes peintes (paṭa) dans le Mañjuśrīmūlakalpa*, Buddhica 1: 6, Paris 1930.

The only really serious studies in Tibetan religious art, including considerations of the different styles and foreign influences, are the works of Giuseppe Tucci, *Tibetan Painted Scrolls*, 3 vols., Roma 1949; Giuseppe Tucci, *Indo-Tibetica I, Mc'od-rten e ts'a-ts'a nel Tibet Indiano,* Roma 1932; *Indo-Tibetica III, I templi del Tibet occidentale e il loro simbolismo artistico,* part 1: Spiti e Kunawar, part 2: Tsaparang, Roma 1935 and 1936; Giuseppe Tucci, *Indo-Tibetica IV: Gyantse ed i suoi monasteri,* 3 vols., Roma 1941; Giuseppe Tucci, "A Tibetan Classification of Buddha Images according to their style," *AA* 22 (1959): 179-87; J. van Manen, "On making Earthen Images, Repairing Old Images and Drawing Scroll Pictures in Tibet," *Journal of the Indian School of*

Oriental Art 1 (1933): 105-11; Siegbert Hummel, *Geschichte der tibetischen Kunst,* Leipzig 1953 (this book, like all other writings of this author, should be perused with caution); P. H. Pott, "Tibet." In *Burma, Korea, Tibet,* Kunst der Welt, pp. 151-269, Baden-Baden 1964; Gisbert Combaz, "L'évolution du stūpa en Asie," *MCB2,* (1933): 163-305; 3 (1934/35): 93-144; 4 (1935/36): 1-125 (deals also with Tibetan mchod-rten); J. Hackin, "Sur des illustrations tibétaines d'une légende du Divyāvadāna," *Annales de Musée Guimet, Bibl. de Vulgarisation* 40 (1913): 145-57; J. Hackin, "Some Notes on Tibetan Paintings," *Rupam* 7 (1921): 11-13; J. Hackin, "Les scènes figurées de la vie du Bouddha dans l'iconographie tibétaine," *Mémoires concernant l'Asie Centrale* 2 (1916): 1-116; J. Hackin, "Indian Art in Tibet and Central Asia," *The Influences of Indian Art,* pp. 129-43, London 1925; Karl Khandalavala, "Commentary on Tāranātha's chapter on Buddhist Art," *Marg* 4, no. 1, pp. 61-63.

Prehistoric and early Tibetan art: George N. Roerich, *The Animal Style among the Nomad Tribes of Northern Tibet,* Seminarium Kondakovianum, Prague 1930; Georges de Roerich, "Problems of Tibetan Archaeology," *Urusvati Journal* 1 (1931): 27-34; A. W. MacDonald, "Une note sur les mégalithes tibétains," *JA* (1953): 63-76; P. H. Pott, "A Tibetan Painting from Tun-huang," *Orientalia Neerlandica* (1948): 303-11; Giuseppe Tucci, "Preistoria tibetana." In *Opera minora,* Roma 1971, Vol. 1, pp. 467-470.

Miscellaneous publications on Tibetan iconography and religious art: H. H. Godwin Austen, "On the System Employed in Outlining the Figures of Deities and other Religious Drawings, as Practiced in Ladak, Zaskar, etc.," *JASB* 33 (1864): 151-54; Eugen Pander, *Das Pantheon des Tschangtscha Hutuktu,* edited by Albert Grünwedel, Veröffentlichungen aus dem Museum für Völkerkunde 1, nos. 2-3, Berlin 1890; Albert Grünwedel, *Mythologie des Buddhismus in Tibet und der Mongolei,* Leipzig 1900; S.Ch. Vidyabhusana, "On Certain Tibetan Scrolls and Images Lately Brought from Gyantse," *MASB* 1, no. 1, Calcutta 1905; J. Bacot, "L'art tibétain," *Annales du Musée Guimet, Bibl. de Vulgarisation* 28 (1908): 35-71; J. Hackin, "Notes d'iconographie tibétaine," *Mélanges d'indianisme S. Lévi,* Paris 1911, pp. 313-28; J. Hackin, *L'art tibétain,* Paris 1911; G. B. Gordon, "The Alexander Scott Collection of Art Objects from Tibet and Nepal," *Philadelphia Museum Journal* 5 (1914): 55-57; G. B. Gordon, "Some Art Objects from Tibet," *Philadelphia Museum Journal* 5 (1914): 10-14; J. Hackin, "Les scènes figurées de la vie du Bouddha d'après des peintures tibétaines," *Mémoirs concernant l'Asie Orientale,* Paris 1916; S. H. Ribbach, *Vier Bilder des Padmasambhava,* Mitteilungen aus dem Museum für Völkerkunde in Hamburg, 5. Beiheft, Hamburg 1917; J. van Manen, "Concerning a Bon Image," *JPASB* (1922): 195 ff.; O. C. Gangoly and J. van Manen, "A Tibetan-Nepalese Image of Maitreya," *Rupam* 11 (1922): 1ff.; J. Hackin, *Guide-Catalogue du Musée Guimet,* Paris 1923; L. Adam, *Hochasiatische Kunst,* Stuttgart 1923; J. Bacot, *Décoration tibétaine/Kunstgewerbe in Tibet,* Berlin-Paris 1924; L. Adam, *Buddhastatuen,* Stuttgart 1925; A. Ghose, "Tibetan Paintings," *Rupam* 27 (1926): 83-86; P. Rousseau, "L'art du Tibet," *RAA* (1927); H. Lee Shuttleworth, *Lhalung Temple, Spyi-ti,* Memoirs of the

Archaeological Survey of India, vol. 39, Calcutta 1929; G. de Roerich, "Le Bouddha et seize grand Arhats," *RAA* (1929/30); J. Hackin, *La sculpture indienne et tibétaine au Musée Guimet,* Paris 1931; A. v. Staël-Holstein, "On Two Tibetan Pictures, Representing Some of the Spiritual Ancestors of the Dalai Lama and of the Panchen Lama," *Bulletin of the National Library of Peiping,* 1932; R. Linossier, "Les peintures tibétaines de la collection Loo," *EORL* vol. 1, pp. 1-97, Paris 1932; T. A. Joyce, "Objects from Lhasa, Collected by Sir James MacDonald," *British Museum Quarterly* 7 (1932): 54ff.; R. H. van Gulik, *Hayagrīva,* the Mantrayanic Aspect of the Horse-Cult in China and Tibet, International Archives for Ethnology, vol. 33, supplementum, Leiden 1933; C. Pascalis, *La collection tibétaine du Musée Guimet,* Hanoi 1935; A. Kühn, "Zwei Darstellungen des Padmasambhava," *AA* 5 (1935): 117-26; Rahula Sankrityayana, "Buddhist Painting in Tibet," *Asia Magazine* 37 (1937): pp. 776-80; Rahula Sankrityayana, "Technique in Tibetan Painting," *Marg* 16 (1963): 30-33; E. H. C. Walsh, "The Image of Buddha in the Jo-wo-khang Temple at Lhasa," *JRAS* (1938): 535-40; Ferdinand D. Lessing, *Yung Ho Kung. An Iconography of the Lamaist Cathedral in Peking,* the Sino-Swedish Expedition VIII, 1, Stockholm 1942; John R. Krueger, *Index to F. D. Lessing's Lamaist Iconography of the Peking Temple Yung-Ho-Kung,* Bloomington 1966; F. A. Peter, "The 'Rin-ḥbyung'," *JASB* IX (1943): 1-27; P. H. Pott, "A Remarkable Piece of Tibetan Ritual Painting," *International Archives for Ethnology* 43 (1943): 215-43; Schuyler Cammann, "Tibetan Painting, Freer Gallery," *Gazette des Beaux Arts* 6 and 25, Paris 1944; Giuseppe Tucci, "Tibetan Book Covers," *Art and Thought* 1948; Mario Bussagli, "Bronze Objects Collected by Prof. G. Tucci in Tibet," *AA* 12 (1949): 331-47; Eleanor Olson, "Tibetan Collection and other Lamaist Articles," *The Newark Museum,* vols. 1-5, Newark 1950-71; Anagarika Govinda, "Solar and Lunar Symbolism in the Development of Stupa Architecture," *Marg* 4 (1950): 185ff.; Siegbert Hummel, "Die Gloriolen in der lamaistischen Malerei," *AS,* 1950, no. 4, René Nebesky-Wojkowitz, "Ein Beitrag zur tibetischen Ikonographie," *AV* 5 (1950): 138-58; Schuyler Cammann, "Suggested Origin of the Tibetan Mandala Paintings," *The Art Quarterly,* no. 2, 1950; Siegbert Hummel, *Lamaistische Studien,* Leipzig 1950; René Nebesky-Wojkowitz, "A Contribution to Mahayana Iconography," *Stepping Stones* (Darjeeling) 2 (1951): 77-82; P. H. Pott, *Introduction to the Tibetan Collection of the National Museum of Ethnology,* Leiden 1951; Eleanor Olson, "A Tibetan Emblem of Sovereignty," *Oriental Art Magazine* 3, no. 3, London 1951; Toni Schmid, *The Cotton-Clad Mila: the Tibetan Poet-Saint's Life in Picture,* Stockholm 1952; P. H. Pott, "The Tibetan and Nepalese Collections of the Baroda Museum," *Bulletin of the Baroda Museum and Picture Gallery* 9 (1953): 1-7; W. J. G. van Meurs, *Tibetan Temple Paintings,* 2nd ed., with an introduction by P. H. Pott, Leiden 1953; Siegfried Morenz und Johannes Schubert, *Der Gott auf der Blüte,* AA, Supplementum 12, Ascona 1954 (concerning the lotus in Egyptian and Tibetan art); Siegbert Hummel, *Tibetisches Kunsthandwerk in Metall,* Leipzig 1954; Siegbert Hummel, *Die Lamaistische Kunst in der Umwelt von Tibet,* Leipzig 1955; R. A. Stein, "Architecture et pensée réligieuse en

Extrême-Orient," *AAs* 4 (1957): 163-86; L. Jísl, *Tibetan Art,* London 1958; E. Bryner, *Thirteen Tibetan Tankas,* Colorado 1959; Toni Schmid, *The Eighty-five Siddhas,* Stockholm 1958; R. A. Stein, "Peintures tibétaines de la vie de Gesar," *AAs* 5 (1958): 243-71; Antoinette K. Gordon, *The Iconography of Tibetan Lamaism,* Tokyo 1959; Toni Schmid, *Saviours of Mankind, I, Dalai Lamas and Former Incarnations of Avalokiteśvara,* The Sino-Swedish Expedition VIII 9, Stockholm 1961; Alice Getty, *The Gods of Northern Buddhism,* 2nd ed., Oxford 1963; Raghu Vira and Lokesh Chandra, *A New Tibeto-Mongol Pantheon,* 17 vols., Satapitaka series 21, New Delhi 1961-67; Antoinette K. Gordon, *Tibetan Religious Art,* 2nd ed. New York 1963; Hugh Richardson, "Early Burial Grounds in Tibet and Tibetan Decorative Art of the 8th and 9th Centuries," *CAJ* 8 (1963): 73-92; Toni Schmid, *Saviours of Mankind, II, Panchen Lamas and Former Incarnations of Amitâyus,* the Sino-Swedish Expedition 46, Stockholm 1964; Walter Eugene Clark, *Two Lamaistic Pantheons,* 2nd ed., 2 vols., New York 1965; P. H. Pott, *Yoga and Yantra. Their Interrelation and Their Significance for Indian Archaeology,* The Hague 1966 (deals also with Tibetan materials); Helmut Hoffmann, *Symbolik der tibetischen Religionen,* Stuttgart 1967; David Snellgrove and Hugh Richardson, *A Cultural History of Tibet,* New York and Washington 1968; Werner Schulemann, "Der Inhalt eines tibetischen *mc'od rten,*" *ZS* 3 (1969): 55-76; Pratapaditya Pal, *The Art of Tibet,* New York 1969; Pratapaditya Pal and Hsien-ch'i Tseng, *Lamaist Art,* Museum of Fine Arts, Boston, n.d.; Jampa Kalsang, "Grundsätzliches zur Füllung von *mc'od rten,*" *ZS* 3 (1969): 51-53; Philip Denwood, "Forts and Castles-an Aspect of Tibetan Architecture," *Shambhala,* Occasional Papers no. 1, pp. 7-17, Tring/Herts 1971; Madanjeet Singh, *Himalayan Art,* London and Melbourne 1968.

XI. TIBET IN EXILE

When, after his adventurous flight, the Dalai Lama found asylum in India in March 1959, he was accompanied only by the most aged members of his Lhasa government and his brave bodyguard of warlike Khampas. Gradually, however, many other monastic and lay officials and many high lamas of the various Tibetan Buddhist schools followed him to India. Among the increasing numbers of Tibetans who began to emigrate to India, Bhutan, Sikkim, and Nepal, only a few belonged to the titled or landed aristocracy. The majority of these refugees had been farmers on tiny estates; the remainder were small traders, nomads, and monks. Their exodus clarifies beyond the slightest doubt the attitude and feelings of the ordinary Tibetan toward the Chinese communist occupation. To those in exile the Dalai Lama remains undisputedly the supreme authority, leader, and guide in spiritual and worldly matters. The Tibetans declared this when they risked their lives to follow him into exile; and they declare it even today by their acceptance of the authority of his administration, which is in fact the government of Tibet in exile whether or not it is recognized as such by other nations. The Dalai Lama remains the symbol of Tibet to the some 85,000 refugees now living outside their lost homeland.

The Dalai Lama himself was strongly aware of this when he wrote in his book *My Land and My People*: "In the face of the destruction of my people and all that they live for, I devote myself in exile to the only course of action left to me: to remind the world, through the United Nations and now through this book, of what is happening in Tibet; to care for Tibetans who have escaped with me to freedom; and to plan for the future." Upon another occasion he said: "Wherever I am the Tibetan people will always look upon me as the government of Tibet."

The greatest problem for the Dalai Lama is the rehabilitation and resettlement of the Tibetans. For this, huge sums of money are needed, which India, still faced with its own refugee problems, and the small countries of Nepal, Bhutan, and Sikkim, can ill afford. Nevertheless, by April 1959 a Central Relief Committee for Tibetans had emerged in India under president Acharya J. B. Kripalani. In the beginning, of course, the refugees were placed in reception camps such as that of Buxaduar in west Bengal, whose climate they found unsuitable. Later the majority of the refugees, both men and women, worked in some 95 road construction camps; and even at present a considerable number are still there awaiting professional training and resettlement. Because about 66 percent of the refugees had been farmers, the Indian authorities tried to accelerate a program for their resettlement. The most important centers were in Bylakuppe, the Canvery Valley and Mundgod in Mysore (planned for a total of

234 XI. Tibet in Exile

4,500 refugees), Chandragiri in Orissa, Mainpat in Madhya Pradesh, and Changland and Tezu in the Northeastern Frontier Agency (NEFA), part of the eastern Himalayan borderland. Certainly the conditions of the settlers were arduous in the beginning, but recent reports show that an improvement is under way. The government of Bhutan has established a new settlement at Bumthang which should absorb about 1,000 people. Another 2,000 refugees are to be rehabilitated at Rosowa, Lo, and Kathmandu in Nepal under the supervision of the United Nations' High Commissioner for Refugees. These activities could obviously not be funded by the host countries alone. Considerable funds have been raised by private groups (in Europe as well as in the United States), by national Red Cross Societies, and especially by the international but European-inspired foundation of the so-called "Common Project," chaired by Prince Bernhard of the Netherlands. This organization hopes to resettle 27,000 Tibetan refugees in Indian agriculture and industry.

Smaller groups of skilled Tibetans formed with the help of the Indian and Nepalese governments and assisted by organizations established by the Dalai Lama himself have found suitable employment in handicraft centers. The most important of these are located in Dalhousie, Darjeeling (sponsored by the Tibetan authorities), and Patan (Nepal). These centers produce rugs, shoes, boots, fur hats, brocades, paintings (so-called thang-kas), belts, metal engravings, and jewelry. The main problem for these centers, which dispose of modest financial means, is the procurement of raw materials and the marketing of their products.

Another problem facing Tibet is the settlement and upkeep of the approximately 5,000 monks whose task it is to maintain Tibetan religion and culture, a matter of great concern for the Dalai Lama. At Buxaduar a religious academy has been established. After initial difficulties, the lamas were provided with books and manuscripts required for their services and educational work. Meanwhile a number of Tibetan printing offices have been established, which produce new copies of important traditional literature.

The worst problem is obtaining aid for the old and handicapped who are no longer able to work. Only recently the office of the United Nations' High Commissioner for Refugees made a commitment to set up two homes for the aged, which together will accommodate 1,000 persons. Food for this group has been assured by the government of India.

The Tibetan Schools Society, an autonomous body under the Indian Ministry of Education, is operating seven boarding schools for the education of 4,170 children, and six day schools for 1,736. There still remain, however, large groups of children not receiving education of any kind.

About 1,000 Tibetans now live outside the Indian subcontinent: in the United States, where some young Tibetans are working for the Great Northern Paper Company in Millinocket, Maine; in Japan; and in several European countries. For some years twenty Tibetan boys have been trained in technical skills in Copenhagen, Denmark.

The most successful effort to resettle Tibetans has been made in Switzerland, where the National Red Cross and the Swiss people have accommodated over 400 Tibetans and created a "Tibet House" in the Pestalozzi Children's Village for orphans.

Because of the untiring efforts of the Dalai Lama a Tibetan administration has gradually taken shape in India to meet the needs of Tibetans living outside Chinese-occupied territory, a very heavy burden in view of the meager financial resources available. This administration is a reorganized form of the old Tibetan government although trends toward modernization have taken place, such as a decentralization of the government into separate departments, each with its own responsibilities and administrative functions. These developments were codified in a new constitution promulgated at Dharamsala, the Dalai Lama's residence in exile, on 10 March 1963. This constitution will also be introduced in Tibet itself if and when international developments again allow home rule for the Tibetans. For the time being the constitution is instrumental in maintaining continuity and the religious and secular identity of the Tibetans.

The constitution is a bulky and elaborate document characterized by a distinct trend toward modernization. Democratic development is exemplified in the totally altered composition of the legislative body, the Tibetan National Assembly. Thus:

> The National Assembly shall consist of
> a)   75 percent of the members elected by the people in the territorial constituencies;
> b)   10 percent of the members elected by Regional and District Councils in accordance with the laws enacted in this behalf;
> c)   10 percent of the members elected by the monasteries and other religious institutions in accordance with the laws enacted in this behalf;
> d)   5 percent of the members nominated directly by His Holiness the Dalai Lama. Such persons shall be selected for their distinguished services in the fields of art, science, and literature.

Another important innovation in the constitution concerns the period of regency, from the death of a Dalai Lama until his successor assumes power at the age of 18. To grant full powers to the regent during this interval has several times proven disastrous in the history of Tibet. Henceforth the Council of Regency shall consist of three members elected by the National Assembly, one of whom shall be an ecclesiastic representative.

Since the Dalai Lama's exile, his administration has been based at Dharamsala, Himachal Pradesh, and consists of the following bodies:

1. The *Kashag* Cabinet
2. A body of seventeen elected representatives of the people who perform administrative functions
3. The Tibetan National Working Committee.

The *Kashag* consists of the Dalai Lama's most senior officials and makes policy decisions on matters relating to the administrative departments of the Tibetan government. At present it consists of five departmental directors. It also generally supervises the Tibet Offices in New Delhi, New York, and Geneva.

The Council of Religious and Cultural Affairs looks after the spiritual and cultural activities of Tibetan refugees in India, Nepal, Bhutan, and Sikkim. It also maintains close contact with Tibetan lamas overseas and with Buddhists of other countries. Moreover, it generally serves as an authoritative medium of information for those interested in Buddhism and its historical development in Tibet.

The Home and Rehabilitation Office looks after the rehabilitation of Tibetan refugees, a program which includes agricultural settlement projects in the mountains at Bylakuppe and Mundgod in Mysore, Mainpat in Madhya Pradesh, Chandragiri in Orissa, and Tezu and Changland in NEFA. It also supervises the handicraft centers where smaller communities of Tibetans are trained and rehabilitated. All other rehabilitation projects such as those begun and sponsored by private organizations (e.g., in Switzerland) come under its purview; and to protect the interest of the refugees, the Office is always represented on the committees which oversee these projects.

Another function of the Home and Rehabilitation Office is to look after the general welfare of all Tibetans. Through its representatives at the road camps, it keeps in constant touch with the thousands of road laborers who have yet to be rehabilitated and represents them in the Public Works Department of the government of India in matters concerning regular payment of wages, payment compensation for accidents on the job, and settlement projects. It keeps in touch with those refugees who have been settled, whether in India or abroad, and compiles information on the refugee situation for the use of the government of India and private donor agencies.

The Council of Tibetan Education is directly responsible for the education of the Tibetan refugee children in India, Nepal, Bhutan, and Sikkim, operating primarily through the Tibetan School Society, a special body set up under the Department of Education of the government of India at the request of the Dalai Lama. This society, sponsored by the Indian government, attempts to provide a modern education for Tibetan children while simultaneously keeping alive a knowledge of their language, history, religion, and culture.

BIBLIOGRAPHY

Tibetans in Exile 1959-1969. A report on ten years of rehabilitation in India, compiled by the office of H. H. the Dalai Lama, Dharamsala 1969; *Die Leiden eines Volkes.* *Die Tragödie Tibets und der tibetischen Flüchtlinge,* Herausgegeben von der Schweizer Tibethilfe Solothurn, Solothurn 1961 (this book deals especially with the Tibetan refugees in Europe: Great Britain, Denmark, West Germany, and more specifically, Switzerland); James O. Mays, "Dilemma of the Dalai Lama," *TSB* 4/1 (1970): 35-44, Bloomington, Indiana; Ernest Gross, "The Tibetan Refugee Problem," *TSB* 3 (1969): 37-41; Ernest Dale, "Tibetan Immigration into the United States," *TSB* 3 (1969): 42-45; H. H. the Dalai Lama, "Future of the Tibetans," *Indian Review* (Feb./March 1967): 64-65; H. H. the Dalai Lama, *My Land and My People,* London 1962; *Tibet 1950-1967,* published by Union Research Institute, Hong Kong 1968 (contains the complete text of the new constitution promulgated by the Dalai Lama on 10 March 1967, pp. 530-54).

CHRONOLOGICAL TABLE

Tibet	*Contemporary events in foreign countries*
before 600 A.D.: Foundation of Tibetan empire by gNam-ri Srongstsan.	
	618-906: T'ang dynasty of China.
ca. 620-649: Srong-btsan sgam-po. Conquest of Zhang-zhung. Creation of the Tibetan script.	
	627-649: T'ai-tsung.
641: Tibetan emperor marries T'ang princess Wen-ch'eng.	
649-679: Mang-srong Mang-btsan. Conquest of T'u-yü-hun (A-zha).	
670-692: First Tibetan colonial empire in eastern Turkestan.	
676-704: 'Du-srong Mang-po-rje.	
692: Temporary loss of eastern Turkestan.	
704-755: Mes-ag-tshoms.	
710: emperor marries Chinese princess Chin-ch'eng.	
	751: Battle near Talas River: Chinese defeated by Muslim allies of Tibetans.
755-797: Khri-srong lde-brtsan.	755-757: Rebellion of An Lu-shan.
	763: Tibetan Conquest of Chinese Capital and peace treaty with Tibetans.
ca. 775: Foundation of bSam-yas.	775-785: Abbasid Caliph al-Mahdi.
779: Buddhism becomes state religion.	
	785-809: Caliph Harûn ar-Rashîd, at first Tibetan ally, but after 789 ally of Chinese.

790-ca. 860: Second Tibetan colonial empire in eastern Turkestan.

792-794: Buddhist debate at bSam-yas: expulsion of Chinese monks.

797-799: Mu-ne btsan-po.

799-815: Sad-na-legs. Increasing influence of Buddhist monks in state government.

From ca. 800: Later Caliph al-Ma'mûn governor of Khorasan. Battles with Tibetans.

809-813: caliph al-Amîn.

813-833: Reign of caliph al-Ma'mûn.

815-838: Ral-pa-can. Increase of clerical influence and translation of many Buddhist scriptures.

821-824: Mu-tsung of T'ang.

822: Sino-Tibetan treaty guaranteeing most of Tibetan colonial possessions.

838-842: gLang-darma. Bon restoration and persecution of Buddhism. After murder of emperor, competition of his sons Yum-brtan and 'Od-srungs. Beginning of disintegration of Tibetan empire.

866: Tibetan "Great Minister" defeated by Chinese. Loss of colonial empire and feudal anarchy in Tibet. Foundation of western Tibetan dynasty in Gu-ge in late 9th century: beginning of "second introduction of Buddhism" in central Tibet. Klu-mes (ca. 950-1025) leading instigator of these activities.

970: Ye-shes-'od, king of western Tibet sends Rin-chen bzang-po to Kashmir for Buddhist studies.

10th to 13th centuries: Si-hia dynasty to northeast of Tibet. Therefore no direct contact with China proper.

1012-1096: Mar-pa, founder of bKa-brgyud-pa school.

1040: Atīsha of Vikramashīlā monastery invited by kings of Gu-ge.

1040-1123: Mi-la ras-pa.

1042-1045: Missionary activity of
Atīsha in western and central Tibet.

1057: Foundation of monastery of
Rva-sgrengs by 'Brom-ston. Development of bKa-gdams-pa school.

1073: Foundation of Sa-skya by
'Khon dkon-mchog rgyal-po.

1076: Buddhist synod at Tabo in
western Tibet.

1158: Foundation of gDan-sa-mthil
monastery and bKa-brgyud- sub-
sect of Phag-mo gru-pa.

1179: Foundation of 'Bri-gung and
another sub-sect of the bKa-
brgyud-pa.

1182-1251: Sa-skya Paṇḍita.

1189: Origin of Karma-pa school.　　1189-1227: Chingis Khan universal
　　　　　　　　　　　　　　　　　ruler of Mongols.

　　　　　　　　　　　　　　　　　1209: Chingis Khan's conquest of Si-
　　　　　　　　　　　　　　　　　hia.

1235-1280: 'Phags-pa of Sa-skya.

1247: Sa-skya hierarch pays visit to
Mongol prince Godan.

　　　　　　　　　　　　　　　　　1280-1367: Mongol Yüan dynasty of
　　　　　　　　　　　　　　　　　China.

1260: 'Phags-pa visits Mongol emper-
or Khubilai. He receives title of
"Imperial teacher" and temporal
overlordship of all Tibet (13 districts).

　　　　　　　　　　　　　　　　　1279-1294: Khubilai Khan, Mongol
　　　　　　　　　　　　　　　　　emperor of China.

1290: 'Bri-gung sacked by Sa-skya-pa.

1290-1364: Bu-ston, great scholar,
systematizes Buddhist canon of
scriptures.

ca. 1350: Byang-chub rgyal-mtshan of Phag-mo-gru-pa assumes power over central Tibet; Sa-skya hegemony ends.

1357-1419: bTsong-kha-pa, reformer of Tibetan Buddhism and founder of dGe-lugs-pa school. Foundation of important dGe-lugs-pa monasteries.

1368-1444: Ming dynasty of China.

1391: dGe'dun grub-pa, nephew of bTsong-kha-pa, becomes abbot of dGa-ldan, and first rGyal-ba rin-po-che (incarnation of Avalokiteshvara).

1403-1424: Yung-lo emperor of China.

1409: dGa-ldan.

1414: bKa-shis lhun-po.

1416: 'Bras-spungs.

1419: Se-ra theg-che-gling.

1470-1543: Dayan Khan of Mongols.

1475-1542: dGe-'dun rgya-mtsho, second rGyal-ba rin-po-che. Decline of Phag-mo gru-pa power, rise of Rin-spungs-pa of gTsang, who patronize Karma-pa sect.

1543-1588: bSod-nams rgya-mtsho, Third rGyal-ba rin-po-che. In 1578 he was invited by Altan khan of Tümet and initiated second conversion of Mongols. Altan khan bestowed on him title of Dalai Lama.

1543-1583: Altan Khan, ruler of Tümet Mongols.

1570-1662: Blo-bzang Chos-kyi rgyal-mtshan, former teacher of Dalai Lama, is installed as Paṇ-chen rin-po-che, which creates another incarnation chain (of Buddha Amitābha), traced back to bTsong-kha-pa's disciple, mKhas-grub-rje.

1587: Official alliance between princes of gTsang and the Karma-pa hierarch against dGe-lugs-pa.

1589-1617: Yon-tan rGya-mtsho, fourth Dalai Lama (a Mongol).

First half of 17th century: Jesuit and Capuchin missionaries in Lhasa and other parts of Tibet.

1617-1682: Ngag-dbang bLo-bzang rGya-mtsho, Fifth Dalai Lama, called "Great Fifth".

1641-1642: Gu-shri Khan of Khoshot subdues Bon-po king of Be-ri and king of gTsang and hands over religious and secular power in Tibet to Dalai Lama. The Khoshot khan and his dynasty remain protectors of Tibet.

1644-1911: Manchu Ch'ing dynasty of China.

1651-1653: Dalai Lama visits China.

1661-1722: K'ang-hsi emperor of China.

1679: Appointment of regent Sangs-rgyas rgya-mtsho by Dalai Lama.

1683: After war with Ladakh, Mana-sarovar area and Gu-ge are ceded and henceforth belong to jurisdiction of Lhasa.

1683-1706: Sixth Dalai Lama. Regent conceals death of "Great Fifth" for political reasons and keeps young new incarnation a secret.

1697: Enthronization of Sixth Dalai Lama.

1705: Invasion of Lhasa by Khoshot Mongols. Sangs-rgyas rgya-mtsho killed.

1706: Lha-bzang of Khoshot deposes young Dalai Lama and enthrones monk Pad-dkar 'dzin-pa, who is not acknowledged by majority of Tibetans. Captured Tshangs-dbyangs rgya-mtsho dies in Koko Nor region.

1708-1757: Seventh Dalai Lama bsKal-bzang rgya-mtsho, born near Li-thang.

1716: Jesuit Father Desideri in Lhasa.

1717: Sacking of Lhasa by Dzungar Mongols.

1720: Establishment of Chinese protectorate in Tibet. Khang-chen-nas rules on behalf of Chinese.

1735-1796: Ch'ien-lung emperor of China.

1740-1747: Rule of Pho-lha-nas under overlordship of Chinese.

1750: 'Gyur-med rnam-rgyal, son and successor of Pho-lha-nas, after conspiring with the Dzungars is killed by Chinese resident (*amban*).

1751: Dalai Lama assumes power under supervision of two Chinese *ambans*.

1758-1804: Eighth Dalai Lama 'Jam-dpal rgya-mtsho.

1774-1775: British-Indian mission of George Bogle to third Pan-chen rin-po-che.

1783: Mission of Samuel Turner.

1788: Invasion of Nepalese Gurkhas.

1790-1792: Second invasion of Gurkhas, who were eventually defeated by Chinese.

1806-1815: Ninth Dalai Lama Lung-rtogs rgya-mtsho.

1816-1837: Tenth Dalai Lama mKhas-grub rgya-mtsho.

1835-1842: Conquest of Ladakh by Raja of Jammu.

1854-1856: Tibeto-Nepalese conflict.

1856-1875: Twelfth Dalai Lama 'Phrin-las rgya-mtsho.

1876-1933: Thirteenth Dalai Lama Thub-bstan rgya-mtsho. Russia tries to get foothold with help of Buriat lama Dojiev.

1890: Annexation of Sikkim by British.

1904: British invasion of Tibet under Colonel Younghusband. Flight of Dalai Lama to Mongolia, followed by visit to Peking.

1910: Chinese invasion of Lhasa, flight of Dalai Lama to British India. Chao Erh-feng, governor of Szechwan, tries to annex south-eastern Tibetan territory as far as Giamda.

1911: Surrender of Chinese garrison of Lhasa.

1911: Revolution in China. End of Manchu rule.

1912: Dalai Lama returns to Lhasa and reigns in state of de facto independence.

1912-1916: Chinese Republic under Yüan Shih-k'ai.

1914: Tripartite convention of Simla (British, Chinese, and Tibetans). Dalai Lama strives until the end of his life for recognition of independent status of Tibet.

1928-1949: Chiang Kai-shek and the Kuomintang in power.

1934: Reting Rin-po-che regent of Tibet.

1935: Birth of Fourteenth Dalai Lama bsTan-'dzin rgya-mtsho.

1941: Reting Rin-po-che, perhaps a partisan of Chinese, deposed and replaced by sTag-brag rin-po-che.

1947: India becomes independent.

1949: Proclamation of People's Republic of China.

1950: October, Chinese invasion of Tibet.

1950: Temporary stay of Dalai Lama at Yatung near the Indian border.

1952: Return of Dalai Lama and his attempt at cooperation with Chinese who had promised internal Tibetan autonomy.

1959: After breaking of Chinese promises outbreak of great Tibetan revolt which is suppressed. Dalai Lama finds asylum in India.

1963: Promulgation of new constitution by exiled government of Dalai Lama.